About the Author

SØREN KIERKEGAARD (1813–55) continues to exercise a wide influence on philosophy, literature, and theology. After a youth spent cultivating the lifestyle of a Romantic aesthete, he finished his studies at the University of Copenhagen with the dissertation *On the Concept of Irony.* Many of his books were published under exotic pseudonyms and explored different dimensions of life outside Christianity. These include *The Present Age, Either/Or, Fear and Trembling,* and *The Concept of Anxiety.* He also wrote a number of more directly devotional works, including *Spiritual Writings* and *Works of Love,* but in the last years of his life he attacked the established Church in a series of polemical leaflets.

WORKS OF
LOVE

WORKS OF LOVE

Søren Kierkegaard

Translated by
HOWARD AND
EDNA HONG

Foreword by
GEORGE PATTISON

HARPER**PERENNIAL** ✕ MODERN**THOUGHT**

NEW YORK • LONDON • TORONTO • SYDNEY • NEW DELHI • AUCKLAND

HarperCollins books may be purchased for educational, business, or sales
promotional use. For information, please e-mail the Special Markets Depart-
ment at SPsales@harpercollins.com.

FIRST HARPER TORCHBOOK EDITION PUBLISHED 1964.
FIRST HARPER PERENNIAL MODERN THOUGHT EDITION PUBLISHED 2009.

Library of Congress Cataloging-in-Publication Data is available upon request.

ISBN 978-0-06-171327-9

23 24 25 26 27 LBC 39 38 37 36 35

FOREWORD
TO THE HARPER PERENNIAL MODERN THOUGHT EDITION

Kierkegaard's *Works of Love* was published by Copenhagen's university bookseller C. A. Reitzel on September 29, 1847, just over a month after the author had given the finished manuscript to the printer. *Works of Love* was one of only two of Kierkegaard's books to go into a second edition in his lifetime and, unlike some of his other works, it clearly spoke to Kierkegaard's contemporaries—and it has remained one of the most widely read and most extensively discussed of his many writings. Never has this been more true than in the past decade.[*] In this short introduction, I shall explore why this is so under three headings: 1. How *Works of Love* was written and its place in Kierkegaard's authorship; 2. What *Works of Love* is about and how it has been received; 3. How to read *Works of Love*.

HOW *WORKS OF LOVE* WAS WRITTEN, AND ITS PLACE IN KIERKEGAARD'S AUTHORSHIP

Søren Kierkegaard (1813–55) is best known to posterity in two somewhat distinct respects: first, as a radical Christian critic of established Christianity and, second, as the proponent of a new approach to philosophy that would come to be called existentialism.

In the decades after his death and in the early twentieth century, it was the first of these two identities that was most to the fore, especially in connection with the series of newspaper articles and pamphlets that he published in the last two years of his life and that constituted a violent satire on the established Church. Although this was in the first instance directed specifically against the church of his native land of Denmark, the issues raised in these small works would send shockwaves across Europe. As the title of the first English edition of these writings suggests, it was an "Attack on 'Christendom'"

---

[*] See, for example, M. Jamie Ferreira, *Love's Grateful Striving: A Commentary on Kierkegaard's "Works of Love,"* Oxford, Oxford University Press, 2001; Robert L. Perkins (ed.), *International Kierkegaard Commentary: Works of Love,* Mercer University Press, Macon GA, 1999; I. Dalferth (ed.), *Ethik der Liebe,* Tübingen, Mohr Siebeck, 2002.

and not just on some more or less local failures on the part of Danish Church leaders. Nor were the effects of the attack limited to the European context with its established or national Churches. On the contrary, it raised fundamental questions about the accommodation of Christianity to the world and the social acceptability of the Christian gospel, questions that were relevant to any situation in which being a Christian had become socially "normal."

Shortly after World War I, however, another Kierkegaard became known to the world. This was the Kierkegaard whose philosophical critique of the Hegelian system and psychological analyses of human existence became a major source for the philosophical and artistic movement known as existentialism. Many of the themes of existentialism were derived directly or indirectly from Kierkegaard, including such topics as anxiety, paradox, the absurd, the leap of faith, the temporality of human existence, and, not least, the specifically modern sense of the term "existence" itself. If the sources for Kierkegaard-the-critic-of-Christendom were mostly the polemical writings he published under his own name, the sources for existentialism were largely drawn from the series of works that he published between 1843 and 1846 under a series of pseudonyms, works such as *Either/Or, Repetition, Fear and Trembling, The Concept of Anxiety,* and *Concluding Unscientific Postscript.* As opposed to the newspaper articles and pamphlets, these were densely written works, often involving complex philosophical arguments that referenced a sometimes overwhelmingly rich supply of modern and classical sources. Even though they often contain a great deal of humor, vivid imagery, and lively parables, these works shaped the prevalent image of Kierkegaard as a hardcore representative of the European intellectual tradition, serious to the point of heaviness—the polar opposite of a "popular" thinker.

But there was also a third Kierkegaard, a Kierkegaard who never achieved quite the same level of acclaim as the first two but who has had a steady if low-level presence in the ongoing reception of his life and work. This was the Kierkegaard who, at the same time as he was publishing his pseudonymous works, wrote a series of what he called "edifying" (or "upbuilding") discourses, meditations on religious subjects that read a bit like sermons but which (he insisted) made no claims to represent Christian teaching in an authoritative way. Where the pseudonymous works discussed such topics as anxiety, absurdity, and despair, the upbuilding works spoke of prayer,

patience, humility, purity of heart, and hope, and offered their readers deeply reflective interpretations of the scriptural texts on which
they were based. Even after the pseudonymous authorship was finished, Kierkegaard continued to produce works of this kind, publishing a large collection titled *Upbuilding Discourses in Various Spirits*
early in 1847.

What is remarkable about *Works of Love* is that it is the one book
in which all these aspects of Kierkegaard's authorship flow together
into a single work. Although published under his own name, *Works of
Love* continues and deepens a number of the themes of the pseudonymous writings; at the same time, it is a specifically Christian work,
written in the form of "discourses"; and, finally, it offers early signs
of the attack on Christendom that would dominate his final writings.
In this sense it may fairly be said that *Works of Love* is the central work
in Kierkegaard's entire authorship—and perhaps it is no coincidence
that it was also written at virtually the midpoint of his writing ca-
reer. (The first period of his authorship comprises the pseudonymous
works and the accompanying upbuilding discourses and takes us up
to 1846; the second, more explicitly religious phase begins in 1847
and leads up to the final "attack on Christendom" of 1854–5. *Works
of Love* is thus neatly positioned so as to give a vantage point from
which to look back over the early authorship, as well as forward to
what would follow.)

This is also a work in which we see a supremely confident Kierkegaard, a writer who knows what he is doing and where he is going.
Although many of the early works took several years to gestate or
be assembled out of diverse notes, *Works of Love* seems to have been
written in a short six-month period between January and July 1847.
Upbuilding Discourses in Various Spirits had been delivered to the print-
ers on January 24, and just a few days later Kierkegaard makes a
note in his journals that seems to be the germ of what would become
Works of Love. He imagines that since the upbuilding discourses had
dealt at length with questions of religious inwardness, his readers
will now expect him to deal with the other side of the religious life,
namely "sociality." His initial response is to dismiss this, but then
he adds, "But, on the other hand, I owe it to myself to acknowledge
before God that in a certain sense there's some truth in it. . . . Now I
have the theme for my next book. It is to be called *Works of Love*."* On

---

* *Søren Kierkegaards Skrifter* (Copenhagen: Gad, 2003) Vol. 20, p. 86.

August 2 another entry speaks of his having finished the fair copy, though it seems not to have been handed over to the printer until two weeks after that.

Not that Kierkegaard knew *exactly* where he was going from the beginning. He had some important hesitations over the subtitle, and at one point he considered publishing what appears here as two parts in two separate books (indeed the first Danish edition gives each part a separate title page, and Part Two starts with new pagination, even though they were bound and sold as a single book). Nevertheless, there is little to suggest serious hesitation or modification of the original concept once he began writing in earnest: it was a straight run from beginning to end—something that is reflected in the consistency of thought and style in the book itself.

Kierkegaard being Kierkegaard and a man of many parts, we should not suppose this was the only thing occupying him during these six months (though it would be enough for most writers!). Also in this period he composed extensive drafts for a series of lectures (which he never gave) on the nature of religious communication, began work on his next collection of discourses (which would become the *Christian Discourses* of 1848), and, in a completely different key, wrote an essay "The Crisis and a Crisis in the Life of an Actress." This last was one of his most brilliant aesthetic writings, being a tribute to the interpretation of Shakespeare's Juliet by the leading lady of the Danish stage, Johanne Luise Heiberg. It contained highly perceptive remarks on the nature of acting expressed with such humor, precision, and elegance as to make it not only readable but even performable.* Although Kierkegaard agonized about the publication of this review (he seems not to have been sure whether it was appropriate for a "religious" writer such as he had become to be publishing such "aesthetic" works), it is perhaps important for us as readers of *Works of Love* to bear in mind that the man who is writing this book about love was at the same time deeply steeped in literary and theatrical representations of love and that his book contains multiple allusions to these, as well as to his own experiences and observations. Might not his reflections on the king and the beggar, for example, allude to the encounter between Lear and the crazed "Poor Tom" in Shakespeare's *King Lear*? *Works*

---

* In 2006 I had the privilege of seeing the text performed by Ghita Nørby, one of the leading stars of Danish film and theatre.

of Love is not just an exposition of Christian teaching: it is also an interpretation of and a response to the whole understanding of love in a culture shaped by modern literature and modern mores. But with this comment, we turn to the question of what *Works of Love* is about.

What *Works of Love* Is About and How It Has Been Received

Works of Love is all about love. But love is not only a many-splendored thing; it is also something for which the language provides many words. C. S. Lewis wrote about there being "four loves," but for Kierkegaard there are two main forms of love that occupy the best part of his attention. For these two forms he uses the Danish words "*Kærlighed*" (translated here as "love") and "*Elskov*" (translated here as "erotic love"). These may broadly be interpreted as, respectively, the love that Christians are commanded to practice ("You shall love the Lord your God . . . and your neighbor as yourself") and the spontaneous love that lovers, parents, children, and friends feel for one another. One way of understanding the central argument of *Works of Love* is therefore to see it as recommending the Christian love at the expense of spontaneous (or, as we might also call it, natural or preferential) love—as if practicing *Kærlighed*/Christian love requires us to root out and destroy all traces of *Elskov*/natural love.

Something like that was argued in a very influential twentieth-century work of moral theology that had a big impact on the way in which Kierkegaard's *Works of Love* has been read (and on the wider understanding of the nature and task of Christian ethics). That was the study *Agape and Eros*, by the Swedish theologian Anders Nygren, translated into English in the 1930s. Although Nygren does not discuss Kierkegaard directly, it seems fairly certain that his key terms "*agape*" and "*eros*" transcribe his Danish predecessor's version of the two basic types of love. *Agape* (often translated "charity") is a term that Nygren (and many following him) believe to have been distinctive to the New Testament. As such, he states that it is "the fundamental motif of Christianity," i.e., it is what distinguishes Christianity from all other views of life. However, from the beginning it found itself opposed by another, ostensibly similar but in reality utterly different idea: that of the Platonic "*eros*." Nygren sums up: "Of all the views that have confronted the Christian idea of love, or *agape*, and have forced it to a decision—whether to the decision of a life-and-death struggle or of a settlement by compromise—by far the most important is that view of love which finds its most complete and classical expression the Platonic conception of *eros*."* These views are also designated as theocentric (God-centered) and egocentric respectively.

This might seem a plausible way of interpreting Kierkegaard's teaching in *Works of Love*. Undoubtedly Kierkegaard has many critical things to say about "erotic" or preferential love, and in numerous telling examples demonstrates how what often passes for love is really only a disguised form of egoism. Recent philosophy has spoken of Marx, Nietzsche, and Freud as "masters of suspicion" with regard to their ability to pierce the foggy self-delusions of middle-class moralities and expose the self-interest at work in our value systems—but Kierkegaard is up there with them in his power to divest egoism of the respectable disguises behind which it likes to hide. At the same time, Kierkegaard does insist on the higher value of the commanded love that expresses itself in indiscriminate love towards "the neighbor."

Yet (for once!), Kierkegaard does not insist on an either/or. It is certainly not the case that we can only become practitioners of commanded love by rooting out or crushing the spontaneous human loves we all know from daily experience. Now there are certainly passages that could be quoted in support of such a view (see, for example, the criticism of the poetic view of love in Chapter II.B), yet it is also clear that it is one of the merits of commanded love that it *supports* and *strengthens* spontaneous love. It is in this sense that we have to read the passage in Chapter II.A about how Christian love gives security and constancy to spontaneous love because it grounds it in the eternal (p. 44ff.). This passage bears being read in tandem with an earlier work, *Either/Or* Part II, in which the fictional Assessor Vilhelm argues for the superiority of married love over a life of serial affairs because (he claims) the marriage relationship rests on a vow before God and this vow gives to love the permanence of the eternal. Or, remembering that Kierkegaard is at the same time writing an essay about a Shakespearean actress, we could see this whole section as a reflection on the meaning of the Bard's line that "love is not love that alters when it alteration finds." The point, then, is not to deny the

---

* See A. Nygren, *Agape and Eros*, London, SPCK, 1957, p. 30.

value of the love we experience when we fall in love but to provide a basis on which such love can truly flourish.*

Nor, despite his eye for the selfishness à deux that characterizes many married relationships, does Kierkegaard see Christian love as incompatible with family life. In a rather remarkable passage near the beginning of the discourse "Love Builds Up," he explains the term "up-building" by reference to a number of examples. So, "When we see a large family cramped into close quarters and at the same time see that they inhabit a cozy, friendly, spacious place, then we say it is up-building to see, because we see the love which must be in each and every individual, since one unloving person is enough to occupy the whole place alone" (p. 203). This seems not merely to affirm the spontaneous love of family life, it almost affirms what C. S. Lewis would call "*storgē*," the animal-like love that manifests itself in children huddling together in a heap. It is striking that the word translated here as "cozy" is the Danish word "*hyggelig,*" an everyday word that some claim is untranslatable but which emphasizes just the quality of intimacy, comfort, and, yes, coziness that we find in certain basic forms of family life. The fact that Kierkegaard cites this as an example of what is upbuilding about love makes it impossible for us to accuse him of denying the value of the normal, everyday human aspect of love. Commanded love is there to support and nurture what is best in such natural love, not to uproot or destroy it.**

Of course, Kierkegaard's account is premised on Christian assumptions. As the original subtitle tells us, it is a work of "Christian Reflections," prefaced by a prayer, and it consists of meditations on a series of carefully chosen scripture texts; furthermore, Christ himself is said to be the prime example and "prototype" (p. 247) for all who are truly concerned to practice the self-denying love that "seeks not its own." Yet the argument is not dogmatic or exclusive. In addition to both explicit and allusive appeals to scripture, Kierkegaard also alludes throughout the text to classical philosophy and above all to Socrates, to whom he refers simply as "that simple wise man of ancient times" (p. 342). Close examination of the text

---

* A sensitive study of how *Works of Love* can be used to expose the selfishness of erotic love but at the same to provide a surer basis for human love is Amy Laura Hall's *Kierkegaard and the Treachery of Love*, Cambridge, Cambridge University Press, 2002

** A similar lesson could be drawn from the discourse on "The Work of Love in Remembering One Dead."

will, indeed, show that Socrates serves Kierkegaard as a subsidiary model for authentic loving. Far from the Platonic *eros* being excluded, Kierkegaard's aim is to incorporate it into the Christian task.

Some readers will sense the presence of another, more recent philosopher in *Works of Love*, namely Immanuel Kant. The specifically Kantian part of Kierkegaard's project is his insistence on the disinterested nature of love and the requirement for purity of intention in what Kierkegaard calls love and Kant called "willing the good." But Kierkegaard seems to push this requirement to a level beyond that insisted on by the German philosopher. Although the title of the book and many passages within it emphasize that love must, after all, *do* something, the value of what is done seems, ultimately, to rest on the intention of the agent. Even if I bring about a good outcome for the other, it can only be regarded as a work of love if I did it in love, with the intention of love.

This focus on intention has provoked some of the strongest criticisms of Kierkegaard, such as those of the Danish philosopher Knud Løgstrup and the Frankfurt philosopher Theodor Adorno. Although their objections are differently articulated, both see Kierkegaard as ultimately ignoring the real relationship with the neighbor and the real, concrete social and human concerns that love has to confront and work through if it is to be effective. There is no space here to do justice to this challenge,* but we should note Kierkegaard's own insistence that the issue is not one of intention versus the relief of real needs. Love will do what it can to relieve the need of the other, but the quantitative scope of what is given or done is not the exclusive measure of love. The wealthy benefactor who is able to disburse many millions is not necessarily more concerned by the plight of the other than a person who is unable to do anything practical. In Kierkegaard's dramatic retelling of the parable of the Good Samaritan (p. 300), even if two men had been struck down by robbers and were left in such a state that neither was capable of doing anything to help the other, there would still be a difference between the one who only worried about his own plight and the one who was anxious to do whatever he could for his friend. Intentions do matter to who we are and what our behavior actually means.

---

* See the discussion in my *The Philosophy of Kierkegaard*, Montreal-McGill-Queen's, 2005, pp. 115-26.

I have noted that *Works of Love* contains important anticipations of the last polemical writings denouncing the failures of Christendom. Already in Chapter II.A we are put on notice that what is known to the world as "Christianity" may not be the genuine article, and the penultimate chapter ("The Work of Love in Praising Love") laments the character of an age in which "'Man' has again become 'the measure of everything' and completely in the understanding of the moment. All communication must be contrived opportunely into a light pamphlet and . . . be so contrived that it can be presented in at most an hour before a gathering which spends half an hour for noises of approval or disapproval and for the other half-hour is too confused to gather the ideas. Children are brought up to regard this as the highest: to be heard and to be admired for an hour" (p. 338). Kierkegaard, of course, never watched television, never heard the phrase "dumbing down," and knew nothing of "celebrity culture"—but he had already analyzed the foibles of a society in which such tendencies are rampant. And if we are to sum up *Works of Love*, perhaps it is in the end simply an exceptionally eloquent call not to be distracted by the populism of modern culture and society but to live by conscience—or, more specifically, by conscience in the service of love.

How to Read *Works of Love*

We have seen that, at the same time that he was writing *Works of Love*, Kierkegaard was also preparing lectures on the nature of ethical and religious communication. Socrates played a key role in that text also, and he is repeatedly used there as the exemplar of how to teach ethics—not as a theory or academic discipline but as *life*. Insisting on what he called the "indirect method," in which (like Socrates) the teacher refrains from giving direct instruction but lets the pupils work the question out for themselves, Kierkegaard regarded this as integral to Christian communication also. It is therefore unsatisfactory to think we can "understand" *Works of Love* (or any other Kierkegaardian work) simply by summarizing its "message." *Works of Love* is a book to be read and reread, pondered and practiced. It may well turn up on reading lists for college courses in ethics or theology, and students may be required to allot it its place in the history of ideas and to debate the strengths and weaknesses of its arguments, but that is not what it was written for.

As the original subtitle tells us, *Works of Love* is written "in the form of discourses," a point which leads to two further comments.

First, it is only in a certain sense a single "book." As we have seen, it was originally published with each part having its own title page and pagination, but the discourse format breaks it down even more. Although (especially in Part One) there is often a clear link between one discourse and the next, each is a self-sufficient entity that can be read and appreciated on its own. We are not to finish one and hurry on to the next, but are to consider how each can be made fruitful in its own terms. Perhaps if we really got the most out of just one of these discourses, that would justify having bought the whole book (and, Kierkegaard might add, if just one reader out of all the thousands who bought it were to do this, that would be enough to justify his having written it). Second, the term "discourses" has a very specific meaning for Kierkegaard: discourses do not contain arguments or authoritative teachings but invite the readers to reflect on the subject matter and to internalize it in the light of their own questions and concerns. The point is not so much to communicate the author's ideas as to set the reader's self-reflection in motion, wherever it may lead. Kierkegaard frequently quoted the parable told to King David by the prophet Nathan, ending with the charge "You are the man!" (2 Samuel 12:7), and in this spirit we may say that all of the illustrations, stories, images, thoughts, and reflections offered in *Works of Love* really come into their own when we apply them to our own lives and allow them to interrogate the sincerity or adequacy of our moral practices or to provoke us to works of love.

Whereas Kierkegaard's earlier discourses had been prefaced by the term "upbuilding," he now uses the term translated "reflections." He says about this that "they must not so much move, mollify, reassure, persuade as *awaken* and provoke men and sharpen thought." He adds, "An edifying discourse about love presupposes that men know essentially what love is and seeks to win them to it, to move them. But this is in fact not the case. Therefore the 'reflections' must first fetch them up out of the cellar, call to them, turn their comfortable way of thinking topsy-turvy with the dialectic of truth" (p. 13). What can one add? You have been warned! *Works of Love* is the kind of book that can change your life. Read it—but then, "go and do likewise."

HOWARD AND EDNA HONG

Howard and Edna Hong, the translators of this edition, made a unique and lasting achievement to Kierkegaard studies in the English-speaking world. Eventually they would finish the first complete English translation of all Kierkegaard's published works, as well as a compendious selection from the unpublished journals and papers. In addition, they established a research library at St. Olaf College in Northfield, Minnesota, that has developed into a truly remarkable center of international research and fellowship. In addition to re-creating Kierkegaard's own library, the Hong and Hong Library has a unique collection of secondary works, and each year it hosts a flock of summer visitors from around the world and also supports longer-term residential fellows. Edna Hong died in 2007, but the joint achievement of the Hongs will certainly live on, as the reissue of this translation bears witness.

GEORGE PATTISON
Oxford University
July 2008

In Kierkegaard's *Journals* there are direct references to *Works of Love* as well as comments about it in relation to his entire authorship. From the author himself, therefore, the reader may have the best introduction to the work itself: its character and purpose and the best mode of approach.

In approaching this and any other of Kierkegaard's writings, one should keep in mind distinctions and relationships between the signed works and the pseudonymous works. In general, the signed works have a more religious character, in contrast to the esthetic-philosophical character of the pseudonymous works ("in the direction of the religious"). There is an important distinction, however, between Christian address or discourse (*Christelige Tale*) and Christian sermon on the one hand, and between edifying address or discourse (*opbyggelige Tale*) and reflections (*Overveielser*) on the other hand.

A Christian Address deals to a certain extent with doubt—A Sermon operates absolutely and entirely through authority, that of Holy Writ and of Christ's apostles. It is therefore neither more nor less than heresy to entertain doubt in a sermon, however well one might be able to handle it.

The preface to my *Christian Discourses* [*Taler*], therefore, contains the phrase: If a sufferer who has also *run wild in many thoughts*.

A sermon presupposes a priest (ordination); a Christian Address can be by a layman.

People try to persuade us that the objections against Christianity spring from doubt. That is a complete misunderstanding. The objections against Christianity spring from insubordination, the dislike of obedience, rebellion against all authority. As a result people have hitherto been beating the air in their struggle against objections, because they have fought intellectually with doubt instead of fighting morally with rebellion.[1]

Again, an edifying discourse may be in the more universal categories of the religious or the more specifically Christian categories. *Works of Love* Kierkegaard calls "some Christian reflections [*nogle*

Christelige Overveielser]." That the difference between edifying discourse and Christian reflections is not a difference of the decisive
categories but lies in the purpose and tone is made clear in another
Journal entry written in the year (1847) during which *Works of Love*
was published.

> Reflections do not presuppose the qualifying concepts as given
> and understood; therefore they must not so much move, mollify,
> reassure, persuade as *awaken* and provoke men and sharpen thought.
> The time of reflections is indeed prior to action, and their purpose
> therefore is to rightly set all the elements into motion. Reflections
> ought to be a " gadfly "; therefore their tone ought to be quite
> different from that of edifying discourse, which rests in mood, but
> reflections ought in the good sense to be impatient, high-spirited
> in mood. Irony is necessary here and the even more significant
> ingredient of the comic. One may well laugh once in a while, if
> only to make the thought clearer and more striking. An edifying
> discourse about love presupposes that men know essentially what
> love is and seeks to win them to it, to move them. But this is in
> fact not the case. Therefore the " reflections " must first fetch
> them up out of the cellar, call to them, turn their comfortable way
> of thinking topsy-turvy with the dialectic of truth.[2]

Elsewhere in the *Journals*[3] for the same year Kierkegaard refers to
the fact that the term *reflections* had already been used as a cue in the
introduction to one of the Christian discourses (in English translation
The Gospel of Suffering). *To reflect* or *to ponder* (*at overveie*), he had pointed
out, is derived from the word and the idea of *weighing* (*at veie*). We
weigh things on scales, but the scales are essentially indifferent and
simply respond to the greater weight on one side or the other. But
when the term becomes figurative in referring to a man's weighing,
it means to reflect, to ponder, and a human being does more than
weigh indifferently.

> . . . he reflects, he is higher than the fact of weighing, he rises
> above the weighing, he chooses. Therefore we are justified in
> saying that the expression, to ponder, if one only insists on it,
> finally indicates the essential in human nature, its composition and
> its advantage. For in order to weigh there must be two magni-
> tudes; hence the reflective man, merely in order to be able to
> weigh, must be so made up that he has two magnitudes. This is
> also the case; he is compounded of the temporal and the eternal.
> Temporal existence and eternity are in the spiritual sense the

magnitudes which are to be weighed. But in order to reflect, the
man again must himself be or have a third with respect to the
two magnitudes. This is the choice: he weighs, he reflects, he
chooses.[4]

On the basis of Kierkegaard's own stated intentions in writing
reflections and his frequent reference to Socrates in *Works of Love* we
can justifiably think of this work as being Socratic in its intended
relationship to the reader: for self-examination, for self-knowledge
within the categories of Christian ethics. " The majority of men," he
wrote, " are subjective towards themselves and objective towards all
others, terribly objective sometimes—but the real task is in fact to
be objective towards oneself and subjective towards all others."[5] The
initial purpose of the work for the reader is, therefore, to be an aid in
his becoming objective about his own subjectivity, about his own
existence.

Just as Kierkegaard saw his entire authorship as being instrumental
in his own essential education, he trusted that for the one who reads
(even though there may be only a few[6]), that is, for " that single
individual," there might be some assistance in his own fundamental
education. The relationship of the reader to the work is therefore
properly autobiographical, *not* in the too frequent improper sense of
a historico-psychological approach to this and other works in order
to dig out clues to Kierkegaard's life,[7] but in order to become aware
of clues to one's own life, its shape and direction. It would not, however, be improper to put the ultimate purpose of the work for the
reader in Kierkegaard's own words about himself the day he finished
16th (August, 1847) the manuscript of *Works of Love*: " I now feel the
need of approaching nearer to myself in a deeper sense, by approaching
nearer to God in the understanding of myself. I must remain on the
spot and be *renewed inwardly*."[8] The intellectual task of reflection and
the coming to greater self-knowledge were not a resting point for the
author, nor are they intended to be conclusive but rather preparatory
for the reader.

" Something is stirring within me which points to a metamorphosis.
For that very reason I dare not go to Berlin, for that would be to
procure an abortion. I shall therefore remain quiet, in no way
working too strenuously, hardly even strenuously, not begin on a
new book, but try to understand myself, and really think out the
idea of my melancholy together with God here and now. That
is how I must get rid of my melancholy and bring Christianity

closer to me. Hitherto I have defended myself against my melancholy with intellectual work, which keeps it away—now, in the faith that God has forgotten in forgiveness what guilt there may be, I must try to forget it myself, but not in distraction, not at a distance from it but in God; I must see to it that in thinking of God I learn to think that he has forgotten it, and thus myself learn to dare to forget it in forgiveness."[9]

When one is aware of this kind of ethico-religious intention of the work or becomes aware of the way these reflections speak to him who reads, one recalls a sentence Kierkegaard uses early (p. 35) in the opening section about the phrase *as yourself*: " Yes, no wrestler can wrap himself around his opponent as this command wraps itself about self-love." This characterises the whole work. The development of the reflections moves towards closing escape hatches and running down equivocations and uncovering evasions as it sharpens distinctions and lays bare implications in concepts and existential positions. The reader comes to understand the reason for the length of the work and does not complain, " Why doesn't he say it and be done with it? " —because he realises that the work is directed to the individual who is to work his own conscious way with the help of the reading and that it is not primarily a presentation of a writer's neatly bundled opinions. And this takes time and the elaboration of meanings, so that the work can find the reader where he is and so wrap itself around him. That is why in our translation we have resisted the temptation to break up paragraphs and sentences to make them " easier." For Kierkegaard carefully developed both thought and form[10] to prevent easy and superficial reading, requiring the either/or of thoughtful reading or no illusion of having really read at all. Both substance and appropriate form are best appreciated and appropriated by the reader who reads as the author hoped he would (" I think continuously of the reader who reads aloud "), because reading aloud helps us to realise that we do not primarily have an author to consider but ourselves— merely prompted in our reflections by an author.

Works of Love, then, aims primarily at finding a reader where he is. The substance within which the reader comes to see himself is a positive love-ethic, in complementary contrast to the ethical volume *Purity of Heart*, which maintains a substantial openness in delineating the ethical integrity of the person, the ethical consciousness as quali- tatively distinguished from the episodic immediacy of the esthetic life. In *Works of Love* love in its works (for it is a deed, not volatile, lovely feeling)[11] is the highest good of ethical vision. But we do not know or we have forgotten what love is.[12] Christian love is not simply the same as erotic love and friendship or the heightening of the immediacy of these interests. Rather it is ethico-religious love which dethrones and catches up immediacy's love, for one's beloved and friend are also neighbours. A century before Anders Nygren (*Eros and Agape*), Denis de Rougemont (*Love in the Western World*) and Father D'Arcy (*The Mind and Heart of Love*) made their important though more detached studies, Kierkegaard had undertaken the philosopher-theologian's task of making distinctions—such as between love and love, the lovely and unlovely objects of erotic love and of Christian love, love as subjective inclination and love as the presupposing of love in the object of love. This task he does so well, yet always by way of prompting the reader, that the reader comes to know his own love —or lovelessness—more profoundly.

Just as the fundamental distinction in the love of the Christian love ethic separates it from anything like the sentimental ethic of a Rousseau or a David Hume, the implicit distinction between an imperative ethic (as in *Purity of Heart* and in *Either/Or, Unscientific Postscript*, and parts of *Fear and Trembling*) and an indicative ethic distinguishes the Christian love ethic from an immanental philosophical ethic and exclusively imperative religious ethic on the one hand and from an unprincipled " Christian pragmatism " of " opportunism with furrowed brow " on the other. F. J. Billeskov Jansen points out that Kierkegaard (pseudonym: Vigilius Haufniensis) in *The Concept of Dread* calls for " a new ethic " and that *Works of Love* constitutes the presentation of " *his* Christian ethics."[13] That which makes it Christian ethics is not only the distinction between love and love, inclination and " thou shalt love," ethical ideals and " the pattern," but its being ultimately the mature indicative ethics of Christianity rooted in and motivated by the love of God for men, for a man, for every man. Since perhaps most individuals live in a diluted sociological morality and stand in need of the rigour and vision of the ethical imperative of vision and demand, this aspect of *Works of Love* will appear dominant. Fundamental, however, is the primacy of God, the God of love and forgiveness, in whose love and forgiveness the person in faith is restored and renewed and returned to the expressive ethic of gratitude in existence. " It is indeed God in heaven who through the apostle says, ' Be reconciled '; it is not man who says to God: ' Forgive us.' No, God loved us first; and again it was God who came first a second

time, since it had to do with reconciliation—although from the standpoint of justice he certainly was the one who could well have waited "
(p. 383). This is the mature, indicative, essentially Christian ethic of
the Conclusion:

> ... we shall now conclude by introducing John the apostle, saying:
> " Beloved, let us love one another." These words, which conse-
> quently have apostolic authority, also have, if you will consider
> them, a middle tone or a middle mood with respect to the con-
> trasts in love itself, which has its basis in that they are said by one
> who was perfected in love. You do not hear in these words the
> rigorousness of duty; the apostle does not say, " You *shall* love
> one another "; but neither do you hear the intensity of inclination,
> of poet-passion. There is something transfigured and blessed in
> these words, but also a sadness which broods over life and is
> tempered by the eternal. It is as if the apostle said, " Dear me,
> what is all this which would hinder you from loving; what is all
> this which you can win by self-love: the commandment is that
> you *shall* love, but when you understand life and yourself, then it
> is as if you should not need to be commanded, because to love
> human beings is still the only thing worth living for; without this
> love you really do not live; to love human beings is also the only
> salutary consolation for both time and eternity, and to love human
> beings is the only true sign that you are a Christian "—truly, a
> profession of faith is not enough. Christianly understood, love is
> commanded; but the commandment of love is the old command-
> ment, which is always new. It is not with the love-commandment
> as with a human command, which becomes old with the years or
> is changed by the mutual agreement of those who should obey it.
> No, the love-commandment remains new until the last day, just
> as new even on the last day when it has become most ancient.
> Consequently the commandment is not altered in the slightest
> way, least of all by an apostle. The only change can be, then,
> that the lover becomes more and more intimate with the com-
> mandment, becomes more and more one with the commandment,
> which he loves: therefore he is able to speak so mildly, so sadly,
> almost as if it had been forgotten that love is the commandment.
> If, however, you forget that it is the apostle of love who speaks,
> then you misunderstand him, for such words are not the beginning
> of the discourse on love but are the consummation of love. There-
> fore we do not dare talk this way. That which is truth in the

mouth of the veteran, perfected apostle could in the mouth of a beginner easily be flirtation whereby he would seek to leave the commandment's school much too soon and escape the *school-yoke*. We introduce the apostle speaking; we do not make his words into our own but make ourselves into hearers of: " Beloved, let us love one another."[14]

In a *Journal* fragment we find this same theocentricity of love which is repeatedly echoed in *Works of Love*:

> . . . a mystery deeper than any thought which has arisen in the heart of a human being, that God is one who hates all ceremonies, that one dares without further ado (*ex tempore*) to speak to him, without being announced, *etc.*, in the joy of life and in the meshes of sorrow, that one always has occasion to thank him, and when one forgets this he loves enough to remind one of it. I build upon this: how proportionately God shares with man, for it must be far more difficult for him to make himself so small that a human being really can love him.
>
> And when one has not a single human being who understands him, then he is willing to hear and he can remember better than all men, better than one himself. And when one's thoughts are so confused that one does not know whether he is coming or going, he has not forgotten even the slightest thing one has prayed him to remember; and if this were not so, everything would be indifferent, whether one himself could remember or not.[15]

If this central characteristic of Christian ethics, the primacy of God in whom is grounded the indicative as well as the imperative of Christian ethics, may be called theocentric otherness, there is also a social otherness in the emphasis upon love to the neighbour. This is not an ethic of socio-political structures but an ethic of social-structures-at-hand, whatever the larger socio-political structures might be. Those who say that Kierkegaard had no consciousness of anything but a purely private individualistic ethic cannot digest this work, nor, when properly understood, his other ethical works, but least of all this. That he himself was aware of this kind of critique is evident in a *Journal* entry prior to the writing of *Works of Love*:

> " In spite of everything men ought to have learned about my maieutic carefulness, in addition to proceeding slowly and continually letting it seem as if I knew nothing more, not the next thing—now on the occasion of my new Edifying Discourses they will presumably bawl out that I do not know what comes next,

that I know nothing about sociality. The fools! Yet on the other hand I owe it to myself to confess before God that in a certain sense there is some truth in it, only not as men understand it, namely that always when I have first presented one aspect sharply and clearly, then I affirm the validity of the other even more strongly. Now I have the theme of the next book. It will be called *Works of Love*."[16]

Because of these and other important aspects of the content of this work, important to the single individual who reads and understands "slowly but then also easily," and important, also, though secondarily, to one "interested" in the authorship, the translators are happy to share in the re-publication of this significant work after it has been out of print in English for some years. In this task they gratefully acknowledge the helpful critical reading of portions of the manuscript by Mary Hinderlie, assistance by Dr. Gregor Malantschuk and Fru M. Michelsen on certain problems in translation and the notes, and the final typing done by Carol Ann Bjornstad.

                              HOWARD AND EDNA HONG

Vesterskovhus
Næsbyholm, Denmark

AUTHOR'S PREFACE

These Christian reflections,[1] which are the fruit of much reflection, will be understood slowly but then also easily; yet they surely will become very difficult if someone by hasty and curious reading makes them very difficult for himself. "That single individual" [Hiin Enkelte],[2] who first ponders whether he will read or not, will ponder lovingly, if he decides to read, whether or not the difficulty and the ease, when they are thoughtfully placed together on the scales, are rightly related, so that Christianity is not misrepresented by making either the difficulty or the ease too great.

These are *Christian reflections*; therefore they are not about *love* but about the *works of love*.

These are reflections on the *works of love*—not as if hereby all love's works were mentioned and described—far from it, nor even as if a single one described were described[3] once and for all—God be praised, far from it! That which in its vast abundance is *essentially* inexhaustible is also *essentially* indescribable in its smallest act, simply because essentially it is everywhere wholly present and *essentially* cannot be described.

Autumn 1847

S.K.

PRAYER

How could love be rightly discussed if You were forgotten, O God of Love, source of all love in heaven and on earth, You who spared nothing but gave all in love, You who are love, so that one who loves is what he is only by being in You! How could love properly be discussed if You were forgotten, You who made manifest what love is, You, our Saviour and Redeemer, who gave Yourself to save all! How could love be rightly discussed if You were forgotten, O Spirit of Love, You who take nothing for Your own but remind us of that sacrifice of love, remind the believer to love as he is loved, and his neighbour as himself! O Eternal Love, You who are everywhere present and never without witness wherever You are called upon, be not without witness in what is said here about love or about the works of love. There are only a few acts which human language specifically and narrowly calls works of love, but heaven is such that no act can be pleasing there unless it is an act of love—sincere in self-renunciation, impelled by love itself, and for this very reason claiming no compensation.

Part One

I

Love's Hidden Life and Its Recognisability

by Its Fruits

" For each tree is known by its own fruit. For figs are not
gathered from thorns, nor are grapes picked from a bramble
bush." *Luke* 6: 44

If it were true—as conceited shrewdness, proud of not being deceived,
thinks—that one should believe nothing which he cannot see by means
of his physical eyes, then first and foremost one ought to give up
believing in love. If one did this and did it out of fear of being deceived,
would not one then be deceived? Indeed, one can be deceived in many
ways; one can be deceived in believing what is untrue, but on the
other hand, one is also deceived in not believing what is true; one
can be deceived by appearances, but one can also be deceived by the
superficiality of shrewdness, by the flattering conceit which is absolutely
certain that it cannot be deceived. Which deception is most dangerous?
Whose recovery is more doubtful, that of him who does not see or of
him who sees and still does not see? Which is more difficult, to awaken
one who sleeps or to awaken one who, awake, dreams that he is awake?
Which sight is more sorrowful, that which immediately and un-
restrainedly moves to tears, like the sight of one unhappily deceived
in love, or that which in a certain sense could tempt laughter, the sight
of one who is self-deceived, whose foolish conceit of not being deceived
is ludicrous, something to be laughed at, if its ludicrousness were not
a still stronger expression for horror by signifying that he is not worth
a tear?

   To cheat oneself out of love is the most terrible deception; it is an
eternal loss for which there is no reparation, either in time or in

eternity. For usually, whatever variations there may be, when there is talk about being deceived in love the one deceived is still related to love, and the deception is simply that it is not present where it was thought to be; but one who is self-deceived has locked himself out and continues to lock himself out from love. There is also talk about being deceived by life or in life; but he who self-deceptively cheated himself out of living—his loss is irredeemable. One who throughout his whole life has been deceived by life—for him the eternal can treasure rich compensation; but the person who has deceived himself has prevented himself from winning the eternal. He who because of love became a sacrifice to human deceit—what has he really lost when in eternity it turns out that love endures; whereas the deception is no more! But one who ingeniously deceived himself by cleverly falling into the snare of cleverness, alas, even if throughout his entire life he has in his own conceit considered himself happy, what has he not lost when in eternity it appears that he deceived himself! In the temporal world a man may succeed in getting along without love; he may succeed in slipping through life without discovering the self-deception; he may have the terrible success, in his conceit, of becoming proud of it; but in eternity he cannot dispense with love and cannot escape discovering that he has lost everything. How earnest existence is, how terrible it is, precisely when in chastisement it permits the wilful person to counsel himself, permits him to live on proud of—being deceived—until finally he is permitted to verify that he has deceived himself for eternity! The eternal does not let itself be mocked; it is rather that which does not need to use might but almightily uses a little mockery in order to punish the presumptuous in a terrible way. What is it that really binds the temporal and the eternal? What is it other than love, which therefore is before everything else and remains when all else is past. But just because love is the bond of the eternal and just because the temporal and the eternal are heterogeneous, to the earthly prudence of temporality love may seem to be a burden, and therefore in the temporal world it may seem a great relief to the sensualist to cast this bond of eternity away.

One who is self-deceived thinks, of course, that he is able to console himself, yes, to have more than conquered; a fool's conceit hides for him how inconsolable his life is. That he " has ceased sorrowing " we will not deny, but, nevertheless, what gain is this when salvation consists precisely in his beginning to sorrow earnestly over himself! Perhaps one who is self-deceived even thinks he is able to console others, who would become a sacrifice to the deceit of perfidy; but what madness, when he who himself has lost the eternal wants to heal him who is at the extremity of sickness unto death. Perhaps the self-deceived, by an odd self-contradiction, even thinks he is being sympathetic with one who is unhappily deceived. But if you scrutinise his comforting words and healing wisdom, you will know love by its fruits—by the bitterness of mockery, by the sharpness of "good sense," by the poisonous spirit of distrust, by the penetrating chill of callousness—that is, by the fruits it will be known that there is no love in this kind of sympathy.

By its fruits one recognises the tree. " Are grapes gathered from thorns, or figs from thistles? " (Matthew 7: 16). If you expect to gather them there, you will not only pick in vain but the thorns will show you that you pick in vain. *For every tree is recognised by its* OWN *fruit.* It may well be that there are two fruits which very closely resemble each other; the one is healthful and good-tasting, the other is bitter and poisonous; sometimes, too, the poisonous fruit is good-tasting and the healthful fruit somewhat bitter in taste. In the same way love also is known by its *own* fruit. If one makes a mistake, it must be either because one does not know the fruit or because one does not know how to discriminate rightly in particular instances. For example, one may make the mistake of calling love that which is really self-love: when one loudly protests that he cannot live without his beloved but will hear nothing about love's task and demand, which is that he deny himself and give up the self-love of erotic love. Or a man may make the mistake of calling by the name of love that which is weak indulgence, the mistake of calling spoiled whimpering, or corrupting attachments, or essential vanity, or selfish associations, or flattery's bribery, or momentary appearances, or temporal relationships by the name of love. There is a flower called the flower of eternity, but there is also, remarkably, a so-called everlasting flower which, like perishable flowers, blooms only at a certain time of the year—what a mistake to call the latter a flower of eternity! And yet it is so deceptive at the moment of blossoming. But every tree is known by its own fruit. So also is love known by its own fruit and the love of which Christianity speaks is known by its own fruit—revealing that it has within itself the truth of the eternal. All other love, whether humanly speaking it withers early and is altered or lovingly preserves itself for a round of time—such love is still transient; it merely blossoms. This is precisely its weakness and tragedy, whether it blossoms for an hour or for seventy years—it merely blossoms; but Christian love is eternal. Therefore no one, if he understands himself, would think of saying of Christian love that it blossoms; no poet, if he understands himself, would think of celebrating it in song. For what the poet shall celebrate must have in it the anguish which is the riddle of his own life: it must blossom and, alas, must perish. But Christian love abides and for that very reason *is* Christian love. For what perishes blossoms and what blossoms perishes, but that which *has being* cannot be sung about—it must be believed and it must be lived.

Yet when one says that love is recognised by its fruits, one also says thereby that love itself is in a certain sense in hiding and therefore can be known only by its revealing fruits. This is precisely the case. Every life, love's life also, is as such hidden and reveals itself in another form. The life of a plant is hidden; the fruit is the manifestation. The life of thought is hidden; the utterance of speech is the manifestation. The sacred words read above therefore have a double meaning; although they hiddenly speak only of one; openly there is only one thought contained in the statement, but there is also another hidden in it.

Let us, then, bring out both thoughts for consideration, since we shall now speak about:

LOVE'S HIDDEN LIFE AND ITS RECOGNISABILITY BY ITS FRUITS.

From whence comes love, where does it have its origin and its source; where is the place, its stronghold, from which it proceeds? Certainly this place is hidden or is in that which is hidden. There is a place in a human being's most inward depths; from this place proceeds the life of love, for "from the heart proceeds life."[4] But this place you cannot see, no matter how far you thrust in; the source withdraws itself into remoteness and hiding; even if you have thrust in as far as possible, the source is still always a bit farther in, like the source of a spring which just when you are nearest to it is farther away. From this place love proceeds in manifold ways, but by none of these ways can you thrust your way in to its hidden beginning. As God dwells in the light[5] from which streams every beam which lights the world and yet no one can penetrate back by these paths to see God, for the path of light changes to darkness when one turns toward the light: so love dwells in the hidden or is hidden in the inmost depths. As the flow of a spring lures by the murmuring persuasion of its rippling, yes, almost begs one to go along the path and not curiously wish to penetrate in to discover its source and reveal its secret; as the rays of the sun invite men to observe by their help the glory of the world but reproachfully punish with blindness the presumptuous who try to turn about in order inquisitively and impudently to discover the origin of the light; as faith, beckoning, offers to be man's companion on life's way but turns to stone the impudent who turn about impudently to grasp it: so also is it the desire and prayer of love that its concealed source and its hidden life in the most inward depths may remain a secret, that no one inquisitively and impudently will disturbingly thrust his way in to see what he cannot see anyway, the joy and blessing of which, however, he forfeits by his curiosity. The suffering is always most painful when the doctor is obliged in operating to penetrate in to the more vital, the hidden parts of the body; in the same way the suffering is most painful and most devastating when someone, instead of rejoicing in the manifestations of love, wants the pleasure of penetrating in to it, that is, by disturbing it.

The hidden life of love is in the most inward depths, unfathomable, and still has an unfathomable relationship with the whole of existence. As the quiet lake is fed deep down by the flow of hidden springs, which no eye sees, so a human being's love is grounded, still more deeply, in God's love. If there were no spring at the bottom, if God were not love, then there would be neither a little lake nor a man's love. As the still waters begin obscurely in the deep spring, so a man's love mysteriously begins in God's love. As the quiet lake invites you to look at it but the mirror of darkness prevents you from seeing through it, so love's mysterious ground in God's love prevents you from seeing its source. When you think you are seeing it, then it is a reflection which deceives you, as if it were the bottom, this which only conceals the deeper bottom. As the clever cover to a treasure appears to be the floor, in order completely to hide the treasure, so the reflection deceptively appears to be the depth of the source—but only conceals that which is still deeper.

In this way the life of love is hidden, but its hidden life is itself in motion and has the eternal in itself. As the still waters, however quietly they lie, are really running water, for is not the well-spring at the bottom: so love flows, however still it is in its hiddenness. But the still waters can dry up if the springs stop; the life of love, on the other hand, has an eternal spring. This life is fresh and everlasting. No cold can freeze it—it is too warm for that; and no heat can dry it up—it is too fresh in its own coolness for that. But hidden it is, and when the Gospel speaks about the recognisability of this life by its fruits, then the meaning is above all not that one should disquiet and disturb this hiddenness or give himself over to observation or investigative intro-spection, something which only "grieves the spirit"[6] and retards growth.

Yet this hidden life of love is knowable *by its fruits*—yes, there is a need in love to be recognisable by its fruits. How beautiful it is—that what betokens the deepest poverty likewise signifies the greatest riches! Need, to have need, and to be needy—how reluctantly a man wishes this to be said of him! And yet we pay the highest compliment when we say of a poet—" It is a need for him to write," of an orator—" It is a need for him to speak," of a girl—" It is a need for her to love." Alas, even the most needy person who has ever lived—if he still has had love—how rich his life has been in comparison with him, the only really poor person, who lived out his life and never felt the need of anything! It is a girl's greatest riches that she needs the beloved. It is the religious man's highest and true wealth that he needs God. Ask them—ask the girl if she could be just as happy if she could dispense with her beloved; ask the religious man if he understands or desires that he could just as well dispense with God! It is the same with the recognisability of love by its fruits, which, for the very same reason, when the relationship is right, are said to press through out of need—an indication of abundance. It would be the greatest torture, if love really could contain such a self-contradiction, for love to require itself to keep hidden, to require its own unrecognisability. Would it not be as if a plant, sensitive to the vigour and blessing of life in itself, did not dare let it become known and kept the blessing to itself as if it were a curse—alas, as a secret in its inexplicable withering away. But this is not so at all. For even if a single, particular expression of love, a single impulse of the heart, were, out of love, forced back into painful concealment—this same life of love would find yet another expression for itself and would still become recognisable by its fruits. O you quiet martyrs of unhappy erotic love—to be sure it remained a secret that out of love you suffered in hiding love; it never became known, for so great was your love which brought this sacrifice—yet your love was known by its fruits! And perhaps those very fruits would be the most precious, those which were matured by the quiet fire of secret pain.

The tree is known by its *fruits*; to be sure, the tree is also known by its *leaves*, but the fruit is still its essential mark. If, therefore, one knew by the leaves that a tree was of a certain kind but in the fruit season found that it bore no fruit—then one would know that it really was not the tree which according to the leaves it appeared to be. The recognisability of love is just like this. The apostle John says (I John 3: 18), "Little children, let us not love in word or speech but in deed and in truth." How can we better compare this love in words and speech than with the leaves of the tree; for words and expressions and the inventions of speech can also be a mark of love, but they are uncertain. The same words in one person's mouth can be very significant and reliable, in another's mouth as the vague whisper of leaves; the same words in one man's mouth can be like "blessed nourishing grain," in another's like the unfruitful beauty of the leaves. Yet because of this one should not repress the words, any more than one should hide visible emotion when it is genuine, for this can be just as unkind a wrong as holding back from a man what is due him. Your friend, your beloved, your child, or whoever is the object of your love, has a claim upon its expression also in words when it really moves you inwardly. The emotion is not your possession but the other's. The expression of it is his due, since in the emotion you belong to him who moves you and makes you conscious of belonging to him. When the heart is full you should not grudgingly and loftily, short-changing the other, injure him by pressing your lips together in silence; you should let the mouth speak out of the abundance of the heart;[7] you should not be ashamed of your feelings and still less of honestly giving to each one his due.[8] Nevertheless, one should not love in word and with devices of speech, and neither should one regard them as sure marks of love. On the contrary, by such fruits or by their being merely leaves, one should know that love has not had time for growth. Sirach says in warning (6, 4), "Eat up your leaves, and you will lose your fruit and leave yourself standing like a dried-up tree";[9] for precisely by words and techniques of speech as the only fruit of love one knows that a man has ripped off the leaves out of season and thereby gets no fruit, not to speak of something more terrible, that occasionally one recognises the deceiver by his very own words and manner of speaking. Consequently, immature and deceitful love is known by the fact that words and techniques of speech are its only fruit.

It is said of certain plants that they must form hearts; the same must be said of a man's love: if it is really to bear fruit and consequently be recognisable by its fruit, it must *form a heart*. Love, to be sure, proceeds from the heart, but let us not in our haste about this forget the eternal truth that love forms the heart.[10] Every man experiences the transient excitements of an inconstant heart, but to have a heart in this natural sense is infinitely different from forming a heart in the eternal sense. How rarely the eternal gets enough control over a man so that the love establishes itself in him eternally or forms his heart. Yet it is the essential condition for bearing love's own fruit by which it is known. As love itself is not to be seen (for that reason must one believe in it), neither is it unconditionally and directly to be known by any one expression.—There is no word in human language, not a single one, not the most sacred word, of which we could say: when a man uses this word, it is unconditionally proved thereby that there is love in him. Rather, it is true that a word from one person can convince us that there is love in him and the opposite word from another can convince that there is love in him also. It is true that one and the same word can convince us that love dwells in the person who uttered it and not in another who nevertheless uttered the same word.— There is no deed, not a single one, not even the best, of which we dare to say unconditionally: he who does this thereby unconditionally demonstrates love. It depends upon *how* the deed is done. There are, indeed, acts which in a special sense are called works of love. But, in truth, because one makes charitable contributions, because he visits the widow and clothes the naked—his love is not necessarily demonstrated or made recognisable by such deeds, for one can perform works of love in an unloving, yes, even in a self-loving way, and when this is so, the works of love are nevertheless not the work of love. You certainly have seen this sad state of affairs often enough. Perhaps you have sometimes also caught yourself in it, something every honest man will confess about himself, simply because he is not unkind and callous enough to overlook what is essential, in preoccupation with *what* he does to forget *how* he does it. Alas, Luther is supposed to have said that not once in his life had he prayed entirely undisturbed by any distracting thoughts. In the same way the honest man confesses that never, however often and however many times he willingly and gladly has given charity, that never has he done it except in frailty, perhaps confused by an accidental impression, perhaps in capricious partiality, perhaps to save face, perhaps with averted glance (but not in the Biblical sense),[11] perhaps without the left hand's knowing about it (yet in thoughtlessness), perhaps thinking about his own troubles (instead of thinking about the troubles of the poor), perhaps seeking alleviation by giving charity (instead of wanting to alleviate the need)—in such ways the works of love would not in the highest sense become a work of love.— Consequently, how the word is said and, above all, how it is meant, consequently, how the deed is done: this is the decisive factor in determining and recognising love by its fruits. But here again it holds true that there is nothing, no *in such a way*, of which it can unconditionally be said that it unconditionally proves the presence of love **or** that it unconditionally proves there is no love.

Nevertheless, it remains fixed and firm that love shall be known by its fruits. But the holy words of our text are not spoken to encourage us to get busy judging one another; they are rather spoken warningly to the individual, to you, my reader, and to me, to encourage each one not to let his love become unfruitful but to work so that it is capable of being recognised by its fruits, whether these are recognised by others or not. For one is not to work in order that love becomes known by its fruits but to work to make love capable of being recognised by its fruits. In this endeavour one must watch himself so that this, the recognition of love, does not become more important to him than the one important thing: that it has fruits and therefore can be known. The prudent counsel one can give to a man, the circumspection one can recommend to prevent being deceived by others—this is one thing; another and far more important thing is the gospel's summons to the individual to consider that the tree is known by its fruits and that it is he or his love which in the gospel is compared to the tree. It does not say in the gospel—as shrewd talk would have it—" You or anyone shall know the tree by its fruits," but it says, " The tree shall be known by its fruits." The interpretation is that you, you who read the words of the gospel, you are the tree. What the prophet Nathan[12] added to the parable, " You are the man," the gospel needs not add, since it is already contained in the form of the statement and in its being a word of the gospel. For the divine authority of the Gospel speaks not to one man about another man, not to you, the reader, about me, or to me about you—no, when the gospel speaks it speaks to the single individual. It does not speak *about* us men, you and me, but it speaks *to* us men, you and me, and it speaks *about* the requirement that love shall be known by its fruits.

Therefore, if any overexcited and enthusiastic or hypocritical person were to teach that love is such a hidden feeling that it is above bearing fruit or such a hidden feeling that the fruits proved nothing for or against, yes, even that poisonous fruits proved nothing—then we should remember the words of the gospel, " The tree shall be known by its fruits." We shall, not in order to attack but to defend ourselves against such persons, remember that what is true of every word of the gospel is true here, that " He who acts according to my teachings is like a man who builds upon a rock."[13] " When the heavy rains come " and destroy the proud frailty of sensitive love, " when the storm blows and snags" the web of hypocrisy—then shall true love be known by its fruits. In truth, love shall be recognisable by its fruits, but still it does not follow from this that you are to take it upon yourself to be the man who knows. Furthermore, the tree shall be recognisable by its fruits, but it does not follow from this that there is one tree which shall take it upon itself to judge the others; on the contrary, it is always the individual tree which ought—to bear fruit. A man ought not to be afraid either of him who can slay the body[14] or of the hypocrite. There is only one whom a human being should fear—that is God; and there is only one a man should be afraid of—that is himself. Truly, he who in fear and trembling towards God has been afraid of himself has never been deceived by a hypocrite. But he who gets busy tracking down hypocrites, whether he succeeds or not, should be certain that this also is not hypocrisy, for such investigations are hardly the fruits of love. He, on the other hand, whose love really bears its *own* fruit will, without wishing it and without trying, unmask or even shame every hypocrite who comes near him; but one who loves will perhaps not even be conscious of all this. The most mediocre defence against hypocrisy is prudence; well, it is hardly a defence, rather a dangerous neighbour of hypocrisy. The best defence against hypocrisy is love; yes, it is not only a defence but a yawning abyss; in all eternity it has nothing to do with hypocrisy. This also is a fruit whereby love is known—it secures the lover against falling into the snare of the hypocrite.

But now even if it is true that love is recognisable by its fruits, let us not, for all that, impatiently, suspiciously, judgingly demand continually and perpetually to see the fruits in the relationship of love with one another. The first emphasis developed in these reflections was that one must believe in love; otherwise one will never become aware that it exists. But now we return again to the first point and say, repeating: believe in love! This is the first and last thing to be said about love if one is to know what love is. At first it was said in contrast to the presumptuous practicality which wants to deny the existence of love; now, however, after the recognisability of love by its fruits has been developed, it is said in opposition to the morbid, anxious, shrewd meanheartedness which in petty, miserable mistrust insists upon seeing the fruits. Do not forget that it would be a beautiful, a noble, a holy fruit by which love in you would become known if in relation to another person, whose life perhaps bears poorer fruit, you were loving enough to see it as more beautiful than it is. If mistrust can see something as less than it actually is, love also can see something as greater than it is —Do not forget that even when you are happy over the fruits of love, when by them you know that love dwells in this other person, do not forget that it is still more blessed to believe in love. Precisely this is a new expression for the depth of love—that when one has learned to know it by its fruits, one again returns to the beginning—to believe in love—and returns to it as the highest. For indeed the life of love is recognisable by its fruits, which make it manifest, but the life itself is still more than the single fruit and more than all the fruits which one could enumerate at any moment. Therefore the last, the most blessed, the absolutely convincing evidence of love remains: love itself, which is known and recognised by the love in another. Like is known only by like. Only he who abides in love can recognise love, and in the same way his love is to be known.

II A

You *Shall* Love

"And a second is like it, You shall love your neighbour as yourself." *Matthew* 22: 39

Every discourse, especially the opening portion, usually postulates something from which it then proceeds. One who wishes to deliberate on a discourse or assertion does well to find first this presupposition in order that he may begin with it. Our quoted text also contains a presupposition which comes at the end, to be sure, but it is nevertheless the beginning. When it is said: "You shall love your neighbour as yourself," therein is contained what is presupposed, that every man loves himself. Christianity, which by no means begins, as do certain high-flying thinkers,[15] without presuppositions—nor with a flattering presupposition, either!—therefore makes this postulate. Indeed, do we dare deny what Christianity presupposes? But on the other hand, is it possible for anyone to misunderstand Christianity, as if it were its intention to teach what worldly cleverness unanimously, alas, and yet contentiously, teaches, "that everyone is closest to himself"—is it possible for anyone to misunderstand this, as if it were the intention of Christianity to proclaim self-love as a prescriptive right? On the contrary, it is its purpose to wrest self-love away from us human beings. This implies loving one's self; but if one must love his neighbour *as himself*, then the command, like a pick, wrenches open the lock of self-love and thereby wrests it away from a man. If the command to love one's neighbour were expressed in a way different from this little phrase *as yourself*, which is so easy to wield and yet at the same time has the tension of the eternal, then the command would not be able to master self-love in this way. This *as yourself* does not waver in

34

its aim, and with the firmness of the eternal it critically penetrates to the innermost hiding place where a man loves himself; it does not leave self-love the slightest excuse or the tiniest escape-hatch. How remarkable! There could be lengthy and discerning addresses on how a man ought to love his neighbour; and when the addresses were over, self-love would still be able to hit upon excuses and find ways out, because the subject had not been entirely exhausted, all circumstances had not been taken into account, because continually something had been forgotten, or something had not been accurately or bindingly enough expressed and described. But this *as yourself*—yes, no wrestler can wrap himself around his opponent as this command wraps itself about self-love, which cannot move from the spot. Truly, when self-love has struggled with this phrase, which nevertheless is so easy to understand that no one needs to rack his brain over it, then will it realise that it has struggled with one that is stronger. As Jacob limped[16] after having struggled with God, so shall self-love be broken if it has struggled with this phrase, which nevertheless does not seek to teach a man not to love himself but in fact rather seeks to teach him proper self-love. How remarkable! What struggle is so protracted, so terrifying, so involved as self-love's war to defend itself, and yet Christianity decides it all with one single blow. The whole thing is as quick as a turn of the hand; every thing is decided, like the eternal decision of resurrection, " in a moment, in the twinkling of an eye." (I Corinthians 15: 52). Christianity presupposes that men love themselves and adds to this only the phrase about neighbours *as yourself*. And yet there is the difference of the eternal between the first and the last.

But, after all, should this be the highest? Should it not be possible to love a person *more than oneself*? Indeed, this sort of talk, born of poetic enthusiasm, is heard in the world. Could it then be true, perhaps, that Christianity is not capable of soaring so high, and therefore (presumably because it directs itself to simple, every-day men) it is left standing wretchedly with the demand to love one's neighbours *as oneself*, just as it sets the apparently very unpoetic *neighbour*[17] as the object of love instead of *a lover, a friend*, the celebrated objects of lofty love (for certainly no poet has sung of love to one's neighbour any more than of loving *as oneself*)—could this perhaps be so? Or should we, since we nevertheless make a concession to this *celebrated* love in comparison with this *commanded* love, look upon Christianity's interpretation and understanding of life as inferior because it more soberly and steadily holds itself down to earth, perhaps in the same sense as the commonplace: " Love me little, love me long"? Far from it. Christianity knows far better than any poet what love is and what it is to love. For this very reason it also knows what perhaps escapes the poet, that the love they celebrate is secretly self-love and in this very way their intoxicated expression—to love another man more than oneself—can be explained. Erotic love is still not the eternal; it is the beautiful giddiness of infinity; its highest expression is the rashness of riddles. Out of this comes its attempting an even more dizzy expression —"to love a human being more than God." This rashness pleases the poet beyond measure; it is sweet music in his ears; it inspires him to song. Alas, Christianity teaches that this is mockery of God.—The same holds true of friendship as of erotic love, insofar as this also is based on favouritism: to love this single human being above all others, to love him in distinction from all others. The object of both erotic love and friendship has therefore also the favourite's name, *the beloved*, *the friend*, who is loved in distinction from the rest of the world. On the other hand, the Christian teaching is to love one's neighbour, to love all mankind, all men, even enemies, and not to make exceptions, neither in favouritism nor in aversion.

There is only one whom a man can with the truth of the eternal love above himself—that is God. Therefore it is not said: " Thou shalt love God as thyself," but rather, " Thou shalt love the Lord thy God with all thy heart, with all thy soul, and all thy mind." A man should love God in unconditional *obedience* and love him in *adoration*. It would be ungodliness if any man dared love himself in this way, or dared love another person in this way, or dared to let another person love him in this way. If your beloved or friend asked something of you which out of honest love and in concern you had decided was harmful to him, then you must take the responsibility if you express love by complying instead of expressing love by denying the fullfillment of the desire. But God you are to love in unconditional obedience, even if what he demands of you may seem to you to be to your own harm—yes, harmful to his cause. For the wisdom of God is not to be compared with yours, and God's governance is not, in duty bound, answerable to your prudence. All you have to do is to obey in love. A human being, on the other hand, you ought only—yet, no, this is indeed the highest—therefore a human being you ought to love as you love yourself. If you can perceive what is best for him better than he himself, you shall not be excused because the harmful thing was his own desire, what he himself asked for. If this were not the case, then there could quite properly be talk about loving another person more than one's self, for this would mean—in spite of one's own insight that it was harmful to him—doing it *in compliance* because he asked for it or *in adoration* because he desired it. But you have no right to do this; you bear the responsibility if you do it, just as the other bears the responsibility if he in the same way should misuse his relationship to you.

Therefore—*as yourself.* Suppose the most cunning deceiver who has ever lived (or we could imagine him as more cunning than anyone who has ever lived), in order, if possible, to have the opportunity of using many words and becoming loquacious (for then the deceiver would quickly conquer), were temptingly to question the *royal law*[18] year in and year out, " How shall I love my neighbour? ": then the terse command, unchanged, will continue to repeat the short phrase, "as yourself." And if any deceiver has—deceived himself throughout his whole life by all sorts of verbosity concerning this subject, the eternal will only hold him to the terse word of the law, *as yourself.* No one, to be sure, will be able to escape this command. If its *as yourself* comes as close to the life of self-love as is possible, then *one's neighbour* is again a qualification as fatally close to self-love as possible. Self-love itself perceives that it is an impossibility to shirk this. The only escape is the one which the Pharisees in their time also tried in order to justify themselves: to let it be doubtful who one's neighbour is—in order to get him out of one's life.

Who, then, is one's neighbour? The word is clearly derived from *neahgebur* [near-dweller]; consequently your neighbour is he who dwells nearer than anyone else, yet not in the sense of partiality, for to love him who through favouritism is nearer to you than all others is self-love—" Do not the heathens also do the same? "[19] Your neighbour, then, is nearer to you than all others. But is he also nearer to you than you are to yourself? No, that he is not, but he is just as near or ought to be just as near to you as you are to yourself. The concept of *neighbour* really means a duplicating of one's own self. *Neighbour* is what philosophers would call the *other,* that by which the selfishness in self-love is to be tested. As far as thought is concerned the *neighbour* or *other* need not even exist. If a man living on a desert island formed his mind according to the command, he could by forsaking self-love be said to love his neighbour. To be sure, *neighbour* in itself is manifold, for *neighbour* means *all men*; and yet in another sense one person is enough in order that you may practise the law. In a selfish sense it is impossible in being a self consciously to be two. In this self-love must be alone. Nor are three needed, for if there are two, it means that there is another person whom you in a Christian sense love *as yourself* or in whom you love your *neighbour* so that you thereby love all men. But what selfishness absolutely cannot endure is duplication, and the words of the command *as yourself* are simply duplication. The ardent lover can by no means, either by reason of or in the power of his ardour, endure duplication, which here would mean giving up his erotic love if the beloved required it. The lover therefore does not love the beloved *as himself*, for he makes demands, but this *as yourself* makes the demand rather on him—alas, and yet the lover still thinks he loves the other person more than himself.

In this way *one's neighbour* is as close to the life of self-love as possible. If there are only two people, the other person is the neighbour. If there are millions, everyone of these is one's neighbour, that is, again, one who is closer than *the friend* and *the beloved*, inasmuch as these, as objects of partiality, lie so close to one's self-love. Of the fact that one's neighbour exists in this way and is so near one is usually conscious only when one wants justice done in relationship to him, when one thinks he can get something out of him. If anyone with this view asks, " Who is my neighbour? " then Christ's reply to the Pharisee contains the answer only in singular way, for in the answer the question is first turned around to mean essentially: in what manner is one to ask the question? After having told the parable of the merciful Samaritan (Luke 10 : 36), Christ says to the Pharisee, " Which of these three, do you think, proved neighbour to the man who fell among the robbers? " The Pharisee answers *correctly*, " The one who showed mercy on him." This means that by recognising your duty you easily discover who your neighbour is. The Pharisee's answer is contained in Christ's question, which by its form necessitated the Pharisee's answering in this way. He towards whom I have a duty is my neighbour, and when I fullfil my duty I prove that I am a neighbour. Christ does not speak about recognising one's neighbour but about being a neighbour oneself, about proving oneself to be a neighbour, something the Samaritan showed by his compassion. By this he did not prove that the assaulted man was his neighbour but that he was a neighbour of the one assaulted. The Levite and the priest were in a stricter sense neighbours of the assaulted man, but they wished to ignore it. On the other hand, the Samaritan, who because of prejudice was predestined to misunder-tanding, nevertheless understood rightly that he was a neighbour of the assaulted man. Choosing a lover, finding a friend, yes, that is a long, hard job, but one's neighbour is easy to recognise, easy to find—if one himself will only recognise his duty.

The command reads thus, " You shall love your neighbour as yourself," but if the command is properly understood, it also says the opposite: " *You shall love yourself in the right way.*" If anyone, therefore, refuses to learn from Christianity how to love himself in the right way, he cannot love his neighbour either. He can perhaps cling to one or more men " through thick and thin," as it is called, but this is, by no means, loving one's neighbour. To love oneself in the right way and to love one's neighbour correspond perfectly to one another; fundamentally they are one and the same thing. When the law's *as yourself* has wrested from you the self-love which Christianity sadly enough must presuppose to be in every man, then and then only have you learned how to love yourself. The law is, therefore: you shall love yourself in the same way as you love your neighbour when you love him as yourself. Whoever has any knowledge of men will certainly admit that whenever he has desired the capacity of moving others to relinquish self-love, he has also frequently been constrained to wish that it were possible to teach them to love themselves. When the activist wastes his time and powers in the service of vain, inconsequential accomplishments, is it not because he has not rightly learned how to love himself? When the frivolous person throws himself, almost like a nonentity, into the folly of the moment, is it not because he does not understand how to love himself rightly? When the melancholic dejectedly desires to be rid of life, of himself, is this not because he will not learn earnestly and rigorously to love himself? When a man surrenders himself to despair because the world or some person has left him faithlessly betrayed, what then is his fault (his innocent suffering is not referred to here) except that he does not love himself in the right way? When a man in self-torment thinks to do God a service by martyring himself, what is his sin except not willing to love himself in the right way? Alas, and when a man presumptuously lays violent hands on himself, is not his sin just this that he does not rightly love himself in genuine understanding of how a man *ought* to love himself? There is a lot of talk in the world about treachery and faith-lessness—and, God help us, it is all too true—but still let us never because of this forget that every man has in himself the most dangerous traitor of all. This treachery, whether it consists in selfishly loving one-self or in selfishly not willing to love oneself in the right way—this treachery is certainly concealed. No outcry goes up about it such as otherwise goes up in cases of treachery and faithlessness. But is it not therefore all the more important that the teaching of Christianity should be brought to mind again and again, the teaching that a man should love his neighbour as himself, that is, as he ought to love himself.

The command of love to one's neighbour therefore speaks in one and the same phrase, *as yourself*, about this neighbour-love and about love to oneself. And now the introduction to this discourse ends with what it desires to make the object of consideration: the commands of love to one's neighbour and of love to oneself become synonymous not only through this *as yourself* but still more through the phrase "you *shall*." Of this we shall speak:

YOU *shall* LOVE,

for the very mark of Christian love and its distinguishing characteristic is this, that it contains the apparent contradiction: to love is duty.

You *shall* love—this, then, is the word of the *royal law*. And truly, my reader, if you are capable of forming a conception of the conditions in the world before these words were spoken, or if you strive to understand yourself and give heed to the lives and dispositions of those who, although they call themselves Christians, really live within pagan concepts—then in relation to this Christian imperative, as in relation to everything Christian, you will humbly confess with the wonder of faith that such a command did not spring up in any human heart. Now after it has been commanded throughout Christianity's eighteen centuries and previously in Judaism; now when everyone is instructed in this and, spiritually understood, is like someone brought up in his parents' comfortable house and almost made to forget that daily bread is a gift; now when by those brought up in it Christianity is slighted in favour of all kinds of novelties, as when good food is slighted in favour of confections by someone who has never been hungry; now when Christianity is presupposed, presupposed as known by all, as given, and is alluded to—in order to proceed further—now this law of love is repeated by everyone as a matter of course, and yet how seldom, perhaps, is it observed! How seldom, perhaps, does a Christian earnestly and gratefully ponder with comprehension what his condition would have been if Christianity had not come into the world! What courage it takes to say for the first time, " You *shall* love," or, more correctly, what divine authority it takes to turn natural man's conceptions and ideas upside-down with this phrase! For there at the boundary where human speech halts and courage forsakes one, there revelation breaks forth with divine creativeness and proclaims what is not difficult to understand in the sense of profundity or human parallels, but which still did not rise up in any human heart. It really is not difficult to understand, provided it has been expressed; indeed, it wants only to be understood in order to be practised—but it did not arise in any man's heart. Take a pagan who is not spoiled by having learned thoughtlessly to patter out Christianity by rote or is not spoiled by imagining himself to be a Christian—and this command " You *shall* love " will not only surprise him but will disturb him and be an offence to him. For this very reason that which is the mark of Christianity— "All things are made new" [20]—also fits this command of love. The command is not something new in an accidental sense, nor a novelty in the sense of something curious, nor some new something in the temporal sense. Love had also existed in paganism; but this obligation to love is an alteration by the eternal—and all things are made new. What a difference there is between the interplay of the powers of feelings, of urges, of inclinations, and of passions, in short, the interplay of the powers of the spontaneous life, the artistically celebrated glory of the immediate life in smiles or in tears, in desires or in wants, what a difference there is between this and the earnestness of the eternal, the earnestness of the command in spirit and in truth, in uprightness and self-renunciation!

But human ungratefulness—what else has such a short memory! Because the highest good is now offered to everyone, men take it as nothing, discern nothing in it, to say nothing of becoming personally aware of its extraordinary quality, just as if the highest good had lost something because every man has or may have the same.—If a family possesses some costly treasure of historical significance, generation after generation the parents tell the children, and the children their children again, how it all happened. Because Christianity for so many centuries now has become the possession of the whole generation, shall all telling of the eternal change which takes place in the world through Christianity therefore cease? Is not every generation just as close, that is, just as duty-bound to make this clear to itself? Is the change less significant because it is now eighteen centuries later? Has it also become less significant that there is a God because for many centuries there have lived generations who believed on him? Has it therefore become less significant for me—whether or not I believe? And for one who lives in our time, eighteen centuries later, is it less significant to become a Christian just because it is eighteen centuries since Christianity entered the world? And if it is not so very long ago since one became a Christian, he must certainly be able to remember what he was like before he became a Christian and consequently know what a change has taken place in him—if the change of becoming a Christian has taken place in him. Therefore there is no need of a world-historical exposition of paganism as if it were eighteen centuries since the fall of paganism; for it is not so very long since both you, reader, and I were pagans, were pagans—that is, if we have become Christians at all.

This is the most tragic and ungodly kind of deception, through ingratitude to allow oneself to be cheated out of the highest, which one thinks he possesses, but which, alas, one really does not possess at all. For what is the highest possession, the possession of everything, if I never get a genuine awareness of possessing it and of what it is that I possess![21] According to the Bible, he who has earthly goods shall be like him who does not have them. I wonder if this is true also in relationship to the highest—to have it and still be like him who does not have it. I wonder if it holds true—but, no, let us not trick anyone with this question, as if it were *possible* to have the highest in this way; let us rightly consider that it is an impossibility. Worldly goods are inconsequential things and therefore Scripture teaches that they, when one possesses them, shall be possessed as inconsequential things; but the highest neither *can* nor should be possessed as something inconsequential. Worldly goods are in an external sense actualities; therefore one can possess them, although at the same time he is as one who does not possess them. But the goods of the spirit are only in inwardness, exist only *as possessed*, and therefore one cannot, if one really possesses them, be as one who does not possess them. On the contrary, if one is such a person, he does not possess them at all. If anyone thinks he has faith and yet is indifferent towards this possession, is neither cold nor hot, he can be certain that he does not have faith. If anyone thinks he is Christian and yet is indifferent towards his being a Christian, then he really is not one at all. What would we think of a man who affirmed that he was in love and also that it was a matter of indifference to him?

Therefore when we talk about Christianity, let us not, now or at any time, forget its primal character—namely, that it did not originate in any human heart.[22] Let us not forget to speak about it with that originality of faith which, if a man has it, does not believe because others have believed but because this man has been seized by that which has seized countless men before him, yet not thereby in a less original way! A tool which a craftsman uses becomes dull through the years, and a spring loses its tension and becomes weak, but that which has the tension of the eternal retains it totally unchanged throughout all time. When a strength-tester has been used for a long time, even the weak can eventually meet the test; but the eternal's standard of strength—whether or not a man has faith—a standard by which every man shall be tested, remains totally unchanged through all ages.— When Christ says (Matthew 10 : 17), " Beware of men," I wonder if this is not also meant: Beware of men, lest by men—that is, by ever-lasting comparison with other men, by customs and externals—you let yourself be tricked out of the highest good. For the chicaneries of a betrayer are not very dangerous, since one is the more readily alerted to them; but this, to have the highest good in a sort of indifferent fellowship, in the indolence of habit, yes, in the indolence of a habit which even sets up the generation in place of the individual, making the generation the recipient and the individual a sharer automatically on the strength of this—this is a terrible thing. Certainly the highest good shall not be booty; you shall not selfishly have it for yourself, for what you can have only for yourself alone is never the highest good. But even if in the deepest sense you have the highest good in common with everyone (and precisely this is the highest; this you can have in common with all), you shall, believing, nevertheless have it for yourself so that you keep it while everyone else, perhaps, also keeps it—but, in addition, even though everyone else gave it up! Guard yourself against men also in this way: " Be shrewd as serpents " in order to preserve the secret of faith for yourself, even though you hope and desire and work that every one may do as you do; " Be innocent as doves,"[23] for faith is this very simplicity. You shall not use ingenuity in order to make faith into something else, but, wise among men, you shall use ingenuity in order to protect the secret of faith in you, guarding yourself against men. Is a password no secret just because everyone knows it, individually, because it is confided to everyone and preserved by everyone as a secret? The secret of a password, however, is one thing to-day and another to-morrow. But the essence of faith is to be a secret, to be for the single individual; if it is not preserved as a secret by each individual, even when he professes it, he believes not at all.

Is there perhaps something lacking in faith since in this way it is and continues to be and ought to be a secret? Is this not also the case with erotic love, is it not rather the transient emotions which become manifest immediately and dwindle away and the deep impression which always maintains secrecy, so that we even say, and rightly so, that the falling in love which does not make a man secretive is not real falling in love? Secret falling in love can be an image of faith; but the hidden man's imperishable inwardness in faith is life itself. He who shrewd as a serpent guards himself against men in order that, simple as a dove, he may preserve the secret of faith, he also has, as the Scriptures say (Mark 9 : 50) "salt in himself"; but if he does not guard himself against men, the salt loses its strength and wherewith shall it then be salted? Even if it does happen that the secrecy of erotic love becomes a man's downfall, faith is eternal and is always the saving secret! Consider, for example, the woman with hæmorrhages:[24] she did not push herself forward in order to touch Christ's robe; she told no one else what she had in mind and what she believed—she said very softly to herself, " If I only touch the hem of his robe I shall be healed." The secret she kept to herself; it was the secret of faith which saved her both for time and eternity. This secret you can have for yourself also when you forthrightly profess the faith, and when you lie weak on your sick-bed and cannot move a limb, when you cannot even move your tongue, you can still have this secret within you.

The primal character of faith is related to the originality of Christianity. Lengthy descriptions of paganism, its errors, its distinctive characteristics, are not at all necessary; the marks of Christianity are contained in Christianity itself. Make a test: forget Christianity for a moment and think of what you ordinarily know as love; call to mind what you read in the poets, what you yourself can find out, and then see if it ever has occurred to you to think this: you *shall* love. Be honest—but lest this disturb you, I will honestly admit that many, many times in my life I have been startled in wonder over the fact that love thereby at times seemed to lose everything, even though it gains everything. Be honest, admit that to most people, perhaps, the poets' glowing descriptions of erotic love, of friendship, seem far higher than this poor: " You *shall* love."

" You shall love." *Only when it is a duty to love, only then is love eternally secured against every change, eternally made free in blessed independence, eternally and happily secured against despair.*

However joyous, however happy, however indescribably confident instinctive and inclinational love, spontaneous love, can be in itself, it still feels precisely in its most beautiful moment the need to establish itself, if possible, more securely. Therefore the two pledge; they pledge fidelity or friendship to one another. And when we talk most solemnly we do not say of the two: " They love one another"; we say " They pledged fidelity" or " They pledged friendship to one another." By what, then, do they swear this love? We shall not confuse the issue and be distracted by calling to mind the great variety of invocations used by the poets, the spokesmen of this love—for in relation to erotic love it is the poet who makes the two promise, the poet who joins the two, the poet who prophesies an Eden for the two and lets them swear —in short, the poet is the priest. Does this love swear, then, by something which is higher than itself? No, this it does not do. Precisely this is the beautiful, touching, enigmatic, poetic misunderstanding— that the two do not themselves discover it, and for this very reason the poet is their sole beloved confidant, because he does not discover it either. When erotic love swears fidelity, it really gives to itself the significance by which it swears; it is love itself which casts the lustre over that by which it swears. Therefore it not only does not swear by something higher but really swears by something which is less than itself. This love is indescribably rich in its own loving misunderstanding; just because it is itself an infinite richness, an unlimited certainty, when it wishes to swear it swears by something poor but does not itself realise this. The result is that this swearing, which should be and honestly thinks itself to be the highest seriousness, is nevertheless a most beguiling jest. And this mysterious friend, the poet, who as the closest confidant has the best understanding of this love, does not understand it either. Yet it is easy to understand that if one is really to swear, he must swear by something higher; then God in heaven is the only one who is truly in a position to swear by himself. But the poet cannot understand this—that is, the individual who is a poet can well understand it, but insofar as he is a poet he cannot understand it, inasmuch as the *poet* cannot understand it; for the poet understands everything, in riddles, and marvellously explains everything, in riddles, but he cannot understand himself, or understand that he himself is a riddle. If he were compelled to understand this, he would, if he did not become indignant and embittered, sadly say: would that this understanding had not been forced on me—it disturbs what is most beautiful to me, it disturbs my life, and yet I can make no use of it. Thus far the poet is right in the matter, for true understanding means the decisive settlement of the life-problems of his existence. There are, then, two riddles: the first is the love of the two persons, and the second is the poet's explanation of it, or that the poet's explanation is also a riddle.

In such a way erotic love swears, and then the two add an Eden—they will love each other "for ever." If this is not added, the poet will not join the two; he turns away, indifferent, from such time-bound love, or mocking he turns against it, since he belongs eternally to this eternal love. There are, then, really two unions, first of the two who will love each other for ever, and then of the poet, who wants to belong to the two for ever. And the poet is right in this that when two persons will not love one another for ever, their love is not worth talking about, even less worthy of artistic celebration. But the poet does not detect the misunderstanding: that the two swear *by their love* to love each other for ever instead of swearing *by the eternal* their love to one another. The eternal is the higher. If one is to swear, then one must swear by the higher; but if one swears by the eternal, then one swears by duty—that "one *shall* love." Alas, but this favourite of the lovers, the poet, he who is even rarer than the real lovers whom his longing seeks, he who himself is love's marvel, he is also like the delicate child—he cannot endure this *shall* and as soon as it is mentioned he either becomes impatient or he begins to weep.

Therefore this spontaneous love has, according to the beautiful understanding of the imagination, the eternal in itself, but it is not consciously grounded upon the eternal and consequently can be *changed*. Even if it does not change, it still can be changed, for it is indeed happiness or good fortune, but what is true of fortune is true of happiness, which, if one thinks of the eternal, cannot be thought of without sadness, just as it is said with a shudder: "Happiness is when it has been."[25] That is to say, as long as it lasted or was in existence change was possible; only after it is gone can one say that it lasted. "Count no man happy while he is living." As long as he is living his happiness can change; only when he is dead and happiness had not left him while he lived, only then is it certain that he was happy. That which merely exists, having undergone no change, is continually confronted by the possibility of change; change may occur at any time; even in the last moment it can happen, and only when life has come to an end can one say: change did not take place—or perhaps it did. Whatever has undergone no change certainly has *continuance*, but it does not have *continuity*; insofar as it has continuance, it exists, but insofar as it has not won enduring continuity amid change, it cannot become contemporaneous with itself and is either happily unconscious of this misalignment or is disposed to sorrow. Only the eternal can be and become and remain contemporaneous with every age; temporality, on the other hand, divides within itself, and the present cannot become contemporary with the future, or the future with the past, or the past with the present. Of that which has won continuity in undergoing change, one can not only say when it has existed, " It existed," but one can say, " It had continuity throughout its existence." Just this is the safeguard, and the relationship is entirely different from that of happiness or good fortune. When love has undergone the transformation of the eternal by being made duty, it has won continuity, and then it follows of itself that it survives. It is not self-evident that what exists in this moment will exist in the next moment, but it is self-evident that the continuous survives. We say that something survives the test, and we praise it when it has survived the test; but this is said about the imperfect, for the survival of the continuous will not and cannot reveal itself by surviving a test—it is indeed the continuous—and only the transient can give itself the appearance of continuity by surviving a test. No one would think of saying that sterling silver [Prøve Sølv] must survive the test [Prøve] of time, for it is, after all, sterling silver. Thus it is also with regard to love. The love which simply exists, however fortunate, however blissful, however satisfying, however poetic it is, still must survive the test of the years. But the love which has undergone the transformation of the eternal by becoming duty has won continuity; it is sterling silver. Is such enduring love perhaps less useful, less applicable in life? Is, then, sterling silver less useful? Indeed not. Speech, involuntarily, and thought, consciously, honour sterling silver in a characteristic way merely by saying, " One uses it." There is no talk at all about testing; one does not insult it by wishing to test it; one knows in advance that sterling silver endures. Therefore when one uses a less reliable alloy, one is compelled to be more scrupulous and to speak less simply; one is compelled almost ambiguously to use double-talk and say, " One uses it, and while one uses it he also tests it," for it is always possible that it may undergo a change.

Consequently, *only when it is a duty to love, only then is love eternally secure.* This security of the eternal casts out all anxiety and makes the love perfect, perfectly secure. For in that love which has only existence, however confident it may be, there is still an anxiety, anxiety over the possibility of change. Such love does not itself understand any more than the poet that this is anxiety, for the anxiety is hidden; the only expression is a burning passion, whereby is merely hinted that anxiety is hidden at the bottom. Otherwise why is it that spontaneous love is so inclined to—yes, so in love with—making a test of the love? This is just because love has not, by becoming a duty, in the deepest sense undergone *the test*. From this comes what the poet would call sweet unrest, which more and more foolhardily wants to make the test. The lover wants to test the beloved. The friend wants to test the friend. Testing certainly has its basis in love, but this violently flaming desire to test and this hankering desire to be put to the test explain that the love itself is unconsciously uncertain. Here again is an enigmatic misunderstanding in this spontaneous love and in the poet's explanation. The lovers and the poet think that this urge to test love is precisely an expression of how certain it is. But is this really so? It is quite right that one does not care to test what is unimportant to him; but from this it certainly does not follow that wanting to test the beloved is an expression of certainty. The two love one another; they love one another for all eternity; they are so certain—that they put it to a test. Is this the highest certainty? Is not this relationship just like that of love's swearing and swearing again by what is lower than love? In this way the lovers' highest expression for the constancy of their love is an expression of its merely existing; and one tests that which merely has existence, one puts it to the test. But when it is a duty to love, neither is a test needed nor the insulting foolhardiness of wanting to test, because if love is higher than every test it has already more than passed the test in the same sense that faith "more than conquers."[26] Testing is always related to possibility; there is always the possibility that what is being tested will not pass the test. Therefore if one would test whether he has faith or would try to get faith, it really means he will prevent himself from getting faith; he will bring himself into the unrest of covetousness where faith is never won, for " You *shall* believe." If a believer were to ask God to put his faith to a test, this would not be an expression of the believer's having faith in an extraordinarily high degree (to think this is a poetic misunderstanding, as it is also a misunderstanding to have faith in an *extraordinary* degree, since the ordinary degree is the highest), but it would be an expression of his having no faith at all, for " You *shall* believe." Never has any greater security been found and never shall the peace of the eternal be found in anything other than in this " You shall." The idea of testing, however congenial it may be, is an unquiet thought, and it is the disquietude which makes one fancy that this is a higher proof. For testing is in itself inventive and is not to be exhausted any more than human knowledge has ever been able to calculate all the contingencies; on the other hand, as the earnest one says so well, " Faith has encompassed all contingencies." When one *shall*, it is for ever decided; and when you will understand that you *shall* love, your love is for ever secure.

By this " You shall " love is also for ever secured *against every change*. For that love which has only existence can be changed; it can be changed *within itself*, and it can be changed *into something else*.

Spontaneous love can be changed within itself; it can be changed to its opposite, to *hate*. Hate is a love which has become its opposite, a ruined love. Deep down love is continually aflame, but it is the flame of hate. When love is first burned out, the flame of hate is also put out for the first time. Just as we say of the tongue, that " It is the same tongue with which we bless and curse,"[27] so may one also say that it is the same love which loves and hates. But just because it is the same love, just for that reason it is not in the eternal sense the true love which *unchanged remains the same*; rather, this spontaneous love is fundamentally *the same* even when *changed*. True love, which has undergone the transformation of the eternal by becoming duty, is never changed, it has integrity; it loves—and never hates; it never hates the beloved. It might seem as if this spontaneous love were the stronger because it can do both, because it can *both* love and hate; it might seem as if it had an entirely different power over its object when it says, " If you will not love me, I will hate you "—but this is only an illusion. Even if changeableness is indeed a stronger power than unchangeableness, then who is stronger, he who says, " If you do not love me, I will hate you," or he who says, "If you hate me, I will still continue to love you?" Certainly it is terrifying and terrible when love is changed into hate, but for whom is it really terrible? I wonder if it is not most terrible for the one concerned, the one within whom love has turned to hate!

Spontaneous love can be changed within itself; by spontaneous combustion it can become *jealousy*; from the greatest happiness it can become the greatest torment. The heat of spontaneous love is so dangerous—no matter how great its passion is—so dangerous that this heat can easily become a fever. Spontaneity is, as it were, the fermenting element, so called because it has not yet undergone a change and therefore has not separated from itself the poison which engenders the heat in the fermenting element. If love kindles itself with this poison instead of expelling it, jealousy appears—alas, as the word itself [*Iversyge*] says, it is a zealousness for becoming sick, a sickness from zealousness. The jealous man does not hate the object of love, far from it; but he tortures himself with the flame of requited love which with purifying power should cleanse his love. The jealous man picks up— almost like a beggar—every beam of love in the beloved, but through the burning glass of jealousy he focuses all these beams of love upon his own love, and he is slowly consumed. On the other hand, the love which has undergone the change of the eternal by becoming duty does not know jealousy; it does not merely love as it is loved—but it loves. Jealousy loves as it is loved. Anxiously tortured by thoughts as to whether it is being loved, it is just as jealous about its own love, about the possibility of its being disproportionate in relation to the other's indifference, as it is jealous of the manifestation of the other's love. Anxiously tortured by preoccupation with itself, it dares neither absolutely trust the beloved nor wholeheartedly surrender itself, lest it give too much and thereby continually burn itself as one burns himself on that which is not burning—except in the contact of anxiety. Spontaneous combustion is comparable. It would seem as if spontaneous love were an entirely different kind of fire since it can become jealousy. Alas, but this fire is a dreadful thing. It would seem as if jealousy might hold its object far more securely since it watches with a hundred eyes, and simple love can have only one eye, as it were, for its love. But I wonder if multiplicity is stronger than unity. I wonder if a heart torn asunder is stronger than a whole, undivided heart. I wonder if a continually anxious grasp holds its object more securely than the unified power of simplicity? How, then, is this simple love secured against jealousy? I wonder if it is not by avoiding comparisons in loving? It does not begin by spontaneously loving according to preference—it just loves. Therefore it can never reach the point of morbidly loving in accordance with comparisons—it just loves.

Spontaneous love can be changed *into something else*. It can be changed through the years—something seen often enough. Thus love loses its ardour, its joy, its desire, its originative power, its living freshness. As the river which sprang out of rocks disperses farther down in the sluggishness of the dead-waters, so is love exhausted in the lukewarmness and indifference of habit. Alas, of all the enemies habit is perhaps the most cunning, and it is cunning enough never to let itself be seen, for he who sees the habit is saved from the habit. Habit is not like other enemies which one sees and against which one strives and defends himself. The struggle is really with oneself in order that one sees it. There is a preying creature, known for its cunning, which slyly falls upon the sleeping. While it sucks blood from the sleeping prey, it fans and cools him and makes his sleeping still more pleasant. Such is habit—or it is even worse; for the vampire seeks its prey among the sleeping, but it has no means to lull to sleep those who are awake. Habit, however, can do this. It slinks, sleep-lulling, upon a man, and then drains the blood of the sleeper while it coolingly fans him and makes sleep still more pleasant to him.—In this way spontaneous love can be changed into something else and made unrecognisable—for love is still recognisable in hate and jealousy. Just as when a forgotten dream flashes by again, one himself becomes aware that habit has changed him; he wants to make up for it, but he does not know where he can go to buy new oil[28] to rekindle his love. Then he becomes despondent, annoyed, weary of himself, weary of his love, weary of its being as paltry as it is, weary of not being able to get it transformed—alas, for he had not heeded the transformation of the eternal in time, and now he has lost the capacity to endure the cure. At times one sorrowfully sees a poverty-stricken man who had once lived prosperously, and still, how much more sorrowful than this is the change which one sees in a love changed almost to loathsomeness! —If, on the other hand, love undergoes the transformation of the eternal by becoming duty, it does not become characterised by habit; habit can never get power over it. To what is said of eternal life, that there is no sighing and no tears, one can add: there is no habit; certainly this is not saying anything less glorious. If you will save your soul or your love from habit's cunning—yes, men believe there are many ways of keeping oneself awake and secure, but there is really only one: the eternal's " You shall." Let the thunder of a hundred cannon remind you three times daily to resist the force of habit. Like that powerful Eastern emperor,[29] keep a slave who reminds you daily— keep hundreds. Have a friend who reminds you every time he sees you. Have a wife who, in love, reminds you early and late—but be careful that all this also does not become a habit! For you can become accustomed to hearing the thunder of a hundred cannon so that you can sit at the table and hear the most trivial, insignificant things far more clearly than the thunder of the hundred cannon—which you have become accustomed to hearing. And you can become so accustomed to having a hundred slaves remind you every day that you no longer hear, because through habit you have acquired the ear which hears and still does not hear. No, only the eternal's " You shall " and the hearing ear which will hear this "shall" can save you from habit. Habit is the most miserable transformation, but on the other hand one can accustom himself to every change; only the eternal, and consequently that which has undergone the transformation of the eternal by becoming duty, is the unchangeable, but the unchangeable simply cannot become habit. However fast a habit fixes itself, it never becomes the unchangeable, even if the person becomes incorrigible. Habit is always that which *ought to be changed*; the unchangeable, on the contrary, is that which neither *can* nor *ought* to be changed! But the eternal never becomes old and never becomes habit.

Only when it is a duty to love, only then is love made eternally free in blessed independence. Is, then, spontaneous love not free? Has the lover no freedom at all in his love? But, on the other hand, should it be the purpose of the discourse to eulogise the miserable independence of self-love, which remains independent because it did not have the courage to bind itself and therefore remains independent through its cowardliness? Should it praise this miserable independence which swings suspended because it finds no foothold and is like him "who strolls here and there, an armed highwayman who turns in wherever twilight finds him? " Should it praise the miserable independence which independently submits to no bonds—at least not visibly? Far from it. On the contrary, in the foregoing portion we have pointed out that the manifestation of the highest riches is to have a need; therefore to have a need in freedom is the true expression of freedom. He in whom love is a need certainly feels himself free in his love, and the very one who feels himself entirely dependent, so that he would lose everything by losing the beloved, that very one is independent. Yet there is one condition—that he does not confuse love with possession of the beloved. If one were to say, " Either love or die" and thereby signify that life without loving is not worth living, we should say he is absolutely right. But if he understood it to mean possession of the beloved and consequently to mean either to possess the beloved or die, either win this friend or die, then we must say that such a misconceived love is dependent. As soon as love, in its relation to its object, does not in that relationship relate just as much to itself, although it still is entirely dependent, then it is dependent in a false sense, then the law of its existence is outside itself, and therefore it is in a contemptible sense, in an earthly, in a temporal sense, dependent. But the love which has undergone the transformation of the eternal by becoming duty and which loves because it *shall* love—this love is independent; it has the law of its existence in the relationship of love itself to the eternal. This love can never become dependent in a false sense, for the only thing it is dependent upon is duty, and duty alone makes for genuine freedom. Spontaneous love makes a man free and in the next moment dependent. It is as with a man's existence. By coming into existence, by becoming a *self*,[30] he becomes free, but in the next moment he is dependent on this self. Duty, however, makes a man dependent and at the same moment eternally independent. " Only law can give freedom." Alas, we often think that freedom exists and that it is law which binds freedom. Yet it is just the opposite; without law freedom does not exist at all, and it is law which gives freedom. We also think that it is law which makes distinctions, because where there is no law there is no distinction. Yet it is just the opposite—when it is law which makes distinctions, it is in fact the law which makes everyone equal before the law.

In this way the " You shall " makes love free in blessed independence; such a love stands and does not fall with variations in the object of love; it stands and falls with eternity's law, but therefore it never falls. Such a love is not dependent on this or on that. It is dependent on the one thing—that alone which makes for freedom—and therefore it is eternally independent. But nothing can be compared with this independence. Sometimes the world praises a proud independence which thinks it has no need of being loved, if at the same time it "needs other men—not in order to be loved by them, but in order to love them, in order nevertheless to have someone to love." How false is this independence! It feels no *need* of being loved, and yet *needs* someone to love; consequently it stands in need of another person— in order to gratify its proud self-esteem. Is this not like the vanity which thinks it can dispense with the world and still needs the world, that is, needs the world to become conscious of the fact that vanity does not need the world! But the love which has undergone the transformation of the eternal by becoming duty feels unambiguously a need to be loved, and this need is therefore in eternally harmonising accord with the " You shall." But it can do without it if it *ought* to, while it still continues to love: is not this independence? This independence is dependent only on love itself through the *ought* of the eternal; it is not dependent on anything else, and therefore it is not dependent on the object of love as soon as it appears to be something else. Yet such a situation does not mean that this independent love has then ceased, has changed into proud self-approval—this is dependence. No, love abides; it is independent. Unchangeableness is true independence; every change—be it the swoon of weakness or the strut of pride, be it sighing or self-satisfied—is dependence. If when another says, " I cannot love you any longer " one proudly answers, " Then I can also get along without loving you."—Is this independence? Alas, it is dependence, for whether he shall continue to love or not is dependent on whether the other will love. But he who answers, " Then I *will* still continue to love you nevertheless "—his love is made eternally free in blessed independence. He does not say it proudly—dependent on his pride—no, he says it humbly, humbling himself under the eternal's " You shall "; for that very reason he is independent.

Only when it is a duty to love, only then is love eternally and happily secured against despair.[31] Spontaneous love can become unhappy, can reach the point of despair. Again this might seem to be an expression of the strength of this love, that it has the power of despair, but this is mere appearance. Despair's power, however highly it is regarded, is nevertheless impotence; its utmost is nothing more nor less than its defeat. Yet this—that spontaneous love can reach the point of despair—proves that it is in despair, that even when it is happy it loves with the power of despair—loves another person "more than himself, more than God." Of despair it must be said: only he can despair who is in despair. When spontaneous love despairs over misfortune, it only reveals that it was in despair, that in happiness it had also been in despair. The despair lies in relating oneself with infinite passion to a single individual, for with infinite passion one can relate oneself—if one is not in despair— only to the eternal. Spontaneous love is in despair in this way; but when it becomes happy, as it is called, its state of desperation is hidden; when it becomes unhappy it is revealed—that it was in despair. On the other hand, the love which has undergone the transformation of the eternal by becoming duty can never despair, simply because it *is* not in despair. Despair is not something which can happen to a man, an event such as fortune or misfortune. Despair is a disrelationship in one's inmost being; no fate or event can penetrate so far and so deep; events can only make manifest—that the disrelationship was there. For this reason there is only one assurance against despair: to undergo the transformation of the eternal through duty's " You shall "; every- one who has not undergone this transformation is in despair. Good fortune and prosperity can hide it; misfortune and difficulties, on the other hand, do not make him despair, as he thinks, but make manifest —that he was in despair. If one speaks otherwise, it is because one carelessly confuses the highest concepts. That which makes a man despair is not misfortune, but it is this: that he lacks the eternal. Despair is to lack the eternal; despair consists in not having undergone the transformation of the eternal through duty's " You shall." Despair is not, therefore, the loss of the beloved—that is misfortune, pain, and suffering; but despair is the lack of the eternal.

How, then, can this love which is commanded be secured against despair? Very simply—by the command—by this " You shall love." It consists first and foremost in this that you must not love in such a manner that the loss of the beloved would make manifest that you were in despair—that is, you absolutely must not love despairingly. Is loving thereby forbidden? By no méans. It would be strange, indeed, if the command which says, " You shall love," were by its own order to forbid loving. Therefore the command only forbids loving in a manner which is not bidden. Essentially the command is not negative, but positive—it commands that you shall love. Therefore love's command does not secure itself against despair by means of feeble, lukewarm grounds of comfort; that one must not take things too seriously, *etc*. Indeed, is such wretched prudence which "has ceased to sorrow" any less despair than the lover's despair? Is it not rather a worse kind of despair! No, love's command forbids despair—by commanding one to love. Who would have this courage without the eternal; who is prepared to say this " You shall " without the eternal, which, in the very moment when love wants to despair over its unhappiness, commands one to love. Where can this command have its base except in the eternal? For when it is made impossible to possess the beloved in time, the eternal says, " You shall love "; that is, the eternal then rescues love precisely by making it eternal. Let it be death which separates the two—then when the bereaved one sinks in despair, what can be of help? Temporal help is a still more doleful kind of despair; then it is the eternal which helps. When it says " You shall love," it says, " Your love has an eternal worth." But it does not say this comfortingly, for that would not help; it says this commandingly, precisely because there is danger afoot. And when the eternal says, " You shall love," it becomes the eternal's responsibility to make sure that it can be done. What is all other consolation compared with that of the eternal! What is all other soul-care compared to that of the eternal! If it were to speak more mildly and say, " Console your-self," the sorrowing one would certainly have objections ready, but—yes, it is not because the eternal will proudly tolerate no objection—out of concern for the sorrowing one it commands, " You shall love." Marvellous words of comfort, marvellous compassion—because humanly speaking it is very odd, almost a mockery, to say to the despairing one that he *ought* to do that which is his only desire, but whose impossibility[32] brings him to despair. Is any other proof needed that the love-command is of divine origin? If you have tried it, or if you would try it, go to such a sorrowing person in the moment when the loss of the beloved is about to overpower him, and discover then what you can find to say. Confess that you want to bring consolation. The one thing you will not think of saying is, " You shall love." And on the other hand, see if it does not almost provoke the sorrowing one the very moment it is said, because it seems the most unsuitable thing to say on such an occasion. But you who have had this earnest experience, you who in the dark moment found emptiness and loathsomeness in the human grounds of consolation—but no consolation—you who discovered in a dreadful way that not even the exhortation of the eternal could keep you from sinking—you learned to love this " You shall " which saves from despair. What you perhaps often verified in lesser relationships, that true up-building consists in rigorous speaking, this you now learned in the deepest sense—that only the " You shall " eternally and happily rescues from despair. Eternally happy—yes, for only he is saved from despair who is eternally saved from despair. The love which has undergone the transformation of the eternal by becoming duty is not exempted from misfortune, but it is saved from despair, in fortune and misfortune equally saved from despair.

Behold, passion inflames, worldly sagacity cools, but neither this heat nor this cold nor the blending of this heat and this cold is the pure air of the eternal. There is something fiery in this heat and some-thing sharp in this cold and in the blending something nondescript or an unconscious deceitfulness, as in the dangerous part of Spring. But this " You shall love " takes all the unsoundness away and preserves for eternity what is sound. So it is everywhere—this " You shall " of the eternal is the saving element, purifying, elevating. Sit with one who deeply mourns. There is relief for a moment if you have the ability to give to passion the expression of despair—something not even the mourner can do—but it is still false. It can be refreshingly tempting for a moment if at the same time you have the knowledge and experience to hold out a prospect where the mourner sees none—but it is still false. But this " You shall sorrow" is both true and beautiful. I do not have the right to harden myself against the pains of life, for I *ought* to sorrow; but neither have I the right to despair, for I *ought* to sorrow; furthermore, neither do I have the right to stop sorrowing, for I *ought* to sorrow. So it is also with love. You have no right to harden yourself against this emotion, for you *ought* to love; but neither do you have the right to love despairingly, for you *ought* to love; just as little do you have the right to misuse this emotion in you, for you *ought* to love. You ought to preserve the love and you ought to preserve yourself and in and by preserving yourself to preserve the love. There where the merely human wants to storm forth, the command still holds; there where the merely human would lose courage, the command strengthens; there where the merely human would become tired and clever, the command flames up and gives wisdom. The command consumes and burns out what is unsound in your love, but through the command you shall be able to kindle it again when humanly considered it would cease. When you think you can easily give counsel, take the command as your counsel; but when you do not know how to counsel, the command shall prevail so that everything nevertheless comes out well.

II B

You Shall Love Your *Neighbour*

*It is in fact Christian love which discovers and knows that one's neighbour
exists and that—it is one and the same thing—everyone is one's neighbour.
If it were not a duty to love, then there would be no concept of neighbour
at all. But only when one loves his neighbour, only then is the selfishness
of preferential love rooted out and the equality of the eternal preserved.*

The objection is often made against Christianity—though in different
manners and moods, with various passions and purposes—that it
displaces erotic love and friendship.[33] Then, again, men have wanted
to defend Christianity and to that end appealed to its doctrine that
one ought to love God with his whole heart and his neighbour as
himself. When the argument is carried on in this manner, it is quite
indifferent whether one agrees or disagrees, just as a fight with air and
an agreement with air are equally meaningless. One should rather
take pains to clarify the point of contention in order calmly to admit
in the defence that Christianity has thrust erotic love and friendship
from the throne, the love rooted in mood and inclination, preferential
love, in order to establish spiritual love in its place, love to one's
neighbour, a love which in all earnestness and truth is inwardly more
tender in the union of two persons than erotic love is and more faithful
in the sincerity of close relationship than the most famous friendship.
One must rather take pains to make very clear that the praise of erotic
love and friendship belong to paganism, that the *poet* really belongs to
paganism since his task belongs to it—in order with the sure spirit of
conviction to give to Christianity what belongs to Christianity, love
to one's neighbour, of which love not a trace is found in paganism.
One must rather take care to discern and divide rightly, in order, if
possible, to occasion the individual to choose, instead of confusing and

combining and thereby hindering the individual from getting a definite impression of which is which. Above all, one must refrain from defending Christianity, rather than consciously or unconsciously wanting to uphold everything—also what is non-Christian.

Everyone who earnestly and with insight thinks on these things will easily see that the question for discussion must be posed in this way: are erotic love and friendship the highest love or must this love be dethroned? Erotic love and friendship are related to passion, but all passion, whether it attacks or defends itself, fights in one manner only: either—or: "Either I exist and am the highest or I do not exist at all —either all or nothing." Confusion and bewilderment (which paganism and the poet are opposed to just as much as Christianity is) develops when the defence amounts to this—that Christianity certainly teaches a higher love but *in addition* praises friendship and erotic love. To talk thus is a double betrayal—inasmuch as the speaker has neither the spirit of the poet nor the spirit of Christianity. Concerning relationships of the spirit, one cannot—if one wants to avoid talking foolishly—talk like a shopkeeper who has the best grade of goods and in addition a medium grade, which he can *also* highly recommend as being almost as good. No, if it is certain that Christianity teaches that love to God and one's neighbour is true love, then it is also certain that as it has thrust down "every proud obstacle to the knowledge of God and takes every thought captive to obey Christ"[34]—that it likewise has also thrust down erotic love and friendship. Would it not be remarkable—if Christianity were such a confusing and bewildering subject as many a defence (often worse than any attack) would make it into—would it not be remarkable, then, that in the whole New Testament there is not found a word about love in the sense in which the poet sings of it and paganism defined it; would it not be remarkable that in the whole New Testament there is not found a single word about friendship in the sense in which the poet sings of it and paganism cultivated it. Or let the poet who himself understands what it is to be a poet go through what the New Testament teaches about love, and he will be plunged into despair because he will not find a single word which could inspire him. And if, for all that, any so-called poet did find a word and used it, then it would be a deceitful, guilt-laden use, for instead of respecting Christianity, he would be stealing a precious word and distorting the meaning in his use of it. Let the poet search the New Testament for a word about friendship which could please him, and he will search vainly unto despair. But let a Christian search, one who wants to love his neighbour; he certainly will not search in vain; he will find each word stronger and more authoritative than the last, serving to kindle this love in him and to keep him in this love.

The poet will seek in vain. But is a poet, then, not a Christian? We have not said this, nor do we say it, either, but say only that *qua* poet he is not a Christian. Yet a distinction must be drawn, for there are also godly poets. But these do not celebrate erotic love and friendship; their songs are to the glory of God, songs of faith and hope and love.[35] Nor do these poets sing of love in the sense a poet sings of erotic love, for love to one's neighbour is not to be sung about—it is to be fullfilled in reality. Even if there were nothing else to hinder the poet from artistically celebrating love to one's neighbour in song, it is quite enough that with invisible letters behind every word in Holy Scriptures a disturbing notice confronts him—for there it reads: go and do likewise. Does this sound like an artistic challenge, inviting him to sing? —Consequently the religious poet is a special case, but it holds true of the secular poet that *qua* poet he is not a Christian. And it is the secular poet we usually think of when we speak of poets. That the poet lives within Christianity does not alter the matter. Whether *he* is a Christian is not for us to decide, but *qua* poet he is not a Christian. It might well seem that since Christendom has existed so long now it must have penetrated all relationships—and all of us.[36] But this is an illusion. Because Christianity has existed so long, it cannot thereby be said that it is we who have lived so long or have been Christians so long. The poet's very existence within Christianity and the place which is accorded to him are an earnest reminder (rudeness and envious attacks on him are certainly not *Christian* objections or misgivings concerning his presence) of how much is taken for granted and how easily we are tempted to fancy ourselves far in advance of ourselves. Whereas, alas, the Christian proclamation very often is scarcely listened to, everybody listens to the poet, admires him, learns from him, is enchanted by him; whereas, alas, men quickly forget what the pastor has said, how accurately and how long they remember what the poet has said, especially what he has said with the help of the actor! The significance of this cannot be that men should seek to get rid of the poet, perhaps by force, for this would result only in a new illusion. What good would it be if there were no poets if in Christendom there were still so many who are contented with the understanding of existence which the poet presides over—and so many who long for the poet! Neither is it required of a Christian that he, in blind and unwise zeal, should go so far that he could no longer bear to read a poet—any more than it is required that a Christian should not eat ordinary food with others or that he should live apart from others in seclusion's hermitage. No, but the Christian must understand everything differently from the non-Christian, must understand himself in that he knows how to make the distinction. A man would not be able to live every moment exclusively in the highest Christian ideals any more than he could live only on the food from the Lord's table. Therefore simply let the poet be, let the individual poet be admired as he deserves, if he really is a poet, but also let the single one in Christendom try his Christian convictions by the help of this test: how does he relate himself to the poet, what does he think of him, how does he read him, how does he admire him? Such things are hardly ever discussed these days. Alas to many people this discussion will seem to be neither Christian nor earnest enough, just because it has to do with such things which nevertheless—note this—occupy men so much six days of the week, and even more of their time on the seventh day than do godly things. Meanwhile we are confident—because from childhood we have been well educated and trained in Christianity and also because in these more mature years we have dedicated our days and our best powers to this service, even though we always repeat that our voice is "without authority"[37]—we have confidence in the knowledge particularly of what should be said in these times and of how it should be said. We are all baptized and instructed in Christianity; there can consequently be no talk about professing Christ in contrast to the non-Christian. It is, however, both beneficial and necessary that the single individual carefully and consciously scrutinises himself and, if possible, helps others (insofar as one man can help another, for God is the true helper)[38] to become Christian in a deeper and deeper sense. The word *Christendom* as a common designation for a whole nation is a superscription which easily says too much and therefore easily leads the individual to believe too much about himself. It is a custom—at least in other places—that signs stand along the highway indicating where the road leads. Suppose that just as one sets out on a journey he sees on such a sign that the road leads to the distant place which is his destination: has he therefore reached the place? So it is also with this road-sign *Christendom*. It designates the direction, but has one therefore reached the goal, or is one always only—on the way? Is it an advance along the road to go on that road for an hour once a week and for six days of the week to live in entirely different categories and make no attempt to understand how all this can hang together? Is it genuine earnestness, then, to be silent about the problem of integrity and relationships in order to talk very solemnly about very serious things, which might just as well be brought along into the confusion, if, out of sheer earnestness, one does not show the relationship to these serious matters. Who has the more difficult task: the teacher who lectures on earnest things a meteor's distance from everyday life—or the learner who should put it to use? Is only this a fraud, to be silent about serious matters? Is it not just as dangerous a fraud to speak of these things—but under certain conditions—and portray them—but in a light altogether different from reality's daily life? If it is true, then, that all of secular life, its pomp, its diversions, its charm, can in so many ways imprison and ensnare a man, what is the earnest thing to do—either from sheer earnestness to be silent in the church about things, or earnestly to speak about them there in order, if possible, to fortify men against the dangers of the world? Should it really be impossible to talk about things of the world in a solemn and truly earnest manner? If it were impossible, does it follow that it should be suppressed in the religious discourse? Certainly not, for the implication is that such things should be prohibited in religious discourse only on the most solemn occasions.

Therefore we will test the Christian conviction on the poet. What does the poet teach about love and friendship? The question is not about this or that particular poet, but only about the poet, that is, only about him as far as he is faithful as a poet to himself and to his task. If such a so-called poet has lost faith in the artistic worth of erotic love and friendship and in its interpretation and has supplanted it by something else, he is not a poet, and perhaps the something else which he sets in its place is not Christian either, and the whole thing is a blunder. Erotic love is based on disposition which, explained as inclination, has its highest, its unconditional, artistically unconditional, unique expression in that there is only one beloved in the whole world, and that only this one time of erotic love is genuine love, is everything, and the next time nothing. Usually one says, proverbially, that the first try does not count. Here, on the other hand, the one time is unconditionally the whole; the next time is unconditionally the ruin of everything. This is poesy, and the emphasis rests decisively in the highest expression of passionateness—to be or not to be. To love a second time is not really to love, and to poetry this is an abomination. If a so-called poet wants to make us believe that erotic love can be repeated in the same person, if a so-called poet wants to occupy himself with gifted foolishness, which presumably would exhaust passion's mysteriousness in the *why* of cleverness, then he is not a poet. Nor is that Christian which he puts in place of the poetic. Christian love teaches love of all men, unconditionally all. Just as decidedly as erotic love strains in the direction of the one and only beloved, just as decidedly and powerfully does Christian love press in the opposite direction. If in the context of Christian love one wishes to make an exception of a single person whom he does not want to love, such love is not "also Christian love" but is decidedly not Christian love. Yet there is this kind of confusion in so-called Christendom—the poets have given up the passion of erotic love, they yield, they slacken the tension of passion, they strike a bargain (by adding on) and are of the opinion that a man, in the sense of erotic love, can love many times, so that consequently there are many beloveds. Christian love also yields, slackens the tension of eternity, strikes compromises, and is of the opinion that when one loves a great deal, then it is Christian love. Thus *both* poetic and Christian love have become confused, and the replacement is *neither* the poetic *nor* the Christian.[39] Passion [40] always has this unconditional characteristic—that it excludes the third; that is to say, a third factor means confusion. To love without passion is an impossibility. Therefore the distinction between erotic love and Christian love is the one possible eternal distinction in passion. Another difference between erotic love and Christian love can not be imagined. If, therefore, one occasionally presumes to understand his life with the help of the poet and with the help of Christianity's explanation, presumes the ability to understand these two explanations together—and then in such a way that meaning would come into his life—then he is under a delusion. The poet and Christianity explain things in opposite ways. The poet idolises the inclinations and is therefore quite right—since he always has only erotic love in mind—in saying that to command love is the greatest foolishness and the most preposterous kind of talk. Christianity, which constantly thinks only of Christian love, is also quite right when it dethrones inclination and sets this *shall* in its place.

The poet and Christianity give explanations which are quite opposed, or more accurately expressed, the poet really explains nothing, for he explains love and friendship—in riddles. He explains love and friendship as riddles, but Christianity explains love eternal. From this one again sees that it is an impossibility to love according to both explanations simultaneously, for the greatest possible contradiction between the two explanations is this, that the one is no explanation and the other is the explanation.

As the poet understands them, love and friendship contain no ethical task. Love and friendship are good fortune. Poetically understood (and certainly the poet is an excellent judge of fortune) it is good fortune, the highest good fortune, to fall in love, to find the one and only beloved; it is good fortune, almost as great, to find the one and only friend. Then the highest task is to be properly grateful for one's good fortune. But the task can never be an *obligation* to find the beloved or to find this friend. This is out of the question—something the poet well understands. Consequently, the task is dependent upon whether fortune will give one the task; but ethically understood this is simply a way of saying that there is no task at all. On the other hand, when one has the *obligation* to love his neighbour, then there is the task, the ethical task, which is the origin of all tasks. Just because Christianity is the true ethic, it knows how to shorten deliberations and cut short prolix introductions, to remove all provisional waiting and preclude all waste of time. Christianity is involved in the task immediately, because it has brought the task along. There is, indeed, great debate going on in the world about what should be called the highest good. But whatever it is called at the moment, whatever variations there are, it is unbelievable how many prolixities are involved in grasping it. Christianity, however, teaches a man immediately the shortest way to find the highest good: shut your door and pray to God—for God is still the highest. And when a man will go out into the world, he can go a long way—and go in vain—he can wander the world around— and in vain—all in order to find the beloved or the friend. But Christianity never suffers a man to go in vain, not even a single step, for when you open the door which you shut in order to pray to God, the first person you meet as you go out is your neighbour whom you *shall* love. Wonderful! Perhaps a girl tries inquisitively and superstitiously to find out her fate, to get a glimpse of her intended, and deceptive cleverness makes her believe that when she has done this and this and that, she shall recognise him by his being the first person she sees on such and such a day. I wonder, then, if it should be so difficult to get to see one's neighbour also—if one does not make it difficult for himself to see him—for Christianity has made it for ever impossible to make a mistake about him. There is in the whole world not a single person who can be recognised with such ease and certainty as one's neighbour. You can never confuse him with anyone else, for indeed all men are your neighbour. If you confuse another man with your neighbour, there is essentially no mistake in this, for the other man is your neighbour also; the mistake lies in you, that you will not understand who your neighbour is. If you save a man's life in the dark, supposing him to be your friend, but he is your neighbour, this again is no mistake; alas, the mistake would be only in your wanting to save only your friend. If your friend complains that, in his opinion, you did for a neighbour what he thought you would do only for him, be at rest, it is your friend who makes the mistake.

The point at issue between the poet and Christianity may be stated precisely in this way: *erotic love and friendship are preferential and the passion of preference.* Christian love is self-renunciation's love and therefore trusts in this *shall.* To exhaust these passions would make one's head swim. But the most passionate boundlessness of preference in excluding others is to love only the one and only; self-renunciation's boundlessness in giving itself is not to exclude a single one.

In other times when men were still earnest about understanding Christianity in relationship to life, they thought Christianity was in some way opposed to erotic love because it is based upon spontaneous inclinations. They thought that Christianity, which as spirit has made a cleft between body and spirit, despised love as sensuality. But this was a misunderstanding, an extravagance of spirituality.[41] Moreover, it may easily be shown that Christianity is far from unreasonably wishing to turn the sensuous against a man by teaching him extravagance. Does not Paul say it is better to marry than to burn![42] No, for the very reason that Christianity in truth is spirit, it understands the sensuous as something quite different from what men bluntly call the sensual. Just as it has not forbidden men to eat and drink, so has it not been scandalised by a drive men have not given themselves. Sensuality, the flesh, Christianity understands as selfishness. No conflict between body and spirit can be imagined, unless there is a rebellious spirit on the side of the body with which the spirit then struggles. In the same way no conflict can be thought of as existing between spirit and a stone, between spirit and a tree. Therefore self-love, egocentricity, is sensuality. Consequently Christianity has misgivings about erotic love and friendship because preference in passion or passionate preference is really another form of self-love. Paganism had never dreamed of this. Because paganism never had an inkling of self-renunciation's love of one's neighbour, whom one *shall* love, it therefore reckoned thus: self-love is abhorrent because it is love of self, but erotic love and friendship, which are passionate preferences for other people, are genuine love. But Christianity, which has made manifest what love is, reckons otherwise. Self-love and passionate preferences are essentially the same; but love of one's neighbour—that is genuine love. To love the beloved, asks Christianity—is that loving, and adds, " Do not the pagans do likewise? " If because of this someone thinks that the difference between Christianity and paganism is that in Christianity the beloved and the friend are loved with an entirely different tenderness and fidelity than in paganism, he misunderstands. Does not paganism also offer examples of love and friendship so perfect that the poet instructively goes back to them? But no one in paganism loved his neighbour—no one suspected that there was such a being. Therefore what paganism called love, in contrast to self-love, was preference. But if passionate preference is essentially another form of self-love, one again sees the truth in the saying of the worthy father, " The virtues of paganism are glittering vices."[43]

That passionate preference is another form of self-love will now be shown, together with its opposite, that self-renunciation's love loves one's neighbour, whom one *shall* love. Just as self-love centres exclusively about this *self*—whereby it is self-love, just so does erotic love's passionate preference centre around the one and only beloved and friendship's passionate preference around the friend. The beloved and the friend are therefore called, remarkably and significantly enough, the *other-self*, the *other-I*—for one's neighbour is the *other-you*, or more accurately, the third-man of equality. The other-self, the other-I. But wherein lies self-love? It lies in the I, in the self. Would not self-love, then, still remain in loving the other-self, the other-I? Certainly one need not be an extraordinary judge of human nature in order with the help of these clues to make discoveries about erotic love and friendship, discoveries provocative for others and humiliating for one's self. The fire in self-love is spontaneously ignited; the I ignites itself by itself. But in erotic love and friendship, poetically understood, there is also self-ignition. Truly enough one may say that it is only occasionally—and then morbidly—that jealousy *shows* itself, but this is no proof that it is not always fundamentally present in love and friendship. Test it. Bring a neighbour between the lover and the beloved as the middle term whom one shall love; bring a neighbour between friend and friend as the middle term whom one shall love—and you will immediately see jealousy. Nevertheless *neighbour* is definitely the

middle-term of self-renunciation which steps in between self-love's **I** and
I and also comes between erotic love's and friendship's I and the other-
I. That it is self-love when a faithless person jilts the beloved and leaves
the friend in the lurch, paganism saw also—and the poet sees it. But
only Christianity sees as self-love the devotion of the lover's surrender
to the one and only, whereby the beloved is held firmly. Yet how can
devotion and *boundless abandon* be *self-love*? Indeed, when it is devotion
to the other-I, the other-myself.—Let a poet describe what erotic love
in a person must be if it is to be called erotic love. He will say much
that we shall not dwell upon here, but then he will add: " and there
must be admiration; the lover must admire the beloved." The
neighbour, however, has never been presented as an object of
admiration. Christianity has never taught that one must admire his
neighbour—one shall love him. Consequently there must be admiration
in erotic love's relationship, and the greater, the more intense the
admiration is, the better, says the poet. Now, to admire another
person certainly is not self-love, but to be loved by the one and only
object of admiration, must not this relationship turn back in a selfish
way to the I which loves—loves its other-I? It is this way with friendship, too. To admire another person certainly is not love, but to be the
one and only friend of this rarest object of admiration, must not this
relationship turn back in a doubtful way to the I from which it
proceeded? Is it not an obvious danger for self-love to have a one and
only object for its admiration when in return this one and only object
of admiration makes one the one and only object of his own love or
his friendship?

Love of one's neighbour, on the other hand, is self-renouncing love,
and self-renunciation casts out all preferential love just as it casts out
all self-love—otherwise self-renunciation would also make distinctions
and would nourish preference for preference. If passionate preference
had no other selfishness about it, it still would have this, that consciously
or unconsciously there is a wilfulness about it—unconsciously insofar
as it is in the power of natural predispositions, consciously insofar as it
utterly surrenders itself to this power and consents to it. However
hidden, however unconscious this wilfulness is in its impassioned
yielding to its "one and only," the arbitrariness is nevertheless there.
The one and only object is not found by obedience to the royal law,
" You shall love," but by choosing, yes, by unconditionally selecting
a one and only individual, but Christian love also has a one and only
object, one's neighbour, but one's neighbour is as far as possible from

being only one person, one and only, infinitely removed from this, for one's neighbour is all men. When the lover or the friend can love only this one person in the whole world (something delightful to the poet's ears), there is in this tremendous devotion a tremendous wilfulness, and the lover in this onrushing, inordinate devotion really relates himself to himself in self-love. Self-renunciation would eradicate this self-loving and self-willing by the " You shall " of the eternal. And self-renunciation, which presses in as a judge to try self-love, is therefore double-edged in that it cuts off both sides equally. It knows very well that there is a self-love which one may call faithless self-love, but it knows just as well that there is a self-love which may be called devoted self-love. The task of self-renunciation is therefore a double one, relating itself to the difference between these two variants. For the faithless self-love which wants to shirk there is the task: devote yourself. For the devoted self-love, the task is: give up this devotion. That which delights the poet indescribably, namely, that the lover says, " I cannot love anyone else, I cannot give up loving, I cannot give up this love, for it would be the death of me and I would die of love "—this does not satisfy self-renunciation at all and it will not tolerate that such a devotion be honoured by the name of love, since it is self-love. Thus self-renunciation first judges and then sets the task: love your neighbour; him *shall* you love.

Wherever Christianity is, there is also self-renunciation, which is Christianity's essential form. In order to be related to Christianity one must first and foremost become sober, but self-renunciation is precisely the way by which a human being becomes sober in an eternal sense. On the other hand, wherever Christianity is absent, the intoxication of self-feeling is the most intense, and the height of this intoxication is most admired. Love and friendship are the very height of self-feeling, the I intoxicated in the other-I. The more securely the two I's come together to become one I, the more this united I selfishly cuts itself off from all others. At the peak of love and friendship the two really become one self, one I. This is explainable only because in this exclusive love there are natural determinants (tendencies, inclinations) and self-love, which selfishly can unite the two in a new selfish self.[44] Spiritual love, on the other hand, takes away from myself all natural determinants and all self-love. Therefore love for my neighbour cannot make me one with the neighbour in a united self. Love to one's neighbour is love between two individual beings, each eternally qualified as spirit. Love to one's neighbour is spiritual love, but two spirits are never able to become a single self in a selfish way. In erotic love and friendship the two love one another in virtue of differences or in virtue of likenesses which are grounded in differences (as when two friends love one another on the basis of likeness in customs, character, occupation, education, etc., consequently on the basis of the likeness by which they are different from other men or in which they are like each other as different from other men). In this way the two can selfishly become one self. Neither one of them has yet the spiritual qualifications of a *self*;[45] neither has yet learned to love himself Christianly. In erotic love the I is qualified as body-psyche-spirit, the beloved qualified as body-psyche-spirit. In friendship the I is qualified as psyche-spirit and the friend is qualified as psyche-spirit. Only in love to one's neighbour is the self, which loves, spiritually qualified simply as spirit and his neighbour as purely spiritual. Therefore what was said at the beginning of this discourse does not hold good at all for erotic love and friendship, that only one human being recognised as one's neighbour is necessary in order to cure a man of self-love—if in this human being he loves his neighbour. In love and friendship one's neighbour is not loved but one's other-self, or the first I once again, but more intensely. Although self-love is condemnable, frequently it seems as if men do not have strength enough to agree about self-love; then it really makes its first open appearance when the other-self has been found and the two I's find in this relationship strength for the self-feeling of self-love. If anyone thinks that by falling in love or by finding a friend he has learned Christian love, he is in profound error. No, if one is in love and in such a way that the poet will say of him, " He is really in love" —yes, then the command of love can be changed a little when it is spoken to him and yet the same thing will be said. The command of love can say to him: love your neighbour as you love your beloved. And yet, does he not love the beloved *as himself*, as required by the command which speaks of one's neighbour? Certainly he does, but the beloved whom he loves *as himself* is not his neighbour; the beloved is his other-I. Whether we talk of the first-I or the other-I, we do not come a step closer to one's neighbour, for one's neighbour is the first-*Thou*.[46] The one whom self-love in the strictest sense loves is also basically the other-I, for the other-I is oneself, and this is indeed self-love. In the same way it is self-love to love the other-I which is the beloved or the friend. Just as self-love in the strictest sense has been characterised as self-deification, so love and friendship (as the poet understands it, and with his understanding this love stands and falls) are essentially idolatry. Fundamentally love to God is decisive; from this arises love to one's neighbour; but of this paganism was not aware. Men left God out; men considered erotic love and friendship to be love and shunned self-love. But the Christian love-command requires one to love God above all and then to love one's neighbour. In love and friendship preference is the middle term; in love to one's neighbour God is the middle term. Love God above all else and then love your neighbour and in your neighbour every man. Only by loving God above all else can one love his neighbour in the next human being. The next human being—he is one's neighbour—this the next human being in the sense that the next human being is every other human being. Understood in this way, the discourse was right when it stated at the beginning that if one loves his neighbour in a single other human being he loves all men.⁴⁷

Love to one's neighbour is therefore eternal equality in loving, but this eternal equality is the opposite of exclusive love or preference. This needs no elaborate development. Equality is just this, not to make distinctions, and eternal equality is absolutely not to make the slightest distinction, is unqualifiedly not to make the slightest distinction. Exclusive love or preference, on the other hand, means to make distinctions, passionate distinctions, unqualifiedly to make distinctions.

Has not Christianity, then, since by its " You shall " it thrust love and friendship from the throne, set something far higher in its place? Something far higher—yet let us speak with caution, with the caution of orthodoxy. Men have confused Christianity in many ways, but among them is this way of calling it the highest, the deepest, and thereby making it appear that the purely human was related to Christianity as the high or the higher to the highest or supremely highest. But this is a deceptive way of speaking which untruthfully and improperly lets Christianity in a meddlesome way try to ingratiate itself with human curiosity and craving for knowledge. Is there anything at all for which humanity as such—is there anything for which the natural man has greater desire than for the highest! When a mere newsmonger blazons abroad that his newest news is of the highest significance, then the gathering of hangers-on proceeds merrily in the world, which from time immemorial has had an indescribable partiality for and has felt a deep need of—being deceived. No, Christianity is certainly the highest and the supremely highest, but, mark well, to the natural man it is an offence.⁴⁹ He who in describing Christianity as the highest omits the middle term, offence, sins against it: he commits an effrontery, more abominable than if a modest housewife were to dress like a strip-teaser, even more appalling than if John,[50] the rigorous judge, were to dress like a Beau Brummel. Christianity is in itself too profound, in its movements too serious, for dancing and skipping in such free-wheeling frivolity of talk about the higher, the highest, the supremely highest. Through offence goes the way to Christianity. By this is not meant that the approach to Christianity should make one offended by Christianity—this would be another way of hindering oneself from grasping Christianity—but offence guards the approach to Christianity. Blessed is he who is not offended by it.

So it is also with this command to love one's neighbour. Only acknowledge it, or if it is disturbing to you to have it put in this way, I will admit that many times it has thrust me back and that I am yet very far from the illusion that I fullfill this command, which to flesh and blood is offence, and to wisdom foolishness. Are you, my reader, perhaps what is called an educated person? Well, I too am educated. But if you think to come closer to this highest by the help of *education*, you make a great mistake. Precisely at this point the error is rooted, for we all desire education, and education repeatedly has *the highest* in its vocabulary. Yes, no bird which has learned only one word cries out more continuously this single word and no crow caws more continuously its own name than education cries out about the highest. But Christianity is by no means *the highest* of education, and Christianity disciplines precisely by this repulsion of offence. This you can easily see, for do you believe that your education or the enthusiasm of any man for gaining an education has taught either of you to love your neighbour? Alas, have not this education and the enthusiasm with which it is coveted rather developed a new kind of distinction, a distinction between the educated and the non-educated? Only observe what is said among the educated about love and friendship, the degree of similarity in education a friend must have, how educated a girl must be and precisely in what way. Read the poets, who hardly know how to defend their frankness against the mighty domination of education, who hardly dare believe in the power of love to break the bonds of all distinctions. Does it seem to you that such talk or such poetry or a life attuned to such talk and such poetry brings a man closer to loving his neighbour? Here again the marks of offence stand out. Imagine the most educated person, one of whom we all admiringly say: " He is so educated." Then think of Christianity, which says to him: " You shall love your neighbour! " Of course, a certain courteousness in social intercourse, a politeness towards all men, a friendly condescension to the poor, a frank attitude towards the mighty, a beautifully controlled freedom of spirit—yes, that is education—do you think it is also loving one's neighbour?

One's neighbour is one's equal. One's neighbour is not the beloved, for whom you have passionate preference, nor your friend, for whom you have passionate preference. Nor is your neighbour, if you are well educated, the well-educated person with whom you have cultural equality—for with your neighbour you have before God the equality of humanity. Nor is your neighbour one who is of higher social status than you, that is, insofar as he is of higher social status he is not your neighbour, for to love him because he is of higher status than you can very easily be preference and to that extent self-love. Nor is your neighbour one who is inferior to you, that is, insofar as he is inferior he is not your neighbour, for to love one because he is inferior to you can very easily be partiality's condescension and to that extent self-love. No, to love one's neighbour means equality. It is encouraging in your relationship to people of distinction that in them you *shall* love your neighbour. In relation to those inferior it is humbling that in them you are not to love the inferior but *shall* love your neighbour. If you do this there is salvation, for you *shall* do it. Your neighbour is every man, for on the basis of distinctions he is not your neighbour, nor on the basis of likeness to you as being different from other men. He is your neighbour on the basis of equality with you before God; but this equality absolutely every man has, and he has it absolutely.

II C

You Shall Love Your Neighbour

Go, then, and do this—take away distinctions and similarities of distinctions—so that you can love your neighbour. Take away the distinctions of preference so that you can love your neighbour. But you are not to cease loving the beloved because of this—far from it. If this were so, the word *neighbour* would be the greatest fraud ever discovered, if you, in order to love your neighbour, must begin by ceasing to love those for whom you have a preference. Moreover, it would also be a contradiction, for, if one's neighbour is all men, then no one can be excluded—shall we now say, least of all the beloved? No, for this is the language of preference. Consequently, it is only the partiality which should be taken away—and yet it is not to be introduced again into the relationship with one's neighbour so that with extravagant preference you love your neighbour in contrast to your beloved. No, as they say to the solitary person, " Take care that you are not led into the snare of self-love," so it is necessary to say to the two lovers, " Take care that you are not led by erotic love itself into the snare of self-love." For the more decisively and exclusively preference centres upon one single person, the farther it is from loving the neighbour. You, husband, do not lead your wife into the temptation of forgetting your neighbour because of love for you; you, wife, do not lead your husband into this temptation! The lovers think that in erotic love they have the highest good, but it is not so, for therein they still do not have the eternal secured by the eternal. To be sure, the poet promises the lovers immortality if they are true lovers, but who is the poet; how good is his signature—he who cannot vouch for himself? The *royal law*, on the other hand, the love-command, promises life, eternal life, and this command simply says, " You shall love your neighbour." Just as this command will teach every man how he ought to love himself, likewise will it also teach erotic love and friendship what genuine love is: in love towards yourself preserve love to your neighbour, in erotic love and friendship preserve love to your neighbour. It may perhaps offend you—well, you know it anyway, that Christianity is always accompanied by signs of offence. Nevertheless believe it. Do not believe that the teacher who never extinguished a single smoking candle would extinguish any noble fire within a man; believe that he who was love will teach every man to love; believe that if all the song writers united in one song to the praise of erotic love and friendship, what they would have to say would be nothing in comparison with the command, "You shall love; you shall love your neighbour as yourself!" Do not stop believing because the command almost offends you, because the discourse does not sound as flattering as that of the poet who courts your favour with his songs, because it repels and terrifies as if it would frighten you out of the beloved haunts of preference—do not for that reason cease to believe in it. Consider that just because the command and the discourse are what they are, for that very reason the object can be the object of faith! Do not give yourself over to the notion that you might compromise, that by loving some men, relatives and friends, you would love your neighbour—for this would mean giving up the poet without grasping what is Christian, and it was to prevent this compromise that the discourse set you between the poet's pride, which scorns all compromise, and the divine majesty of the royal command, which regards any compromise as blameworthy. No, love your beloved faithfully and tenderly, but let love to your neighbour be the sanctifier in your covenant of union with God; love your friend honestly and devotedly, but let love to your neighbour be what you learn from each other in the intimacy of friendship with God! Death erases all distinctions, but preference is always related to distinctions; yet the way to life and to the eternal goes through death and through the extinction of distinctions. Therefore only love to one's neighbour truly leads to life. As Christianity's glad proclamation is contained in the doctrine about man's kinship with God, so its task is man's likeness to God. But God is love;[51] therefore we can resemble God only in loving, just as, according to the apostle's words, we can only " be God's co-workers—in love."[52] Insofar as you love your beloved, you are not like unto God, for in God there is no partiality, something you have reflected on many times to your humiliation, and also at times to your rehabilitation. Insofar as you love your friend, you are not like unto God, because before God there is no distinction. But when you love your neighbour, then you are like unto God.

Therefore go and do likewise. Forsake all distinctions so that you can love your neighbour. Alas, perhaps it is not necessary to say this to you at all. Perhaps you have found no beloved in this world, no friend along the way, and you walk alone. Or perhaps God took from your side[53] and gave you a beloved, but death came and took her from your side; it came again and took your friend but gave you none in return, and now you walk alone; you have no beloved to cover your weak side and no friend at your right hand. Or perhaps life separated you, even though all of you remained unchanged—in the solitariness of separation. Or, alas, perhaps change separated you and you walk sorrowfully alone because you found what you sought but then found that what you found—changed! How inconsolable! Yes, just ask the poet how inconsolable it is to live alone, to have lived alone, without being loved and without having any beloved. Just ask the poet if he knows of anything other than comfortlessness when death comes between the lovers, or when life separates friend from friend, or when change separates them as enemies from each other. For doubtless the poet loves solitude—he loves it so that in solitude he may discover the lost happiness of erotic love and friendship, just as one goes to a dark place in order to see the wonder of the stars. And yet, if a man were blameless in not having found a beloved, if he were blameless in having looked in vain for a friend, if the loss, the separation, and the change were not his fault, does the poet know of anything else than comfortlessness? But the poet himself has succumbed to change when he, the prophet of joy, does not know of anything else on the day of need than the mournful lament of comfortlessness. Or would you not call it change? Would you call it fidelity on the part of the poet that he inconsolably sorrows with the inconsolably sorrowing—well, we won't quarrel about that! But if you will compare this human fidelity with the faithfulness of heaven and the eternal, you will certainly concede that there is a change. For heaven not only rejoices—above any poet —with the joyful; heaven not only sorrows with the sorrowing—no, heaven has something new, a holier joy, in readiness for the sorrowing. Thus Christianity always has consolation, and its consolation is different from all human consolation in that human consolation recognises itself to be a substitute for lost joy—and Christian consolation *is joy itself*. Humanly speaking, consolation is a more recent invention. First came pain and suffering and the loss of joy, and then, afterwards, alas, after a long time, man hit upon the way of consolation. The same is true in the life of the individual. First comes pain and suffering and the loss of joy, and then afterward, alas, sometimes long afterward, comes consolation. But Christian consolation can never be said to come afterward, for since it is the consolation of the eternal, it is older than all temporal joy. As soon as this consolation comes, it comes with the head-start of the eternal and swallows up, as it were, pain, for pain and the loss of joy are momentary—even if the moment were a year— and the momentary is drowned in the eternal. Neither is Christian consolation a substitute compensation for lost joy, since it is joy itself. All other joy is essentially only disconsolateness in comparison with Christianity's consolation. Man's life was not and is not so perfect on this earth that the joy of the eternal could be proclaimed to him simply as joy which he had and which he has wasted. For that reason the joy of the eternal can be proclaimed to him only as consolation. As the human eye cannot bear to look directly at the sun except through dark glasses, so man cannot bear the joy of the eternal except through the dimness of being proclaimed as consolation.—Consequently, whatever your fate in erotic love and friendship, whatever your privation, what- ever your loss, whatever the desolation of your life which you confide to the poet, the highest still stands: love your neighbour! As already shown, you can easily find him; him you can never lose. The beloved can treat you in such a way that he is lost to you, and you can lose a friend, but whatever a neighbour does to you, you can never lose him. To be sure, you can also continue to love your beloved and your friend no matter how they treat you, but you cannot truthfully continue to call them beloved and friend when they, sorry to say, have really changed. No change, however, can take your neighbour from you, for it is not your neighbour who holds you fast—it is your love which holds your neighbour fast. If your love for your neighbour remains unchanged, then your neighbour also remains unchanged just by being. Death itself cannot deprive you of your neighbour either, for if it takes one, life immediately gives you another. Death can deprive you of a friend, because in loving a friend you really cling to your friend, but in loving your neighbour you cling to God: therefore death cannot deprive you of your neighbour.—If, therefore, you have lost everything of erotic love and friendship, if you have never had any of this happiness—in loving your neighbour you still have the best left.

Love to one's neighbour has the very perfection of the eternal. Is it really perfection belonging to love that its object is the superior, the remarkable, the unique? I should think that this would be a perfection belonging to the object, and the perfection of the object would evoke a subtle suspicion concerning the perfection of the love. Is it an excellence in your love that it can love *only* the extraordinary, the rare? I should think it would be a merit belonging to the extraordinary and the rare that it is extraordinary and rare, but not a merit of the love for it. Are you not of the same opinion? Have you never meditated upon God's love? If it were love's merit to love the extraordinary, then God would be—if I dare say so—perplexed, for to him the extraordinary does not exist at all. The merit of being able to love *only* the extraordinary is therefore more like an accusation, not against the extraordinary nor against love, but against the love which can love *only* the extraordinary. Is it the merit of a man's delicate health that he can feel well in *only* one place in the world, surrounded by every favourable condition? When you see a person who has thus arranged matters in life, what is it you praise? No doubt the comfortableness of his surroundings. But have you not noticed that every word eulogising this magnificence really sounds like a joke on the poor fellow who can live *only* in this luxurious environment? Consequently, perfection in the object is not perfection in the love. Precisely because one's neighbour has none of the excellences which the beloved, a friend, a cultured person, an admired one, and a rare and extraordinary one have in high degree—for that very reason love to one's neighbour has all the perfections which love to a beloved one, a friend, a cultured person, an admired one, a rare and extraordinary one, does not have. Let men debate as much as they wish about which object of love is the most perfect—there can never be any doubt that love to one's neighbour is the most perfect love. All other love, therefore, is imperfect in that there are two questions and thereby a certain duplicity: there is first a question about the object and then about the love, or there is a question about both the object and the love. But concerning love to one's neighbour there is only one question, that about love. And there is only one answer of the eternal: this is genuine love, for love to one's neighbour is not related as a type to other types of love. Erotic love is determined by the object; friendship is determined by the object; only love to one's neighbour is determined by love. Since one's neighbour is every man, unconditionally every man, all distinctions are indeed removed from the object. Therefore genuine love is recognisable by this, that its object is without any of the more definite qualifications of difference, which means that this love is recognisable only by love.

Is not this the highest perfection? Insofar as love can and may be recognised by something else, then this something else, in the relationship itself, is like a suspicion about the love, that it is not comprehensive enough and therefore not in an eternal sense infinite. This something else, unconscious to love itself, is a disposition to morbidity. In this suspicion, therefore, lies hidden the anxiety which makes erotic love and friendship dependent upon their objects, the anxiety which can kindle jealousy, the anxiety which can bring one to despair. But love to one's neighbour does not contain a suspicion about the relationship and therefore cannot become suspiciousness in the one who loves. Yet this love is not proudly independent of its object. Its equality does not appear in love's proudly turning back into itself, indifferent towards the object. No, its equality appears in love's humbly turning itself outwards, embracing all, yet loving everyone in particular but no one in partiality.

Let us consider what has already been developed, that in a human being love is a need, is the expression of riches. In fact, the deeper this need is, the greater are the riches; if the need is infinite, then the riches are also infinite. If a man's love-need is to love one single person, it must be said, even if one concedes that this need is riches, that he really needs this person. On the other hand, if the love-need in a man is to love all, there is a real need, and it is so great that it could almost produce its own object of love. In the first case the emphasis is on the speciality of the object, in the second on the essentiality of the need, and only in this latter sense is need an expression of riches. Only in this latter sense are the object of love and the love-need related equally in an infinite way, for the first person is the best person and every human being is one's neighbour, or, in the sense of *speciality* there is no object of love; whereas in the infinite sense every human being is the object of love. When one feels the need of talking with one particular person, he really needs this person; but when this need of conversing is so great that he must speak, so that if he were transported to a desert island or put in solitary confinement and the need of conversing were so great that every human being was the special person he wanted to talk with—then the need would be riches. For him in whom there is love to his neighbour, love is a need, the deepest need. He does not have need of men just to have someone to love, but he needs to love men. Yet there is no pride or haughtiness in this wealth, for God is the middle term and the "shall" of the eternal binds and guides the great need so that it does not run wild and turn into pride. But there are

no limits to the objects of love, for one's neighbour is all men, unconditionally every human being.

Therefore he who in truth loves his neighbour loves also his enemy.
The distinction *friend or enemy* is a distinction in the object of love, but
the object of love to one's neighbour is without distinction. One's
neighbour is the absolutely unrecognisable distinction between man
and man; it is eternal equality before God—enemies, too, have this
equality. Men think that it is impossible for a human being to love
his enemies, for enemies are hardly able to endure the sight of one
another. Well, then, shut your eyes—and your enemy looks just like
your neighbour. Shut your eyes and remember the command that *you*
shall love; then you are to love—your enemy? No. Then love your
neighbour, for you cannot see that he is your enemy. When you shut
your eyes, you do not see the distinctions of earthly existence, but
enmity is also one of the distinctions of earthly existence. And when
you shut your eyes, your mind is not diverted and confused just when
you are to listen to the words of the command. And when your mind
is not disturbed and confused by looking at the object of your love and
the distinction of your object, then you become all ears for the words
of the command, which speak one thing and one thing only to you,
that *you* ought to love your neighbour. Now, when your eyes are closed
and you have become all ears for the command, you are on the way
of perfection in loving your neighbour.

It is veritably true, then (the previous exposition has already shown
that *neighbour* is the unqualified category of spirit), that one sees his
neighbour only with closed eyes or by looking *away from* all distinctions.
The sensual eye always sees distinctions and pays attention *to* the
distinctions. Therefore worldly prudence shouts early and late: " Look
before you love." Ah, if one shall love his neighbour in truth, it follows
above all that one must not look around, for this prudence in scrutinis-
ing the object will result in your never getting to see your neighbour,
because he is every man, the first the best, taken quite blindly. The
poet scorns the sighted blindness of prudence, which teaches that one
should be careful about whom he loves. He teaches that love makes
one blind. In a mysterious, obscure manner, according to the poet's
view, the lover should find his object or fall in love and thus become—
blind from love, blind to every fault, blind to every imperfection in the
beloved, blind to everything else than this beloved—but nevertheless
not blind to this one's being the one and only one in the whole world.
When this is the case, erotic love certainly does make a man blind,

but it also makes him very particular not to mistake any other person for his beloved. Consequently, with regard to this beloved, it makes him blind by teaching him to make an enormous distinction between this one and only one and all other men. But love to one's neighbour makes a man blind in the deepest and noblest and holiest sense, so that he blindly loves every man, just as the lover loves his beloved.

Love to one's neighbour has the perfection of the eternal—*this is perhaps why at times it seems to fit in so imperfectly with earthly relationships and with earthly temporal distinctions, why it is easily misunderstood and exposed to hate, and why in any case it is very thankless to love one's neighbour.*

Even the person who is otherwise not inclined to praise God and Christianity does so when with a shudder he reflects on the dreadfulness in paganism or a caste system whereby men are inhumanly separated man from man through the distinctions of earthly life, when he reflects on how this ungodliness inhumanly teaches one man to disclaim relationship with another, teaches him presumptuously and insanely to say of another man that he does not exist, that " He is not born."[54] Then even he praises Christianity, which has saved men from this sort of evil by deeply and eternally unforgettably stamping the imprint of kinship between man and man, because kinship of all men is secured by every individual's equal kinship with and relationship to God in Christ, because the Christian doctrine addresses itself equally to every individual and teaches him that God has created him and Christ has redeemed him, because the Christian doctrine calls every man aside and says to him, " Shut your door and pray to God and you have the utmost a human being can have; love your Saviour, and you have everything, both in life and death; then pay no attention to the differences, for they make no difference. I wonder if a person looking from a mountain peak at the clouds below is disturbed by the sight; I wonder if he is disturbed by the thunderstorm which rages below in the low regions of the earth? Just so high has Christianity set every man, absolutely every human being—because before Christ just as in the sight of God there is no aggregate, no mass; the innumerable are for him numbered—they are unmitigated individuals. Just so high has Christianity placed every man in order that he should not damage his soul by preening himself over or grovelling under the differences in earthly existence. For Christianity *has not taken distinctions* away—any more than Christ himself would or would pray God to *take the disciples out of the world*[55]—and these remain one and the same thing. Never in Christendom, therefore, just as never in paganism, has there lived any man who has not been attired in or clothed with the distinctions of earthly life. Just as the Christian does not and cannot live without the body, so he cannot live without the distinctions of earthly life which belong to each individual, whether by virtue of birth, position, circumstance, education, *etc.*—no one of us is pure or essential man. Christianity is too earnest to present fables about pure man—it wants only to make men pure. Christianity is no fairy tale—even if the eternal happiness which it promises is more glorious than what any fairy tale offers. Neither is it an ingenious fragment of the imagination intended to be difficult to understand, nor does it impose the conditions of—an idle head and an empty mind.

Consequently, Christianity has once and for all dispelled this horror belonging to paganism, but the distinctions of earthly existence it has not taken away. These must continue as long as time continues and must continue to tempt every man who enters into the world, for by being a Christian he does not become free from distinctions, but by winning the victory over the temptation of distinctions he becomes a Christian. In so-called Christendom, therefore, the distinctions of earthly existence still continually tempt; alas, very likely they more than tempt, so that one behaves arrogantly and another defiantly envies. Both ways are rebellion, rebellion against what is Christian. Far be it from us to strengthen anyone in the presumptuous delusion that only the mighty and the famous are the guilty ones, for if the poor and weak merely aspire defiantly for the superiority denied them in earthly existence instead of humbly aspiring for Christianity's blessed equality, this also damages the soul. Christianity is not blind, nor is it one-sided; with the quietness of the eternal it looks equably on all the distinctions of earthly life, but it does not contentiously take sides with any single one. It sees—and with real distress—that earthly busy-ness and the false prophets of secularism will in the name of Christianity conjure up the illusion of perfect equality, as if only the high and mighty make much of the distinctions of earthly existence, as if the poor were entitled to do everything in order to attain equality—only not by way of becoming Christians in earnestness and truth. I wonder if one can come closer to Christian likeness and equality that way?

Christianity, then, will not take differences away, neither the distinction of poverty nor that of social position. But on the other hand, Christianity will not in partiality side with any temporal distinction, either the lowliest or the most acceptable in the eyes of the world. Whether the temporal distinction which a man falls in love with by fastening himself carnally to it is in the eyes of the world revolting and disturbing or is in the eyes of the world innocent and lovable does not concern Christianity at all; it makes no earthly distinction. It is not concerned with the means whereby he damages his soul, but it is concerned with his doing damage to his soul—by means of a triviality? Perhaps. But damaging one's soul is certainly no triviality. Between the extremes of fashionable life and poverty there lies a great throng of specific qualifications of earthly differences, but in none of those more specific and therefore less conspicuous distinctions does Christianity make an exception. Differences are like an enormous net in which the temporal is held. The meshes in this net are additional variations; one man seems more caught and bound in existence than another; but all these differences, the distinction between one difference and another and the comparing of these differences, do not concern Christianity at all, not in the least; such preoccupation and concern are nothing other than worldliness. Christianity and worldliness never come to an understanding with one another, even for a moment—although to the less observing they may deceptively seem to. To bring about likeness among men, to apportion the conditions of temporal existence equally, if possible, to all men, this is a task which pre-eminently occupies the secular world. Yet even what one may call well-intended secular striving along these lines never comes to an understanding with Christianity. This well-meaning worldliness is piously—if one may say so—convinced that there must be one temporal condition, one earthly distinction—which one discovers with the aid of calculations and surveys or some other preferred device—in which there is equality.[56] If this condition were to become one and the same for all men, then likeness would have been achieved. On the one hand, this cannot be accomplished and, on the other, the likeness of everyone's sharing the same temporal distinction is by no means Christian equality. Earthly likeness, if it was possible, is not Christian equality. And perfect achievement of earthly likeness is an impossibility. Well-meaning worldliness really confesses this itself. It rejoices when it succeeds in making temporal conditions similar for more and more, but it recognises that its struggle is a pious wish, that it has taken on an enormous task, that its prospects are remote—if it rightly understood itself it would perceive that its vision will never be achieved in time, that even if this struggle were continued for millennia it would never attain its goal. Christianity, on the other hand, aided by the short-cut of the eternal, is immediately at the goal: it allows all distinctions to stand, but it teaches the equality of the eternal. It teaches that everyone shall *lift himself above* earthly distinctions. Notice carefully how equably it speaks. It does not say that it is the poor who shall lift themselves above earthly distinctions, while the mighty should perhaps come down from their elevation—ah, no, such talk is not equable, and the likeness which is obtained by the mighty climbing down and the poor climbing up is not Christian equality; this is worldly likeness. No, if one stands at the top, even if one is the king, he shall *lift himself above* the distinction of his high position, and the beggar shall *lift himself above* the distinction of his poverty. Christianity lets all the distinctions of earthly existence stand, but in the command of love, in loving one's neighbour, this equality of lifting oneself above the distinctions of earthly existence is implicit.

Because every man, the poor fully as much as the prominent and powerful, can in his own characteristic manner lose his soul by not Christianly willing to lift himself above the distinctions of earthly existence, and alas, because it happens to both and in various ways—because this is the situation, willing to love one's neighbour is often exposed to double, to multiplied dangers. Everyone who in despair has clung to one or another of the distinctions of earthly existence so that he centres his life in it—not in God—also demands that everyone who possesses this same distinction shall stick together with him—not in the good (for the good does not form an association, does not unite two or a hundred or all men in an association), but in an ungodly association against the universally human. Persons in despair consider it traitorous to want to have fellowship with others, with all men. On the other hand, these other men are also differentiated in terms of other temporal distinctions and very likely misunderstand when anyone who does not belong to their group wants to associate with them. Through a misunderstanding, both strife and harmony are strangely involved simultaneously in the distinctions of earthly existence; one wants to do away with a particular distinction, but he desires another in its place. Distinction can, as the word signifies, mean important distinction or the utmost distinction, but everyone who struggles against distinction in this way that he wants to have one set aside and another in its place really works for distinction. He, then, who will love his neighbour, he who consequently does not concern himself about eliminating this or that distinction or about mundanely eliminating all distinctions but concerns himself devoutly with permeating his distinction with the sanctifying thought of Christian equality, such a person easily becomes like one who does not fit in with earthly existence, not even with so-called Christendom; he is readily exposed to attacks from all sides; he easily becomes like a lost sheep among ravenous wolves. Wherever he looks he naturally sees distinction (for, as said, no man is pure man, but the Christian lifts himself above distinctions); and they who have mundanely fastened themselves to a temporal distinction, whatever it is, are like ravenous wolves.

Let us take a few examples of the distinctions of earthly existence in order to make this matter clear. Let us proceed very carefully. And may your patience in reading correspond to my diligence and time in writing, for since being an author is my only work and my only task, I both can and am obliged to use a careful—fussy, if you so will—but certainly a serviceable precision which others are not able to use since they, in addition to not being authors, must use their perhaps longer days, perhaps richer gifts, and their perhaps greater working-strength in other ways.—You see, the times are past when the powerful and prominent alone were men, and the others—human slaves and serfs. We are indebted to Christianity for this. But from this it does not follow that prominence and power can no longer become a snare for a man in that he makes something of these distinctions, damages his soul, and forgets what it is to love his neighbour. If this should happen now, it certainly must come about in a more hidden and secret manner, but basically it is still the same thing. Whether in the enjoyment of his haughtiness and pride one openly gives other people to understand that they do not exist for him, whether in the nourishment of his arrogance one wants them to be sensitive to this by demanding an expression of slavish subjection from them, or whether stealthily and secretly, simply by avoiding any contact with them (perhaps also out of fear that openness would incite men and put him in a dangerous situation), one expresses that they do not exist for him—these are basically one and the same thing. The inhumanness and unChristian-ness of this does not consist in the manner in which it is done but in wanting to deny one's relationship in the human race with all men, with absolutely every man. Alas, alas, to keep oneself pure and unspotted from the world is the task and doctrine of Christianity—would that we did it—but in a worldly manner to close oneself off as if therein lay the most glorious of all distinctions, this is nothing less than corruption. It is not rude labour which corrupts—if it is done in purity of heart; and it is not meagre living conditions which corrupt—if you devoutly aim to lead a quiet life; but silk and ermine can corrupt if they have occasioned a man to damage his soul. It is corruption when the poor man shrivels up in his poverty so that he lacks the courage to will to be built up by Christianity. It is also corruption when a prominent man wraps himself in his prominence in such a way that he shrinks from being built up by Christianity. And it is also corruption if he whose distinction is to be like the majority of people never comes out of this distinction through Christian elevation.

Therefore this distinguished corruption teaches the man of distinction that he exists only for distinguished men, that he shall live only in their social circle, that he must not exist for other men, just as they must not exist for him. But he must be circumspect, as it is called, in order with smoothness and dexterity to avoid getting people excited; that is to say, the secret and the art of the secret consist in keeping this secret to oneself. This avoidance of disturbance must not be an expression for the relationship, and it must not be done in a striking manner that might awaken attention. No, the evasiveness must be for the purpose of shielding oneself and therefore must be practised so carefully that no one becomes aware of it, to say nothing of being offended by it. Consequently he will go about as if with closed eyes (alas, but not in the Christian sense) when he travels amid the human throng. Proudly, and yet quietly, he will flit, as it were, from one distinguished circle to another. He must not look at those other men— lest he be seen; yet behind this screen his eyes will be all attention, just in case he should happen to meet a fellow-being or an even more distinguished person. His glance will float vaguely about, sweeping over all these men so that no one may catch his eye and remind him of their kinship. He must never be seen among less important people, at least never in their company, and if this cannot be avoided, it must appear as a stately condescension—although in the subtlest guise in order not to offend and hurt. He must be prepared to employ extreme courtesy towards common people, but he must never associate with them as equals, for thereby expression would be given to his being—a human being—whereas he is a distinguished personage. And if he can do this easily, smoothly, tastefully, elusively and yet always keeping his secret (that those other men do not really exist for him and he does not exist for them), then this refined corruption will confirm him as being—a well-bred man. Yes, the world has changed—and corruption has also changed. Yet it would be jumping to a conclusion if one believed that the world has become good because it has changed. Consider one of those proud, defiant figures who delighted in the ungodly game of openly letting "those mortals" feel their paltriness—how surprised he would be to find out to what extent public-relations has now become necessary to keep this secret. Alas, but the world has changed, and gradually as the world changes the forms of corruption also become more cunning, more difficult to point out—but they certainly do not become better!

So it is with distinguished corruption. And if there were a distinguished person whose life, as a result of birth and conditions, definitely belonged within this same earthly distinction, a distinguished person who would not consent to this contentious plot against the universally human, that is, against his neighbour, if he could not find it in his heart to do this, if he, clearly perceiving the consequences, nevertheless trusted in God for strength to bear these consequences, since he lacked strength—to harden his heart: experience would certainly teach him what he was risking. First of all, distinguished corruption would accuse him of being a traitor and an egotist—because he would love his neighbour; for solidarity with corruption—this is love and loyalty and honesty and devotion! If, then, as it so often happens, the common people, again from the point of view of their distinctions, misunderstood and misjudged him, this one who did not belong to their synagogue, and rewarded him with mockery and insult—because he would love his neighbour!—well, then he would stand in double danger. If instead he had sought to become a leader of the common folk in a rebellion to stamp out all distinctions of quality, they perhaps would have honoured and loved him. But this he would not do. He would merely express what to him was a Christian need—to love his neighbour. And for that very reason his fate would become very precarious, for that very reason the double danger.

Now if this distinguished corruption should triumphantly ridicule him, should scoffingly and condemningly say: " This he has richly deserved"—it would certainly use his name as a scarecrow to prevent inexperienced, distinguished young people from going astray, astray—from the good form of high-class corruption. And many of the better ones among the upper class, over whom the good form of high-class corruption still exercised power, would not dare to defend him, would not dare refrain from laughing with the "council of the scornful ";[57] it would indeed be extraordinary if anyone dared to defend him. It is quite conceivable that an inspired, eloquent distinguished person could in the upper-class circles advocate love to one's neighbour, but when it came to something real he would be unable to subject his mind obediently to the view he had perhaps victoriously championed. But to champion an opposite viewpoint from within and behind the partitions of distinction, a viewpoint which in a Christian sense (not in a rebellious sense) will take the distinctions away, means nevertheless a maintenance of the distinctions. In company with scholars or within an environment which insures and elevates his distinction as such, a scholar would perhaps be willing to lecture enthusiastically on the doctrine of the equality of all men, but this means a continued maintenance of the distinction. In company with rich men, in an environment which makes the advantage of wealth conspicuous, a rich man would perhaps be willing to make every concession to the likeness of all men, but this would mean the continued maintenance of the distinction. The superior person, who in upper-class society could perhaps drive all opposition victoriously from the field, would very likely in a refined and cowardly manner avoid contact with reality's opposition to distinction.—" To walk with God "—we use this expression as a felicitation—if this superior one among the men of distinction should walk with God among men instead of proudly escaping, then he would perhaps seek to hide from himself and also from God what he had come to see, except what God saw—that he hid. When one walks with God, he no doubt walks free from danger, but one is also constrained to see and to see in a unique way. When you walk in company with God you need to see only one single person in misery, and you will not be able to escape what Christianity will have you understand, human likeness. Alas, but the superior person would perhaps not quite dare risk going through with this journey in company with God and the impression it gives; he would perhaps take his leave—although he might still champion the Christian viewpoint in distinguished society the same evening. Yes, walking with God (and it is really only in this company that one discovers his neighbour, for God is the middle term) in order to learn to know life and one's self is an earnest walk.[58] Then honour, power, and glory lose their worldly gloss: in company with God you cannot rejoice over them in a worldly way. If you stick together (for sticking together is not for the good) with certain other people who have a special position and special conditions in life, even if it is only with your wife, then worldliness tempts. Even if it does not have great meaning in your eyes, it tempts you comparatively in respect of persons; it tempts you perhaps for her sake. But when you walk with God, hold only to him and understand God within everything you understand; then you will discover—shall I say to your own disadvantage—then you will discover your neighbour, since God will constrain you to love him—shall I say to your own disadvantage—for loving one's neighbour is a thankless task!

It is one thing to let ideas strive with ideas; it is one thing to battle and be victorious in a dispute; it is something else to be victorious over one's own mind when one battles in the reality of life. For however close one battling idea comes to another in life, however close one combatant comes to the other in an argument, all this strife is still at a distance and like shadow-boxing. On the other hand, the measure of a man's fundamental disposition is this: how far is what he understands from what he does, how great is the distance between his understanding and his action. Fundamentally we understand all the highest things. A child, the simplest man, the wisest, all understand the highest things and everyone the same, for this is, if I may put it so, one lesson we have all been assigned. But what makes the difference is whether we understand it at a distance—then we do not act accordingly—or close at hand —then we do act accordingly and "cannot do otherwise," cannot keep from doing it, as Luther, who understood the radical reduction of the distance between required action and words when he said, " I cannot do otherwise. God help me. Amen."[59]—In the quiet hour's remoteness from the confusion of life and the world, every man understands what the highest is. When he departs, he has understood it. If good weather seems to abound for him in life, he understands it; but when confusion begins, understanding flees—or reveals that this understanding was at a distance. To sit in a room where everything is so still that one can hear a grain of sand fall and then to understand the highest—this everyone can do; but, speaking figuratively, to have to sit in the kettle which the coppersmith is hammering and then to have the same understanding—well, then understanding must have been very close at hand, otherwise it would show itself to be at a distance—because one was absent from his understanding.—In the still hour's remoteness from the confusion of life, a child, the simplest person, and the wisest one all understand, and almost with equal ease, what every man ought to do—what every man should do. But if, in the confusion of life, there is only a question about what *he* ought to do, then it appears, perhaps, that his understanding is at a distance—it is at the distance of humanity from him.—In the remoteness of an argument from action, in the remoteness of a magnanimous vow from action, in the distance of repentance from action, every man understands the highest. Within the security of conditions unchanged through old habit, every one can understand that a change should be made, for this understanding is at a distance—is not unchangedness an enormous distance from the change? Alas, in the world there is perpetually the agitated question about what the one can do and that one can do and this one cannot do; the eternal in speaking about the highest assumes calmly that every man can do it, and merely asks therefore, whether or not he has done it. From the distance of superior condescension the distinguished man understands equality between man and man; from the distance of concealed patronising the scholar and the gentleman understand equality between man and man; from within a little concession to variations of fortune, the man whose distinction is to be like most men understands equality between man and man—at a distance all of them recognise the neighbour, but only God knows how many recognise him in actuality, that is, close at hand. But at a distance one's neighbour is only a figment of the imagination —he who by being close at hand, the first one the best, is uncondi- tionally every man. At a distance one's neighbour is a shadow which in imagination enters every man's thought and walks by—but alas, one perhaps does not discover that the man who at the same moment actually walks by him is his neighbour. At a distance every man recognises his neighbour, and yet it is impossible to see him at a distance. If you do not see him so close that you unconditionally before God see him in every man, you do not see him at all.

Let us now consider the distinction of insignificance. The times are past when those called the poor and insignificant had no conception of themselves or only the conception of being slaves, not merely poor and insignificant men but essentially not men at all. The wild rebellion and terror which followed on the heels of that horror are perhaps also over, but I wonder if corruption may not dwell hidden in a man? Thus a corrupt insignificance will induce the insignificant man to see his enemy in the powerful and important, in everyone who is favoured by some advantage. But use caution, it says, for these enemies still have so much power that it could be dangerous to break with them. There- fore this corruption will not teach the lower ranks to create disturbances or to repress entirely every expression of deference or to permit revelation of the secret, but it will teach that this must be done and yet not be done, that it should be done and yet in such a way that the powerful will derive no pleasure from it, and at the same time they will not be able to say that anything has been withheld from them. There- fore even in homage there will be a crafty defiance which secretly can provoke, a sullenness which secretly disavows what the mouth confesses, a sort of hoarseness of suppressed envy in the jubilation which honours the mighty. No force shall be used—it would be dangerous; no break must be made—it would be dangerous. But a disguise of hidden exasperation and a remote intimation of painful dejection will transform the power and glory and eminence into a plague for the mighty, the honoured, the eminent, who nevertheless cannot find anything specific to complain about, for precisely therein lies the art and the secret.

And if there were an unimportant person into whose heart this secret envy did not come and who would not let corruption from without get this power over him, an insignificant man who without craven submission, without fear of men, modestly, but above all with joy, gave every earthly advantage its due, happier and more joyful for the giving, many times more, perhaps, than he can be who receives—if there were such a man, he also would discover the double danger[60]. His peers would perhaps thrust him away as a traitor, scorn him as slave-minded, alas, and the favoured ones would perhaps misunderstand him and deride him as a climber. What in the previous relationship would perhaps be regarded as too unimportant for the important —to love one's neighbour—would perhaps here be regarded as too presumptuous for the unimportant—to love one's neighbour.—Thus it is dangerous to want to love one's neighbour. For there are plenty of distinctions in the world; differences are everywhere present in temporal existence, which means just that, differences and multiplicity. Perhaps a man might also have success, by virtue of his differences, in fitting into all differences through a compliant, accommodating adjustment which deducts a little here and exacts a little elsewhere. *But the equality of eternity*, to will to love one's neighbour, *seems both too little and too much, and therefore it is as if this love to one's neighbour did not fit properly within the relationships of earthly existence.*

Imagine a man who gave a banquet feast and invited to it the halt, the blind, cripples, and beggars. Now far be it from me to believe anything else about the world than that it would find this beautiful even though eccentric. But imagine that this man who gave the feast had a friend to whom he said, "Yesterday I gave a great feast!" Is it not true that the friend would first and foremost wonder that he had not been among those invited? But when he found out who the guests had been—now, far be it from me to believe anything else about this friend than that he would find it beautiful even though eccentric. Yet he would wonder and would perhaps say, " It is a strange use of language to call such a gathering a feast: a feast—where friends are not present, a feast—where the concern is not for the choiceness of the wine, the quality of the company, the number of servants who waited on a table." One could call such a meal a charitable gesture, the friend would think, but not a feast. For however good the food which they received may have been, even if it had not merely been, like the food in the poor house, "substantial and edible," but really choice and costly, yes, even if they had had ten kinds of wine—the company itself, the organisation of the whole, a certain lack, I know not what, would prevent calling such a thing a feast; it all runs contrary to language-usage—which makes distinctions. Suppose, now, that the man who had given the feast answered, " I thought I had language-usage on my side. Do we not read in Luke's gospel (14 : 12-13) these words of Christ: ' When you give a dinner or a banquet, do not invite your friends or your brothers or your kinsmen or rich neighbours, lest they also invite you in return, and you be repaid. But when you give a feast, invite the poor, the maimed, the lame, the blind.' Not only is the word *feast* used in this manner, but in the beginning a less festive expression, *dinner* or *banquet* is used. The word *feast* is first used when the discussion is about inviting the poor and crippled. Do you not think that this is what Christ meant, that this inviting of the poor and crippled is not only what we should do but that it is something far more festive than eating a dinner or supper with friends and relatives and rich neighbours; this ought not to be called a banquet or a feast, because inviting the poor makes the feast. But I well perceive that our ways of using language are different, for in accordance with common language-usage the list of those invited to a feast is something like this: friends, brothers, relatives, rich neighbours—who can repay one's hospitality. But so scrupulous is Christian equality and its use of language that it demands not only that you shall feed the poor—it requires that you shall call it a feast. Yet, if in the actuality of daily life you will hold fast to this strict language-usage and do not think that Christianly understood it is a matter of indifference under what name food is handed to the poor, then men will certainly laugh you to scorn. But let them laugh; they laughed at Tobit, too. Willing to love one's neighbour is always exposed to double danger, as we see in the example of Tobit. Under punishment of death, the king had forbidden burial of the dead. But Tobit feared God more than the king, loved those who had died more than life—he buried them. This was the first danger. And then when Tobit had risked this heroic deed—then " his neighbours mocked him ' (Book of Tobit 2 : 8). This was the second danger. . . ." So spoke the man who had given the feast. Was he not right, my reader? Nevertheless, should there not be additional objections to his behaviour? Why was he so obstinate in inviting only the lame and the poor? Why did he, as it were, purposely, yes, defiantly, refrain from inviting his friends and relatives? He could just as well have invited them all. Undeniably, and if he were obstinate in this way, then we would praise neither him nor his use of language. But according to the word of the gospel, the meaning is this—the others would not come. Therefore the friend's amazement over not being invited ceased as soon as he heard what sort of company it had been. If the man—according to his friend's use of language—had given a feast and had not invited him, he would have become angry. But now he did not become angry—for he would not have come anyway.

Does it seem to you, my reader, that the preceding paragraphs are only an argument over the use of the word *feast*? Or do you perceive that the issue concerns loving one's neighbour? He who feeds the poor but yet is not victorious over his own mind in such a way that he calls this feeding a feast sees in the poor and unimportant only the poor and unimportant. He who gives a *feast* sees in the poor and unimportant his neighbours—however ridiculous this may seem in the eyes of the world. Alas, it is not rare that one hears the world's complaint over this or that man for not being earnest enough, but the question is what the world understands by earnestness, whether it does not more or less understand thereby the bustle of temporal concern. The question is whether the world by this constant confounding of earnestness and vanity is not in spite of its earnestness so jocular that if it got a notion of earnestness in the highest sense, thereby seeing that one would act earnestly—the question is whether the world would not quite involuntarily break into laughter. So earnest is the world! If the manifold and manifoldly complex distinctions of temporal existence did not make it just as difficult to see whether one loves his neighbour as to see *humanity*, the world would always have material enough for laughter—if there otherwise were a sufficient number who loved their neighbour. To love one's neighbour means, while remaining within the earthly distinctions allotted to one, essentially to will to exist equally for every human being without exception. To will to exist openly for other men only in the basis of the advantages of one's earthly distinction is pride and arrogance, but the clever invention of not willing to exist for others at all in order secretly to enjoy the advantage of one's distinctions in the company of one's peers is cowardly pride. In both instances there is discord. But he who loves his neighbour is tranquil. He is made tranquil by being content with the earthly distinction allotted to him, whether it be important or unimportant; moreover, he lets every earthly distinction retain its significance and be taken for what it is and ought to be worth in this life, for one shall not covet what is his neighbour's, neither his wife nor his donkey, nor, consequently, the advantages granted him in life.[61] If they are denied to you, you shall rejoice that they are granted to him. Thus he who loves his neighbour is made tranquil. He neither cravenly shuns those mightier than he, but he loves his neighbour; nor does he proudly shun the less significant, but he loves his neighbour and wishes essentially to be equal to all men, whether he is actually known to many or not. Undeniably this is quite a stretch of one's wings, but this is not a proud flight which soars above the world; it is self-renunciation's humble and difficult flight along the earth. It is far easier and far more comfortable to sneak through life by living in stately seclusion if one is a distinguished person, or in quiet obscurity, if one is an insignificant person. Yes, one can—however strange it is—seem to get on even better through this sneaky manner of life, because one exposes himself to much less opposition. But even if it is rather pleasant for flesh and blood to avoid opposition, I wonder if it is a consolation likewise at the time of death? At the hour of death there is only this one consolation, that one has not avoided opposition but has survived it. What a man achieves or does not achieve is not within his power. He is not the One who shall steer the world; he has one and only one thing to do—to obey. Therefore everyone ought first and foremost (instead of asking what position is most comfortable for him, what connections are most advantageous to him) to place himself at the point where Governance can use him, if it so pleases Governance. That point is simply to love one's neighbour or to exist on an essentially equal basis for every man. Every other position is schismatic, however advantageous and convenient and seemingly significant this other position may be; Governance cannot use the man who has oriented himself in this way, for he is really in revolt against Governance. But he who takes this overlooked, this scorned, disdained sound position without clinging to his earthly distinctions, without forming a party with a single person, existing on an essentially equal basis for every man, he shall, even if he seemingly achieves nothing, even if he becomes exposed to the mockery of the insignificant and the jests of the distinguished or to the mockery and jests of both—may yet at the time of death dare to speak consolingly to his soul, " I have done what was mine to do. Whether or not I have accomplished anything, I do not know. I do not know if I have done anyone any good. But I do know that I have existed for them; I know that because they have scoffed at me. And this is my consolation that I shall not take with me into the grave the secret that I, in order to have good, undisturbed, and comfortable days in this life, had repudiated kinship with other men, with the insignificant in order to live in superior reserve, with the superior in order to live in hidden obscurity." Let the one who by the help of his connections and by not existing for all men has achieved so much, let him watch out that death does not change his life for him when it reminds him of his liability. For he who did what he was supposed to do in order to make men aware, the insignificant or the significant, he who learning, acting, striving, existed equally for all men, he has no liability if men by persecuting him reveal—that they had become aware. He has no liability. No, he has even been of some benefit, because the prerequisite for benefit is first and foremost to become aware. But the one who cravenly existed only within the walls of his clique, where he accomplished so very much and won so many advantages, he who cravenly did not dare make men aware, neither the insignificant nor the significant, because he had a suspicion that the awareness of men is an ambiguous good—if one has had any truth to communicate and cravenly kept his celebrated activity within the security of the respect of persons: he bears the responsibility—for not having loved his neighbour. If such a person were to say, " Well, what good is it to order one's life according to such a standard? " I would answer, " What good do you think such excuses will be in eternity? " For the requirement of the eternal is infinitely higher than ever so clever an excuse. I wonder whether a single one of those whom Governance has employed as instruments in the service of truth (and let us not forget that every human being shall and ought to be this, at least he shall and ought to order his life in such a way that he could be an instrument) has ordered his life otherwise than by existing equally for every man. No person of this kind has ever clanned together with the insignificant or clanned together with the significant, but he has existed equally for the significant and insignificant. Truly, only by loving one's neighbour can a man achieve the highest, for the highest is the capability of being an instrument in the hand of Governance. As previously stated, everyone who has placed himself in any other

position, everyone who has organised parties and established connections or is a member of a party or a clique, steers according to his own
reckoning and all his accomplishment, were it even the remodelling
of a world, is a delusion. He will not have great joy from it in eternity
either, for possibly Governance did utilise the accomplishment, but,
alas, it did not employ him as an instrument. He was a self-willed
person, conceited in his own cleverness, and Governance makes use
of the strivings of such a person, also, by taking his arduous labours
and letting him have his just reward.—However ridiculous, however
backward, however inexpedient loving one's neighbour may seem in
the world, it is still the highest a man is capable of doing. But *the
highest* has never quite fitted into the relationships of earthly life—it
is *both too little and too much.*

Consider for a moment the world which lies before you in all its
variegated multiplicity; it is like looking at a play, only the plot is
vastly more complicated. Every individual in this innumerable throng
is by his differences a particular something; he exhibits a definiteness
but essentially he is something other than this—but this we do not get
to see here in life. Here we see only what rôle the individual plays and
how he does it. It is like a play. But when the curtain falls, the one
who played the king, and the one who played the beggar, and all the
others—they are all quite alike, all one and the same: actors. And
when in death the curtain falls on the stage of actuality (for it is a
confused use of language if one speaks about the curtain being rolled
up on the stage of the eternal at the time of death, because the eternal
is no stage—it is truth), then they also are all one; they are human
beings. All are that which they essentially were, something we did not
see because of the difference we see; they are human beings. The stage
of art is like an enchanted world. But just suppose that some evening
a common absent-mindedness confused all the actors so they thought
they really were what they were representing. Would this not be, in
contrast to the enchantment of art, what one might call the enchantment of an evil spirit, a bewitchment? And likewise suppose that in the
enchantment of actuality (for we are, indeed, all enchanted, each one
bewitched by his own distinctions) our fundamental ideas became
confused so that we thought ourselves essentially to be the rôles we
play. Alas, but is this not the case? It seems to be forgotten that the
distinctions of earthly existence are only like an actor's costume or like
a travelling cloak and that every individual should watchfully and
carefully keep the fastening cords of this outer garment loosely tied,

never in obstinate knots, so that in the moment of transformation the garment can easily be cast off, and yet we all have enough knowledge of art to be offended if an actor, when he is supposed to cast off his disguise in the moment of transformation, runs out on the stage before getting the cords loose. But, alas, in actual life one laces the outer garment of distinction so tightly that it completely conceals the external character of this garment of distinction, and the inner glory of equality never, or very rarely, shines through, something it should do and ought to do constantly. For the actor's art is deceptive; the art is the deception. The ability to deceive is its greatness; permitting oneself to be deceived is just as great. Therefore one must be able to see and not want to see the actor through the costume. Therefore it is the height of artistry when the actor becomes one with the rôle he plays, because this is the height of deception. But the actuality of life, even if it is not the truth as the eternal is truth, ought nevertheless to partake of the truth, and therefore that other person who everyone essentially is should always shine through the disguise. Alas, but in actual life the individual develops in temporal growth simultaneously with his individual differences; this is in contrast to eternal growth, which grows away from distinctions. The individual grows misshaped; every such individual is, in the view of the eternal, a cripple. Alas, in actuality the individual grows simultaneously with his differences so that death at last must use force to tear them from him.—Yet if one were in truth to love his neighbour, he would be reminded every moment that the differences are a disguise. As previously said, Christianity has not wanted to storm forth to abolish distinctions, neither the distinction of prominence nor that of insignificance, nor has it wanted in a worldly manner to make a worldly compromise between distinctions; but it wills that differences shall hang loosely about the individual, loosely as the cloak the king casts off in order to show who he is, loosely as the ragged costume in which a supernatural being has disguised itself. When distinctions hang loosely in this way, then there steadily shines in every individual that essential other person, that which is common to all men, the eternal likeness, the equality. If this were true, if every individual lived in this manner, then temporality would have reached its utmost. It cannot be like the eternal. But this expectant solemnity which, without stopping the stream of life, every day renews itself by the eternal and by the equality of the eternal, every day saves the soul from the differences in which it still remains: this would be the reflection of eternity. If then in actual life you were actually to see the sovereign, gladly and respectfully bring him your homage; but for all that you should see in the sovereign the inner glory, the equality of glory which his magnificence only conceals. If then you were to see the beggar—perhaps suffering in sorrow over him more than he himself, you should nevertheless also see in him the inner glory, the equality of glory, which his wretched outer garments conceal. Yes, then you should see—wherever you turned your eye— your neighbour. For no man exists or has existed from the beginning of the world who is the neighbour in the sense that the king is king, the scholar a scholar, your relative your relative—that is, in a particular sense or, which is the same, in the sense of distinction. No, every man is your neighbour. In being king, beggar, scholar, rich man, poor man, male, female, *etc.*, we do not resemble each other—therein we are all different. But in being a neighbour we are all unconditionally like each other. Distinction is temporality's confusing element which marks every man as different, but neighbour is eternity's mark—on every man. Take many sheets of paper and write something different on each one—then they do not resemble each other. But then take again every single sheet; do not let yourself be confused by the differentiating inscriptions; hold each one up to the light and you see the same water-mark on them all. Thus is neighbour the common mark, but you see it only by help of the light of the eternal when it shines through distinction. [62]

My reader, doubtless this must seem glorious to you and you must have thought of it in this way whenever in silent exaltation you devoted yourself to meditation and let the thought of the eternal rule; yet do not simply remain at a distance from this understanding. Should it not seem just as glorious that you for your part resolve to make the agreement with God that you will cling to him in order to stick to this understanding, that is, in order to express in your life that you with him hold to this understanding as the only essential, whatever may befall you in life for the sake of this understanding—should it even cost you your life—that you with God hold fast to it as your victory over all vexations and all wrongs? Remember that he who in order to will one thing in truth chooses to will the good in truth, remember that he has this holy comfort: one suffers only once but is victorious for eternity. —The poet knows how to talk much about the dedication of erotic love about what an ennobling power it casts over a man falling in love and being loved, about what a transfiguration takes place in his whole existence, about, according to the poet's view, what a heavenly difference there must be between the one who has fallen in love and one who has never felt the transformation of erotic love. O, true dedication, however, is to give up all demands on life, all demands on power and honour and advantage, all demands—but the happiness of erotic love and friendship is among the very greatest demands—consequently to give up all demands in order to understand what an enormous demand God and the eternal make upon one himself. He who will receive this understanding is ready to love his neighbour. A man's life begins with the delusion that a long, long time and a whole world lie in the distance before him, begins with the rash fancy that he has ample time for the fullfillment of all his expectations. The poet is the smooth-talking, enthusiastic confidant of this rash but beautiful fancy. But when a man in the infinite transformation himself discovers the eternal so near to life that there is not the distance of one single wish, of one single evasion, of one single moment from what *he* in this *now*, in this second, in this holy moment *ought* to do—then he is on the way to becoming a Christian. It is characteristic of childhood to say: *Me want—me—me.* It is characteristic of youth to say, " *I*—and *I*—and *I*." The mark of maturity and the dedication of the eternal is to will to understand that this *I* has no significance if it does not become the *you*, the *thou*, to whom the eternal incessantly speaks and says: " *You shall, you* shall, *you* shall." It is youthful to want to be the only I in the whole world. Maturity is to understand this *you* as addressed to oneself, even though it were not said to a single other person. *You* shall; *you* shall love your neighbour. O, my reader, it is not to *you* I speak. It is to me, to whom the eternal says: " *You* shall."

III A

Love Is the Fullfilling of the Law

(*Romans 13: 10*)

"To promise is honourable, but to keep a promise is onerous," says an old proverb [65]—but by what right? It is perfectly clear that to keep a promise is honourable, and so the proverb is right in saying that to keep a promise is honourable and likewise onerous. But what, then, becomes of the promising? The proverb, according to the suggested explanation, does not say anything about what it is. Perhaps this promising, then, is nothing at all. Perhaps it is less than nothing. Perhaps the proverb even advises against promising, as if it would say, Do not waste any time on promising; keeping the promise, which is the point of honour, is troublesome enough. And certainly promising is far from honour even if the promise is by no means dishonourably intended. Is there not something dubious in giving *promising* the name of honour, dubious in a world which deceitfully promises so much, in a generation which is all too ready to promise and to deceive itself honourably by promising? Is there not something dubious about the proverb's own concern, inasmuch as another proverb, which also has some acquaintance with the world and mankind, knows from experience that "Money lent and paid back according to promise is money found." Therefore one might rather go to the opposite extreme and say "to promise is dishonourable," assuming that it is characteristic of true faithfulness that it does not make promises, that it does not waste time by promising, does not deceive itself by promising, does not demand double pay, first for the promise and then for fullfilling the promise. In contrast, one might prefer trying to concentrate attention solely and decisively, on the keeping, while, as in a preamble, an inspiring admonition from authority warns against the promising.

There is found in Holy Scriptures (Matthew 21 : 28-31) a parable which is seldom treated in godly discourse and which nevertheless is very instructive and inspiring. Let us dwell on it a bit. There was a "man who had two sons."[66] Therein he resembles the father of the prodigal son, who also had two sons; yes, the likeness between these two fathers is still greater, for one of the sons of the father whom we are now discussing was also a prodigal son, whose story we shall now hear. The father "went to the first and said, ' Son, go and work in the vineyard today.' And he answered, ' I will not '; but afterward he repented and went. And he went to the second and said the same; and he answered, ' I go, sir,' but did not go. Which of the two did the will of his father? " We could also ask in another manner: which of these two was the prodigal son? I wonder if it was not the one who said " Yes," the obedient one who not only said " Yes," but said, " I go, sir," as if to show his unqualified, dutiful submission to his father's will. I wonder if it was not the one who said " Yes," he who secretly went about, a lost soul, in such a way that this would not easily become generally known of him as of the prodigal son who wasted his goods with the prostitutes and ended by watching the swine, but also by being won back in the end. I wonder if he who said " Yes," he who in a remarkable manner resembles the brother of the prodigal son, whose righteousness is made suspect in the gospel, although he still called himself the righteous one or the good son, I wonder if perhaps this brother (we have a special word in our language which for the sake of brevity we could apply to him: a *yes-brother*, a *yes-man*) did not also regard himself as being the good son—did not he also say " Yes "? Did he not say, " Sir, I will "?—and to promise is honourable, says the old proverb.

But the other brother said " No." Such a *no*, which nevertheless means that one does precisely what one said " No " to, can sometimes have its roots in a peculiarity which is not inexplicable. In such a sham *no* sometimes hides a kind of honour which is strange and exiled in the world. It may be that the speaker has become so nauseated by hearing again and again this *yes* which means that one does not do what one says that he has come to say " No " when others say " Yes " in order then to do what the yes-men omit, the doing; or it may be that the speaker has a concerned distrust of himself and therefore avoids promising anything in order that he shall not promise too much; or it may be that the speaker in his honest zeal to do the right thing wishes to prevent the hypocritical show of a promise. But the *no* in the gospel is not said in any of these oblique ways; it is really disobedience on the part of the son, but he repents and goes and does his father's will.

But what does the parable wish to point up? I wonder if it is not to show the danger of too great a hurry in saying " Yes," even if it is meant at the moment. The yes-brother is not presented as one who *was* a deceiver when he said " Yes," but as one who *became* a deceiver because he did not hold to his promise, more accurately, as one who by his very eagerness in promising became a deceiver—that is to say, the promise became his snare. Had he not promised, he perhaps would more likely have done it. When one says " Yes " or promises something, he very easily deceives himself and easily deceives others also, as if one already had done what one promised, or as if by promising one had at least done part of what one promises to do, or as if the promise itself were something meritorious. Then when one does not do what he promised, it is a long way back to the truth again and to an approach to beginning to do a little of what he promised. Alas, what one promised to do was perhaps expansive enough, but now by the help of the unfullfilled promise one had become separated from the beginning by the distance of an illusion. Now it is no longer as it was in that moment when one made a mistake on the way and instead of beginning the work swung around it with the help of the promise. One must retrace this whole detour before one again approaches the beginning. On the other hand, the way which leads from having said " No," the way through repentance to doing the good, is much shorter and much easier to find. The " Yes" of the promise is sleep-inducing but the " No " uttered and consequently heard by oneself is stimulating, and repentance may not be far away. He who says, " Sir, I will," is in the same moment pleased with himself. He who says " No " becomes almost afraid of himself. But this difference is very significant in the first moment and very decisive in the next moment; yet the first moment is the judgment of the moment and the second moment is the judgment of the eternal. For that reason the world is much inclined to promises, for the worldly is the immediate, and a promise appears very fine at the moment; for that very reason the eternal is suspicious of promises, as it is suspicious of all that is immediate. Suppose that neither of the brothers went to do his father's will, the one who said " No " was constantly nearer to doing his father's will insofar as he was nearer to becoming aware that he did not do his father's will. A *no* does not hide anything, but a *yes* very easily becomes a deception, a self-deception, which of all difficulties is the most difficult to conquer.

Ah, it is all too true that " The road to hell is paved with good intentions," and certainly the most dangerous thing for a man is to go backwards with the help of good intentions, also with the help of promises. It is very difficult to discover that it really is a regression. When a man turns his back upon someone and walks away, it is so easy to see that he walks away, but when a man hits upon a method of turning his face towards the one he is walking away from, hits upon a method of walking backwards while with appearance and glance and salutations he greets the person, giving assurances again and again that he is coming immediately, or incessantly saying " Here I am "— although he gets farther and farther away by walking backwards— then it is not so easy to become aware. And so it is with the one who, rich in good intentions and quick to promise, retreats backwards farther and farther from the good. With the help of intentions and promises he maintains an orientation towards the good, he is turned towards the good, and with this orientation towards the good he moves backwards farther and farther away from it. With every renewed intention and promise it seems as if he takes a step forward, and yet he not only remains standing still but really takes a step backward. The intention taken in vain, the unfullfilled promise leaves a residue of despondency, dejection, which perhaps soon again flares up in more passionate protestations of intention, which leave behind only greater languor. As a drunkard constantly requires stronger and stronger stimulation—in order to become intoxicated, likewise the one who has fallen into intentions and promises constantly requires more and more stimulation—in order to walk backward. We do not laud the son who said " No," but we endeavour to learn from the gospel how dangerous it is to say, " Sir, I will." A promise with respect to action is somewhat like a changeling—one needs to be very watchful. In the very moment a child is born the mother's joy is greatest, because her pain is over. When because of her joy she is less watchful—so says superstition—the hostile powers come and put a changeling in the child's place. In the significant initial moment when one should begin, but for that very reason a dangerous time, the enemy forces come and slip in a changeling promise, thus hindering one from making a genuine beginning. Alas, how many have been deceived in this manner, yes, as if bewitched!

For this reason it is very important for a man, in all his relationships and respecting all his tasks, that attention be undividedly concentrated entirely on essential and important things. So must it be also with love, lest at any moment it gets a chance to seem to be anything other than what it is or appearances take hold and become a snare, lest love comes to take its time or in flattering fancy to pat itself on the back. Instead it will immediately get under way with the task and be constrained to understand that every previous moment was a wasted moment, more than just a waste of time, for it will understand that every other expression of it is retardation and retreat. This is precisely stated in the words of our text:

LOVE IS THE FULLFILLING OF THE LAW,[67]

and these words we will now make the object of our consideration.

If anyone asks, " What is love? " Paul answers, " It is the fullfilling of the law," and straightway every further question is precluded by that answer. For the law—alas, it is already a very complex matter; but the fullfilling of the law—well, you yourself recognise that if this is to be attained there is not one moment to waste. Frequently in this world the question " What is love? " has been asked out of curiosity, and frequently there has been an idle fellow who in answering has latched on to the curious fellow, and these two, curiosity and idleness, think so much of each other they almost never tire of each other or of asking and answering. But Paul does not become engaged with the questioner, least of all in prolix discussions. On the contrary, he imprisons with his answer, imprisons the questioner in obedience under the law. In his answer he gives instantaneous direction and impetus to act accordingly. This answer of Paul's is not exceptional; the same thing is true of all Paul's answers and of all the answers of Christ. This mode of answering, to swing away from the questions, orientation towards the remote in order instantaneously to bring the task to the questioner— what he has to do, as near to life as possible—is characteristically Christian. That simple wise man of old,[68] who in the service of understanding judged paganism, understood the art of questioning, how by his questions to imprison every one who answered in ignorance. But Christianity, which does not relate itself to apprehension but to action, has the characteristic of answering and in the answer imprisoning everyone in the task. For that reason it was dangerous for the Pharisees and the sophists and the hairsplitters and the daydreamers to ask questions of Jesus. Indeed, the questioner always got an answer, but in the answer he also got to know, in a certain sense, much too much; he received an imprisoning answer which did not ingeniously indulge in prolix conversation about the question, but with divine authority grasped the questioner and obliged him to act accordingly; whereas the questioner perhaps only desired to remain at the vast distance of curiosity or inquisitiveness or definition from himself and from—doing the truth. How many have not asked " What is Truth? " and at bottom hoped that vast spaces would intervene before truth came so close to him that in the immediate now it would determine his duty for action at that very moment. When the Pharisee, "desiring to justify himself," asked, " Who is my neighbour? " [69] he surely thought that it would develop into a very prolix inquiry, that it would perhaps take a very long time and then perhaps end with the admission that it is impossible to determine with absolute accuracy the concept of *neighbour*—for this very reason he asked the question, in order to find an escape, to waste time, to justify himself. But God catches the wise in their foolishness, [70] and Christ imprisoned the questioner in the answer which contained the task. And thus it is with all of Christ's answers. Not with prolix discourse does he warn against futile questions which only give rise to quarrelling and evasions; alas, prolix discourse against such questions is not much better than the object of its opposition. No, as he taught so does he answer, with divine authority, for authority means precisely to set the task. The hypocritical questioner received the answer he deserved, but not the answer he wished; he did not get an answer which could nourish his curiosity, nor an answer he could run around with, for the answer contains the remarkable quality that when it is told further it immediately imprisons the individual to whom it is told, binds him in particular to the task. Even if someone would presumptuously attempt to tell one or another of Christ's answers as an anecdote, it is no good, it cannot be done—the answer imprisons by binding to the task the person to whom it is told. An ingenious answer which addresses itself to human ingenuity is essentially indifferent as to who says it or to whom it is said. Every answer of Christ has the very opposite quality, which nevertheless is two-fold: it is infinitely important that it is Christ who has spoken it, and when it is spoken to an individual it is precisely to *him* that it is spoken. The whole emphasis of the eternal lies in its being spoken to him, even if it is in a sense spoken to all individuals. Ingenuity is turned in upon itself and to that extent is blind; it does not know whether anyone is looking at it or not, and it approaches no one too closely in scrutiny; divine authority, on the other hand, is like the single eye; it constrains the person addressed to see who is talking with him and then fastens its piercing look on him and says with this glance, " It is you to whom this is said." It is for this reason that men readily employ ingenuity and profundity—then they can play Blind-man's Buff, but they are afraid of authority.

For that reason, perhaps, men are not quite willing to have anything to do with Paul's answer, which, as said before, is imprisoning. As soon as anything else is answered to the question " What is love? " questions of time, intervals, and spare moments are introduced, whereby concession is made to curiosity, idleness, and selfishness. But if love is the fullfilling of the law, then there is no time even for a promise, for promising is here used as an expression for the last device which seeks to give love a wrong direction away from acting, away from *immediately* undertaking the task. The promise lies right at the beginning and resembles deception without, however, being that. Even if this promise of love were not so easily a momentary stimulation, which in the next moment is a deception, a momentary blazing-up which is followed by languor, a leap forward which leads backward, an anticipation which, retarded, blocks its own way, an introduction which does not lead into the matter—even if this were not so, the promise is still a loitering, a dreaming or gratifying or wondering or flighty or fanciful loitering by the side of love, as if it must first gather itself together, or as if it were thinking it over, or as if it marvelled at itself or at what it should be capable of, the promise is a loitering at the side of love and therefore is a game, a game which can become dangerous, for in all earnestness love is the fullfilling of the law. But Christian love, which gives everything away, precisely for this reason has nothing to give away, no moment of time and no promise. Yet this is no busyness,[71] least of all a worldly busyness, and worldliness and busyness are inseparable ideas. For what is it to be busy? One ordinarily thinks that the manner in which a man is occupied determines whether he should be called busy or not. But this is not so. It is only within a narrower aspect of the definition that the manner is the determining factor—and this only after the object is first defined. He who occupies himself only with the eternal, unceasingly every moment—if this were possible—is not busy. Consequently he who really occupies himself with the eternal is never busy. To be busy means, divided and scattered (depending upon the object which occupies one), to occupy oneself with all the manifold things in which it is practically impossible for a man to be whole,[72] whole entirely or whole in any single part, something only a lunatic can successfully do. To be busy means, divided and scattered, to occupy oneself with what makes a man divided and scattered. But Christian love, which is the fullfilling of the law, is whole and collected in its every expression, and yet it is sheer action. Consequently it is just as far from inaction as it is from busyness. It never becomes engrossed in anything beforehand and never gives a promise in place of action. It never draws satisfaction from imagining that it has finished. It never loiters delighting in itself; it never sits idly marvelling at itself. It is not that secret, private, mysterious feeling behind the lattice of the inexplicable, which the poet wants to lure to the window, not a soul-mood which fondly knows no laws, wants to know none, or wants to have its own law and hearkens only to singing—it is pure action and its every deed is holy, for it is the fullfilling of the law.

This, then, is Christian love. Even if it is not or was not thus in any man (yet every Christian by abiding in love works that his love might become this), it nevertheless was thus in Him who was love, in our Lord Jesus Christ. The same apostle therefore says of him (Romans 10 : 4): " Christ is the end of the law." What the law was unable to produce—as little as it could save a man—that Christ was. Whereas the law with its demand thereby became the destruction of all, because they were not what it demanded and only learned to recognise sin through it, Christ became the law's destruction because he was what it demanded. Its destruction, its consummation—for when the demand is fullfilled, the demand exists only in the fullfillment, but consequently it does not exist as a demand. Just as thirst when it is satisfied exists only in the solace of refreshment, so Christ came not to abolish the law but to fullfill it; therefore from that time on it exists in the perfect fullfillment.

Yes, he was love, and his love was the fullfilling of the law. " No one could convict him of any sin," [73] not even the law, which knows everything in the conscience. " No guile was found on his lips," [74] but everything in him was truth. There was not the distance of a moment of a feeling, of an intention between his love and the law's demand for its fullfillment. He did not say " No " as the one brother did; neither did he say " Yes " as the other brother, for his good was to do his Father's will. Thus he was one with the Father, one with every single demand of the law, so that fullfilling it was a need, his only life-necessity. —Love in him was pure action. There was no moment, not a single one in his life, when love in him was merely the inactivity of feeling, which hunts for words while it lets time slip by, or a mood, which is self-satisfying, dwelling on itself with no task to perform—no, his love was pure action. Even when he wept, this was not passing time, for although Jerusalem did not know what belonged to its peace, he knew; if those sorrowing at Lazarus's grave did not know what was going to happen, he knew what he would do.—His love was completely present in the least things as in the greatest; it did not gather its strength in single great moments as if the hours of everyday life were outside the requirements of the law. It was equally present in every moment, no greater when he breathed his last on the cross than when he suffered himself to be born. It was the same love which said, " Mary has chosen the good portion "[75] and the same love which rebuked with a glance—or forgave—Peter.[76] It was the same love when he received the disciples who joyfully returned home after performing miracles in his name[77] and the same love when he found them sleeping.[78]—In his love there was no demand on any other man or on any other man's time, energy, assistance, service, love-in-return, for what Christ demanded of him was only the other man's gain, and he demanded it only for the other man's sake; no one lived with him who loved himself as deeply as Christ loved him. In his love there was no compromising, excusing, partisan agreement with any man, except the agreement which in him was accord with the law's infinite demand. In Christ's love no exemption was claimed for himself, not the slightest, not a farthing's.—Christ's love made no differentiation, not the tenderest differentiation between his mother and other men, for he pointed to his disciples and said, " These are my mother."[79] Nor did his love make the distinction of disciples, for his only wish was that every man would become his disciple, and this he desired for every individual's own sake. And again his love made no distinctions among the disciples, for his divine-human love was equal to all men, willing to save them all, and equal towards all who would permit themselves to be saved.—His life was pure love, and yet his whole life was one single workday; he did not rest before *the* night came when he *could* no longer work;[80] before that time his work did not alternate with the alternation of day and night, for if he did not work he watched in prayer.—Such was his fullfilling of the law. As a reward he demanded nothing, for his only demand, the only purpose of his whole life from birth to death, was in guiltlessness to offer himself—something which even the law, when it demands the utmost, dares not demand.—In this way he was the fullfilling of the law. He had, as it were, only one fellow-witness, one who was by no means able to follow him, a fellow-witness who was attentive and sleepless enough to scrutinise him; it was the law itself, which followed him step by step, hour after hour, with its infinite demand; but he was the fullfilling of the law.—How poverty-stricken never to have loved! Ah! but even the person who becomes richest in his love—his whole wealth is only poverty compared to this fullfillment. And yet, not so—let us never forget that there is an eternal difference between Christ and every Christian. Even though the law is abolished, it stands here, still with power, and fixes an eternal yawning abyss between the God-man and every other human being, who cannot even comprehend but can only believe what the divine law must concede—that he was the fullfilling of the law. Every Christian believes this and believingly appropriates it for himself, but no one has known this except for the law and Him who was the fullfilling of the law. For only in his strongest moment can a human being understand that what is present weakly enough in his strongest moment was far more strongly and yet equally present in every moment, but in the next moment he cannot understand it, and therefore he must believe and hold fast in faith so that his life may not become confused by understanding at one time and not understanding at other times.

Christ was the fullfilling of *the law*. From him we should learn how to understand this thought, for he was *the explanation*. Only when the explanation *is* what it explains, when the one who explains is that which is explained, when the explanation is the transfiguration,[81] only then is there the right relationship. Alas, we are not able to explain in this way. If we can do nothing else, we can learn humility from this in our relation to God. Our earthly life, which is weak and infirm, must distinguish between explaining and being, and this frailty of ours is an essential expression of how we are related to God. Let a man, humanly speaking, love God in the uprightness of his heart—alas, God has nevertheless loved him first, God is an eternity previous—man is that far behind. And so it is with every task of the eternal. When, after a long time a man reaches the point of beginning, how infinitely much was wasted beforehand, even if for a moment we were to forget all the deficiencies and imperfections in the task which at long last is begun! Let a man, humanly speaking, in uprightness of heart seek first the Kingdom of God and his righteousness—O, how long a time passes before he learns just to understand this correctly, and consequently how infinitely long from the time he *first* seeks the Kingdom of God and his righteousness! And so at every point wasted time precedes every human beginning. In the context of human relationships we usually speak of the regrettable fact that a man must go into debt in order to begin an enterprise   In relationship to God every man begins with an infinite debt, even if we forget the debt which is added daily after the beginning. All too often this is forgotten in life, and why, indeed, except that God also is forgotten. Thus one man compares himself with another, and the one who has understood something more than others praises himself for being somebody. Would that he would understand for himself that before God he is nothing. And now that men are so eager to be somebody, what wonder that they, however much they talk about God's love, are very reluctant to have anything to do with him, for the very reason that his demand and his standard reduce them to nothing.

Use one-tenth of the power which is granted to you, use it to the utmost; then turn your back to God and compare yourself with other men—and in a very short time you will be an alien among men. But turn about, turn to God, use the ten tenth-parts, exploit if possible the most extreme last resort—and you will still be as nothing, an infinite distance from having approached anything, in infinite debt! For that reason one can say that in a certain sense it does not help to talk to a man about the highest good, because quite another revolution must take place than any which talking can produce. If you want to be well off and nevertheless score easy success in being a somebody, then forget God, [8] never let it appear and never let it become really clear to you that it is he who has created you from nothing; proceed on the presupposition that a man does not have time to waste reflecting about him to whom one infinitely and unconditionally owes all—nor is one person entitled to ask another about this—therefore let this be forgotten and join the clamour of the crowd, laugh or cry, be busy from morning to night, be loved and respected and regarded as a friend, as a public official, as a king, as a pall-bearer; above everything else be an earnest man by forgetting what is most earnest of all—to relate oneself to God, to become as nothing. Oh, but bear in mind—still it does not help to talk—yet would to God that you might understand what you have lost, that you might understand that this becoming-as-nothing before God is blessed in such a way that you would at every moment seek again this becoming-as-nothing more strongly, more warmly, more inwardly than the blood seeks again the place from which it is pressed out, but to worldly shrewdness this is and must be the greatest foolishness. Therefore never hold fast to God (one must talk this way if he is to expose plainly the secret of vacillation, which with false words also pretends to hold fast to God)—" Never hold fast to God, for by holding fast to him you lose what no man who holds fast to the world (not even the man who has lost the most) ever lost: you lose absolutely everything." And this is true, in another sense, because the world cannot in fact take everything, simply because it cannot give everything—only God can do that, God, who takes everything, everything, everything, in order to give everything, who does not take by instalments a little or much or exceedingly much but takes absolutely everything if you in truth hold fast to him. " Flee from him, therefore. A king can be dangerous enough to approach if you desire to amount to anything; the proximity of a mightily endowed spirit is dangerous; but God is infinitely more dangerous to approach."

Yet, if God is to be left out and be forgotten, I do not know what it can mean to discuss such an expression or what meaning outside of loathsome meaninglessness there could possibly be in a discussion of this expression: love is the fullfilling of the law. So let us not timorously and traitorously to ourselves avoid understanding, as if we feared— what the natural man certainly does fear, however much he talks about his aspiration for knowledge and insight—as if we feared getting to know too much, for to talk about love being the fullfilling of the law is once again an impossibility without simultaneously recognising one's own guilt and making every man guilty.

Love is the fullfilling of the law, *for in spite of all its many provisions the law is still somewhat indeterminate*, but love is the fullfillment. The law is like a ponderous speaker who cannot say everything in spite of all his efforts, but love is the fullfillment.

It might seem strange to say that the law is indeterminate, for it has its very strength in determinate provisions; it possesses and governs all determinations. Yet it is true, and therein lies the weakness of the law. As a shadow is weak in comparison to the powerful actual object, so is the law; and just as there is always something indefinite in a shadow, there is also an indefiniteness in the outline of the law, however accurately it is delineated. Therefore Holy Scriptures declare, the law is "a shadow of things to come," [83] for the law is not a shadow which follows the reality of love; the fact is that the law is embodied in love, but the law is the shadow of things to come. When an artist devises a plan, a sketch of a work, however exact the sketch is, there is always something indeterminate. Only when the work is finished, only then can one say, " Now there is not the slightest indeterminateness, not of a single line, of a single point." There is, therefore, only one composition which is completely determined—the work itself; but this only means that no sketch is or can be entirely and absolutely determined. Thus the law is a sketch; love the fullfillment and the complete definition. In love the law is completely defined. There is only one

power which can complete the work for which the law is a sketch—
that is love. Yet the law and love, just like the sketch and the work,
are by one and the same artist, are of one and the same origin. They
do not quarrel with each other any more than the work of art which
corresponds completely to the sketch quarrels with it, because the work
of art is still more definite than all the provisions of the sketch.

Therefore Paul says in another place (I Timothy 1 : 5), " Love is
the sum of the commandments." [84] But in what sense is this said? It
is said in the same sense as saying that love is the fullfilling of the law.
In another sense the sum comprises all the single commandments, thou
shalt not steal, *etc.* But try to find the sum in that way, however long
you continue to count, and you will see it is useless labour, because
the concept of the law is inexhaustible, endless, and unlimited in its
provisions; every provision brings forth a still more exact explication
of itself, and then again by reference and relation to the new provision
a still more exacting provision, and so on *ad infinitum.* The relation of
love to the law is like the relation of understanding [85] to faith. The
understanding reckons and reckons, calculates and calculates, but it
never attains the certainty which faith has. So it is with the law: it
defines and defines but never reaches the sum, which is love. When
one speaks of a sum, the very expression seems to invite counting, but
when a man has become tired of counting and nevertheless is all the
more eager to find the sum, he understands that this word must have a
deeper meaning. Similarly, when the law has hounded a man with all
its provisions and has hunted him weary, because there are provisions
everywhere, and yet every provision, even the most definite, still has
such indefiniteness that it can become even more definite (for there is
perpetual indefiniteness in the provisions and the undying disquietude
of their multiplicity)—then a man learns to understand that there must
be something else which is the fullfillment of the law.—But there is no
quarrel between the law and love, no more than there is between the
sum and that of which it is the sum, no more than there is a quarrel
between the vain attempt to find the sum and the happy discovery,
the happy conclusion, that it has been found.

Under the law man groans. Wherever he looks he sees only
demands, never a boundary—like one who looks out over the ocean
and sees wave after wave, but never a boundary. Wherever he looks
he meets only severity, which in its infinitude can always become more
severe, never the boundary where it becomes mildness. The law
starves out, as it were; one never gets his fill by its help, for its character

is precisely to take away, to demand, to exact to the uttermost, and the continuous regression of indefiniteness in the multiplicity of all its provisions constitutes an inexorable collection-statement of demands. With every provision the law demands something, and yet there is no limit to the provisions. The law is therefore the very contradiction of life, but life is fullfillment. The law resembles death. But I wonder if life and death do not know essentially one and the same thing; for just as accurately as life knows everything which gives life, just so accurately does death know everything which gives life; consequently, there is in a certain sense no quarrel between law and love in respect to knowledge, but love gives and law takes, or, to express the relationship more concretely in proper order, law requires and love gives. There is not a provision of the law, not a single one, which love wishes to do away with; on the contrary, love gives them for the first time complete fullness and definiteness. In love all the provisions of the law are even more definite than in the law. There is no quarrel, then, any more than between hunger and the blessing which satisfies it.

Love is the fullfilling of the law, for love is no shirker of tasks, no indulgence which, demanding exemption or giving exemption, coddling or being coddled, sneaks in between love and the fullfilling of the law, as if love were an idle feeling too superior to express itself in action, a pretentious incapability which neither can nor will give satisfaction. Only foolishness speaks this way about love—as if there were a quarrel between law and love, which there certainly is, but *in* love there is no quarrel between the law and love, which is the fullfilling of the law— as if there were an essential difference between the law's demand and love, which there certainly is, but not *in* love, in which the fullfillment is absolutely one and the same with the demand. Only foolishness drives a wedge between the law and love, thinking that it speaks wisely when it talks between them or even speaks ill of one to the other.

The fullfilling of the law—but what law are we talking about? Our text is the *apostolic* word; we are talking about *Christian love*, consequently we can be speaking here only about *God's law*. The world (insofar as there is yet a difference between this and what we have called "foolishness") and God, worldly wisdom and Christianity, are of one mind in this that there is a law which love shall fullfill in order to be love; but they are not of one mind about what constitutes the law, and this disagreement constitutes an infinite difference. *Worldly wisdom thinks that love is a relationship between man and man. Christianity teaches that love is a relationship between: man - God - man, that is, that*

God is the middle term. However beautiful the love-relationship has been between two or more people, however complete all their enjoyment and all their bliss in mutual devotion and affection have been for them, even if all men have praised this relationship—if God and the relationship to God have been left out, then, Christianly understood, this has not been love but a mutual and enchanting illusion of love. *For to love God is to love oneself in truth; to help another human being to love God is to love another man; to be helped by another human being to love God is to be loved.* Worldly wisdom certainly is not of the opinion that one who loves shall himself arbitrarily determine what he will understand by love. Love is indeed affection and devotion. Therefore the world thinks that the object of love (be it a beloved, a friend, the lovers, an association, or one's contemporaries—we shall hereafter for sake of brevity call them *the beloved*) shall judge whether or not affection and devotion are evidenced and whether or not the evidenced devotion and affection are love. Consequently the matter depends upon whether men, who are to judge, know how to judge correctly. If the object of love, the judge, does not have for himself before God a true idea of what it is to love himself, that it is to love God, then the beloved has no true idea, either, of what it is to be loved by another human being, that it is to be helped to love God. When this is the case, the beloved will consider an untrue kind of affection and devotion to be true love and the true love to be no love at all. The merely human judgment about love if not true judgment, for to love God is true self-love. But when God is the middle term in judging love, final and double judgment is still forthcoming, a judgment which first of all begins, although basically it alone is decisive, where human judgment has finished and has decided if it is or is not love. The judgment is this: divinely understood, is it really love to show devotion such as is demanded by the object of love? Next, is it love, divinely understood, on the part of the object of love to demand such devotion? Every man is God's servant; therefore he dare not belong to anyone in love unless in the same love he belongs to God, and he dare not possess anyone in love unless he and the other belong to God in this same love; a man dare not belong to another human being as if the other were everything to him; a man dare not permit another to belong to him in such a way that he is everything to the other. If there were a relationship of love between two or more people, a relationship so happy, so perfect, that the poet must needs exult over it—yes, so blissful that one who was not a poet would become one from wonder and joy over this sight—the matter is by no means ended. For now Christianity steps in and asks about the God-relationship, asks whether each individual is related to God, and then whether the love-relationship is related to God. If this is not the case, then Christianity, which still is the defender of love, or precisely because it is that, will in God's name have no scruples about splitting this relationship until the lovers understand it. And if only one participant understands it, then Christianity, which still is the defender of love, will have no scruples about splitting the relationship asunder in God's name until the lovers understand this. And if only one understands it, then shall Christianity, which still is the defender of love, have no scruples about leading him out into the horror of a conflict such as no poet ever dreams about or has ever dared to portray. For the poet can have no more to do with the Christian demand *to love one's enemy* any more, even less if less were possible, than he can have anything to do with the Christian demand to *hate the beloved* out of love and in love. Yet Christianity does not hesitate in God's name to strain the relationship so tensely. Christianity does this not merely to collect, as it were, God's debt (since God is indeed the servant's lord and master) but does it also out of love for the lovers, for to love God is to love oneself, to love another man as God is to deceive oneself, and furthermore, to permit another person to love one as if he were God is to deceive this other person. So high—humanly speaking to a kind of madness—can Christianity press the demand of love if love is to be the fulfilling of the law. Therefore it teaches that the Christian shall, if it is demanded, be capable of hating his father and mother and sister and beloved. —I wonder if in this sense he would really hate them? O, such atrociousness is far from Christianity! But certainly in the sense that love, faithful and upright love divinely understood, may be regarded by the lovers, by close relatives, and by contemporaries as hate, because they will not understand what it is to love oneself, that it really is to love God, and that to be loved is to be helped by another person to love God, whether or not in the process it turns out that the lover finds himself hated. Worldly wisdom has a long list of various expressions for affection and devotion. I wonder if among them there are also found: out of love to hate the beloved, out of love to hate the beloved and thereby oneself, out of love to hate one's contemporaries and thereby his own life. Worldly wisdom knows a great many and a great variety of cases of unhappy love. I wonder if among these you find the suffering which has to appear to hate the beloved, which has to use hate as the last and only expression for its love, or the suffering which

in reward for its love has to be hated by the beloved because there is
the infinite difference of Christian truth between what the one person
and the other understands by love?—No matter what the world before
the time of Christianity had seen of unhappy love—love's collision with
the horror of circumstances, its collision with that which within the
same fundamental conception of the nature of love is the opposite of
love, its collision with partially different views still within the common
fundamental conception—the world before the time of Christianity
never saw the possibility of a collision in love between two views
separated by a world of difference: the divine and the merely human
conceptions. But if there is such a collision, then, divinely understood,
love means precisely to hold fast to the true, eternal conception and
to love in the power of this conception, although the one or ones who
are loved, if they have a merely human concept, may regard it as hate.
Let us talk in a purely human manner about the highest. Unfortunately
one is tempted in so-called Christendom to imagine that one has faith,
without having an impression of what this means, at least not enough
to be noticeable. Let us talk in a purely human manner about the
highest, yet never forgetting that the one the discussion is about is
separated by an eternal difference from every man—Christ's life is
really the only unhappy love. He was, divinely understood, love; he
loved in the power of the divine conception of what love is; he loved
the whole race. He did not dare—out of love—to give up this conception, for this would mean to betray the race. For this reason his
whole life was a terrible collision with the merely human conception of
what love is. It was the ungodly world which crucified him, but even
his disciples did not understand him and continuously sought, so it
seemed, to win him to their idea of what love is, so that once he had to
say to Peter, " Get behind me, Satan. [86] O, the unfathomable suffering
of this dreadful collision: that the most upright and faithful disciple,
when he, not only well meaning but burning with love, desires to
counsel for the best, desires only to express how deeply he loves the
master, that this disciple, then, because his conception of love is
unsound, speaks in such a way that the master must say to him, " You
do not know it, but to me your words are as if Satan were speaking."
Thus Christianity came into the world; with Christianity came the
divine explanation of what love is. We often complain about misunderstanding, especially when it is most bitterly blended with love, when
we recognise in its every utterance that love is unhappily present, that
we are really loved but are not understood, that everything is made so

bitter because it is done out of love but through a misunderstanding: but to become misunderstood in such a way as no human being has ever, ever been misunderstood by another human being, to become misunderstood as Christ was misunderstood—and then to be love as Christ was love! One assumes that it was only ungodliness which had to collide with Christ. [87] What a misunderstanding! No, humanly speaking, the best and most affectionate man who has lived had to collide with him, had to misunderstand him, for the first thing this finest man had to learn from him was what love is, divinely understood. Christ's love was not, humanly understood, devoted, anything but; he did not make himself unhappy, humanly speaking, in order to make his own happy. No, he made himself and his own as unhappy, humanly speaking, as possible. This was the one who had it in his power to establish the kingdom of Israel and make everything good for himself and his own, something every contemporary could see plainly enough. Since he could have done it, since he did not will to do it—consequently the defect must have lain in him, in his heart, that he would not sacrifice his ideas, his fancies, but instead cruelly sacrificed himself and his own, that is, forfeited his own life and the lives of those he loved! He founded no kingdom on earth; neither did he sacrifice himself so the apostles could inherit the gains. No, it was—humanly speaking— madness: he sacrificed himself—in order to make the beloved as unhappy as himself. Was it really love—to gather a number of simple, poor men about himself, win their devotion and love as no one's love had ever been won, to let it seem to them for a time as if now the prospects of fulfilling their proudest dream were opening—only to reconsider suddenly and change the plan, only to plunge himself from these seductive heights into the abyss of all dangers without being stirred by their prayers, without taking the least regard for them, only to give himself without resistance into the power of his enemies, to be nailed to the cross like a criminal, amid mockery and scorn, while the world rejoiced! Was it really love to be separated from his disciples in this way, to leave them abandoned in a world which for his sake might hate them, to toss them like lost sheep among ravenous wolves whose blood-thirst he himself had incited against them—was it really love? What then, did this man want, what did he want of these unwary, upright, even though provincial men whom he so horribly deceived? Why did he die without confessing that he deceived them? As it was, he died with the claim that it nevertheless was for love—alas, while the disciples with crushed hearts, yet with moving faith, did not presume to have any opinion about his conduct, probably because he had overpowered them, even though others easily perceived that he (whatever else he was), perhaps even yet to escape being regarded as an enthusiast, acted like a deceiver as far as his disciples were concerned. And yet he was love and nevertheless did everything out of love and would make man eternally happy—and by what means? By relationship to God—for he was love. Yes, he was love, and he knew in himself and in God that it was the sacrifice of reconciliation which he brought, that he genuinely loved the disciples, loved the whole race of man, everyone who would let himself be saved!

The fundamental untruth in the merely human conception of love is that love is withdrawn from the relationship to God and thereby from the relationship to the law which is referred to in the expression, " Love is the fullfilling of the law." By a strange misunderstanding one may be inclined to think that love to one's neighbour should not be withdrawn from the God-relationship but rather erotic love and friendship, as if Christianity were a fraction, as if it should not penetrate all relationships, as if the doctrine about love to one's neighbour were not intended for this very thing, thereby transforming love and friendship, although through a strange misunderstanding many may think they need God's help to love their neighbour, the least lovable object, but, however, that they get along best by themselves in relationship to erotic love and friendship, as if, alas, God's intermingling here were a disturbing and unfortunate factor. But no love and no expression of love may secularly and merely humanly be deprived of the relationship to God. Love is a passion of the emotions, but in this emotion man, even before he relates himself to the object of love, should relate himself to God and thereby learn the demand that love is the fullfilling of the law. Love is a relationship to another human being or to other human beings, but it is by no means and by no means dares to be a marital, a merely human accord, a relationship (no matter how faithful and tender it is just, between man and man. Everyone as an individual, before he relates himself in love to a beloved, to a friend, to lovers, to contemporaries, must first relate himself to God and the God-demand. As soon as one leaves out the God-relationship the merely human conception of what the participants wish to understand by love, what they wish to require of each other, and their mutual judgment in the power thereof become the highest judgment. Not only shall the person who unconditionally has a call from God not belong to a woman, in order not to be obstructed by wanting to please her, but also the person who in love belongs to a woman shall first and foremost absolutely belong to God, shall not first seek to please his wife, but shall strive first that his love may please God. Consequently it is not the wife who shall teach the husband how he should love her, or the husband his wife, or a friend his friend, or associates their associates, but it is God who shall teach every individual how he should love, if his love shall even barely be related to the law which the apostle talks about when he says, " Love is the fullfilling of the law." It follows quite naturally that one who has only a worldly or a merely human conception of what love is must come to regard as self-love and unkindness precisely that which, Christianly understood, is love. When, however, the God-relationship determines what constitutes love between man and man, then love is prevented from stopping in some illusion or self-deception, and simultaneously the demand for self-denial and sacrifice is again made infinite. The love which does not lead to God, the love which does not have the single goal of leading the lovers to love God, such love comes to a standstill in the merely human judgment of what constitutes love and love's sacrifice and devotion; it comes to a standstill and thereby escapes the possibility of the horror of the ultimate and most terrible collision: that in the love-relationship there is an infinite difference between the conceptions of what love is. According to a purely human way of looking at things, this collision can never happen, for understood merely humanly the basic idea of what love is must essentially be held in common. Only Christianly understood is the collision possible, for it is a collision between the Christian and the purely human. Yet Christianity knows how to steer through this difficulty, and no doctrine has ever taught constancy in love as has Christianity. Unalterably and resolutely, precisely for the sake of the lovers, it teaches one to hold fast to the true idea of what love is and then willingly to discover that as a reward for his love he is hated by his beloved—for there is, indeed, an infinite difference, an eternity's difference in language, between what the one understands by love and what the other understands by it. To conform to the beloved's idea of love is, humanly speaking, loving, and if one does this he becomes loved. But to run counter to the beloved's merely human conception of love, in order to hold fast to God's conception, to deny desire and to that extent also what the lover himself must wish, understood in purely human terms—this is the collision. A purely human conception of love can never comprehend that anyone, through being loved as completely as possible by another person, would be able to stand in the other person's way. And still,

Christianly understood, this very thing is possible, for to be loved thus can be a hindrance to the lover's God-relationship. But what is to be done? For such a beloved to caution against it will really not help much, inasmuch as he would thereby only become more lovable—and the lover consequently even more deceived. Christianity knows how to remove the collision, yet without removing love. It demands only this sacrifice (in many cases it is the greatest sacrifice possible and is always very great): being willing to discover that the reward for his love is to be hated. Wherever a man is loved in such a way, admired by others so that he comes to be dangerous to their God-relationship, there is the collision; but wherever this collision is, there is also the requirement of a sacrifice which the merely human conception of love does not suspect. For the Christian view means this: truly to love oneself is to love God; truly to love another person is with every sacrifice (even to become hated) to help the other person love God or in loving God.

This is no doubt easy to understand, but in the world this view meets with great difficulties, because a contradictory view of what love is, a worldly, a purely human, but for all that an ingenious and poetically developed view, either declares that all this about a God-relationship is really a figment of the imagination, a bit of backwardness, or in talking about love it keeps silent about the God-relationship. Just as attempts are made nowadays in so many ways to free men from all bonds, beneficial ones as well, so men seek to free the emotional relationship between man and man from the bond which binds him to God and binds him in everything, in every expression of life. In respect to love there is a desire to teach men something quite new, something, however, for which the now antiquated Holy Scriptures already had the significant expression—there is an effort to teach men the freedom which "is without God in the world."[88]   Serfdom's abominable era is past; so there is the intention to go further with the help of this abomination: to abolish man's serfdom in respect to God, to whom every man not by birth, but by creation from nothing, belongs as a bondservant, and in such a way as no bondservant has ever belonged to an earthly master, who nevertheless concedes that thoughts and feelings are free. But he belongs to God in every thought, the most hidden, in every feeling, the most private, in every motion, the most inward. Yet men find this bondservice to be a burdensome imposition and are more or less openly intent upon deposing God in order to enthrone man.[89] In the rights of man?—no, that is not necessary, for God has already done that—consequently it is in the rights of God, for the place becomes vacant when God is dismissed. And now, as a reward for such presumption men will come closer and closer to transforming all existence into doubt or confusion. What, after all, is law? What is the law's demand on a man? Yes, men are going to decide this. Which men? Here doubt begins. Since one man is essentially not superior to another, it is left entirely to me to decide with whom I will ally myself in determining the highest, unless I—still more arbitrarily, if possible—am able and in a position to hit upon a new determination and as a campaigner win a following for it. It is likewise left to my arbitrariness to regard one thing as the law's demand to-day and another to-morrow. Or shall the determination of what is the law's demand perhaps be a compromise, a common conclusion by all men, to which the individual then has to submit? Excellent—if it were possible to find the place and to fix a time for this assembling of all men (all of them living, all?—but what of the dead?), and if it were possible, and this is equally impossible, that they could all agree on one thing! Or is the agreement of a crowd of men, a certain number of votes, sufficient for this decisive determination? How great a number is required? And furthermore, if a purely human determination of the law's demand is the law's demand (but not the individual man's, for then we fall into pure arbitrariness, as indicated), how then does the individual come to begin to act, or is it not left to chance how he comes to begin, instead of everyone's having to begin at the beginning? For in order to begin to act the individual must first find out from *the others* what the law's demand is; but every one of these others must, each as an individual, find this out from *the others*. In such a manner all of human life is transformed to one great excuse—is this perhaps the great, matchless common undertaking, the great achievement of the race? The category *the others* becomes fanciful, and the fancifully sought determination of what the law's demand is becomes a blind hubbub. And now if this inhumanly tedious labour on the common agreement among all men is not finished in one evening but drags along from generation to generation, the way the individual comes to begin will be quite up to chance; it will depend, so to speak, upon when he comes into the game. A few would begin at the beginning but would die before the determination had been half completed. Others would begin midway but would die without seeing the end, which no one really sees, for it comes for the first time when the whole thing is over and world history is ended—then only would one come to know completely what the law's demand is. What a shame that human life should not begin now, rather than just when it is all over, and that consequently all men lead out their lives without full knowledge of what the law's demand is. If of seven men, all charged with having committed a crime which could not have been committed by any others, the seventh man said, " It was not I, it was the others," one would understand " the others " to mean the six—and so on in the same manner. But if all seven, each individually, said, " It was the others," what then? Is there not conjured up an apparition which has doubled the actual seven and likewise would have us believe that there were even more, although there were only seven? Similarly when a whole generation, every single individual, hits upon saying "the others," a phantasm is conjured up, as if the human race were once again beyond the time of its actual existence, only that it is so difficult to point out the falsity here, a bedazzlement with the appearance of profundity because the generation is innumerable. Yet the relationship is exactly the same as in what one could be tempted to call the fairy story about the Seven and the Seven Others. The relationship is precisely this: if the merely human determination of what the law's demand is shall be the law's demand, one helps himself up and along with the assistance of that fanciful giddiness *the others*, and down below men support each other by associating together a little. To be sure, the human race has another existence, but not in fancy. Its other existence is its existence in God, or more correctly, this is its first existence, wherein every individual finds out from God the law's demand; its actual existence is its second existence. To what can we compare this confused state which we have described? I wonder if it is not a mutiny? Or should we hesitate to call it this if it was the whole generation which at a given time became guilty of it and we then—note well—add that it is a mutiny against God? Or is morality an accidental matter so that when a great number do wrong or we all do it, wrong is then right? This explanation would only be a repetition of mutinous thought or mutinous thoughtlessness, for if it is men instead of God who ultimately decide what the law's demand is, the one who forgets God's law is not only personally guilty of insurrection against God but he is also a contributor to the success of the mutiny. Who could stop such a mutiny, if it existed? Should we perhaps repeat the mutiny's delusion (only in a new pattern) and each one individually say: " I cannot stop it; the others must "? I wonder if every individual is not duty bound towards God to stop the mutiny, not, of course, with shouts and con-ceited importance, not by domineering and wanting to force others to

obey God, but by unconditionally obeying as an individual, by unconditionally holding fast to the God-relationship and the God-demand
and thereby expressing for his part that God exists and is the only
master, and that he, on the other hand, is unconditionally obedient to
Him?—Only then is there substance and meaning and truth and
reality in existence, when all of us, each one individually, if I dare say
so, receive our instructions at one place and each one individually
unconditionally obeys one and the same command. Since it is one and
the same command, one man could, in a sense, find it out from another
—if it were certain, or at least certain enough, that this other man
communicated the right thing. This, however, would still be disorder
striving against God's order, because God, for the sake of certainty and
universality and responsibility, wants every individual to find out from
him the law's demand. When this is true, there is a holding-on place
in existence, for God has hold of it. There is no whirling about, for
every individual begins, not with *the others*, consequently not with
escapes and excuses, but begins with the God-relationship, and therefore he stands fast, and he thereby also diminishes, as far as he can
reach, the dizziness which is the beginning of mutiny.

So it is also with the law of love—there is substance and truth and
a holding-on place in existence when we all—each individually—find
out from God what the demand is according to which we must direct
our lives, and when, in addition, all of us, each one individually,
defend ourselves against human confusion (yet it follows as a matter of
course that if we all did this there would be no confusion), yes, if
necessary, defend ourselves against the beloved, the friend, our nearest
and dearest, who still are special objects of love, insofar as these in any
way want to teach us another explanation or side-track us, but thank
them if they want to help us to the right path. Let us not forget this;
let us not deceive or be deceived by vague and hazy ideas of what love
is but heed God's explanation, indifferent to what the beloved and
friend and lovers think or do not think, yet not indifferent but rather
deeply concerned if they do not agree with us, but still undisturbedly
and unchangingly continuing to love them.

There really is strife between what the world and what God understand by love. It is easy enough to bring about an apparent harmony
(as is already apparent in the use of one and the same word: *love*); it
is more difficult, however, accurately to discover the disharmony, but
this difficulty is unavoidable in order for us to recognise the truth.
From the world one frequently hears the saying: look out for number

one—this is the soundest practical wisdom in the world. Obviously this saying does not contribute much to the best idea of the world, for it is hardly a good world in which self-love is the highest wisdom or that which brings the greatest advantage. But even if the world regards self-love as the most practical wisdom, it does not follow that it could not by way of compensation regard love as more noble. And so it does, except that the world does not understand what love is. Again, it is easy enough to bring about an apparent harmony between God's and the world's conceptions of love—it is already apparent in the use of this common expression that love is something noble. But nevertheless there is a concealed misunderstanding. What is the point in praising love as something noble (which Christianity also does) when the world understands something different by *love* and something else again by *nobility*! No, if the world is to be explicit, it must say, " Not only is self-love the wisest course, but if you want to be loved by the world, if you want it to praise your love and you as a noble person, you must, Christianly understood, be selfish, for what the world calls love is selfishness." The distinction which the world makes is namely this: if a person wants to be all by himself in being selfish—which, after all, is very rarely seen—the world calls it selfishness, but if in selfishness he wants to form a group with several other selfish people, especially with many other selfish people, the world calls it love. The world can never go any further in characterising what love is, because it has neither God nor one's neighbour as a middle term. What the world honours and loves under the name of love is group-selfishness. The group also demands sacrifice and devotion from the one whom it is to call loving. It demands that he shall sacrifice a portion of his own selfishness in order to maintain the united group-selfishness, and it demands that he shall sacrifice the God-relationship in order to unite in a worldly way with the group which locks God out or at most takes him along for the sake of appearance. God, on the other hand, understands love to be sacrificing love, sacrificing love in the divine sense, love which sacrifices everything in order to make room for God, even if a heavy sacrifice were to become still heavier because no one understands it, which in yet another sense belongs to true sacrifice. The sacrifice which is understood by men has its reward in the approval of men and to that extent is no true sacrifice, for a true sacrifice must unconditionally be without reward. Therefore, in understanding the words of the apostle —that love is the fullfilling of the law—we dare not assent to that superficial talk which maintains that a man who really has love will also be loved by men. He will more likely be criticised for self-love, [90] simply because he will not love men in the way whereby they selfishly love themselves. The facts are these: extreme self-love the world also calls selfishness; the self-love of a group the world calls love; a noble sacrificial, high-minded human love, which still is not Christian love, is ridiculed by the world as foolishness; whereas Christian love is hated and detested and persecuted by the world. Let us not again by a reductionist compromise gloss over the incongruities by saying: so it is with the world, but it is otherwise with the Christians. This is quite true, but if every baptized person is a Christian and baptized Christendom is pure Christianity, then the *world* does not exist at all in a Christian country—something which may be proved with the help of lists from the sextons and the police sergeants.—No, there is genuine conflict between what God and the world understand by love. O, it is inspiring to fight for home and fatherland. But certainly it is also inspiring to fight for God, something one does when before God, in the presence of God, he holds fast in the God-relationship and to its characterisation of what love is! True enough, God does not stand in need of any man any more than he stands in need of a whole generation or of everything, which at any moment it may exist is for him as the nothing out of which he created it. Nevertheless he who fights the good fight to express that God is and is the Lord whose declaration must be obeyed unconditionally—he fights for God.

The God-relationship is the mark whereby love towards men is recognised as genuine love. As soon as a love-relationship does not lead me to God, and as soon as I in a love-relationship do not lead another person to God, this love, even if it were the most blissful and joyous attachment, even if it were the highest good in the lover's earthly life, nevertheless is not true love. The world can never get through its head that God in this way not only becomes the third party in every relationship of love but essentially becomes the only loved object, so that it is not the husband who is the wife's beloved, but it is God, and it is the wife who is helped by the husband to love God, and conversely, and so on. The purely human conception of love can never go further than mutuality: that the lover is the beloved and the beloved is the lover. Christianity teaches that such a love has not yet found its proper object: God. The love-relationship is a triangular relationship of the lover, the beloved, love—but love is God. Therefore to love another person means to help him to love God and to be loved means to be helped.

The world's talk about love is confusing. When a youth going out into the world is told " Love and you will be loved," this is quite true —especially if the journey he undertakes is into the eternal, into the land of perfection. But the youth is going out into the world, and therefore it is deceitful to talk this way without reminding him to hold fast to God in order to learn what love is, without reminding him that the world—if it has not learned the same thing from God (but then it would be the land of perfection he travels in)—has a quite different conception. If Christ had not been love and if in him love had not been the fullfilling of the law, I wonder if he would have been crucified? If he had reduced the demand on himself and agreed with those who make love something other than the fullfilling of the law divinely understood, if instead of being the world's teacher and Saviour in love he had shaped his conception of what it is to love in accordance with the world's view, would he not, I wonder, have been loved and praised by all or even (frightful madness!) idolised by devotees? If the apostles had not held fast to the truth that love is the fullfilling of the law, and consequently something different from the fullfillment of human agreements and participation in human society, if they had not held fast to loving men in this sense without wishing to undertake an adaptation to the world's conception of what it is to love—would they, I wonder, have been persecuted? What does the world love and call love, what else but half-measures and an exclusively secular association in worldliness, which, divinely understood, is nothing else than a half-measure. I wonder if anyone has ever been more gossiped about for his self-love than one who has really held fast to the God-requirement and, faithful to this, has loved men and because of this has continued to love them in spite of persecution and misjudgment. Is it not natural, too, that the world is enraged because there is One whom such a man loves more than he loves the world, because there is One towards whom the love of such a man is expressed in love to men? If a man's efforts are spent in winning earthly success, he no doubt complains unjustly about the world if he complains about finding no friend,[91] for at a price one certainly can become loved, win friends, have many or few with whom he—lovingly associates. But when with every sacrifice, the sacrifice of everything, when impoverished, despised, locked out from the synagogue, one's efforts are unconditionally spent in holding fast to God in loving men, then he may well advertise in the paper that he is looking for a friend—stating, however, the conditions and laying particular emphasis on " It is not for the sake of advantage "—but it will be difficult to find anyone. We marvel that Christ chose such insignificant men for apostles. Disregarding what no doubt was a determining factor in the choice, that the less promising the apostle was as a man the greater was the impression of divine authority granted to him, I still wonder if it was not more remarkable that Christ got them at all, that he really succeeded in forming a band of disciples whose qualification was to stick together in a willingness to be scourged, persecuted, mocked, crucified, beheaded, and whose qualification also was not mutual flattery, but on the contrary a mutual helping of each other to humility before God. It might seem like a horrible joke on what the world understands by love, but I wonder, could it not function as a beneficial shock if someone in these times, when so many organisations are formed, advertised that he proposed to form such a society of love. The world can understand that when someone wills to sacrifice everything there are those who, in all indolence, would like to have some advantage from his sacrifices; that sort of participation, which shares in all the profit and in scarcely half the work, is certainly found in the world. It goes without saying that true participation is also found on earth, but wherever you find it you will find it hated and persecuted by the world. Try this. Imagine a man (and you need not even imagine him as possessing that perfection which characterises the magnificent one who, repudiated by men, becomes the glory of his generation), imagine a man who was or became or was and remained so unhappy that earthly advantages and the goods of this world had lost their allure in his eyes, so unhappy that, "weary of sighing" (Psalm 6 : 6), he became, as we read in Holy Scriptures of the unhappy Sara (Tobit 3 : 11), "so despondent that he wanted to hang himself." Imagine, then, that precisely in the darkest hour of his need it became absolutely clear to him that in spite of all his unhappiness, which essentially would not be relieved even if he won all the world's goods, since their possession, by inviting happy enjoyment, would only painfully remind him of his wretchedness, an unhappiness which would not essentially be increased by earthly adversity, which like dark weather in relationship to melancholy would rather harmonise with his mood— imagine, then, that it became absolutely clear to him that there still remained for him the highest: to will to love men, to will to serve the good, to serve truth for truth's sake alone, the only thing which truly could enliven his troubled mind and give him the joy of life for eternity. Imagine such a person in the world and you will perceive that it will go hard with him ; he will not win the world's love, he will not be understood, he will not be loved by the world. In proportion to their greater or lesser affiliation with the world, some men will complain about him, some smile at him, some rather be rid of him because they noticed the sting, some envy him and yet not envy him, some feel themselves attracted to him and yet again repelled, some work against him but yet have everything in readiness to honour him after death, some young people feel swept off their feet like a woman but when they get a little older will not quite understand him any more. But the world would like directly and openly to prove his self-love because he secured no earthly advantage either for himself or for any one else, no, not for a single other man. The world is no better than this: the highest which it recognises and loves, when it attains the highest, is to love the good and mankind, and yet in such a way that one also watches out for one's own and a few others' earthly advantage. What goes beyond that, the world with its best intentions (this, of course, is only a manner of speaking) cannot grasp. One step beyond and you have lost the world's friendship and love. Such is the world and its love. No observer measuring a liquid can more accurately vouch for the degree of its specific gravity than I will vouch for this conception of the world's love. It is not absolutely evil, as it is sometimes passionately represented, nor is it untainted, but to a certain degree is both good and evil. But Christianity understood, this "to a certain degree" is of evil.

This, however, we do not say for the purpose of judging; let us not waste time on that. The discourse seeks, with the help of thought and a little knowledge of human nature to penetrate illusions or to understand those words of the apostle in the context of daily life-relationships, precisely where illusions are most at home. It takes no time at all to become deceived—one can be deceived immediately and remain so for a long time—but to become aware of the deception takes time. It certainly is easier to get a quick fanciful picture of what love is and then be satisfied with the fancy; it is still easier hastily to get a few men to associate together in self-love, to be loved and regarded by them till the end—there is nothing so easy and nothing so sociable as going astray. But if your ultimate and highest purpose is to have life made easy and sociable, then never have anything to do with Christianity. Flee from it, for it will do the very opposite; it will make your life difficult and do this precisely by making you alone before God. No earnest person, therefore, becomes weary of tracking down illusions, because insofar as he is a thinking person he fears most of all to be deluded—however convenient the arrangement might be or however good the associations; and as a Christian he fears most to be lost without knowing it—however flattering, however attractive the conditions and the associations might be.

That such pretentiousness is not love seems so easy to perceive that one would think nobody could entertain such a view. Yet this is not always the case, and here is a good example of an illusion insofar as purely human judgment might be decisive. If the pretentious person himself should presume to call it love, one would certainly raise an objection and then there really would be no illusion. The illusion is present only when others wish to become the object of this pretentiousness, to regard it as love, to praise it as love, and to regard him as one who loves. Without being an exceptional student of men, one would not find it difficult to point out life-relationships in which a man can be situated in such a way that there will be those who will look with favour on him, will commend his love, if in the name of love he demands everything of them. There are men who really know nothing else about love than that it is caressing. Such men want just this—that the one they are to love and cherish should presume upon them. There are men who inhumanly have forgotten that every man should strengthen himself in that likeness to God which is common to all men and that for this reason whether a person is man or woman, richly endowed or poorly endowed, master or slave, beggar or rich man, the relationship between man and man ought and dare never be one in which the one worships and the other is worshipped. This is so easy to see that one very likely thinks this abomination can rise only out of a misuse of superiority, consequently only from the superior one. Alas, it can also arise from the weak, who themselves desire it so that in this way they might have a kind of significance before their superiors. Take the equality of the eternal and its divine erectness away, that is, assume that it is forgotten; then the meek woman in relationship to the over-bearing man, the poorly endowed and yet vain person in relationship to the richly endowed, the poor and yet only worldly-concerned man in relationship to the "all-powerful man," the very subordinate and yet earthly-minded person in relationship to the master—they will know of no other expression for the relationship than to abase themselves and throw themselves away. And since they desire for themselves this abomination, inasmuch as they know nothing higher because they *will* not know anything higher, they will desire it with all their hearts. The desire is to exist in the eyes of the mighty; inasmuch as power is impossible of earthly attainment, prostration becomes the desirable thing. Is it perhaps not apparent that a girl would rather inhumanly cast herself down and adore her idol, beseeching only one thing of him, that he inhumanly demand everything of her, and, this being the case, extolling his love, rather than perceive that before God all these differences between man and man are a jest, vanity, often to one's ruin! And yet the girl would call it selfishness if her idol sought to bring her to this knowledge. Is it not apparent that by forgetting God the weak and abject man has only one desire, that he might cast himself in the dust before his master—in order that he might exist for him, only one desire, that the master would step on him in order that he might praise with gladness the master's gracious love and kind-heartedness! Is it not apparent that the vain person who has completely forgotten God desires only a relationship to a distinguished person and willingly calls the most abject relationship an indication of his love! And if the other will not have it, if he will prevent this sort of relationship by helping him to that holy equality before God, then this is called selfishness. When at first the eternal is taken away from a man or it is within him as if it were not there, the eternal, which can both cool all unhealthy passions in the relationship between man and man and kindle them when temporality will freeze, when at first the eternal is taken away from a man, there is no assurance that he will not think of calling this most abominable affair by the name of love and even passionately crave to be the object of this abomination. One can inhumanly wish to make himself indispensable by his weakness, and therefore, cringing and begging, call another man's pretentiousness love.

But the demand of the eternal will not exempt a man from fullfilling the law of God, even if the whole world would exempt him, even if the whole world would love his pretentiousness but misunderstand his love, because perhaps first through despair can this demand teach the despairing one to hold to God instead of cravenly taking damage upon his soul. The demand of the eternal will prevent love from remaining in any self-deception and from being satisfied with any illusion. It shall be no excuse that men themselves do desire it and themselves call becoming the object of pretentiousness by the names of love and being loved. It is God who has placed love in man, and it is God who shall decide in every case what is love.

But when a friend, a beloved, lovers, and associates notice that you want to learn from God what it is to love instead of learning from them, they will very likely say to you, " Spare yourself. Give up this eccentricity. Why take life so seriously? Cut out the straining, and we

will live a beautiful, rich, and significant life in friendship and joy."
And if you give in to the suggestions of this false friendship, you will be
loved and praised for your love. But if you will not, if in loving you will
be a traitor neither to God nor to yourself nor to the others, you must
expect to be called selfish. For your conviction that truly to love oneself
is to love God and that to love another man is to help him to love God,
for this conviction your friend will very likely not care much. Even if
you say nothing, he notices, you may be sure, that your life contains,
if it is truly related to God's demand, an admonition, a demand on him
—it is this which he wants to do away with. The reward for this is
friendship and the good name of a friend. In the world, unfortunately,
worldliness has so much the upper hand that when one talks about
false friendship people think immediately about deception in respect to
earthly advantages, or faithlessness in regard to earthly interests. This
was not your friend's intention or idea at all. He would only cheat
you out of the God-relationship and have you as a friend help him in
cheating yourself—then through life and death he would stick faithfully
by you in the deception. People speak of the world's falsity and
immediately take it to mean that it deceives one in respect to earthly
goods, disappoints one's great expectations, makes sport of one's daring
plans. But that it can be most dangerously deceiving when in these
respects it honourably maintains everything, almost more than it has
promised—that this is its most dangerous falsity the world seldom
thinks about. It seldom thinks that the world by its upright friendship
(for, indeed, there was false friendship when it deceived one out of
temporal things) will teach one to forget God. They talk about
mortgaging oneself to evil, and if one asks what advantages are offered
in compensation, they name power, honour, the satisfaction of desires,
and the like. But they forget to think and mention that by such a
mortgage one can also succeed in being loved by men and being praised
for his love. Yet this is the case—for the opposite is and was the case,
that they who in love to God loved men became hated in the world.
Just as the world has wanted to tempt a man to forget God by offering
him power and might and then again has treated the same man like
the scum of the earth because he withstood the temptation, so the world
has also temptingly offered an individual its friendship and then hated
him because he would not be its friend. The world would just as soon
not hear anything about the eternal, God's demand to love; still less
does it like to see it expressed in life. But I wonder if the world therefore
calls itself selfish? By no means. What does the world do, then? It

calls him selfish who will hold fast to God. The way out is an old one—to sacrifice the individual when all the others can get some advantage out of it.

God and the world are of one mind in this that love is the fullfilling of the law. The difference is that the world understands law to be something it conceives of by itself, and that the person who agrees to this conception and carries it out is a loving person. How many a man has been corrupted, divinely understood, by a girl's love, simply because, defrauded out of his God-relationship, he became far too faithful to her while she in turn was inexhaustible in her praise of his love? How many a man have relatives and friends corrupted, while yet his ruination was as if it were not, for now he came to be loved and praised for his love—by his relatives and friends? How many a man has been corrupted by the age he lived in, the age which in return idolised his loving disposition because it got him to forget his God-relationship and changed it to something men could noisily parade, shout about, esthetically admire, without being sensitive to any admonition about higher things? Why, I wonder—in order to raise a different and really serious question, and yet not even pointing to the highest pattern but being satisfied with an inferior one, which unfortunately is quite enough even in so-called Christendom[92]—I wonder why that simple wise man[93] of old, when he defended his life, accused of selfishness and worldliness before the judgment seat of thoughtlessness, doomed to death—I wonder why he compared himself to a "gadfly" at the same time that he called himself a gift from the gods, and why, I wonder, did he love young men so deeply? Was it not, first, because he had loved men in some higher way which was open to a pagan, consequently because he had had a quickening influence and had not let himself in any way be charmed by temporality or by any man, or by an obsequious or passionate relationship in erotic love, in friendship, or in compromise with others or with the times, but had preferred to be a selfish person, a teaser whom nobody loved? Was it not, second, because he had perceived that young men still had a receptivity for the divine, a receptivity which is very easily lost in the passage of years, in trade and commerce, in erotic love and friendship, in subjection to merely human judgment and the demands of the times? Consequently, because in virtue of the eternal and that "something divine" he had prevented his love for men from coming to a standstill in self-deception or illusion, consequently, because he had held himself close to the demand, he had been to other men as a demand.

If, then, in any way, even in human frailty, you will aspire to accomplish the apostolic words that love is the fullfilling of the law, then beware of men! I wonder if in a certain sense you should stop loving them? How unreasonable! How then would your love become the fullfilling of the law? But beware that it does not become more important for you that you are looked upon as loving them than that you love them; beware that your being loved does not become more important for you than that wherein you ought to love each other; beware that they do not trick you out of the highest because you cannot bear to be called selfish. Do not appeal to the judgment of men concerning you in order to prove your love, for the judgment of men has validity only as far as it agrees with God's demand; otherwise men are only your accomplices! Learn also, and never forget the teaching, this sad teaching, which is the truth about temporal life, that all love between man and man neither can nor shall be perfectly happy, never dares to be perfectly secure! For, divinely understood, even the happiest love between man and man has still one danger which the purely human conception of love cannot imagine, the danger that earthly love could become too intense, so that the God-relationship is disturbed, the danger that the God-relationship, when humanly speaking there is perfect peace and no danger in sight, can require even this, the happiest love, as a sacrifice. From the possibility of this danger, it follows that you, even in the happiest love-relationship, must always watch apprehensively, although indeed the concern is not that you might become weary of the beloved or the beloved of you, but watch apprehensively lest you too should forget God, or that the beloved might do so, or you yourself. And from the possibility of this danger it follows—to remind you of the introduction to this discussion —how difficult it must be to promise love when to stick to it can mean being hated by the beloved. Only God, who is the one true object of love, is the continuously happy, the continuously blessed object of love. You should not watch apprehensively; watch only in adoration.

Love is the fullfilling of the law. But the law has an inexhaustible multiplicity of provisions; how can we ever finish discussing them? Let us therefore concentrate this multiplicity in that which is decisive. *The demand of the law* must be twofold—*in part a demand for inwardness, in part a demand for perseverance.*

What is this inwardness which is required? The purely human conception of love also requires inwardness, devotedness, sacrifice, but defines it in a purely human way. The devotedness of inwardness is this: with every sacrifice to satisfy the beloved's (the object's) conception of what love is, or on its own responsibility willingly to venture to decide what love is. But divinely understood to love oneself is to love God and truly to love another man is to help him to love God or in loving God. Therefore we see here that inwardness is determined not only by the love-relationship, but by the God-relationship. Therefore the inwardness which is required is the inwardness of self-renunciation which is more accurately defined by reference to one's helping the beloved to love God, not by reference to the beloved's (the object's) conception of love. From this it follows that the love-relationship as such can be the sacrifice which is required.—The inwardness of love must be sacrificial and therefore must not require any reward. The purely human conception of love also teaches that love requires no reward—it only wants to be loved, as if this were no reward, as if this which becomes the whole relationship were not still within the definition of the relationship between man and man. But the inwardness of Christian love is willing to be hated by the beloved (the object) as reward for its love. This shows that such inwardness is essentially a God-relationship; it has no reward, not even that of being loved. In this way it belongs wholly to God, or the person belongs wholly to God. The self-denial, self-reliance, and self-sacrifice which are only an inversion within the world of time within man's range of vision are not truly Christian, are like a jest compared to Christian earnestness, are like a preparatory run toward Christian decisiveness. Men will sacrifice this or that and everything, but they still hope to be understood and thereby to remain in a meaningful human context in which one's sacrifices are recognised and rejoiced over. They will leave everything, but they do not mean thereby to be deprived of the good opinion and understanding of men. The movement of sacrifice becomes, then, a thing of appearance; it makes a show of forsaking the world but nevertheless remains within the world. By no means do we wish to under-value this—alas, even this purely human sacrifice is found rarely enough. But, Christianly understood, we have to say that it gets stuck half-way. It climbs to a high point, for humanly speaking sacrifice indeed ranks high; it casts everything away in order to climb this elevated peak, whose height admiration realises, while sacrifice sees to it that it is seen. But to stand on this elevated peak (for sacrifice is truly elevation) criticised, despised, hated, mocked almost worse than the most base among the debased—consequently, superhumanly straining to attain the elevated point and to stand on the elevation in such a way that it appears to all as if one stood at the lowest point of contempt—this, Christianly understood, is sacrifice, and it is also, humanly understood, madness. There is only one who sees the true connection, and he does not admire it, for God in heaven does not admire any man. On the contrary, while the one who truly sacrifices has only one single stronghold, God, he is nevertheless as if forsaken by God, for he understands that before God he has absolutely no merit, but he also understands as a man that by sacrificing only half of what he sacrificed he would become understood, loved, and admired of men, and yet, in a certain sense, before God have the same significance as the true sacrifice, inasmuch as before God no sacrifice, none at all, has any merit. This, Christianity understood, is sacrifice and at the same time, humanly understood, is madness. Christianly understood, this is what it is to love. If it is true that to love is the greatest happiness, this is the heaviest suffering—if it were not that being related to God is the greatest blessedness.

The other requirement of the law is perseverance of love throughout time. The purely human conception of love makes this demand also; however, Christianly understood, this demand is something different, inasmuch as the required inwardness is something different. The demand for perseverance in time is that the same inwardness of love shall be maintained throughout the duration of time, which, to a degree and in a certain sense, is a new expression for inwardness. As soon as you think you have done enough in your love or loved long enough and now must demand something of another, you discover therewith that your love is in the process of becoming a demand, as if there were, however sacrificial and devoted your love is, nevertheless a frontier where it must show itself basically to be a demand—but love is the fullfilling of the law. This is no great moment of self-denial which we are discussing; the law demands the same inwardness for the duration of time. For the duration of time! But does it not amount to twisting a man's soul, a contradiction in the demand, to make a demand in such different directions at one and the same time—a demand in the direction of length and in the direction of depth? For example, the arrow flies speedily through the air horizontally, but if at the same time it should bore into the earth and continue to fly with the speed of an arrow—oh, what a demand! For example, in a great moment of inspiration the eternal lingers, but when time begins its restless busy-ness, when it keeps on moving—then not to move with time away from the inspiration but precipitously proceed with the hastiness of time and yet slowly with the lingering of the eternal! To be on one's death-bed (and when a man in self-renunciation has had to bring the hardest sacrifice—as reward for his love to be hated by the object of his love—then is he without doubt on his death-bed) and then to have a future, a long life ahead of him, although everything is over—consequently, at one and the same time and at every moment to be on his death-bed and to have to walk forward erect! What a demand! To lie down is precisely the opposite of walking upright, but to lie on one's death-bed is truly the most decisive expression for being down and therefore removed as much as possible from erectness. Have you ever seen a tired traveller, bearing a heavy burden, fighting at every step to keep from sinking to the earth? He holds himself erect with the greatest difficulty; he struggles against collapse. But to be in a state of collapse, to lie down, to lie on one's death-bed—and then to hurry intrepidly forward with upright stride! Remarkable! All this the demand can be —and it can also be a demand for endurance throughout the duration of time.

Alas, in the world of the spirit there is something fraudulent for which there is nothing in the external world that corresponds. We say, for instance, that a child must learn to spell before it can learn to read. It is, for better or for worse, an unavoidable necessity. It has never happened that a child has been induced by appearances or by an illusion to fancy that it could read long before it could spell. But how seductive in the realm of the spirit! For here does not everything begin with the great moment of resolution, of intention, of promise—whereby one reads as fluently as the most accomplished reader presents the best prepared reading? And then comes the next part; then one is supposed to go on to the littlest things, the simple, everyday things which will certainly not make a great impression or help anyone by means of a bold comprehensive plan. Alas, on the contrary, it is like spelling, which separates words and takes them apart; so it is, too, in the long, long hours when one cannot see the meaning of things and waits in vain for connectedness. To struggle with oneself in self-renunciation, especially if one is determined to be victorious, is regarded as a most difficult struggle, and to struggle with time, if one is to be unconditionally victorious, is regarded as an impossibility.

The heaviest burden laid on man (for the burden of sin he lays upon himself) is, in a certain sense, time [94]—do we not say that something long and drawn out can be killing! And yet, on the other hand, what a softening, alleviating, seductive power time has! But this softening, seductive element is indeed a new danger. If a man has been guilty of something—and then some time has passed, especially if during that time he seems to have made some progress towards the better—how mitigated his guilt seems to him! But is this really so? Is it, then, also true that when a thoughtless person has instantaneously forgotten his guilt, it is then forgotten?

Suppose, then, it is possible to discuss these words—that love is the fullfilling of the law—without judging against one's will, but desiring only to judge oneself! Is there any more accurate expression for how infinitely far a man is from fullfilling the demand than this, that the distance is so great he really cannot begin to calculate it, cannot reckon it at all! Not only is much omitted every day, to say nothing about what one is guilty of, but when some time has slipped by, one is not even in a position to state accurately the guilt as it appeared to him, because time changes and softens one's judgment about the past—alas, but no amount of time changes the requirement, the eternal's requirement: love is the fullfilling of the law

III B

Love Is a Matter of Conscience

The aim of our charge is love that issues from a pure heart and a good conscience and sincere faith. (*I Timothy* 1 : 5)

If one were to indicate and describe in one simple word the victory Christianity has won over the world, or even more accurately, the victory in which it has more than overcome the world, the infinite transformation which Christianity aims at (since Christianity has never wanted to conquer in a worldly way), by which everything indeed remains as it was (for Christianity has never been a friend of the trumpery of novelty) and yet in the transformation of infinity becomes new—I know of nothing briefer, but also nothing more decisive, than this: it has made every human relation between man and man a relationship of conscience. [95] Christianity has not wanted to hurl governments from the throne in order to set itself on the throne; [96] in an external sense it has never striven for a place in the world, for it is not of this world (for in the heart-room, if it finds place there, it still takes no position in the world), and nevertheless it has infinitely changed everything which it has permitted and permits to continue. Just as the blood throbs in every nerve, so will Christianity in the relationship of conscience penetrate everything. The change is not in the external, not in the visible, and yet the change is infinite. Just as if a man (as dreamed of in paganism) had a divine fluid in his arteries instead of blood, [97] so does Christianity want to breathe eternal life, the divine, into the human race. For that reason Christians have been called a nation of priests, [98] and for that reason when considering the relationship of conscience one can say that they are a nation of kings. Take the most insignificant, the most looked-down-upon servant, imagine someone we call a poor, simple, impoverished scrub-woman who earns her living by the most lowly labour—she has, Christianly understood, the right, yes, we beseech her most earnestly in the name of Christianity to do it—she has the right, while she carries out her work, talking to herself and to God, something which by no means retards her work, she has the right to say, " I am doing this work for my daily bread, but that I do it as carefully as I do, that I do—for conscience's sake." In a secular sense there is only one man, only one single man who recognises no other duty than the duty of conscience—that is the king. [99] And yet this poor woman, Christianly understood, has the right to say regally to herself before God, " I am doing this for the sake of conscience! " If the woman becomes discontented because no one will listen to such talk, it merely shows that she is not of a Christian mind; otherwise it seems to me to be enough that God has permitted one to talk in this manner with him—greedily to demand freedom of speech in this matter is very self-contradictory foolishness against oneself, for there are certain things, among them in particular the secrets of inwardness, which lose something by being made public and which are completely lost when one makes publication the most important thing. Yes, there are secrets which in such a case not only are lost but immediately become meaningless. Christianity's divine meaning is to say in confidence to every man, " Do not busy yourself with changing the shape of the world or your condition of life, as if you (to continue with the example), instead of being a poor scrub-woman, perhaps could manage to be called *Madam*. No, make Christianity your own, and it will show you a point outside of the world by the help of which you shall move heaven and earth so quietly, so easily, that no one notices it."

This is the miracle of Christianity, more wonderful than changing water into wine, this miracle, without any shifting of thrones, without a hand stirring, of quietly making every man in a divine sense a king, so easily, so deftly, so miraculously that the world in a certain sense does not need to find out about it. In the external world the king should and ought to be the only one who rules according to his conscience, but to obey for the sake of conscience—this shall be permitted to everyone. Yes, no one, no one can prevent this. And there within, far within, where Christianity lives in the relationship of conscience, there everything is changed.

The world makes a great noise merely to bring about a little change, sets heaven and earth in motion for nothing, like the mountain which gives birth to a mouse! Christianity makes the transformation of infinity in all stillness as if it were nothing! It is still in a way which nothing worldly can be, still as only inwardness or the dead can be. What else is Christianity but inwardness!

Thus it is that Christianity transforms every relationship between man and man into a relationship of conscience and thereby also into a relationship of love. This is what we want to consider now: that Christianly understood

LOVE IS A MATTER OF CONSCIENCE.

In the words of the apostle previously read there is clearly contained a double meaning. First, "The sum of the commandments is love." We developed this in the previous discussion, in that we knitted the observation to another verse, that love is the fullfilling of the law. Our text continues: if love is to be the sum of the commandments, it must be from a pure heart and a good conscience and sincere faith. Yet we chose to concentrate our attention on one qualification, that love is a matter of conscience, in which the other two are essentially contained and to which they essentially lead.

That a certain kind of love is Christianly made into a matter of conscience is sufficiently known to everyone. We are speaking of marriage. Before the pastor of the church joins the two in the union which has been their heart's choice—something, however, which he does not ask about—he asks them first, each one separately: have you deliberated on this with God and with your conscience. Consequently the pastor refers love to the conscience, for which reason he speaks like a stranger to them without using the familiar form of address [*Du*]. He lays on the heart of each one individually that it is a matter of conscience; he makes an affair of the heart a matter of the conscience. It cannot be expressed more definitely and more clearly, and yet still another expression for the same view is contained in the form of the question or in addressing the question to each one individually. To ask the individual—this is a more common expression for the relationship of conscience, and therefore it is also Christianity's essential view of the human race, first and foremost to regard the mass individually, every one by himself as the single individual [*den Enkelte*].

Therefore the pastor of the church asks the two, each one individually, whether he has deliberated with God and his conscience. This is the transformation of infinity which in Christianity takes place in erotic love. It is—like all Christian transformations—so gentle, so hidden, because it belongs only to the inwardness of the hidden man, the inviolable being of the quiet spirit. What abominations has the world not seen in the relationship between man and woman—that she, almost like an animal, was a despised creature compared to the male, a creature of another species! What battles there have been to establish women on equal terms with men in the secular world! But Christianity makes only the transformation of infinity and does it, therefore, in all stillness. Outwardly in a way the old remains—for the man shall be the woman's master and she shall be submissive to him, but in inwardness everything is transformed, transformed with the aid of this little question to the woman, whether she has deliberated with her conscience about having this man—for a master, for otherwise she does not get him. Yet the question of conscience about a matter of conscience makes her in inwardness before God absolutely equal with the man. What Christ said about His kingdom, that it is not of this world, holds true of all that is Christian. As a higher order of things it wills to be present everywhere but is not to be grasped; as a friendly spirit it surrounds the lovers everywhere, follows their every step, but cannot be pointed to. In this Christianity wills to be a stranger in life, because it belongs to another world; it is strange in the world, because it is meant to belong to the inner man. Foolish men have foolishly busied themselves in the name of Christianity to make it obvious in the world that women have equal rights with men—Christianity has never demanded or desired this. It has done everything for woman if she Christianly will be satisfied with what is Christian. If she will not, for her loss she gains only a mediocre compensation in the little fragmentary externals she can win by worldly threats.

So it is with marriage. Although Christianity through marriage has made erotic love into a matter of conscience, it still does not seem to follow that it has made love completely a matter of conscience. Yet anyone who has some other view is under a delusion about Christianity. Christianity has not discriminatingly made erotic love a matter of conscience, but because it has made all love a matter of conscience it has made erotic love that, too. Besides, if any kind of love would be difficult to change to a matter of conscience, it would certainly be erotic love, which is based on impulse and inclination, for impulse and inclination seem quite adequate in themselves to decide the question of its presence or absence, and to that extent erotic love seems to have strong objections to Christianity, just as Christianity has to it. When, therefore, two people love each other—something they themselves must know best—and there is nothing else to hinder their union, why then make difficulties, as Christianity nevertheless does, by saying: no, they must first answer the question whether they have deliberated with God and their conscience. Christianity never seeks to make changes in externals; neither does it seek to abolish impulse or inclination; it seeks only to make an infinite change in the inward man.

Christianity wants above all to make the infinite change (which is the hidden man of inwardness oriented in inwardness towards the God-relationship and therein different from the inwardness which is oriented outwards and away), and therefore it also wants to transform all love into a matter of conscience. Therefore one has a wrong notion of Christianity if he thinks there is a certain kind of love which it discriminatingly wants to make a matter of conscience. After all, one cannot make just certain things a matter of conscience; either one must make everything that, as Christianity does, or nothing at all. It is in the nature of the inner power of conscience to spread abroad just like God's omnipresence, which one cannot restrict to a certain place and then say that God is everywhere present by being in this particular place, for that is to deny his omnipresence. In the same way to restrict the conscience-relationship to something in particular is to deny altogether the conscience-relationship.

If we wish to think of a point of commencement in Christianity's doctrine of love (even if it is impossible to determine the point of beginning in a circular motion), then one cannot say that Christianity begins by making erotic love a matter of conscience, as if this matter had first and foremost attracted the concern of the doctrine, which has something quite different to think about than getting folks married. No, Christianity has begun from the bottom and therefore with a spiritual teaching of what love is. To determine what love is, Christianity begins either with God or with the neighbour, which is the essentially Christian doctrine of love, since in love to find one's neighbour a person must start with God and in loving his neighbour he must find God. On the basis of this primary consideration Christianity controls every expression of love and is jealous for itself. One may therefore just as well say that it is the doctrine about man's God-relationship which has made erotic love a matter of conscience as to say that it is the doctrine of love to one's neighbour. Both are equally the Christian opposition to the autonomy of impulse and inclination. Because the man belongs first and foremost to God before he belongs to any other relationship, the first question put to him must be whether he has deliberated with God and his conscience. So also with the woman. And because the man first and foremost, even in his relationship to the beloved woman, is the neighbour, and she to him is first and foremost the neighbour, it must therefore be asked whether he and she have deliberated with their consciences. Christianly understood, there is equality among all men before God, and in the doctrine of love to one's neighbour there is equality between all men before God. People may think that love for one's neighbour already exists if there is worn-out erotic love. No, love to one's neighbour is the ultimate and the highest love and shall therefore be given a place surpassing even the first and highest moment of falling in love.

This is Christianity. Our primary task is so far from getting busy looking for the beloved that, instead, in loving the beloved, we are first to love our neighbour. For impulse and inclination this is truly a strange, chilling upside-downness; yet it is Christianity and no more chilling than the spirit is in relation to the physical or the physical-psychic, and furthermore, it is above all the quality of the spirit to be burning without blazing. The wife shall first and foremost be your neighbour; the fact that she is your wife is then a narrower definition of your special relationship to each other. But what is eternally basic must also be the basis of every expression of what is special.

If this were not so, how could one then find room for the doctrine of love to one's neighbour; and yet people generally forget it altogether. Without being aware of it himself, a person talks like a pagan about erotic love and friendship, arranges his life paganly in these relationships, and then adds a bit of Christianity by loving his neighbour—that is, some other men. But the person who does not pay attention to the fact that his wife is for him the neighbour, and only then his wife, never comes to love his neighbour, no matter how many people he loves, for he has made an exception of his wife. This exception he will then love either all too intensely throughout his whole life or all too passionately at first and then too coolly. To be sure, one's wife is to be loved differently than the friend and the friend differently than the neighbour, but this is not an essential difference, for the fundamental equality lies in the category *neighbour*. The category *neighbour* is just like the category *human being*.[100] Every one of us is a human being and at the same time the heterogeneous individual which he is by particularity; but being a human being is the fundamental qualification. No one should mistake his distinctiveness to the degree that he cravenly or presumptuously forgets that he is a human being. No one should be preoccupied with the differences so that he cowardly or presumptuously forgets that he is a human being; no man is an exception to being a human being by virtue of his particularising differences. He is rather a human being and then a particular human being. Thus Christianity has nothing against a man loving his wife in a special way, but he must never love her in such a special way that she is an exception to being a neighbour, which every human being is, for then he confuses Christianity—his wife does not become for him his neighbour, and thereby all other men do not become his neighbours, either. If there existed one human being who by virtue of particularising differences was an exception to being a human being, then the concept *human being* would be confused: the exception would not be a human being and other men would not be human beings either.

People speak of a man's loving his wife conscientiously or his friend or his intimates, but often they speak in such a manner that what they say involves a great delusion. Christianity teaches that you shall love every man, therefore also your wife and friend, conscientiously; it is indeed a matter of conscience. Usually when they speak of one's loving his wife and friend conscientiously, they mean loving them preferentially in the sense of separateness or, what amounts to the same thing, in the sense of joining together in such a way that they have nothing to do with other men. But such conscientiousness Christianly understood is simply an utter lack of conscience. One also sees that it is the wife and friend who shall determine whether the manifested love is conscientious. Herein is the lie, for it is God who by himself and by means of the middle term *neighbour* scrutinises whether love to wife and friend is conscientious. Only then is your love a matter of conscience. It is clear, however, that one can be truly conscientious only in a matter of conscience, for otherwise one could also talk about being conscientious in receiving stolen goods. Love must first be recognised as a matter of conscience before there can be any talk about loving conscientiously. But love is first qualified as a matter of conscience when either God or the neighbour is the middle term, and neither is present in erotic love and friendship as such. But if love is not qualified as a matter of conscience in erotic love and friendship as such, then the so-called conscientiousness becomes more and more doubtful as the relationship becomes closer and closer.

Christianity is not related as a narrower definition to what in paganism and in general has been called love; it is rather a fundamental change. Christianity has not come into the world to teach this or that modification in how you *in your particularity* should love your wife or friend but to teach how you *in your universal humanity* shall love all men. And, again, it is this change which Christianly transforms erotic love and friendship.

One sometimes hears it said: to ask a person about his love affair is a question of conscience. Often enough this is not understood quite correctly. The reason for its being a question of conscience is that a man in his erotic love belongs first and foremost to God. Therefore no one gets angry when the pastor asks, for he asks in God's name. But this is not usually considered; on the contrary, it is usually thought that erotic love is such an intimate matter that every third person is an intruder—even God—which, Christianly understood, is utter lack of conscience. But a question of conscience regarding a matter in which a man does not relate himself to God is altogether inconceivable, for to relate oneself to God is precisely to have conscience. Therefore a man could not have anything on his conscience if God were not present, for the relationship between the individual and God, the God-relationship, is conscience; for that reason it is dreadful to have even the least thing on one's conscience, because one is immediately involved in the infinite gravity of God.

Love is a matter of conscience and thus is not a matter of impulse and inclination or a matter of feeling or a matter of intellectual calculation.

According to the secular or purely human point of view many different kinds of love are discernible; it knows all about all the particular differences and about the mutually exclusive particular differences; it becomes absorbed in the differences among these differences, absorbed, if such is possible, in the direction of superficiality. With Christianity the opposite is the case. It recognises only one kind of love, spiritual love, and does not busy itself very much in elaborating on the different ways in which this essentially common love can reveal itself. All distinctions between the many different kinds of love are essentially abolished by Christianity.

In the merely human view, love is interpreted either purely in terms of spontaneity, as impulse, inclination (erotic love), as inclination (friendship), as feeling and inclination with one or another discriminating alloy of duty, natural relationship, right, *etc., or* as something which ought to be aspired to and attained because the reason perceives that to be loved and favoured, as well as to have people one loves and favours, is an earthly good. All this is really no concern of Christianity, neither this sort of spontaneity nor this sort of convenience. Christianity lets all this have its validity and significance externally, but at the same time by its doctrine of love, which is not computed on the basis of convenience, it would have the change of infinity take place in the inner being. There is something wonderful and perhaps for many something strange, something incomprehensible in the fact that Christianity's eternal power is so indifferent towards recognition in the external world, something wonderful in that its earnestness is precisely in this—that for the very sake of earnestness inwardness plays the stranger amid worldliness. Indeed, there have been times when people within Christianity thought it was necessary to betray secrecy and thereby gain for Christianity a secular expression in the secular world. For this reason men wanted to abolish marriage and lived securely enough—hidden in the cloister. Yet the hiding place of inwardness, the inwardness of the hidden man, which " holds the mystery of faith " (I Timothy 3 : 9) is a far more secure hiding place. The concealment of the cloister in the solitude of the forest or high on the top of an inaccessible mountain and the quiet hiding place of the cloister-dweller were, therefore, compared to true Christian inwardness, like a child's hiding himself—in order that someone should come and find him. The hidden occupant of the cloister informed the world that he had hidden himself, that is, he had, Christianly understood, not hidden himself in earnest but played at hiding. By a similar misunderstanding

of Christianity, with a similar childishness, men thought it was
Christian to tell the secret, to express in a worldly way Christianity's
indifference towards friendship, towards the family-relationship,
towards patriotism—which, nevertheless, is untrue, for in a worldly sense
Christianity is not indifferent to anything; on the contrary it is wholly
spiritually concerned for everything. But to express one's indifference
in such a way that one is eager for outsiders to find out—this is not
indifference at all. Such indifference can be compared to one's going
to another and saying, " I don't care about you "; whereupon the
other might well answer, " Why do you take the trouble to tell me,
then? " It was childishness; it was a childish way of being distinguished
by virtue of one's christianity. But christianity is to earnest to be distinguished. It does not seek to bring about external changes in the
external; it wants to seize it, purify it, sanctify it, and thus make everything new, while nevertheless everything is old. The Christian may well
marry, may well love his wife, especially in the way he ought to love her,
may well have a friend and love his native land; but in all this there
ought to be a fundamental understanding between him and God in the
Christian sense—this is Christianity. God is not a human being; it is
not important to God to have visible evidences in order to know if his
cause has won or not; he sees in secret equally as well. Far be it from
you to help God learn; rather it is he who should help you learn so
that you become weaned from the secular life which wants visible
evidences. If Christ had felt any need for visible demonstrations, he
certainly would have done something about it and called the twelve
legions of angels.[101] This is precisely what he would not do; on the
contrary, he rebuked the apostles, who wished to see in order to believe,
by saying that they did not know by what spirit they were speaking,
since they insisted on having a decision in terms of externalities.
Decision in terms of externals is just what Christianity does not want
(except insofar as it will establish one or another mark which to the
world is an offence as, for example, the sacraments); rather, by the
very lack of this, it will test faith in the individual, test whether the
individual will keep the secrecy of faith in the individual, test whether
the individual will keep the secrecy of faith and be satisfied with it.
The secular mind always needs to have decision externalised; otherwise it mistrustfully believes that the decision actually does not exist.
But this ground for mistrust is precisely the temptation in which faith
shall be tested. As far as a secular mentality is concerned, a far more
certain way of making sure and of having positive certainty that there

is a God would be to have a picture of him hung up; then one could see—that God is?—or that there is an idol?—which nevertheless does not exist.[102] As far as the secular mentality is concerned, it would have been far more certain, too, if Christ in some external manner, perhaps by a splendid pageant, had sought to prove who he was, instead of taking the shape of a poor servant without once attracting attention thereby; in this way he looked like any other man, and as far as the world is concerned, absolutely failed in his task. But this is precisely the temptation in which faith is tried. It is the same with the Christian conception of love. Worldly misunderstanding, in order to get an external expression, puts pressure on Christian love as spiritual love—but this cannot be externalised, cannot be expressed externally, because of the very fact that it is inwardness. But this is an offence to the world, as is all Christianity, likewise the opposite, that Christianity makes an arbitrary external token to be the only decisive element in the external, such as water in baptism. The world is always against it; where Christianity will have outwardness, worldly Christendom will have inwardness—which can be explained by saying that wherever Christianity is, offence accompanies it.

Christianity knows only one kind of love; spiritual love; but this can lie at the base of and be present in every other expression of love. How wonderful! The Christian conception of life has something in common with the conception of death. Imagine a man who at some time wanted to compile his impressions of all the life-differences among the men he had seen, and then, when he had catalogued them, would say, " I see all these different men, but I do not see man."[103] So it is with Christian love in respect to the different kinds of love. It is in all of them, that is, it can be in all of them, but Christian love itself you cannot point out. Erotic love you know by this that a woman is the beloved, friendship by the friend, love of one's native land by its object; but Christian love you cannot know even by this that it loves the enemy, for this can also be a hidden form of bitterness, as if someone loved his enemy—in order to heap coals of fire on his head. Nor can you know Christian love by hatred of the beloved, for it is really impossible for you to see this if you yourself are not the person concerned and you know love in relationship to God. From God's side, what confidence, in a certain sense, towards a man, what earnestness! We men take care that we have positive and reliable signs by which love is known. But God and Christianity have no infallible signs—is this not a great, yes, the uttermost confidence in men! When in our relationship to a person we renounce dependence upon signs by which his love shall be recognised, we are really saying that we show him boundless confidence, that we will believe in him in spite of all appearances. But why do you suppose God shows such confidence? I wonder if it is not because he sees in secret? What earnestness!

But *you* never see and no man has ever seen Christian love, in the same sense as no one has ever seen *man*. Nevertheless, *man* is the essential qualification, and nevertheless Christian love is the essential love, just as, Christianly understood, there is only one kind of love. To repeat, Christianity has not altered anything in what men previously taught about loving the beloved, the friend, *etc.*, has not added a little or subtracted something, but it has transformed everything, changed the whole of love. Only insofar as there follows from this fundamental change an internal change in erotic love and friendship, only to that extent has it changed these. This it has done by making all love a matter of conscience, which in respect to erotic love and friendship can have just as much significance for the cooling of the passions as it has significance for the inwardness of eternal life.

Love is a matter of conscience and must therefore be from a pure heart and sincere faith.

" A pure heart." Usually we talk in a different way and say that for love and for surrendering oneself in love a free heart is needed. This heart must not belong to anyone else or to anything else; yes, even the hand which gives it must be free; for it shall not be the hand which takes the heart by force and gives it away, but on the contrary it shall be the heart which gives away the hand. And this heart, free as it is, shall then find its whole freedom in giving itself away—the bird you let fly from your hand, the arrow from the drawn bow, the bent branch snapping back as it will—not one of these, nothing, nothing is as free as the free heart when it freely gives itself away. For the bird is free only because you let it go, the arrow speeds forth because it leaves the bowstring, and the branch rises again because the pressure is released, but the free heart does not become free because there is no more opposition; it was free, it had its freedom—and yet, it found its freedom. Beautiful thought, blissful freedom—which finds what it has! —But I am speaking almost as a poet! But this, too, is permissible, if the main issue is not forgotten, if it is done for the purpose of illuminating the main issue—for we take pains to talk ingratiatingly, if that is possible, about what men are generally pleased to hear, in order that no one shall be tempted to think it was stupidity or incompetence which kept us from speaking about it or kept us from speaking about it exclusively as if it were the highest, forgetting the main issue—Christianity.

A pure heart is not in this sense a free heart, or this is not what our discussion is about; for a pure heart is first and foremost a *bound heart*. Therefore it is not so pleasant to speak about this as it is to speak about freedom's blissful self-esteem and self-esteem's blissful delight in the boldness of devotion. A bound heart, yes, in the deepest sense a bound heart—no ship which rides with all its anchors out is as bound as the heart must be which shall be pure—that heart must be bound to God. No king who commits himself to the strictest charter, no man who commits himself to the most demanding obligation, no day-labourer who commits himself for every day, and no private teacher who commits himself for every hour is so bound, because such people can still say to what extent they are committed, but the heart, if it is to be pure, must be limitlessly committed to God. No power can bind in such a way, because the king can be released by death from his charter; the master can die and the day-labourer's obligation ceases; and the instruction period can come to an end—but God never dies, and the bond which binds is never broken.

Thus must the heart be bound. You who burn with the desires of erotic love or with the warmth of friendship, remember that what you say about freedom has never been denied by Christianity; yet this infinite bond must exist first if the beloved's heart and your heart are to be pure! Therefore, first the infinite bond—and then talk about freedom can begin. There is a foreign word which is very often used in scholarly work, but still more in trade and commerce, and is heard very often on the streets and sidewalks, in business circles, and in merchants' mouths—it is the word *priority*. Scholarship speaks much about the priority of God, and merchants talk about priorities. Let us, then, use this foreign word to express the idea in such a way as to assure the right impression. Let us say that Christianity teaches that God has first priority. Scholarship does not speak of God's priority in exactly this way; it will gladly forget what merchants know about priorities: that priority means a demand. God has first priority, and everything, everything a man owns is pledged as collateral to this claim. If you remember this, you can talk about the pleasures of freedom as much as you please. But if you really remember this, the pleasures will not tempt you.

The free heart has no concerns; heedlessly it plunges itself into the delights of attachments; but the heart infinitely bound to God has infinite concern. The person who must every moment exercise the most complex concern is not bound by concern in such a way as is the heart infinitely bound to God. Wherever it is, alone with itself or filled with thoughts of others or in the company of others, whatever else the infinitely bound heart is occupied with, it always has this concern with it. You who talk so beautifully about how much the beloved means to you or you to the beloved, remember that the first concern must be for your soul and for that of your beloved if a pure heart shall be given away in erotic love! This concern is the first and last; there is no separation from this concern without guilt or sin.

The free heart has no history. When it gives itself in devotion, it begins its love-history, happy or unhappy. But the heart bound infinitely to God has a prior history and therefore understands that erotic love and friendship are only an interlude, an inlay in the history of the one and only love, the first and last. You who know how to talk so beautifully about erotic love and friendship, if you understood that this is only a very little snippet within that eternal history, how brief would you be about the brevity of the snippet! You begin your story with the beginning of love and end with the grave. But that eternal love-history is begun far earlier. It began with your beginning, when you came into being out of nothing, and just as you do not become nothing, so your history surely does not end at the grave. When the couch of death is prepared for you,[104] when you have gone to bed never to get up again, and they are only waiting for you to turn on your side to die, and stillness grows about you, and then after a while the friends of the family go away and it becomes quieter, because only the closest ones remain while death comes ever closer, and then the closest ones go quietly away, and it becomes quieter because only the very closest of all remain, and then when the last one has bent over you for the last time and turns away to the other side, for you yourself turn now to the side of death, there is still one who remains by your side, the very last one at the death-bed, he who was the first, God, the living God—if, whatever else it was, your heart was pure, something it became only by loving him.

This is the way we must speak about a pure heart and about love as a matter of conscience. If erotic love and earthly love are the joy of life, so that the happy one in truth says, " Now for the first time I live," then it is the joy of one's life merely to listen to the lover talk about his happiness, about life, that is, its delight; the dead must speak of this conscience-filled love, the dead, note well, who did not grow weary of life but who won the very life-joy of the eternal. But it is one who has died who speaks, alas, and to many this seems so frightening that they do not dare listen to his glad message; whereas everyone gladly listens to the person about whom we say in the sense of superiority: " He is really living." Yet a person who has died is needed, and in the very moment the comrades gladly toast " Long live " to the happy one, the eternal says, " Die "—if, whatever else, the heart shall become pure. To be sure, there have been those who became happy, unspeakably happy or unhappy, in loving someone; but no person's heart ever became pure unless it became pure by loving God.

A sincere faith. What more loathsome combination is possible than love—and falsity! Yet this combination is impossible, for to love falsely is to hate. This is true not only of falsity, but it is impossible to reconcile the least lack of honesty with loving. As soon as there is a lack of honesty, there is also something concealed. In this concealment hides selfish self-love, and inasmuch as this is present in a man he does not love. In honesty the lover presents himself before the beloved. No mirror is as accurate as honesty in catching the smallest trifle, if it is true honesty, or if the lovers express themselves with true faithfulness in the mirror of honesty which love holds between them.

But if two people can thus in honesty become transparent to each other, is it not somewhat arbitrary of Christianity to talk about sincere faith in another sense, insofar as it thereby means honesty before God? If two people are to love each other in sincere faith, is not a prior requirement in each individual of honesty before God just what is needed? Is it dissimulation only when a man consciously deceives others or himself? I wonder if it is not also dissimulation when a man does not know himself.[105] And can such a person promise love out of sincere faith, or can he—hold to what he promises? To be sure he can, but if he cannot promise, can he hold to what he cannot even promise? And a person who does not know himself cannot promise love out of sincere faith.

The concept of confidence involves a reduplication: the one with whom a man has the most intimate relationship, that is, a relationship which is best suited to a confidential communication or communication in confidence—only to him can this man really confide, or have confidence, or communicate in confidence. But confidence itself is related to itself in this way, and thus there remains in confidence an essential unspeakableness, lest one might think that confidence means speaking out. If a wife, humanly speaking, has this most intimate relationship with her husband, she can certainly in confidence communicate one thing and another to her parents; but this confidence is confidence about confidence. The wife will therefore feel she is far from being able to confide everything to them or to confide to them in the way she confides to her husband, with whom she has her most intimate relationship—but also her most confidential relationship—the only one to whom she really can confide respecting her most intimate relationship, which is her relationship with him. External matters or things of no consequence one cannot—or at least only in a trifling or meaningless sense—communicate confidentially; but note, when the wife wishes to communicate to another concerning her most intimate affairs, her relationship to her husband, she herself perceives that there is only one to whom she can fully communicate in confidence, and this one is the same one to whom and with whom she has the relationship.

With whom does a man have his most intimate relationship, to whom can a man have his most intimate relationship? Is it not with God? Consequently all confidence between man and man ultimately becomes only confidence about confidence. Only God *is confidence*, just as he is love. When two persons in all honesty promise to be faithful to each other, is it, then, faithfulness to promise to one another, if beforehand each one promises and has promised faithfulness to someone else? And yet, on the other hand, this is necessary, if in a Christian sense they are to love out of sincere faith. When two men confide completely to each other, is this a complete confiding to each other if each one beforehand confides to a third person? And yet this is necessary if they are to confide completely to each other, even if in every individual's confidence to God there remains the unspeakable, which is the very indication that the relationship to God is the most intimate and the most confidential.

How inviting, how beguiling is all discussion about the confidence of two lovers in each other, and yet there is insincerity in such talk just as there is insincerity in such confidence. But if one is to speak about love out of sincere faith, then one who has died must do the speaking, and it sounds at first as if a breach had come between the two who nevertheless are to be united in the most intimate and confidential association. Yes, it is like a breach between them, and yet it is the confidence of the eternal which is placed between them. Many, many times have two people been happy in a confidential relationship to each other, but never has any man loved out of sincere faith without separation through confidence with God, which yet again is God's consent to the lovers' confidence.—Only when love is from a clean heart and out of sincere faith—only then is it a matter of conscience.

IV

Our Duty to Love Those We See

If any one says, " I love God," and hates his brother, he is a liar; for he who does not love his brother whom he has seen, cannot love God whom he has not seen. (*I John* 4 : 20)

How *deeply* the need for love is grounded in the nature of man! The first observation, if we dare call it that, made about man, an observation made by the only one who could truly make it, by God, and about the first man, expresses just this. For we read in Holy Scriptures: " God said, it is not good that the man be alone."[106] Then woman was *taken* from man's side and *given* to him for community—for love and companionship first take something from a man before they give. All through the ages everyone who has thought deeply over the nature of man has recognised in him this need for community. How often has this been said and repeated again and again, how often have men cried woe upon the solitary person or portrayed the pain and misery of loneliness, how often have men, weary of the corrupting, noisy, confusing life in society, let their thoughts wander out to a solitary place —only to learn again to long for community! Thus man is always turned back to that observation by God, this the first thought about man. In the busy, teeming crowd, which as community is both too much and too little, man becomes weary of society, but the cure is not in making the discovery that God's thought was incorrect. No, the cure is precisely to learn all over again the most important thing, to understand oneself in one's longing for community. So deeply is this need grounded in the nature of man that since the creation of the first man there has been no change, no new discovery made; this selfsame first observation has only been confirmed in various ways, from generation to generation varied in expression, in presentation, in turns of thought.

So deeply is this need grounded in the nature of man and so *essentially* does it belong to being a human being that even He who was One with the Father and in the communion of love with the Father and the Spirit, He who loved the whole race, our Lord Jesus Christ, even He felt in a human way this need to love and be loved by an individual human being. Truly he is the God-man and thus eternally different from every human being, but he nevertheless was also a true human being and tried in everything human. On the other hand, the fact that he experienced this need is the very expression of its belonging essentially to man. He was an actual human being and therefore could participate in everything human. He was not an airy shape who beckoned in the clouds without understanding or wanting to understand what humanly befalls a human being. No, he could have pity on the crowd who lacked food in a purely human way, he who himself had hungered in the wilderness. In the same way he could also participate with men in this need to love and to be loved, participate in a purely human way. We read this in the Gospel of John (21 : 15 ff.): " Jesus said to Simon Peter:[107] ' Simon, son of John, do you love me more than these? ' He said to him, ' Yes, Lord; you know that I love you.' " How moving this is! Christ said: Do you love me *"more than these?"* It is, as it were, a petition for love; thus speaks One to whom it is important to be the most beloved. Peter himself perceived this and the incongruity of it, as when Christ should be baptized by John; therefore Peter did not merely answer, " Yes," but added, " Lord, you know that I love you." Peter's answer indicates the incongruity. Even if a man knows that he is loved, because he has heard the " Yes " before, he is still eager to hear and wants to hear it again, even though he knows it from things other than this " Yes " to which he still again returns, eager to hear it—in yet another sense Christ can be said to know that Peter loved him. Nevertheless, " A second time he said to him, ' Simon, son of John, do you love me? ' He said to him, ' Yes, Lord ; you know that I love you.' " What else was there to answer, since the incongruity became even more perceptible inasmuch as the question was asked again! Christ "said to him the third time, ' Simon, son of John, do you love me? ' Peter was grieved because he said to him the third time, ' Do you love me? ' And he said to him, ' Lord, you know everything; you know that I love you.' " Peter did not answer *yes* any more; nor did he direct the answer to what Christ through experience must have known of Peter's mind: " You know I love you." He answered, " *You know everything;* you know that I love you." Therefore Peter did not answer *yes* again; he almost shrank from this incongruity, for a *yes* is like an actual answer to an actual question by which the questioner finds out something or finds it out more certainly than he knew before. But he who " knows all things," how can he find out anything or by another's assurances find out something more certainly? And yet, if he cannot do this, then he cannot love in a purely human way either, for this is precisely the enigma of love, that there is no higher certainty than the beloved's renewed assurance. Humanly understood, to be absolutely certain of being loved is not to love, since this means to be superior to the relationship between friend and friend. Dreadful contradiction—that he who is God loves humanly; for to love humanly is indeed to love a single human being and to desire to be the most beloved of this individual person. That is why Peter was despondent over the third asking of the question. For in love's direct relationship between man and man, there is a new joy in the question's being asked a third time and a new joy in answering a third time; otherwise the too often repeated question makes one despondent because it seems to betray mistrust. But when he who knows everything asks a third time, finds it necessary to ask a third time, it must be because he knows—since he knows everything—that the love is not strong or heartfelt or ardent enough in the one who is asked, in him who also denied three times. Peter certainly thought this was the reason the Lord found it necessary to ask the question a third time—for it could not be that our Lord felt the need to hear this "yes" a third time—the idea is inconceivable. Even if it were permissible, it is out of the question. But how human! He who did not have one word to answer the high priests who condemned him to death or to Pilate, who held his life in his hands—he asks three times if he is loved; yes, he asks if Peter loves him—"more than these! "

So deeply is love grounded in the nature of man, so essentially does it belong to man—and yet men very often find escapes in order to avoid—this happiness; therefore they manufacture deceptions—in order to deceive themselves or make themselves unhappy. Soon the escape is clothed in the form of sorrow; one grumbles about humanity and over its unhappiness; one finds no one he can love. To grumble about the world and its unhappiness is always easier than to beat one's breast and groan over oneself. Soon the self-deception sounds out in the form of complaint; one complains about men, that they are not worth loving; one "grumbles against"[108] mankind—for it is always easier to be a complainer than the one complained about. Soon the self-deception is the proud self-satisfaction which judges it fruitless to seek someone worthy of his love—for it is always easier to prove one's superiority by being fastidious about everyone else rather than by being severe toward himself. And yet—yet they all agree that this is unhappiness and that this relationship is wrong. And what is it that is wrong, what else but their seeking and rejecting! Such persons do not notice that their talk sounds like a mockery of themselves, because this—that one is unable to find among men an object for his love—indicates that one himself is utterly lacking in love. Is it love to want to find love outside oneself? I thought love meant bringing it along oneself. But he who brings love with him when he seeks an object for his love (and otherwise it is not true that he seeks an object—for his love) will easily, and to the same degree as love in him is great, very easily find the object and find it to be such that it is lovable. For to be able to love a man in spite of his weaknesses and errors and imperfections is not perfect love; it is rather to be able to find him lovable in spite of and together with his weakness and errors and imperfections. Let us understand each other. It is one thing fastidiously to want to eat only the choicest and most delicate dish when it is exquisitely prepared—or even when thus prepared, fastidiously to find one thing or another wrong with it; it is quite different not merely to be able to eat the plainer foods, but to be able to find these plainer dishes to be the most exquisite, for the task does not consist in developing fastidiousness but in educating oneself and his taste. Or, suppose there were two artists, and the one said, " I have travelled much and seen much in the world, but I have sought in vain to find a man worth painting. I have found no face with such perfection of beauty that I could make up my mind to paint it. In every face I have seen one or another little fault. Therefore I seek in vain." Would this indicate that this artist was a great artist? On the other hand, the second one said, " Well, I do not pretend to be a real artist; neither have I travelled in foreign lands. But remaining in the little circle of men who are closest to me, I have not found a face so insignificant or so full of faults that I still could not discern in it a more beautiful side and discover something glorious. Therefore I am happy in the art I practise. It satisfies me without my making any claim to being an artist." Would this not indicate that precisely this one was the artist, one who by bringing a certain something with him found then and there what the much-travelled artist did not find anywhere in the world, perhaps because he did not bring a certain something with him! Consequently the second of the two was the artist. Would it not be sad, too, if what is intended to beautify life could only be a curse upon it, so that *art*, instead of making life beautiful for us, only fastidiously discovers that not one of us is beautiful. Would it not be sadder still, and still more confusing, if love also should be only a curse because its demand could only make it evident that none of us is worth loving, instead of love's being recognised precisely by its loving enough to be able to find some lovableness in all of us, consequently loving enough to be able to love all of us.

It is a sad upside-downness, which, however, is altogether too common, to talk on and on about how the object of love should be in order to be lovable enough, instead of talking about how love should be in order that it can love. It is very common, not only in daily life; indeed, how often do we not see that even one who calls himself a poet puts all his powers into a refined, effeminate, superior fastidiousness which, as far as loving is concerned, inhumanly knows how to reject and reject, assuming as his task in this respect the initiation of men into all the loathsome secrets of fastidiousness—and how many are so minded, are so inclined, are so eager to learn—that is, to get knowledge which really only serves to embitter life for themselves and for others! Is it not true that if one had not learned this kind of thing he would have found much in life to be beautiful or even more beautiful? But when one is first initiated into the contamination of fastidiousness, how difficult it is to win that which is lost, the dowry of good-nature, of love, which God has basically bestowed on every man!

But if no one else can or will, an apostle will always know how to lead us along the right way in this matter, the right way which guides us both to doing what is right to others and to making ourselves happy. Therefore we have chosen a verse from the apostle John: " If any one says, ' I love God,' and hates his brother, he is a liar, for he who does not love his brother whom he has seen, cannot love God whom he has not seen." We shall make these words the subject of our consideration in that we, joyful in the task, choose to talk about

THE DUTY TO LOVE THE MEN WE SEE.

But this is not to be understood as if the discussion were about loving all the men we see, for this is love to one's neighbour, which was previously described. On the contrary, it is to be understood that this discussion is about the duty of finding in the world of actuality those we can love in particular and in loving them to love the men we see. *When this is the duty, the task is not: to find—the lovable object; but the task is: to find the object already given or chosen—lovable, and to be able to continue finding him lovable, no matter how he becomes changed.*

But first of all we shall make a little difficulty for ourselves in regard to the apostle's words just read, a difficulty which worldly shrewdness, perhaps even conceited in its acuteness, could manage to make, whether or not it actually does it. When the apostle says, " He who does not love his brother whom he has seen, cannot love God whom he has not seen,"[109] a clever person could object that this is a deceptive turning of the idea: just because one had made certain of the fact that the brother whom he has seen is not lovable, how could it be concluded from this (that he did not love one whom he recognised as undeserving of love) that there was anything to hinder him from loving God, whom he has not seen? And yet the apostle thinks that there is some hindrance for such a person in loving God, although by the phrase *his brother* he assuredly is not talking about one certain individual, but in the larger sense about loving men. The apostle believes that a divine claim is entered against the credibility of a man's assertion about loving the unseen,[110] when it is apparent that this man does not love what is seen, since it would seem just as fanatic to seek to express one's exclusive love of the unseen by not loving anything seen. It is a divine claim entered against human enthusiasm in respect to loving God, for it is fanatical —even if it is not hypocritical—to want to love the unseen in this way. The matter is quite simple. Man shall begin by loving the unseen, God, for thereby he himself shall learn what it is to love. But the fact that he really loves the unseen shall be indicated precisely by this that he loves the brother he sees. The more he loves the unseen, the more he will love the men he sees. It is not the opposite, that the more he rejects those he sees, the more he loves the unseen, for when this is the case, God is changed to an unreal something, a fancy. Such a thing can occur only to a hypocrite or to a deceiver in order to find an escape, or to one who misrepresents God, as if God were grasping for his own interest and his being loved, rather than that the holy God is gracious and therefore always points away from himself, saying, as it were, " If you wish to love me, love the men you see. Whatever you do for them you do for me." God is too exalted to be able to accept a man's love directly, to say nothing of being able to find pleasure in what pleases a fanatic. If anyone says " Corban "[111] of the gift by which he could help his parents, that is, that it is intended for God, this would not be well-pleasing to God. If you want to show that it is intended for God, then give it away, but with the thought of God. If you want to show that your life is intended as service to God, then let it serve men, yet continually with the thought of God. God is not a part of existence in such a way that he demands his share for himself; he demands everything, but as you bring it you immediately receive, if I may put it this way, an endorsement designating where it should be forwarded, for God demands nothing for himself, although he demands everything from you.—Thus do the words of the Apostle, properly understood, lead right into the subject of the discourse.

When it is a duty to love the men we see, *then one must first and fore-most give up all fanciful and extravagant ideas about a dream-world where the object of love is to be sought and found; that is, one must become sober, win actuality and truth by finding and continuing in the world of actuality as the task assigned to one.*

The most dangerous of all escapes as far as love is concerned is wanting to love only the unseen or that which one has not seen. This escape is so high-flying that it flies over actuality completely; it is so intoxicating that it easily tempts and easily fancies itself to be the highest and most perfect kind of love. It scarcely ever occurs to a man shamelessly to speak evil about loving; more common, however, is the deception whereby men deceive themselves out of really coming to love, simply by talking too enthusiastically about love and what it is to love. This has a far deeper basis than one thinks, otherwise the confusion could not have taken as firm a hold as it has, the confusion of calling a misfortune that which is a fault—namely, not to find any object of love—whereby they further prevent themselves from finding it. If they first perceived that they were at fault, they would certainly find it. It is commonly thought that love is admiration's opened eye which seeks excellency and perfection. This is why men complain that they seek in vain. We will not decide to what extent the individual is or is not justified in this, whether or not what he seeks, the lovable, the excellent, and the perfect, is to be found, whether or not he is confusing seeking with fastidiousness. No, we do not wish to be contentious in this way; we do not wish to contend within this view of love, for this whole conception is a delusion, since love is rather the closed eye of forbearance and gentleness, the closed eye which does not see defects and imperfections.

But the difference between these two conceptions is very essential;

there is a world of difference, the difference of opposites. Only the latter concept is the truth; the former is a delusion. And a delusion, as you know, never stops by itself; it only leads on into greater and greater delusion so that it becomes more and more difficult to find one's way back to the truth. The way of delusion is easy to find, but it is very difficult to find the way back. It is told in the legend of the Mount of Voluptuousness,[112] which is supposed to be somewhere on earth, that no one who found his way to it could find his way back. When, then, a man with a wrong conception of love goes out in the world, he seeks—according to his way of thinking he seeks—to find the object, but, according to his way of thinking, in vain. Yet he does not alter his conception. On the contrary, enriched with the manifold knowledge of fastidiousness, he seeks more and more fastidiously, but, according to his way of thinking, in vain. Yet it does not occur to him that the error could be in him or in the wrong conception. On the contrary, the more refined he becomes in his fastidiousness, the more inflated are the ideas he gets about himself and the perfection of his view—does it not show him clearly how imperfect men are? and this, indeed, can be discovered only with the help of perfection. Meanwhile he is convinced within himself that it is not his fault, that he is not doing this out of any evil or spiteful intention—he who seeks nothing but love. Far be it from him to give up love, he who vividly feels his conception becoming more and more enthusiastic—what, indeed, was ever more enthusiastic than a delusion! He has not stopped the delusion; quite the contrary, he has now by its help grown dizzy—in loving the invisible, a phantasm which one cannot see. Or does it not come to the same thing—to *see* a *phantasm*—and *not* to *see*? Take the phantom away and you see nothing —one admits that himself. But take away seeing, and you see a phantom—one forgets that. But as has been said, he will not give up love, nor will he talk cheaply about it; he will speak enthusiastically about it and preserve it—this love of the invisible. Tragic delusion! It is commonly said that worldly glory and power and wealth and happiness are vapours, and so they are; but that the strongest power in a man, a power which according to its own qualifications is nothing less than this, since it is life and power, that this becomes changed to vapour, and that a person intoxicated in its vapours proudly thinks that he has apprehended the highest, but he has in truth grasped after clouds of fancy which always fly high, over actuality—how dreadful! People usually warn piously against wasting God's gifts, but which of God's gifts can be compared to love, which he implanted in man's heart—alas, and then to see it wasted in this way! The shrewd foolishly think that one wastes his time in loving imperfect, weak men. I should think that this would be making use of one's love, employing it. But to be unable to find an object, to waste love in vainly seeking, to waste it in empty space by loving the invisible—this is truly to waste it.

Be sober, then; come to yourself. Understand that the mistake lies in your conception of love; understand that it should be a demand, a requirement most glorious when the whole of existence cannot satisfy it—any more than you can prove your right to demand satisfaction. At the very moment when you have changed your conception of love and have understood that it is the very reverse of a requirement, that it is a debt to which God binds you—at this very moment you have found actuality.—And this is precisely the duty, to find actuality with closed eyes (for in love you indeed close your eyes to weakness and frailty and imperfection), instead of overlooking actuality with open eyes (well, open or staring like a sleep-walker's). It is the duty, the first condition, in order that in loving you may eventually reach the point of loving the men you see. The condition is that of finding a foothold in actuality. Delusion is always floating; for that reason it sometimes appears quite light and spiritual, because it is so airy. Truth takes a firm step, and for that reason sometimes a difficult one, too. It stands on firm footing, and therefore sometimes appears to be very simple. Here is a significant change: instead of asserting a demand to be fulfilled, to get a duty to do; instead of running about in the world, to take the world, as it were, upon oneself; instead of ardently seeking the delightful fruit of admiration, patiently to have to bear with shortcomings. What a change! And yet it is by this change that love comes into existence, the love which can accomplish the task—in loving to love the men we see.

When it is a duty in loving to love the men one sees, *it holds true that in loving actual individual men one does not slip in a fanciful idea about how one thinks or could wish this man should be.* He who does this does not love the man he sees but again something invisible, or his own imagination, or something of that sort.

There is in loving a certain demeanour which makes of love a dubious mixture of duplicity and fastidiousness. It is one thing to reject and reject and never find any object for one's love; it is another thing to love what one himself calls the object of his love, carefully and honestly fulfilling this duty of loving what one sees. True, there is always the desire, and a worthy desire, too, that the person we are to love may possess endearing perfections; we wish it not only for our own sake but also for the sake of the other person. Above all, it is worthy to wish and pray that the one we love might always behave and be such that we could give our full approval and assent. But in God's name let us not forget that it is not to our credit if he is such a person, still less to our credit to demand it of him—if there should be any talk about anything being to our credit (something which, however, is unseemly, and an unseemly sort of talk as far as love is concerned), then it should be just this, to love with equal faithfulness and tenderness in either case.

But there is a fastidiousness which works continually, as it were, against love and wants to hinder it from loving what it sees, since fastidiousness, unsteady of glance and yet in another sense so particular, volatilizes the actual form or is offensive toward it and then disingenuously demands to see something else. There are men of whom one must say that they have not attained form, that their actuality has not become integrated, because in their innermost being they are at odds as to what they are and what they will to be. But one can also make another man's form wavering or unreal by the manner in which one sees, because the love which should love the man it sees cannot rightly make up its mind but now will have a fault taken away from the object and then a perfection added, as if—I dare say—the bargain still were not concluded. Yet the person who in loving thus is inclined to be fastidious; he does not love the man he sees and easily makes his love as loathsome to himself as he makes it difficult for the beloved.

The beloved or the friend is a human being in the more ordinary sense of the word and exists as such for the rest of us, but for you he should really be only as the beloved if you are to accomplish the duty of loving the person you see. If there is a doubleness in your relationship, so that to you he is in part a particular person in the more usual sense and in part the special beloved, then you do not love the person you see. It is rather as if you had two ears and did not, as is common, listen to one thing with both but listened to one thing with one, to something else with the other. You listen with one ear to what he says, whether it is wise and correct and penetrating and spiritual, etc.—and with the other ear, alas, you hear that it is the beloved's voice. You look at him with one eye, searching, investigating, scanning critically —and only with the other eye, alas, do you see that he is the beloved. But to be divided thus is not loving the person we see. Is it not as if there were a third person always present, even when the two are alone, a third person who coldly scrutinizes and rejects, a third person who disturbs the intimacy, a third person who sometimes, however, must make the person concerned disgusted with himself and his love, that it is so fastidious, a third person who would trouble the beloved if he knew this third person were present! What does it mean that this third person is present? Does it mean that if . . . if this or that is not according to your wish, you could not love? Does the third person therefore mean separation, division, so that consequently the thought of separation is present—in the relationship of confidence—alas, just as when in paganism the destructive principle was insanely included in the unity of the Godhead? Does this third person mean that in a certain sense the love-relationship is no relationship at all, that you stand above the relationship and test the beloved? Do you think that in such a case anything is tested except whether you really have love, or more accurately, is anything decided except that you really do not have love? Life certainly has tests enough, and these tests should reveal the lovers, friend and friend, united in order to endure the testing. But if the test is to be dragged into the relationship, treason has been committed. This secretive reserve or closed-up-ness is certainly the most dangerous kind of faithlessness. Such a person does not break faith, but he keeps in continuous suspension the either/or of being bound by his faith. Is it not faithlessness when your friend gives you his hand and there is an ambiguous something in your handshake, as if it were he who clasped your hand, but the extent to which he corresponded at this moment to your conception of him was so doubtful that your response reflected this ambiguity? Does a relationship genuinely exist if at every moment one begins anew, as it were, to enter into this relationship; is this really loving the person you see, every moment testing him as if it were the first time you saw him? It is disgusting to see the fastidiousness which rejects all food, but it is also disgusting to see the person who actually eats the food which is graciously offered him and yet in a certain sense does not eat but merely samples the food as if he were already satiated or takes the trouble to taste a more delicate dish and is satiated when it comes to more common food.

No, if a man is going to fullfill the task of love by loving the men he sees, he must not merely find those he loves among actual human beings, but he must root out all double-mindedness and fastidiousness in loving them, so that in earnestness and truth he loves them as they are, so that he grasps the task in earnestness and truth: to find lovable the object which has now been given or chosen. We do not mean hereby to glorify a childish infatuation for the accidental characteristics of the beloved, still less a misplaced caressing indulgence. Far from it. The earnestness is precisely in this that the relationship itself wills to strive with integrated powers against imperfection, to conquer deficiencies, to remove the heterogeneous. This is earnestness; fastidiousness makes the relationship itself ambiguous. One does not become alien to the other person because of his weakness or his error, but the union regards the weakness as alien, and to both it is equally important that this be conquered and removed. Because of your beloved's weakness you shall not, as it were, remove yourself from him or make your relationship more remote; on the contrary, the two shall hold together with greater solidarity and inwardness in order to remove the weakness. As soon as the relationship is made ambiguous, you do not love the person you see; it is indeed as if you demanded something else in order to be able to love. On the other hand, when the fault or weakness makes the relationship more inward, not to entrench the fault but to conquer it, then you love the person you see. You see the error, but the fact that your relationship then becomes more inward indicates that you love the person in whom you see the fault or weakness or imperfection.

Just as there are hypocritical tears, hypocritical sighing and complaining over the world, so is there also hypocritical grief over the beloved's weaknesses and imperfections. It is so easy and sweet to wish the beloved to have all possible perfections, and if something is lacking it is again so easy and sweet to sigh and grieve and become self-important in one's supposedly pure and deep concern. On the whole, it is perhaps a more common form of lasciviousness selfishly to wish to make a show of the beloved or friend and to wish to despair over every trifle. But should this be regarded as loving the men one sees? Ah, no, the men we see (and it is the same when others see us) are not perfect. And yet it is very often the case that one develops within himself this queasy weakness which is good only for loving the complete epitome of perfections. And yet, although we human beings are all imperfect, one very rarely sees the sound, strong, capable love which is good for loving imperfect beings, that is, the men we see.

When it is a duty in loving to love the men we see, *there is no limit to love. If the duty is to be fullfilled, love must be limitless. It is unchanged, no matter how the object becomes changed.*

Let us think about what we were reminded of in the introduction to this reflection—the relationship between Christ and Peter. I wonder whether Peter, especially in his relationship to Christ, was an epitome of all perfections, and yet Jesus knew his faults very well! Let us speak in a perfectly human way about this relationship. God knows the common run of insignificant and yet painstakingly collected and painstakingly hoarded trifles which either immediately or, equally tragic, after a long time give us human beings occasion to complain, each one of the other, about self-interest, disloyalty, and treachery. God knows how seldom it usually is that the plaintiff makes even a feeble effort to put himself in the defendant's place so that the judgment, severe and merciless, might not be an overhasty judgment, but might at least be somewhat thoughtful and considered to the extent that it knows precisely of what it judges. God knows how often one sees this sorrowful sight—how passion equips even a perhaps otherwise limited person, when he presumably is the wronged one, with an amazing acuteness, and on the other hand how even a perhaps otherwise intelligent person, when he presumably is the wronged one, is struck dumb as far as any mitigating, excusing, exonerating concept of the wrong is concerned, for this offended passion takes delight in being blindly acute. But we will all agree that if things happened between two friends as between Christ and Peter, there would certainly be reason enough to break—with such a traitor. Suppose that your life were brought into a most critical situation and you had a friend who on his own initiative loudly and solemnly swore loyalty to you, yes, was willing to risk life and blood for you, and this same person in the moment of danger did not fail to appear (it would almost have been more forgivable)—no, he came, he was present; but he did not lift a hand; he stood calmly and looked on. But no, he did not stand unperturbed, for his only thought was to save himself in any way possible; yet he did not take flight (it would almost have been more forgivable)—no, he stood there, like a spectator, a rôle which he secured for himself—by denying you: what then? We will not even follow up the consequences but merely sketch vividly the relationship and talk in a purely human way about it.[113] You stood accused by your enemies, condemned by your enemies; it was literally true that you stood surrounded on every side by enemies. The mighty ones, who perhaps could have understood you, had hardened themselves against you; they hated you. Therefore you stood, accused and condemned— while a blinded, raging mob howled insults at you, even rejoicing insanely in the idea that your blood should come upon them and their children. And this pleased the mighty ones, who themselves usually had deep scorn for the mass. It pleased them, because their hate was gratified by the fact that animal wildness and the most wretched meanness had found in you its plunder and prey. You had reconciled yourself to your fate, understanding that there was not a single word to say, since mockery merely sought an occasion, since a high-spirited word about your innocence would give mockery a new occasion, as if it were defiance, since the clearest proof of your righteousness would embitter the mob and make mockery even more raging, so that an outburst of pain would only give mockery a new occasion, as if it were cowardice. Thus you stood, cast out of human society and yet not cast out, for you stood surrounded by human beings enough, but not one of them saw in you a human being. Yet in another sense they saw a human being in you, for they would not have treated an animal so inhumanly. O, horror, more dreadful than if you had fallen among wild animals. I wonder if the wild, nocturnal howl of beasts of prey is ever so dreadful as the inhumanity of a raging mob. I wonder if one beast of prey in the pack can incite another to a frenzy greater than is natural for the individual beast in the same way as one man among the unrepentant crowd can incite another to a more than animal bloodthirstiness and frenzy. I wonder if even the most bloodthirsty beast's spiteful or flashing glance has this same fire of evil which is kindled in the individual's eye when, incited and inciting, he rages in the frenzied mob!

Thus you stood—accused, condemned, despised; you sought in vain to discover a form which resembled a human being, to say nothing of a kind face which your eye could rest upon. And then you saw him, your friend—but he denied you; and the mockery which had sounded loud enough sounded now as if an echo intensified it a hundred times! If this were to happen to you, is it not true that you would promptly regard it as too high-minded if, instead of thinking about revenge, you turned your eyes away from him and said to yourself, " I would rather not see the traitor before my eyes! "—How differently Christ acted! He did not turn his eyes away from him in order, as it were, to become unaware of Peter's existence; he did not say, " I will not look at the traitor"; he did not leave him to take care of himself. No, he " looked at him." He caught him up immediately in a glance. If it had been possible, he surely would not have avoided speaking to him.

And how did Christ look at Peter? Was it a repelling look, a look of dismissal? No, it was as when a mother sees her child endangered through its own indiscretion; since she cannot approach and snatch the child, she catches him up with a reproachful but also saving look.

Was Peter in danger, then? Alas, who cannot understand how serious it is for a man to have denied his friend. But in the passion of anger the injured friend cannot see that the denier is in danger. Yet he who is called the Saviour of the world always saw clearly where the danger was, that it was Peter who was in danger, Peter who should and must be saved. The Saviour of the world did not make the mistake of regarding his cause lost if Peter did not hurry to help him; rather he saw Peter lost if he did not hurry to save Peter. I wonder if there lives or ever lived a single individual who cannot understand this since it is so clear and self-evident; yet Christ is the only one who saw this at the critical moment, when he himself was the one accused, condemned, scorned, and denied.—Seldom is a man tried in a crisis of life and death, and seldom does a man get opportunity to try the devotion of friendship in such a radical way. But in a more serious moment to find only timorousness and prudence where in the power of friendship you were entitled to expect courage and decision, to find duplicity, fickleness, and evasion instead of openness, determination and steadfastness, to find only chatter instead of a thoughtful grasp of the situation, how difficult, then, in the rush of the moment and of passion to be able to understand immediately just where the danger is, to understand which of the friends is more in danger, you or he who thus leaves you in the lurch. How difficult then to love the man one sees—when the man one sees is so changed!

We are now accustomed to praise Christ's relationship to Peter. Let us take care that this praise is not a delusion, a fancy, because we are incapable of thinking or do not wish to tax our minds by thinking of ourselves as contemporary with the event; consequently we praise Christ in this way, and, on the other hand, insofar as we are able to become contemporary with a similar event, we act and think quite differently. There is no account preserved concerning the opinion of contemporaries, but if you were to meet them, ask them, and you would hear that on this occasion, as on almost every occasion when Christ did something, it was said, " The fool! However desperately lost his cause might be, yet not to have the power of gathering together all his strength for the last time in one single glance which could crush this traitor! What whimpering weakness! Is this acting like a man! " Thus was his action judged, and mockery got a new expression. Or the influential people who presumed to evaluate the relationship said, " Well, why did he seek company with sinners and publicans, his adherents among the lowest class of people. He should have joined with us, with the foremost men of the synagogue. But now he gets his just reward. It just goes to show how one can depend on this sort of man. Yet up to the very end he was resigned as always; he never once became embittered over such shabby faithlessness." Or the clever people, who even thought they were being good-natured, said, " The fact that the high priests had him seized and that he, fanatic that he was, finally saw everything lost must have weakened his mind and broken his courage so that he has collapsed completely into an effeminate and impotent stupor. This explains his forgiving such a traitor, for no man acts in this way! " Alas, it is all too true—no man acts this way. It is precisely for that reason that Christ's life is the only instance in which it is seen that a teacher, in the moment his cause together with his life is lost and everything is forfeited in the most appalling way because of the denial by his disciple—that a teacher by his glance wins in this very moment and in this disciple wins his most zealous follower and thus in great part wins his cause, although it is hidden to all.

Christ's love for Peter was so boundless that in loving Peter he accomplished loving the person one sees. He did not say, " Peter must change first and become another man before I can love him again." No, just the opposite, he said, " Peter is Peter, and I love him; love, if anything, will help him to become another man." Therefore he did not break off the friendship in order perhaps to renew it again when Peter had become another man. No, he preserved the friendship unchanged and in this very way helped Peter to become another man. Do you think that Peter would have been won again without this faithful friendship of Christ? But it is so easy to be a friend when it means nothing more than requiring something in particular from the friend, and if he does not respond to the demand, then to let the friendship go—until it perhaps is renewed when he responds to the demand. Is this the relationship of friendship? Who is closer to helping an erring one than the person who calls himself a friend, even if the offence is committed against the friend! But the friend withdraws and says (yes, as if a third person were talking): when he has turned over a new leaf, he can perhaps become my friend again. And we human beings are not far from regarding even such behaviour as high-minded. But truly, one is far from being able to say of such a friend that in loving he loves the person he sees.

Christ's love was boundless, as it must be if this shall be fullfilled: in loving to love the person one sees. This is very easy to perceive

However much and in whatever way a man is changed, he still is not changed so that he becomes invisible. If this—the impossible—is not the case, we do indeed see him, and the task is to love the person one sees. Usually one thinks that when a man has changed essentially for the worse, he is changed in such a way that one is exempted from loving him. What a confusion in language: to be exempt—from loving—as if it were a matter of compulsion, a burden one wished to cast away! But Christianity asks, " Because of this change, can you no longer see him? " The answer to that must be, " Certainly I can see him. As a matter of fact, I see he is no longer worth loving." But if you see this, you really do not see him (which in another sense you cannot deny doing); you merely see unworthiness, imperfection, and admit thereby that when you loved him you in another sense did not see *him* but saw only his excellence and perfections, which you loved. But Christianly understood, loving is loving the very person one sees. The emphasis is not on loving the perfections one sees in a person, but on loving the person one sees, whether or not one sees perfections or imperfections in this person, yes, however distressingly he has changed, inasmuch as he certainly has not ceased to be the same man. He who loves the perfections he sees in a person does not see the person and therefore ceases to love when the perfections cease, when change steps in, which change, not even the most distressing, nevertheless does not mean that the person ceases to be. Alas, even the wisest and most ingenious purely human conception of love is yet somewhat high-flying and wavering; but Christian love goes from heaven to earth. The direction is thus an opposite one. Christian love is not supposed to vault into heaven, for it comes from heaven and with heaven. It steps down and thereby accomplishes loving the same person through-out all his changes, because it sees the same person in all his changes. Purely human love is always about to fly after or fly away with the beloved's perfections. We say that a seducer steals a girl's heart, but one must say of all merely human love, even when it is most beautiful, that there is something thievish about it, that it even steals the beloved's perfections; whereas Christian love grants the beloved all his im-perfections and weaknesses and in all his changes remains with him, loving the person it sees.

If this were not so, Christ would never have loved, for where could he have found the perfect man! Remarkable! What was this, after all, which for Christ was an obstacle in finding the perfect person? I wonder if it was not the fact that he himself was the perfect one, something we recognise by his limitless love towards the person he saw! What a remarkable criss-crossing of conceptions! With respect to love we speak continually about perfection and the perfect person. With respect to love Christianity also speaks continually about perfection and the perfect person. Alas, but we men talk about finding the perfect person in order to love him. Christianity speaks about being the perfect person who limitlessly loves the person he sees. We men want to look upward in order to look for the perfect object (but the direction is always towards the unseen), but in Christ perfection looked down to earth and loved the person it saw. We ought to learn from Christianity, for it is true in a far more common sense than is usually understood that no one ascends into heaven without him who descends from heaven.[114] However enthusiastic this talk about swinging oneself up into heaven may sound, it is sheer fancy if you do not first Christianly descend from heaven. But Christianly to descend from heaven means limitlessly to love the person you see just as you see him. If, then, you will become perfect in love, strive to fulfil this duty, in loving to love the person one sees, to love him just as you see him, with all his imperfections and weaknesses, love him as you see him when he is utterly changed, when he no longer loves you, when he perhaps turns indifferent away or turns to love someone else, love him as you see him when he betrays and denies you.

V

Our Duty to Be in the Debt of

Love to Each Another

Owe no one anything, except to love one another. (*Romans* 13 :8)

Men have sought in different ways to describe and portray what love is like to a person in love, the state of love, or what it is like to love. One calls love a feeling, a mood, a life, a passion; but since these are broad categories, men have tried to describe it more accurately. Men have called it a want, but note well that the lover always wants that which he nevertheless possesses; men have called it a longing, but note well it is always a longing for that which the lover has—for otherwise it is unhappy love which men describe.—That simple wise man of old has said, " Love is a son of riches and poverty."[115] Who, indeed, has ever been more impoverished than one who has never loved! On the other hand, I wonder if even the poorest wretch who abjectly picks up crumbs and is humbly grateful for a penny really has any idea how little the trifle can be which has infinite worth for the lover, how little the trifle can be which the lover (in his poverty!) most carefully gleans and cautiously saves—as the most precious treasure. I wonder if even the poorest wretch is ever in a position to see things so little that only passion's (love in its poverty) sharpened glance sees them—and enormously enlarged! But the smaller the object which poverty gleans —if it is grateful beyond all measure for it, as if the object were extra-ordinarily large—the greater poverty shows itself to be. Even all the protestations of the most extreme poverty do not prove this as decisively as when the poor man to whom you gave less than a dime thanked you for it with feeling commensurate with gifts of wealth and abundance, with such feeling as if he now had become rich. Alas, it is all too evident that the poor man remained just as poor—therefore it was only his crazy notion that he now had become rich. So poor is love's poverty! A noble man has said about love, " It takes everything and it gives everything." Who indeed receives more than the one who receives the love of a human being! And who gives more than the person who gives a human being his love! On the other hand, I wonder if even envy, when it enviously strips a man of his real or supposed greatness, can penetrate to the innermost layer! Envy is ever so stupid! It never suspects where the strong-box could be or that the strong-box exists in which the truly rich man has hidden his true treasure. It does not suspect that there really is a burglar-proof (consequently also for envy) depository, just as there is treasure which thieves (consequently also envy) are not able to steal. But love can penetrate into the innermost and strip a man in such a way that he has nothing left, nothing at all, so that he understands that he possesses nothing, nothing at all. Remarkable! Envy supposes that it takes everything, and when it has taken it the man says, " I have really lost nothing! " But love can take everything in such a way that the man himself says, " I possess nothing at all."

Yet love is perhaps best described as an infinite debt: when a man is gripped by love, he feels that this is like being in infinite debt. Usually one says that the person who becomes loved comes into debt by being loved. Along the same line we say that children are in love's debt to their parents, because their parents have loved them first and the children's love is only a part-payment on the debt or a repayment. This is true, to be sure. Nevertheless, such talk is all too reminiscent of an actual bookkeeping relationship—a bill is submitted and it must be paid; love is shown to us, and it must be repaid with love. We shall not, then, speak about *one's coming into debt by receiving love.* No, it is the one who loves who is in debt; because he is aware of being gripped by love, he perceives this as being in infinite debt. Remarkable! To give a person one's love is, as has been said, certainly the highest a human being can give—and yet, precisely when he gives his love and precisely by giving it he comes into infinite debt. One can therefore say that this is the *essential characteristic of love: that the lover by giving infinitely comes into—infinite debt.* But this is the relationship of infinitude, and love is infinite. To be sure, by giving money one does not come into debt; it is rather the recipient who becomes indebted. But when the lover gives what is infinitely the highest one human being can give another, his love, he himself comes into infinite debt.

What a beautiful, holy modesty love takes along as a companion! It not only dares not persuade itself to become conscious that its act is meritorious, but it is ashamed even to become conscious of its deed as being part-payment on a debt. It becomes conscious of its giving as an infinite debt which it is impossible to repay, since giving means continually to come into debt.

In this way could one describe love. But Christianity never dwells upon the conditions or upon a description of them; it always hastens to the task or hastens to shape up the task. This is expressed in the words of the apostle just read, " Owe no one anything except to love one another." These words we make the basis of our consideration:

OUR DUTY TO BE IN THE DEBT OF LOVE TO EACH OTHER.

To be in debt! Should this be difficult? Nothing, indeed, is easier than to be in debt! And then also that it should be one's task to be in debt! Usually we think the task is to get out of debt, whatever the debt is, a money debt, a debt of honour, a debt involving a promise— in short, whatever the debt is, the task is always rather to get out of debt, the sooner the better. But here it should be the task, therefore an honour, to be in debt! And if it is a task, there must be action, probably complex, difficult action, but to be in debt is precisely the expression for not doing the slightest thing, an expression for inactivity, indifference, indolence. Yet here this is supposed to be the expression of the greatest contradiction to indifference, an expression of infinite love!

All of this, all these peculiar difficulties which, as it were, pile up against this queer way of speaking imply that the matter must have its own inner coherence, so that a certain prior transformation of mind and thought is necessary in order merely to become aware of what the discussion is about.

Let us begin with a little thought-experiment. If a lover had done something for the beloved, something humanly speaking so extraordinary, lofty, and sacrificial that we men were obliged to say, " This is the utmost one human being can do for another "—this certainly would be beautiful and good. But suppose he added, " See, now I have paid my debt." Would not this be speaking unkindly, coldly, and harshly? Would it not be, if I may say it this way, an indecency which ought never to be heard, never in the good fellowship of true love? If, however, the lover did this noble and sacrificial thing and then added, " But I have one request—let me remain in debt": would not this be speaking in love? Or, if the lover in every sacrifice complied with the beloved's wish and then said, " It is a joy hereby to repay a small part of the debt—in which, however, I still wish to remain "— would not this be speaking in love? Or if he remained absolutely silent about the sacrificial cost simply to avoid the confusion of its seeming for a moment to be the part-payment on a debt—would not this be thinking in love? If this is true, it really is an expression of the incon-ceivability of a literal bookkeeping-relationship, that such a thing is the greatest abomination to love. An accounting can only take place where there is a finite relationship, because the relationship of the finite to the finite can be calculated. But one who loves cannot calculate. When the left hand never gets to know what the right hand does, it is impossible to make an accounting, and likewise when the debt is infinite. To calculate with an infinite magnitude is impossible, for calculation means precisely to utilize finite categories.—Con-sequently for his own sake the lover wishes to be in debt; he does not wish exemption from sacrifice, far from it. Willing, indescribably willing as is the prompting of love, he wants to do everything; he fears only one thing—that he might do everything in such a way that he would get out of debt. This is, correctly understood, the fear; the desire is to be in debt, but it is also the duty, the task. If the love in us human beings is not so perfect that this wish is our wish, the duty will help us to remain in debt.

When it is a duty to remain in the debt of love to everyone, *there must be eternal vigilance, early and late, so that love never comes to dwell upon itself or to compare itself with love in other men or to compare itself with the deeds it has accomplished.*

There is often heard in the world enthusiastic and fervid talk about love, about faith and hope, about goodness of heart, in brief, about all the qualifications of the spirit, talk which portrays and transports with the most glowing expressions, with the most glowing colours. Yet such talk is really a painted back-drop; on closer and more earnest inspection it turns out to be a deception, since it must either flatter the listener or mock him. Sometimes one also hears Christian discourse whose whole secret, considered as discourse and guidance, is this fraudulent enthusiasm. When such a talk is heard and then a person quite simply and honestly (for it certainly is honesty to will to act according to what is said to one, to will to shape his life accordingly) asks, " What shall I do now? How shall I get love to flame up in me this way? "—the speaker must really answer, " That is a curious question; the person in whom there dwells faith, hope, love, and goodness of heart, in him these exist in the manner described, but the person who does not have them—of what use is it to talk to him." Curious! Yet one might think it would be especially important to talk to those who are not like this so that they might become like this. But precisely here is the fraud in the delusion: to speak as if one would guide men and then have to confess that one can talk only *about* those who need no guidance, because they already are the perfection which the talk describes. But *to* whom does one speak this way? Who shall benefit from this talk, which at best has a few individuals *of* whom it speaks—if it is true that such individuals exist at all.

But should such fiction and nonsense be Christianity? If so, primitive Christianity must have been quite in error when in speaking of righteousness and purity it continually addressed itself to sinners and publicans, who certainly are not righteous. Instead of speaking satirically about the righteous who have no need of repentance, Christianity should more properly have flamboyantly eulogized—the righteous! But if this had been done, Christianity would not only have had no one to talk *to*, alas, but no one to talk *about*, either—that is, Christianity would have been reduced to silence. No, least of all has Christianity proclaimed itself a eulogy and has never occupied itself in describing or dwelling upon how a man is right now. It has never made *distinctions* among men so that it could talk about those who at present *are* fortunate enough to be so lovable. Christianity begins immediately with what *every* human being *ought to become*. For that reason Christianity calls itself instruction about the way, and correctly so, for not in vain will anyone ask Christ, who is the way, or Scriptures, which is instruction about the way, what he ought to do: the questioner will immediately learn this—if he himself *wants* to know.

To prevent a misunderstanding, let me say this. Everyone who does not wish to understand the discourse about what one shall do in respect to love, that in reality there is much or, more correctly, every-thing to be done both to gain it and keep it, has placed himself outside of Christianity; he is a pagan who admires good fortune, consequently the accidental, but for that very reason fumbles in the dark.—Yet I wonder if one really gets more light, no matter how many will-o'-the-wisps are wafted about!

There is something to do, therefore. And what must be done in order to be in the debt of love to each other? When a fisherman has caught a fish in his net and wishes to keep it alive, what must he do?

He must immediately put it in water; otherwise it becomes exhausted and dies after a time. And why must he put it in water? Because water is the fish's element, and *everything which shall be kept alive must be kept in its element*. But love's element is infinitude, inexhaustibility, immeasurability. If you will to keep your love, then, by the help of the debt's infinitude, imprisoned in freedom and life, you must take care that it continually remains in its element; otherwise, it droops and dies —not after a time, for it dies at once—which itself is a sign of its perfection, that it can live only in infinitude.

That love's element is infinitude, inexhaustibility, immeasurability no one will deny; it is easy to perceive. Assume—we can at least assume it—that a servant or a man for whose work and inconvenience you can pay does exactly the same thing for you as the one who loves you, so there is not the slightest bit of discoverable difference between the sums of their deeds and service. For all that, there still remains an infinite difference, the difference of immeasurability. In the one instance there is always a bonus, which, strangely enough, is worth *infinitely* much more than that to which it is related as a bonus. This is precisely the idea of *immeasurability*. In everything which the loving one does for you, in the smallest trifle as well as in the greatest sacrifice, he always gives love in addition, and thereby the smallest service, which in the case of the hired servant you would hardly find worth reckoning, becomes immeasurable.—Imagine that a man got the notion of wanting to find out, without loving another person, but just because he wanted to (for the sake of the experiment, then, and not for the sake of duty), whether he could be just as inexhaustible in sacrifice, in service, in expressions of devotion as one who loved this same person. You can easily see that he would not be successful; on the contrary, a difference of immeasurability comes between the two. The person who really loves always has a head-start, an infinite head-start, for every time the experimentalist has worked out, computed, discovered a new expression of devotion, the loving one has already accomplished it, because the loving one needs no calculation and therefore wastes no time in calculating.

But to be and remain in infinite debt is in itself an expression of love's infinitude; thus by remaining in debt it remains in its element. There is a reciprocal relationship here, but infinite on both sides. In one instance it is the beloved who in every expression of the lover's love lovingly discerns immeasurability; on the other hand, it is the lover who feels the immeasurability because he recognizes the debt to be infinite: the infinitely great and infinitely small are one and the same thing. The object of love confesses in love that the lover does infinitely more with a trifle than all the others do with all the greatest sacrifices, and the lover himself confesses that with all possible sacrifices he does infinitely less than he considers the debt to be. What a remarkable like-for-like in this infinitude. The learned are proud of the calculation of infinity, but here is the philosopher's stone: the most trifling expression is infinitely greater than all sacrifices, and all sacrifices are infinitely less than the smallest trifle in making part-payment on the debt.

But what can take love out of its element? *As soon as love concentrates upon itself it is out of its element.* What does that mean, to concentrate on itself? It means to become an object for itself. But an *object* is always a dangerous matter if one is to move forward; an *object* is like a finite fixed point, a boundary, a stopping-place, a dangerous thing for infinitude. Love can never *infinitely* become its own object; nor is there danger in that. For *infinitely* to be an object for itself is to remain in *infinitude* and thus, simply by existing or continuing to exist (since love is a reduplication in itself) is as different from the particularity of natural life as is the reduplication of the spirit. Consequently, if love *concentrates* upon itself, it must become an object for itself in its individual expression, or another and separate love becomes its object, love in this person and love in that person. When the object is thus finite, love concentrates on itself, for *infinitely* to concentrate on itself means precisely a becoming. But when love finitely concentrates on itself, everything is lost. Imagine an arrow flying, as they say, with the speed of an arrow. Imagine that for a second it got a notion of wanting to concentrate on itself, perhaps to see how far it had come, or how high over the earth it skimmed, or how its course was related to that of another arrow which also flew with the speed of an arrow: in that very moment the arrow would fall to the earth.

It is the same with love when it finitely concentrates upon itself or becomes for itself an object, which, more accurately defined, is *comparison*. Love cannot *infinitely* compare itself with itself, for infinite self-comparison would only be a way of saying that it is itself; in such an infinite comparison there is no third factor; love is a reduplication and therefore there is no comparison. All comparison requires a third factor, together with similarity and dissimilarity. If there is no dwelling upon itself, there is no comparison; if there is no comparison, there is no dwelling upon itself either.

But what can comparison's third factor be? A person can compare his love with the love of another. Thus he discovers or thinks he discovers that love in him is greater than that in others or that love is greater in some and less again in others. Very likely he would at first think the comparison to be merely a quick side-glance in passing, requiring neither time nor effort; alas, but the side-glance of comparison discovers all too easily a whole world of relationships and calculations. This is the halting; in this very moment he is on the way out of debt, or perhaps is already out of it—that is, out of love.—Or comparison's third factor can be the deeds already accomplished out of love. In that very moment, counting and weighing out, he is on the way out of debt, or perhaps already, with great self-satisfaction, way out of debt—that is, way out of love.

In comparison everything is lost; love is made finite and the debt something to replay just like every other debt, instead of love's debt having its own characteristic of infinitude, just as a debt of honour has its own characteristic so that one first and foremost, the sooner the better, must see to it that he fullfills it. What does comparison always lose? It loses the moment, the moment which should be filled with an expression of the life of love. But *to lose the moment is to become episodic and momentary*. A moment lost, and the chain of the eternal is broken; a moment lost, and the coherence of the eternal is disturbed; a moment lost, and the eternal is lost—but to lose the eternal is to become episodic and momentary. A moment wasted in comparison—then everything is lost. The moment of comparison is a selfish moment, a moment which wants to be *for* itself; precisely this is the break, the fall—just as concentrating on itself means the fall of the arrow.

In comparison everything is lost; love is made finite, the debt something to repay. Regardless of position, whether or not it be the highest, love expects *by way of comparison* to get status in relationship to others' love or in relationship to its own achievements. Let us understand each other. Suppose it were true—we can indeed assume it for a moment—that it is unworthy and unseemly for the son of the king to associate with a simple man. If he did it, nevertheless, and then in self-defence said, " I am by no means giving up my dignity; indeed, I shall certainly know how to assert myself as the most eminent among these men also." —I wonder if the elegant courtier would not say, " Your Highness, this is a mistake; the unseemliness lies in associating with such men; Your Highness will himself sense that it sounds like mockery when it is said of you, O Prince, that you are the most eminent among these simple men. There is nothing to be won by this comparison, hardly the slightest gain by being uppermost in the comparison, for the relationship itself, the possibility of comparison, is the false move, and only by remaining beyond comparison is there royal dignity." Yet this is merely a joke. But if what is and ought to be infinitude seeks the bad company of familiarity and comparison with finitude, then it is unseemly, undignified, then the degradation is deserved, even though one thinks to be the superior one within the comparison. To love *by the way of comparison* more than all other men, even if this were the case, is: not to love. To love is to remain in infinite debt; the infinitude of the debt is the bond of perfection.

Let me illustrate this by mentioning another relationship of infinitude. Imagine an enthusiast who enthusiastically wills only one thing and enthusiastically wants to sacrifice everything for the good. Imagine that it now happens (which will not happen by *chance* but will unconditionally happen as long as the world is the world) that in the same degree as he works more and more disinterestedly, more and more sacrificially, more and more strenuously, to the same degree the world works more and more against him. Imagine him at this point—if he for one single moment makes the mistake of comparing his striving with the world's reward or makes the mistake of comparing his striving with the achievements already accomplished or makes the mistake of comparing his status with the eminence of those who simply do not seem to burn with enthusiasm—alas, he is lost. Yet the tempter approaches him and says, " Stop your work, take it easy, have a good time, enjoy life in ease, and accept as offered the flattering situation of being one of the greatest enthusiasts "—for the tempter does not speak ill of enthusiasm; he is too smart for that. One does not trick men so easily into abandoning enthusiasm. Meanwhile he will not give in to the tempter, and he renews his efforts. The tempter comes to him again and says, " Stop your work, take it easy, have a good time, and enjoy life in ease by accepting the absolutely most flattering terms, which admittedly can be offered only to you as the greatest enthusiast, terms which make life easier for you and get for you, the enthusiast, the world's admiration, whereas you are now only making your life strenuous and thereby winning the world's opposition." Alas, to be *by comparison* the most enthusiastic one is precisely not to be enthusiastic. Woe to the man who has corrupted his soul with the defilement of comparison so he cannot understand the next person without enormous pride and vanity. The enthusiast says to the tempter, " Get out, and take comparison with you." And this is right. For that very reason we shout to an enthusiast, " Shut your eyes, stop your ears, hold to the demand of infinitude, and no comparison shall sneak in to kill your enthusiasm by making you the most enthusiastic person—by comparison! For even your greatest effort is child's play to the demand of infinitude, under which you shall not be able to become important to yourself, since you simply come to understand how infinitely much more is required of you! " We warn the person who stands on a ship which ploughs ahead with the speed of the storm that he should not look into the waves, for he will become dizzy; thus does comparison between the infinite and the finite make a man dizzy. Watch out, therefore, for the comparison which the world wants to force on you, for the world has no more knowledge of enthusiasm than a capitalist has of love, and you will always find that indolence and stupidity are primarily intent upon making comparisons and upon imprisoning everything in comparison's muddied "realism." Therefore do not look around; " Greet no one on the way" (Luke 10 : 4); do not listen to cries or shouts which will trick you out of your enthusiasm and fool its power into labouring on the treadmill of comparisons. Do not let it disturb you that the world calls your enthusiasm crazy, calls it self-love—in eternity everyone will be compelled to understand what enthusiasm and love are. Do not accept the terms which are offered you—to get the full admiration of the world for half the work; remain in the debt of infinitude; rejoice in the terms: the world's opposition, because you will not bargain. Do not listen, for then it is already too late not to believe it; do not listen to what others fraudulently say of enthusiasm; do not listen, lest you also in some other manner come to harm by believing it, as if every man who *wills* it were not equally near to infinitude and equally near to becoming enthusiastic. For what is enthusiasm, I wonder, if it is not simply willing to do and suffer everything; I wonder if it is not also wanting continually to be in the debt of infinitude? Every time the arrow shall fly forth, the bowstring must be tightened, but every time enthusiasm renews or in renewal maintains its speed, the debt of infinitude must be considered.

So it is also with love. If you will preserve love, you must preserve it in the infinitude of debt. Watch out, therefore, for comparison! He who guards all the world's most precious treasure does not need to watch so carefully that no one gets to know anything about it; for you must also watch out lest you yourself get to know something about love by way of companion. Watch out for comparison! Comparison is the most unholy association into which love can enter; comparison is the most dangerous acquaintance love can make; comparison is the worst of all seductions. And no seducer is so readily at hand; no seducer is everywhere present the way comparison is as soon as your side glance beckons—yet no seduced person says in defence, " Comparison seduced me," for it was he himself who discovered comparison. It is well known how apprehensively, how clumsily, and yet how frightfully laboriously a man walks when he knows he is walking on slippery ice; but it is also well known that a man walks very confidently and firmly on the slippery ice when because of darkness or for some other reason he does not know he is walking on slippery ice. Guard, therefore, against discovering comparison! Comparison is the parasitic growth which takes vitality from the tree: the cursed tree becomes a withered shadow, but the parasitic growth flourishes with unhealthy luxuriance. Comparison is like the neighbour's swampy ground; even if your house is not built upon it, it sinks just the same. Comparison is like the hidden worm which consumes in secret and does not die, at least not before it has taken the life out of love. Comparison is a loathsome rash which has turned in and is eating at the marrow. Watch out, therefore, for comparison in your love!

But if comparison is the only thing which could bring love out of debt or put one on the way out of debt, and if comparison is avoided, then love, healthy and alive, remains—in infinite debt. " To remain in debt " is an infinitely exact and yet infinitely adequate expression for the infinity of love. When one says of a force in nature, for example, that it rushes forward with infinite speed or that it bursts forth with infinite power and abundance, it always seems as if it is nevertheless possible that at some point it must stop or become exhausted. But that which, infinite in itself, also has an infinite debt behind it, is made infinite once again; it has in itself the control which continually sees to it that it does not stop—the debt is once again the propelling power.

When it is a duty to be in the debt of love to each other, *this being in debt is not a fanatical expression, is not a fancy of love, but is action; therefore, with the help of duty, love continues Christianly in action, in the movement of action, and thereby in infinite debt.*

To love means to have come into infinite debt. The desire to be in debt might seem to be merely a notion, a fancy of love, the most extreme expression of all, like a festival wreath. Even the most expensive goblet filled with the rarest wine lacks something—the goblet should be crowned with a garland! Even the loveliest soul in the most charming feminine form still lacks something—the garland which puts on the finishing touch! One must talk this way also when speaking merely humanly about love: this desire to be in debt is the ultimate of festivity, the crowning wreath of festivity, something which in a certain sense is superfluous (for, after all, one does not drink the wreathed goblet, nor is the garland part of the bride) and is for that very reason the beautiful expression of extreme enthusiasm. But only in a human sense is beautiful enthusiasm the ultimate.

But Christianity does not talk fanatically this way about love. It says it is a duty to be in the debt of love but does not, at the point of ultimate and complete intoxication, say this as a giddy idea—for the desire to be in debt is an extreme expression, and yet it might seem to become even more extreme, if possible, by being a duty. However, this extreme expression of erotic love has, against its will, the appearance of paying something on the debt; but if it is a duty to be in debt, the impossibility has soared still higher. To speak, then, of duty, might be likened to that state of intoxication wherein a sudden moment of complete soberness is really an increase of intoxication, for fanaticism becomes still more fanatical when it is expressed calmly and reflectively; the fanciful becomes still more fanciful when it is related with all simplicity as a common incident.—But Christianity does not speak this way. It says quite the same thing about remaining in debt as noble human love passionately says, but it says it in quite another way. Christianity makes no fuss at all over it. Unlike the purely human conception of love, it does not become overwhelmed by the vision. No, it speaks just as earnestly about this as about something which merely human enthusiasm regards as utterly indifferent. It says it is a duty, and thereby takes away from love everything that is inflamed, everything that is momentary and giddy.

Christianity says it is a duty to be in debt and thereby says it is an *act*—not an expression about, not a theoretical *conception of* love. Christianly understood, no man has accomplished the utmost in love; and even if this impossibility were so fullfilled, there would in the same moment, Christianly understood, be a new task. But if in the same moment there is a new task, it is impossible to find out whether one has done the utmost, for the moment in which one might find this out he is engaged in the service of the task, and consequently he is prevented from finding out about the preceding moment; he has no time for it since he is occupied in the *course of action*; whereas even in the most extreme fanaticism there is a kind of loitering.

Christianity understands what it is to act and what it is to keep love incessantly occupied in action. The merely human concept of love admires love and therefore there comes so easily a standstill the moment when there is nothing to do, the idle moment which is the moment of fanaticism. Love according to the view of a merely human conception is like the unusually gifted child in the eyes of simple parents: the child finishes his tasks so quickly that finally the parents are at a loss to find something to keep the child occupied. Love according to the view of a merely human conception is like a fiery, snorting steed which quickly rides the horseman weary instead of the horseman's being able, if necessary, to tire out the horse. And this Christianity can do. Its intention is not to work love weary, far from it, for Christianity knows, in the power of its eternal being and with the earnestness of the eternal, that it can master love, and therefore it speaks so simply and is so earnest about the matter—just as the iron-man bronco-buster, who knows he can throw the horse, is not amazed at its high spirit but says it ought to be high-spirited, for he does not try to break the horse's spirit but through discipline simply improves its high spirit. In the same way Christianity knows how to discipline love and teach it that in every moment there is the task; it knows how to persevere with love so that humbled love will learn that it is not a way of speaking, not a fanaticism to will to remain in debt, but earnestness and truth.

The danger—and this certainly has happened—is that love would want to concentrate on itself by making comparisons. This must be prevented, but when it is prevented *by the help of duty* something else happens, too—love comes to relate itself to the Christian conception, or *Christianly* to the conception of God: the debt-relationship is carried over to the relationship between man and God. It is God who, so to speak, lovingly takes over the demand of love; by loving a person, one who loves comes into infinite debt—but also to God as guardian for the beloved. Now comparison is made impossible, and now love has found its master. There is no more talk about a festive mood and splendid achievement. No more, if I dare say so, shall love play on the childish stage of humanity, which leaves in doubt whether it is in fun or in earnest. Although love in all its expressions turns itself out toward men, where it indeed has its object and its tasks, it nevertheless knows that here is not the place where it shall be judged, but that judgment is there in the depths of inwardness where love is related to God, who is the judge. The situation is like that of a child out among strangers: the child acts according to its upbringing. But whether or not the strangers think well of the child, whether or not it occurs to the child that it behaves better than the other children, the earnestly reared child never forgets that judgment is at home, where the parents judge. And yet the upbringing of a child is not predicated on the child's remaining at home with its parents; on the contrary, it presupposes that the child shall go out into the world. So it is with love, Christianly understood. It is God who, so to speak, brings up love in a man; but God does not do this in order that he might himself rejoice, as it were, in the sight; on the contrary, he does it in order to send love out into the world, continually occupied in the task. Yet earnestly reared love, Christian love, never for a moment forgets where it shall be judged, evening or morning or whenever it might be, in short, every time it comes home for a moment from its tasks it is examined—in order immediately to be sent out again. In the company of the most extreme fanaticism love can loiter a bit before it goes out again, but with God there is no loitering.

You see, understood this way there is earnestness and truth in being in the debt of love to one another. Humanly speaking, even the most honestly intended and most noble fanaticism, even the most fiery and disinterested passion, still is not earnestness, even if it accomplishes amazing things and even if it also wishes to remain in debt. The deficiency of even the noblest human enthusiasm is that being merely human it is *not in the deepest sense powerful in itself, because it has no higher power over it.* Only the God-relationship is earnestness. Earnestness is simply this that the task is constrained to its highest point, because there is one who constrains with the power of the eternal; earnestness means that the enthusiasm has a power beyond itself and a constraint upon itself. The single individual is bound in love's debt to other men, but it is neither this individual man nor other men who shall judge his love. If this is so, the individual must remain in infinite debt. God has the infinite conception of love in truth and infallibility; God is love, consequently the individual must be in debt—as truly as God judges it or as truly as he abides in God, for only in the infinitude of the debt can God abide in him.

He is in debt, and he recognises also that it is his duty to be in debt, his duty to make this confession which, Christianly understood, is not the confession of fanaticism but the confession of a humble, loving soul. The humility lies in making the confession; the love consists in being infinitely willing to do it, because it belongs to love, because there is the intention and coherence of salvation in this confession; the specifically Christian lies in making no commotion at all over this, because it is a duty.

"Owe no one anything except to love one another." No, "Pay everyone everything you owe him; the person to whom you owe a tax, pay the tax; him to whom you owe a fee, pay the fee; to whom fear, fear; to whom honour, honour." Owe no man anything, what you have borrowed from him, what you have promised him, what he rightfully may demand of you in return. If possible, owe no man anything, no obligation, no service, no sympathy in joy or sorrow, no leniency in judging, no help in life, no advice in dangers, no sacrifice, even the most difficult—no, in all these things owe no man anything. But nevertheless be in the debt which amid all this you have by no means desired to get out of and before God have by no means been able to pay off, the debt of love to one another!

Do this! Then only one thing more: "Remember in good time that if you do this or at least strive to do accordingly, it will go hard with you in the world." It is especially important to be reminded of this particularly at the end of this discourse, and in general at the conclusion of this little book so that the discourse does not deceitfully work a fascination. Consequently the world will find this conclusion a complete failure, which again has the significance of proving—that the conclusion is correct.

Sad it is that one sometimes reads and hears Christian sermons which actually leave out the last danger. What is said about faith, love, and humility is absolutely correct and absolutely Christian; but such a sermon must misguide a youth instead of guiding him, for the sermon leaves out what consequently befalls the essentially Christian in the world. The sermon demands that a man shall labour with self-renunciation to develop a Christian consciousness—but then, then, yes, then nothing more is said, or the most critical and relevant qualifications are suppressed; whereas there is talk and assurance about the good having its own reward and its being loved both by God and man. When this Christian consciousness, quite rightly, is lauded as the highest, the youth must certainly believe that if he accomplishes what is demanded or honestly works to accomplish it, it will go well with him in the world. You see, this silence about the last difficulty (namely, that humanly speaking it will fare badly with him in the world and the more so as he develops Christianly) is a deception which either must lead the youth to despair over himself (as if he were directly responsible, as if he were not a true Christian) or despondently to give up striving, as if something quite out of the ordinary had befallen him; whereas what happened to him was only what the Apostle John speaks of as being very ordinary, when he says (I John 3 :13), " Do not wonder, brethren, that the world hates you." The speaker consequently has deceived the youth by being silent about the true relationship, by letting it seem as if, Christianly, there was striving only in one area instead of making clear that true Christian striving always involves a double danger because there is striving in two areas: first in man's inner being, where he must strive with himself, and then, if he makes progress in this striving, outside of man with the world. Alas, perhaps the speaker is afraid to recommend Christianity and the good in this doubtlessly strange but truthful manner—that it has no reward in the world, indeed, that the world works against it. The fact that the good is rewarded with hate, contempt, and persecution perhaps seems to the speaker like a blow on his eloquent mouth after he has praised the good in the most commendatory and especially well-chosen phrases and expressions and thus brought the listener as close as possible to going forth even today and doing accordingly; very likely he feels that it would be a blow in the face and that his masterpiece of elegant eloquence would make a pitiable impression if he should add to his recommendations that the good is rewarded with hate, contempt and persecution. For if this be true, it seems more natural to advise against the good, or, more correctly, one is doing the good precisely by recommending it in this manner. The speaker certainly is in a difficult position. Well-meaning, perhaps, he wants so much to lure men—that he leaves out the last difficulty, that which makes the recommendation very difficult—and now the sermon flows along, a charming discourse, uplifting, transporting, drawing tears. Alas, but this is to deceive, and this certainly has happened. If, on the other hand, the speaker should make use of—the difficult recommendation, he "frightens his listeners away." Perhaps the talk would almost frighten him who, highly admired, respected, and valued, indeed proves that the good Christian has his reward in the world. That he has his reward—although the eternal ten times says the reward is taken away—that he has his reward cannot be denied, but it seems a bit worldly and is not the fullfillment which Christianity promised its followers at the time and by which it *immediately* recommended itself.

Truly we do not want to make a young man arrogant and promptly teach him to get busy criticizing the world; God forbid that any word of ours should contribute to developing this disease in a man. We hope to be able to make his inward life so strenuous that from the very first he has something else to think about, for it is no doubt an unsound hate towards the world which, perhaps without even once having considered the enormous responsibility, wishes to be persecuted. But on the other hand, we are also truly reluctant to deceive a youth by silence about the difficulty, by silence at the very moment we are trying to recommend Christianity, for then and precisely then is the moment to speak. We put our confidence in frankly daring to recommend Christianity along with the postscript that its reward, putting it most mildly, is ingratitude from the world. We regard it as our duty always to speak out *at the time*, so that we do not sometimes recommend Christianity by the omission of some of its essential difficulties and at other times, perhaps on the occasion of a particular text, hit upon a few grounds of comfort for the person who has trials in life. No, precisely when Christianity is recommended most strongly the difficulty must simultaneously be presented. It is unChristian whining if anyone thinks: let us in every way win men for Christianity, and if at some time adversity comes to them, we will have advice at hand, then is the time to talk about it. But right here is the fraud: as if it were possible for a Christian to be able to avoid such adversity in quite the same way as a person has the good fortune of being tried by neither poverty nor sickness. That is, people look on the world's opposition as an accidental relationship to Christianity rather than as an essential relationship: opposition may perhaps come, but it may also, perhaps, never arise. But this view is altogether unChristian. It may well be possible that a pagan at the time of death can justifiably call himself happy because he has slipped through life and even past all misfortunes, but a Christian must be somewhat suspicious about this joy at the moment of death—for, Christianly, the opposition of the world stands in an *essential* relationship to the inwardness of Christianity. In addition, the person who chooses Christianity should in that very moment have an idea of its difficulty so he knows what it is he chooses. Nothing should be promised the youth which Christianity cannot deliver, and Christianity cannot deliver something different from what it has promised from the very first: the ingratitude of the world, opposition, mockery, and always to a higher degree the more earnest a Christian one becomes. This is the final difficulty in being a Christian, and when one recommends Christianity there should be silence least of all about this.

No, if there is silence about the last difficulty, there can really be no talk about Christianity. If the world is not what Christianity originally assumed it to be, Christianity is essentially abolished. What Christianity calls self-renunciation involves precisely and essentially a *double-danger*;[116] otherwise self-renunciation is not Christian self-renunciation. If anyone, therefore, can prove that the world or Christendom has now become essentially good—as if it were the eternal —then I will also prove that Christian self-renunciation is made impossible and Christianity is abolished, just as it will be abolished in eternity where it will have ceased to be a *striving*. The *purely human conception of self-renunciation* is this: give up your selfish desires, longings, and plans—and then you will become appreciated and honoured and loved as a righteous man and wise. One can easily see that this self-renunciation does not approach God or the God-relationship; it remains secularly within the relationship between man and man. *The Christian conception of self-renunciation* is this: give up your selfish desires and longings, give up your arbitrary plans and purposes so that you in truth work disinterestedly for the good—and submit to being abominated almost as a criminal, scorned and ridiculed for this very reason; submit, if it is demanded of you, to being executed as a criminal for this very reason—or, more correctly, do not submit to this, for one can hardly be forced into this, but choose it freely. Christian self-renunciation knows in advance that this will happen and chooses it freely. Christianity has the eternal's conception of what it means to give up one's arbitrary purposes; therefore it does not let the Christian get by at half-price. One readily sees that Christian self-renunciation approaches God and in God has its sole stronghold. Only this way of being forsaken, in double-danger, is Christian self-renunciation. This second danger, or the danger in another area, is the assurance of being in a right God-relationship, that it is genuinely a God-relationship. And even if there were no other part to this double-danger, simply willing to be forsaken in this way is regarded by the world as stupidity and insanity; consequently the world is far from honouring and admiring it. The world looks upon self-renunciation only with shrewd practicality and therefore honours only the self-renunciation which prudentially remains in worldliness. Therefore the world always sees to it that there is a sufficient number of the false notes of counterfeit self-renunciation in circulation—and sometimes, alas, the criss-crossing of relationships and ideas becomes so complicated that it takes a skilled eye to recognise immediately a false note. For one can also take God secularly along within secularism and consequently manage a self-renunciation which has a God-mark and still is false. At times one can even make a good worldly show, as they say, of denying oneself for the sake of God, yet not in this double-dangered abandoned confidence in God, but in such a way that the world understands this man and honours him for it. Yet it is easy to recognise the falsity, for as soon as the double-mark is missing the self-renunciation is not Christian self-renunciation. It is human self-renunciation when the child denies himself while the parents, encouraging and prompting, reach out to embrace him. It is human self-renunciation when a man denies himself and the world opens up to him. But it is Christian self-renunciation when a man denies himself and, because the world precisely for this reason shuts itself up to him, he must as one thrust out by the world seek God's confidence. The double-danger lies precisely in meeting opposition there where he had expected to find support, and he has to turn about twice; whereas the merely human self-renunciation turns once. All self-renunciation which finds support in the world is therefore not Christian self-renunciation. It was with this in mind that the old church fathers said: The virtues of paganism are glittering vices.[117]—*Purely human self-renunciation* is: without fear or regard for oneself to venture into danger—into danger where honour beckons to the victor, where the admiration of contemporaries and onlookers already beckons to the one who simply ventures. One easily sees that this self-renunciation does not reach towards God but remains on the way within the human. *Christian self-renunciation* is: without fear or regard for oneself to venture into the danger in which one's contemporaries, blind, ensnared, and mutually guilty, are not conceivably able (or do not wish) to discern any honour to be won; therefore it is not only dangerous to venture into danger but doubly dangerous because the spectators' mockery awaits the courageous one no matter whether he wins or loses. In the one case the concept of the danger is a mutual given; the contemporaries agree that there is danger, danger in venturing and consequently honour in winning the victory, inasmuch as their concept of danger presupposes their willingness to admire the person who simply ventures. In the other case the courageous must, as it were, discover the danger and struggle to get permission to call dangerous that which the contemporaries are not willing to call danger. Even if they grant it is possible to lose one's life in this danger, they still deny it is a danger, since to their mind it is ridiculousness and therefore doubly ridiculous to lose one's life for the ridiculous. Christianity discovered a danger which is called eternal damnation. This danger the world regards as ridiculous. Now let us imagine a Christian witness. For the sake of this doctrine he risks battle with the mighty ones who hold his life in their hands and who must see in him a disturber—this will indeed cost him his life. At the same time his contemporaries, with whom he does not particularly strive but who are spectators, find it ridiculous to risk death for the sake of such foolishness.[118] Here there is life to lose and truly no honour and admiration to gain! Yet to be forsaken in this way, only in this way to be forsaken is Christian self-renunciation.—If then, the world or Christendom had become essentially good, this self-renunciation would be made impossible, for in such a case the world, being essentially good, would honour and praise the person who denied himself, and would always have the right conception of where and what the real danger is.

We wish to conclude this, as all our discussions which according to our capacities extol Christianity, with this hardly ingratiating recommendation: beware of beginning to do this—if it is not your true and earnest desire to will in truth to deny yourself. We have too earnest a conception of Christianity to entice anyone; we wish rather almost to give warning. The person who truly wishes to make Christianity his own certainly will experience inwardly terrors quite different from a dramatic bit of terror in a sermon; in venturing out he must be committed quite otherwise than he can become with the aid of a bit of the painted falsity of eloquence. We leave it to everyone to test whether this earnest conception of ours seems cold, comfortless, and without enthusiasm. Insofar as one were to talk about his own relationship to the world, this would be another matter, since it is a duty to speak as mildly, as mitigatingly as possible, and even when one does this it is a duty to remain in love's debt. But when we speak to instruct, we do not dare keep silent about something which probably will not gain favour for the discourse in the groping understanding of an enthusiastic youth. Neither do we dare recommend seeking to lift oneself optimistically above the world's opposition and foolishness, for even if it be done as in paganism, it can be done only in paganism, because the pagan does not have Christianity's true, earnest, eternally concerned conception of the truth: for him it is in no way ridiculous that others lack it. Christianly understood, the essential foolishness of the world is not at all ridiculous, no matter how ridiculous it is; for when there is salvation to win or lose, it is no jest whether or not I win it, nor is it ridiculous whether or not anyone forfeits it.

There is, however, a ridiculousness we should guard against:

talking ingratiatingly about Christianity. I wonder if a man handing another man an extremely sharp, polished, two-edged instrument would hand it over with the air, gestures, and expression of one delivering a bouquet of flowers? Would not this be madness? What does one do, then? Convinced of the excellence of the dangerous instrument, one recommends it unreservedly, to be sure, but in such a way that in a certain sense one warns against it. So it is with Christianity. If what is needed is to be done, we should not hesitate, aware of *the highest responsibility*, to preach *in Christian sermons*—yes, precisely *in Christian sermons*—AGAINST Christianity. For we know full well where disaster strikes these days—namely, that by foolish and ingratiating Sunday-talk Christianity has been deceptively transformed into an illusion and we have even been tricked into the fancy that we, just as we are, are Christians. Yet if a man thought he was holding a flower in his hand, a flower which he somewhat idly, somewhat thoughtlessly delighted to look at—and then someone, truly discerning, shouted to him " You poor man, don't you realise you are holding a very sharp, polished two-edged sword! "—I wonder if he would not become terrified for a moment! But, but—I wonder if the person who truthfully said this deceived him or truth? For it would only plunge him deeper into misunderstanding if this man were to be reminded that the flower in his hand was no plain, common flower, but an extremely rare one. No, Christianity is not in a human sense an extremely rare flower, nor is it the rarest of all—such pagan and secular talk remains within merely human conceptions. Christianity is, *divinely* understood, the highest good, and therefore also, humanly understood, an extremely dangerous good, because understood in a purely human way it is so far from being a rare flower that it is an offence and foolishness,[119] now as in the beginning and as long as the world endures.

Wherever Christianity is there is the possibility of offence, but offence is the highest danger. Everyone who in truth has made Christianity or something of Christianity his own has also had to come close to the possibility of offence in such a way that he has seen it—and with this before his eyes he has chosen Christianity. If anything is to be said about Christianity, the discourse must always hold open the possibility of offence, but then it can never come to the point of *directly* recommending Christianity. Therefore the difference between speakers would only be that one speaks in stronger, the other in weaker, the third in the strongest possible expressions of praise. Christianity can be recommended only when at every point the danger is incessantly made clear—how Christianity according to merely human conceptions is foolishness and offence. But by making this clear and evident, a warning is issued. Christianity is that earnest. That which stands in need of the favour of man curries favour with them, but Christianity is so sure of itself and knows with such earnestness and exactness that it is men who stand in need of it, that for this very reason it does not recommend itself directly but first alerts them, as Christ recommended Himself to the apostles by once predicting to them that for his sake they would be hated—yes, that whoever put them to death would think he did God a service.[120]

When Christianity came into the world, it did not need to call attention itself (even though it did so) to the fact that it was an offence, for the world, which took offence, discovered this easily enough. But now, now, when the world has become Christian, Christianity itself must above all pay attention to the offence. If it is true that so many " Christians " in these times miss the point of Christianity, how does it happen except that the possibility of offence—this dreadful thing, please note, escapes them. What wonder then that Christianity and its salvation and tasks can no longer satisfy "the Christians"—they cannot even be offended by it!—When Christianity came into the world it did not need to call attention itself (even though it did so) to the fact that it was contrary to human understanding, for the world discovered that easily enough. But now, now, when Christianity has lived through centuries in extensive intercourse with human understanding,[121] now when a fallen Christianity—like that fallen angel who married mortal women—has married human understanding, now when Christianity and human understanding are on intimate terms: now Christianity above all must itself watch for the collision. If Christianity is going to be preached out of the enchantment of illusion (alas, it is like the fairy-tale about the castle enchanted for one hundred years) and its disfigured alterations, the possibility of offence must again fundamentally be preached to life. Only the possibility of offence (the antidote to apologetics' sleeping potion) is able to waken those who have fallen asleep, is able to break the enchantment so that Christianity is itself again.

Since Holy Scripture says " Woe to the men by whom the temptation comes[122] we confidently say: woe to him who first thought of preaching Christianity without the possibility of offence. Woe to the person who ingratiatingly, flirtatiously, commendingly, convincingly preached to mankind some effeminate something which was supposed to be

Christianity! Woe to the person who could make the miracles reasonable, or at least sketch and publicise the prospects of its being done soon! Woe to the person who betrayed and broke the mystery of faith, distorted it into public wisdom, because he took away the possibility of offence! Woe to the person who could comprehend the mystery of atonement without detecting anything of the possibility of offence; woe again to him because he thought thereby to make God and Christianity something for study and cultivation. Woe to all those unfaithful stewards who sat down and wrote false proofs, winning friends for themselves and Christianity by writing off the possibility of offence in Christianity and inserting foolishness by the hundreds! O, the learning and acumen tragically wasted, O, the time tragically wasted in this enormous work of defending Christianity! Truly, when Christianity simply rises up again, powerful in the possibility of offence, so that this terror can again arouse men: then Christianity will need no defence. On the other hand, the more learned, the more excellent *the defence*, the more Christianity is disfigured, abolished, exhausted like an emasculated man, for the defence simply out of kindness will take the possibility of offence away. But Christianity ought not be defended, it is men who should see whether they can justify themselves and justify for themselves what they choose when Christianity terrifyingly, as it once did, poses for them the choice and terrifyingly constrains them to choose: either to be offended or to accept Christianity. Therefore take away from Christianity the possibility of offence or take away from the forgiveness of sin the battle of an anguished conscience (to which, nevertheless, according to Luther's excellent explanation,[123] this whole doctrine leads), and then lock the churches, the sooner the better, or turn them into places of amusement which stand open all day long!

But although by taking away the possibility of offence men have gotten the whole world Christianised, the curious thing always occurs —the world is offended by the real Christian. Here comes the offence, the possibility of which is after all inseparable from Christianity. Only the confusion is more distressing than ever, for at one time the world was offended by Christianity—that was the intention; but now the world imagines that it is Christian, that it has made Christianity its own without detecting anything of the possibility of offence—and then it is offended by the real Christian. Truly it is difficult to break out of such an illusion. Woe to the flowing pens and the busy tongues, woe to this whole busyness which, because it knows *neither* the one *nor* the other, can so very easily reconcile *both* the one *and* the other.

The Christian world is still always offended by the real Christian. But now the pressure of offence is ordinarily not so strong that it will liquidate him; no, it merely takes the form of mockery and scorn. This is easily explained. When the world was itself conscious of not being Christian, there was something to struggle over; it was a matter of life and death. But now when the world is proudly and calmly self-assured of being Christian, the exaggeration of a true Christian is worth no more than a laugh. The confusion is more distressing than in the first period of Christianity. It was distressing then, but there was meaning in it when the world battled in a life-and-death struggle with Christianity; but the world's present exalted tranquillity in the consciousness of itself being Christian, its cheap bit of jeering, if you please, at the real Christian—all this borders almost on madness. Christianity in its first period never became the object of jeers in this way.

When, then, in this Christian world a man will in some measure strive to accomplish the duty of being in love's debt to each other, he will also be carried out into the utmost difficulty and get the world's opposition to contend with. Alas, the world thinks so little or never of God; that is the reason the world absolutely must misunderstand every life whose most essential and constant thought is thought of God, the thought of where, divinely understood, the danger is and what the demand on a man is! Therefore the Christian world will say of the real Christian: " He lays himself wide open; even when it is quite clear that he is the injured one, it almost seems that he is the one who seeks forgiveness." In him the world will Christianly (for the world is indeed Christian) detect the lack of that essential—Christian hard-heartedness, which busily asserts its rights, affirms itself, repays evil with evil or at least with the proud consciousness of doing good. The world does not at all discern that such a person has an entirely different criterion for his life and that the whole thing is thereby quite easily explained; whereas it certainly remains absolutely meaningless when explained by means of the world's criterion. But since the world essentially does not know and does not want to know that this criterion (the God-relationship) exists, it cannot explain such a person's behaviour except as eccentricity—for that this is Christlikeness can naturally never occur to the world, which as Christian of course knows best what Christianity is. It is eccentric of a person not to be self-interested; it is eccentric of him not to retort; it is eccentric and silly of him to forgive his enemies and almost be fearful of not doing enough for his enemies;

it is eccentric of him always to be in the wrong position, never where there is the appearance of being courageous, magnanimous, disinterested—this is eccentric and affected and half-idiotic, in short, something to laugh at a little, inasmuch as one himself, by being the world, is certain as a Christian of possessing truth and blessedness both here and yonder. The world at best has nothing but a very remote holiday conception of the existence of the God-relationship, not to mention that it should daily qualify a man's life—therefore it must judge as it does. The invisible law for such a person's life, its suffering and its blessedness, simply does not exist for the world: *ergo* it must explain such a life most charitably as eccentricity, just as we call it lunacy when a person suddenly sees a bird which none of the rest of us can see or when a man dances—to music which none else, even with the best intention, is able to hear, or when a man by his walk indicates that he is going out of his way for something—invisible. And this is lunacy, because a bird, if it is actually present, cannot be invisibly present any more than actual music can be inaudible or any more than an actual obstacle in one's path, which compels going around, can be invisible: but God can be invisibly and inaudibly present, and the fact that the world cannot see him does not prove very much.

Let me illustrate this relationship by a simple image which I have frequently used in various ways because it is so fruitful, instructive, and suggestive. When a strictly brought-up child is together with naughty or less good children and does not want to join them in their mischief, which they themselves, for the most part, at least, do not regard as mischief—would the naughty children know how to explain this otherwise than that the child must be a strange and foolish child? They do not see that the situation permits a quite different explanation, that the strictly brought-up child, wherever it is, continually has with him the parents' standards for what it may and may not do. If the parents were visibly present so the naughty children could see them, they would better understand the child, especially if the child appeared sad because of having to obey the parents' orders, for then it would be obvious that the child would more than willingly do as the naughty children did, and it would be easy to perceive, in fact, to see, what is holding the child back. But when the parents are not present, the naughty children cannot understand the strictly brought-up child. They think like this: *either* this child must not like what we other children like but is silly and strange, *or* it has the same likes but does not dare—but why doesn't it dare? The parents are not here. See, here again it is silly and strange. Consequently one cannot promptly call it badness or spite on the part of these children when they judge the strictly brought-up child in this way. No, according to their own lights they perhaps mean very well by it. They do not understand the strictly brought-up child; no, they themselves think well of their naughtiness, and therefore they want the child to join them and be a real boy—just like the others.—The application of this picture is easy. The world just cannot get into its head (and therefore it cannot be) that a Christian should not have the same inclinations and passions the world has. But if he has them, it can even less get it into its head why, out of fear of the invisible, he wants in this silly way to constrain these inclinations, innocent and permissible according to the world's view, even a "duty to fullfill," why he wants to constrain self-love, which the world not only calls innocent but praiseworthy, why he wants to constrain anger, which the world not only regards as natural but as the mark of a man and a man's honour, why he wants to make himself doubly unhappy: first, by not satisfying his inclinations and, second, by reaping as reward the world's ridicule.

One easily sees that self-renunciation is here rightly identified: it has the double-mark. Just because this is the case, because he who wills in earnest to try to comply with this will quite rightly fall into double danger, precisely for this reason we say that it is the *Christian's* duty: to be in the debt of love to one another.

Part Two

I

Love Builds Up

" But love builds up." (*I Corinthians* 8 :1)

All human language about the spiritual, yes, even the divine language of Holy Scriptures, is essentially transferred or metaphorical language. This is quite in order or corresponds to the order of things and of existence, since even though man[1] is spirit from the moment of birth he first becomes conscious as spirit later, and therefore prior to this he has lived for a certain time within sensuous-psychic categories. The first portion of life shall not, however, be cast aside when the spirit awakens, any more than the awakening of spirit announces itself in sensuous or senuous-psychic modes in contrast to the sensuous or sensuous-psychic. The first portion is taken over by spirit, and, thus used, thus laid at the base, it *becomes transferred*. Therefore the spiritual man and the sensuous-psychic man say the same thing in a sense, and yet there remains an infinite difference between what they say, since the latter does not suspect the secret of transferred language, even though he uses the same words, but not metaphorically. There is a world of difference between the two; the one has made a transition or has let himself be led over to the other side; whereas the other has remained on this side. Yet there is something binding which they have in common—they both use the same language. One in whom the spirit is awakened does not therefore leave the visible world. Although now conscious of himself as spirit, he is still continually in the world of the visible and is himself sensuously visible; likewise he also remains in the language, except that it is transferred. Transferred language is, then, not a brand new language; it is rather the language already at hand. Just as spirit is invisible, so also is its language a secret, and the secret rests precisely in this that it uses the same language as the simple man and the child but uses it as transferred. Thereby the spirit denies (but not in a sensuous or sensuous-psychic manner) that it is the sensuous or sensuous-psychic. The distinction is by no means directly apparent. Therefore we quite rightly regard emphasis upon a directly apparent distinction as a sign of false spirituality—which is mere sensuousness; whereas the presence of spirit is the quiet, whispering secret of transferred language—audible to him who has an ear to hear.

One of the transferred terms which Holy Scriptures very frequently uses, or one of the expressions which Holy Scriptures very frequently uses in a transferred way, is the word *edify* or *build up* [*opbygge* in Danish]. It is immediately, yes, it is very up-building to see how Holy Scriptures does not become weary of this simple word, does not seek inventively for variations and new nuances, but, on the contrary, in truly spiritual ways makes thought new in the same old word! It is, yes, it is very up-building to see how Holy Scriptures with this simple word achieves characterisation of the highest, and in the innermost way; it is just like the miracle of feeding the five thousand with scanty supplies which through the blessing provided so bountifully that a surplus remained.[2] It is, yes, it is very up-building when someone succeeds, not in laboriously seeking out new discoveries which should laboriously dislodge the old, but in making a new acquaintance with the old acquaintance by humbly contenting himself with Scriptures and thankfully and inwardly appropriating to himself what has been handed down from the fathers. As children we all have often played "stranger." Truly it is real earnestness when we, spiritually understood, are able to continue this up-building game in earnest and play "stranger" with the old and familiar.

To build up is a transferred expression. With the secret of the spirit in mind, we shall now see *what meaning this expression has in ordinary speech.*[3] *To build up* is composed of *to build* and the adverb *up*, on which the emphasis must be placed. Everyone who *builds up* also *builds*; but not everyone *builds up* who *builds*. When a man *builds* a wing on to his house, one does not say that he *builds up* a wing, but that he *builds it on.* Consequently this *up* seems to point towards the heights, the upward direction, yet this is not the case. When a man builds a sixty-foot structure ten feet higher, we still do not say that he *builds up* the structure ten feet higher—we say: he *builds on.* Here the meaning of the word begins to come more clearly to the fore, since it is evident that it does not depend on height. When, on the other hand, someone has constructed something, however unpretentious and small, from the ground up, we say he *built it up*. To build up means, then, to construct something *from the ground up into the heights*. This *up* certainly points to the heights, but only when the heights also means the opposite—depth—do we say *build up*! Therefore if a man builds high and from the ground but the depth does not properly correspond to the height, then we do say that he *builds up* but also that he builds it up badly; however, we would mean something else by *building badly*. The emphasis in *building up* comes, then, to rest especially on building from the ground up. We do not call underground construction *building up*. We do not speak of *building up* a well. If there is to be talk of *building up*, however high or low the construction may be, it must in any case be *from the ground up*. We therefore may say that a man began to build up a house but he did not finish. But we can never say that one *builds up* even if he manages to construct a lofty structure which does not go from the ground up. How wonderful! This *up* in the expression *build up* indicates height and also its opposite, depth.—For to *build up* means to build from the ground up. Therefore the Scriptures say that the foolish man built his house without a foundation. However, of the man who heard the word for genuine up-building, or who (according to the Scriptures) heard the word and kept it, of him it is said, he is like the man who "*dug deep*" and built his house (Luke 6 : 48). When the rains come and the storms beat upon the house properly built up—then we all rejoice over the *up-building* sight of a house withstanding the shock of the storm. Therefore, as stated, *building up* depends chiefly on building fundamentally. It is laudable that before beginning one calculates " how high he can build up the tower "; but, if he is to *build up*, he then gives heed to digging deeply enough. For even though a tower (if this were possible) were built to the heavens, and if there were not adequate foundation, it would still not be *built up*. To build up entirely without a foundation is impossible. That is called building in the air. Hence, linguistically one speaks quite accurately of *building air-castles*. One does not speak of *building up air-castles;* this would be a careless and absurd use of words. Even in saying something insignificant the individual words must fit together, but such is not the case with the expression *build up* and *in the air*, since here the second takes away the foundation which the first presupposes. The combination would be, therefore, a false exaggeration.

So it is with the expression *build up* in ordinary language. Now we

recall that it is a transferred expression, and we direct our attention
to the subject of the discourse:

LOVE BUILDS UP.

But is *building up* in the spiritual sense such a characteristic predicate
of love that it pertains solely and alone to love? It is generally the case
that a predicate has many objects, all of which equally, even though
in various degrees, have claim to one and the same predicate. If this
is the case with *build up*, would it be incorrect to emphasise it so
particularly in relationship to love as this discussion has done? It
would be an endeavour based on misunderstanding to attribute
usurpation to love, as if it would monopolise or seize for itself what it
shares with others—since to share with others is precisely what love is
willing to do, inasmuch as it "does not insist on its own way" (I
Corinthians 13 : 5). Yet, in truth, *building up* is exclusively characteristic
of love. But on the other hand, this quality of *building up* has the
essential characteristic of giving itself up in everything, of being one
with all—just like love. Thus one sees that love with its characteristic
quality does not set itself apart or pride itself on independence or self-
sufficiency in relationship to another but completely gives of itself.
The characteristic is just this that it exclusively has the attribute of
complete self-giving. There is nothing, nothing, which cannot be done
or said in such a way that it becomes up-building, but whatever it is,
if it does build up, then love is present. Therefore the admonition reads
thus, precisely where difficulty in giving an exact rule is conceded—
"do everything for the sake of building up." One can just as well say:
do everything in love, whereby the very same thing is expressed. One
man may do the very opposite of what another does; but if each one
does the opposite out of love, the opposites build up. There is no word
in the language which builds up in and by itself, and there is no word
in the language which cannot become edifying and which in being
said cannot build up if love is present. Building up is not at all, then,
an exclusive superiority based on individual *talents*, such as brains,
beauty, artistic talent, and the like (such a view would be a love-less
and contentious error!). Rather it is just the opposite: every person,
through his life, his conduct, through his behaviour in common things,
through his relationship with his fellows, through his language, his
expression, should and can build up, and every person would do this
if love were actually in him.

We ourselves observe this, too, for we use the expression *build up* in the widest sense, but we perhaps do not make clear to ourselves that we use the expression most of all only when love is present. Yet it is good language-usage scrupulously to avoid using the expression unless love is present and by this limitation to make its sphere limitless, because everything can be up-building in the same sense that love can be present in everything.—When we see a single person who through praiseworthy simplicity gets along thriftily with little, we honour and extol him, we are made happy and are strengthened in the good by this sight. But when we see a mother with many to care for, one who through simplicity and wise thrift understands in love how amid the little to confer a blessing so that all nevertheless get enough, then we say: such a sight builds up. The up-building is rooted in this that together with the simplicity and thriftiness which we honour we have occasion to witness the loving concern of the mother. On the other hand, we say that there is little edification in the dismal sight of one who in a way goes hungry amid abundance and still has nothing left over for others. We find such a sight revolting; we are disgusted by his luxury; we shudder at the thought of vengeance on such sensuous addiction, hunger amid abundance—but in seeking vainly for the slightest expression of love we are obliged to conclude that the sight is hardly edifying.—When we see a large family cramped into close quarters and at the same time see that they inhabit a cosy, friendly, spacious place, then we say it is up-building to see, because we see the love which must be in each and every individual, since one unloving person is enough to occupy the whole place alone. We call it up-building because we see that there really is room where there is heart-room. On the other hand there is little which builds up in the sight of an unquiet soul dwelling in a palace without finding rest in a single one of the many rooms and yet without being able to give up or get along without a single room.—Is there anything which cannot in this way be up-building? The sight of a sleeping person, one would think, could not be edifying. And yet when you see a child sleeping on its mother's breast and see the mother's love, see that she had, as it were, waited for the moment and now while the child sleeps uses the time to rejoice over the child because she hardly dares let the child notice how inexpressibly she loves it—this is a sight which builds up. If the mother's love is not manifest, you will vainly seek in her face and manner for evidence of mother-love's joy in the child and concern for it, and you will see only inertia and indifference which is glad to be free of the child for a time—then the sight is hardly up-building! Just to see the child sleeping alone is a friendly, warming, peace-giving sight, but it does not build up. If you will nevertheless call it up-building, it is because you see love present anyway, because you see how the love of God encompasses the child.—To see the great artist perfecting his masterpiece is a glorious, elevating sight, but it is not up-building. Suppose this masterpiece were a miraculous piece of work—if then the artist out of love to some person were to dash it to pieces: such a sight would be up-building.

Wherever there is building up, love is present, and wherever love is, there is building up. Therefore Paul says that a loveless man, even though he were to speak in the tongues of men and of angels, would still be like a noisy gong and a clanging cymbal.[4] And what is less edifying than a clanging cymbal! Worldliness, no matter how splendid and acclaimed, is loveless, and therefore does not build up. The most trivial expression or the slightest action builds up if said or done with love or in love. Knowledge puffs up.[5] And yet knowledge and the communication of knowledge can also be edifying; but if they are, it is because love is present. To commend oneself hardly seems edifying, and yet this, too, can build up. Does not Paul do this at times? But he does it in love and therefore, as he himself says, " for up-building."[6] Therefore to speak of what can build up would be the most interminable discourse of all discourses, because everything can build up; it would be the most inexhaustible discourse, alas, as inexhaustible as the most sorrowful complaining which can be carried on in the world—that one sees and hears so little that builds up. If it is rare to see great wealth, it makes no difference; nevertheless, we at least want to see ordinary economic well-being. If it is rare to see a masterpiece, in a certain sense it makes no difference, and in this respect it makes no difference to the majority of men. But building up is quite different. At every moment there live innumerable human beings; it is possible that everything every man undertakes and everything every man says can build up. Alas—and yet it is very rare to see or hear anything which builds up!

Love builds up. Let us now consider what was developed in the introduction wherein we straightway made sure that the discourse would not go astray in choosing an insuperable task, inasmuch as everything can build up. To build up is to construct something from the ground up. In the simple illustration of a house, a building, everyone knows what is meant by ground and foundation. But spiritually understood, what are the ground and foundation of the life of the spirit which are to bear the building? In very fact it is love; love is the origin of everything, and spiritually understood love is the deepest ground of the life of the spirit. Spiritually understood, the foundation is laid in every person in whom there is love. And the edifice which, spiritually understood, is to be constructed, is again love; and it is love which edifies. Love builds up, and it is this which love builds up. In this way the task is limited: the discourse does not spread out into particulars and multiplicities; it does not confusedly begin with something which must arbitrarily be cut off in order to be concluded. No, it concentrates itself and its attention on what is essential, on the one and the same in the many. From the beginning to the end the discourse is on love, for the simple reason that love's most characteristic qualification is to build up. Love is the ground; love is the building; love builds up. To build up is to build up love, and it is love which builds up. At times we talk quite appropriately about building up in a more ordinary sense. In contrast to the corruption which seeks only to tear down or in contrast to the confusion which can only tear down and disintegrate, we say that a capable man is constructive, one who knows how to guide and to lead, one who knows how to instruct effectively in his field, one who is a master in his art. All such persons build up in contrast to tearing down. But all such building up in knowledge, in insight, in expertness, in rectitude, *etc.*, insofar as it does not build up love, is not in the deepest sense up-building. This is because, spiritually, love is the *ground*, and to build up means precisely to construct from the *ground* up.

Therefore when the discourse is about the works of love in building up, it must mean *either* that the lover implants love in the heart of another person *or* that the lover presupposes that love is in the other person's heart and precisely with this presupposition builds up love in him—from the ground up, insofar as in love he presupposes it present as the ground. One of the two must exist for building up. But I wonder whether or not one person can implant love in the heart of another person. No, this is a more-than-human relationship, a relationship unthinkable between man and man; in this sense human love cannot build up. It is God, the creator, who must implant love in each person, he who himself is love. Therefore it is essentially unloving and not at all up-building for anyone presumptuously to conceive of himself as desiring and able to create love in another person; all energetic and self-assertive zeal in this regard neither builds up love nor is itself up-building. The first relationship for up-building is, then, unthinkable.

Therefore we must consider the other relationship. Thus we have achieved a clarification of what it means that love builds up and on this we shall dwell: *the lover presupposes that love is in the other person's heart, and by this very presupposition he builds up love in him—from the ground up, insofar as in love he presupposes it present as the ground.*

Therefore the discourse cannot be about what the lover who desires to build up should do to transform the other person or to constrain love to come forth in him; it is rather about how the lover constrains himself. See, it is already up-building to consider that the lover builds up by constraining himself! Only one lacking in love imagines himself able to build up by constraining the other; the lover continually presupposes that love is present; precisely in this way he builds up. A builder gives little thought to the stone and gravel he is to use for a building. A teacher presupposes that the pupil is ignorant. A disciplinarian presupposes that the other person is corrupted. But the lover, who builds up, has only one mode of progression—to presuppose love. What is to be done further can only be to constrain himself continually to presuppose love. In this way he entices forth the good; he " loves up " [*opelsker*] love; he builds up. For love can and will be treated in only one way—by being loved forth. To love forth love is to build up. But to love forth love means precisely to presuppose that it is present at the base. A man might be tempted to be a builder, a teacher, or a disciplinarian because these seem to be ways to rule over others, but to build up as love does cannot tempt one, for this seems only to be a servant. Therefore only love has the desire to build up, because it is willing to serve.—The builder can point to his work and say, " This is my work," the teacher to his pupil; but love which builds up has nothing to point to, for its very work consists only in presupposing. This is again very up-building to consider. Suppose that a lover did succeed in building up love in another person. When the building stands, the lover stands aside and humbly says, " Indeed, I presupposed this all the time." Alas, the lover has no merit at all. The building does not stand as a monument to the craft of the builder or, like the pupil, as a reminder of the teacher's instruction. The lover has indeed done nothing; he has only presupposed that love was fundamentally present. The lover works very quietly and earnestly, and yet the powers of the eternal are in motion. Love humbly makes itself inconspicuous especially when it works hardest; yes, its work is what makes it as nothing at all. Alas, to busyness and worldliness this is the greatest foolishness—that what in a certain sense is doing nothing

at all should be the most difficult work. And yet it is so. For it is more
difficult to rule one's mind than to occupy a city,[7] and it is more
difficult to build up as love does than to complete the most astonishing
undertaking. If in relationship to oneself it is difficult to rule one's
mind, how difficult it is in relationship to another person to make oneself absolutely nothing, and yet to do everything and suffer everything!
If it is usually difficult to begin without presuppositions, it is in truth
most difficult to begin to build up with the presupposition that love
is present and to end with the same presupposition: thus one's entire
labour is from the outset reduced to nothing in that the presupposition
is, first and last, self-renunciation or that the builder is hidden and is
as nothing. Therefore we can compare this up-building of love only
with the work of nature in secret. While men sleep, the forces of nature
do not sleep, neither day nor night. No one gives a thought to how
they carry on—although everyone delights in the beauty of the meadow
and the fruitfulness of the field. This is the way love conducts itself;
it presupposes that love is present, like the germ in a kernel of grain,
and if it succeeds in bringing it to fruition, love hides itself just as it
was hidden while it worked early and late. That which edifies in nature
is precisely this: you see all this magnificence and then it penetrates
you edifyingly as you begin to reflect on the amazing fact that you do
not see the one who brings it forth. If you could see God with the
physical eye, if he, if I dare say it, stood alongside and said, " It is I
who have brought this forth "—the up-building would then be
dissipated.

Love builds up by presupposing that love is present. In this way
one lover builds up the other, and here where its presence is acknowl-
edged, it is easy enough to presuppose love. But, alas, love is never
completely present in any person; this being the case, it is still possible
to do something other than to presuppose it, to discover one or another
flaw or frailty in him. When someone has unlovingly detected this, he
will perhaps remove it, pull the sliver out, as one says, in order to build
up love properly. But love builds up. To him who loves much is much
forgiven;[8] but the more perfectly the lover presupposes love to exist,
the more perfect is the love which he loves forth. Among all the
relationships in the world there is no other relationship in which there
is such a like-for-like, such an accurate correspondence of yield to what
had been presupposed. One makes no protests, one does not cite
experience, for it would indeed be unloving arbitrarily to set the day
when the result should make its appearance. Love does not understand

such things; it is eternally confident of the fullfillment of the pre-supposition. If this is not the case, love is already on the way to exhaustion.

Love builds up by presupposing that love is fundamentally present. Therefore love also builds up when, humanly speaking, love seems to be absent and where, humanly understood, the first and foremost need is to tear down, certainly not for the sake of gratification but for the sake of salvation. To tear down is the opposite of building up. The contrast never appears more clearly than when the discourse is concerned with love as building up; for in any other discussion about building up there is a similarity to tearing down—it means to do something with another. But when the lover builds up it is the very opposite of tearing down, for the lover does something about himself: he presupposes that love is present in the other person—which is quite the opposite to doing something about the other person. Only too easily does tearing down satisfy the sensual man; to build up in the sense that one does something with the other person can also satisfy sensuality; but to build up by conquering oneself satisfies only love. And yet this is the only mode of building up. But in the well-intentioned zeal to tear down and build up, one forgets that ultimately no man is capable of laying the ground of love in the other person.

Right here the difficulty of the building art practised by love and described in the prized passage from the apostle Paul (I Corinthians 13) emerges, for what is said *there* about love is a precise characterisation of how it conducts itself in building up. " *Love is patient* "; by this it builds up, for patience specifically means perseverance in presupposing that love is fundamentally present. One who judges, even though he does this leisurely, one who judges that the other person lacks love takes the ground-work away—and he cannot build up; for love builds up with patience. Therefore " *It is not irritable or resentful,*" for irritability and resentment deny love in the other person and thereby annihilate, if it were possible, the ground-work. Love, however, which builds up, bears the other person's misunderstanding, his thanklessness, his anger—this is already enough to bear; how then should love also bear irritability and resentment! In the world things are dealt out in such a way that he who bears irritability and resentment does not bear the other person's burdens; but the lover, who does not bear irritability and resentment, bears the burdens. Each one bears his own burdens, the resentful man and the lover; both of them in a certain sense become martyrs, for as a pious man has said: the resentful person is a

martyr, but the devil's. [9] "*Love does not insist on its own way*"; therefore
it builds up. For he who seeks his own way must push everything else
aside; he must demolish in order to make room for his own which he
wants to build up. But love presupposes that love is fundamentally
present; therefore it builds up. "*It does not rejoice at wrong.*" But one
who wants to tear down or at least wants to be prominent through
the idea that it is necessary to tear down must be said to rejoice at
wrong—otherwise there would indeed be nothing to tear down. On the
other hand, love rejoices in presupposing that love is fundamentally
present; therefore it builds up. "*Love bears all things,*" for what is it to
bear all things but in the long run to find in everything the love which is
fundamentally presupposed. When we say of a very healthy man that he
can eat or drink anything, we mean that in his strength he draws nourishment out of poor food (just as the sickly are harmed even by sound food);
we mean that his soundness takes nourishment out of what seems least
nourishing. In the same way love bears all things, continually presupposing that love is still fundamentally present—and thereby it
builds up. "*Love believes all things,*" for to believe all things means
precisely, even though love is not apparent, even though the opposite
is seen, to presuppose that love is nevertheless present fundamentally,
even in the misguided, even in the corrupt, even in the hateful. Mistrust takes the very ground-level away by presupposing that love is not
present; therefore mistrust cannot build up. "*Love hopes all things,*"
but to hope all things means, even though love is not apparent, even
though the opposite is seen, to presuppose that love is nevertheless
fundamentally present and that it will show itself in the deluded, in the
misguided, and even in the lost. Remember that the prodigal son's
father was perhaps the only one who did not know that he had a
prodigal son, for the father's love hoped all things. The brother
promptly saw that he was hopelessly lost. But love builds up, and the
father won the lost son again just because he who hoped all things
presupposed that love was fundamentally present. In spite of the son's
misguided conduct there was no break on the father's side (a break is
just the opposite of building up); he hoped all things; therefore he in
truth built up through his fatherly forgiveness, since the son vividly
grasped the fact that fatherly love had carried through with him and
that there had been no break. "*Love endures all things,*" for to bear all
things means precisely to presuppose that love is fundamentally present.
When we say that a mother endures all the child's naughtiness, do we
mean that as a woman she patiently suffers evil? No, we mean some-

thing else, that she as a mother continually remembers that the child is a child, and therefore she presupposes that the child still loves her and that this love will show itself eventually. Otherwise we should have discussed how patience endures all things, not how love endures all things. For patience endures all things and remains silent. If the mother endured the child's naughtiness in this way, then we would have said that basically the mother and the child have become strangers to one another. Love, however, endures all things, is patiently silent—but in all quietness presupposes that love is nevertheless present in the other person.

In this way love builds up. "*It is not jealous or boastful; it is not arrogant or rude; it is not irritable or resentful.*" It is not boastful over the thought that it should create love in the other person. It is not impatiently resentful and arrogant, almost hopelessly busy with first tearing down in order to build up again. No, it continually presupposes that love is fundamentally present. Therefore to see love build up is unconditionally the most up-building sight, a sight to edify even the angels; therefore it is unconditionally up-building if a man successfully describes: how love builds up. There is many a friendly sight, many gripping, many elevating, many captivating, many persuasive sights and the like, but there is only one up-building sight: to see love build up. Therefore whatever of terror and atrocity you have seen in the world, something you desire only to forget because it depresses your courage and your confidence and gives you a distaste for life and disgust for living—consider only how love builds up and you are built up for living! There are numerous things to discuss, but there is only one up-building subject: how love builds up. Therefore whatever experience you may have had, however embittering, so much so that you may wish never to have been born and the sooner the better to become silent in death—think only of how love edifies, and you will again be built up to speak! There is only one up-building sight and only one up-building subject; yet everything can be said and be done for up-building, for wherever up-building is, there love is, and wherever love is, there is up-building, and as soon as love is present, it builds up.

Love builds up by presupposing that love is present. Have you, my reader, experienced this yourself? If any person has ever spoken to you in such a way or acted toward you in such a way that you really felt yourself built up, it was because you quite vividly perceived that he presupposed love to be present in you. Or what kind of person do you think another man might be who could in truth build you up? Is it not true that you would wish him to have insight, knowledge, talent, and experience? But still you would not consider these to be decisive but rather that he was a reliable, loving person, that is, truly a loving person. Consequently you consider that up-building depends decisively and essentially upon loving or having love to such a degree that one can abandon himself to it. But what, then, is love? Love means to presuppose love; to have love means to presuppose love in others; to be loving means to presuppose that others are loving. Let us understand each other. The qualities a man can possess must be either qualities he has for himself, even if he makes use of them in relationship to others, or qualities for others. Wisdom is a characteristic for oneself; power, talents, knowledge, and such are likewise qualities for oneself. To be wise does not mean to presuppose that others are wise. It may, however, be very wise and true for a truly wise person to assume that all men are far from being wise. Because *wise* is an exclusive characteristic, it is not impossible to suppose that there could be or could have been a wise man who dared say that he assumed all others to be ignorant. In theory (to be wise and to assume that all others are ignorant) there is no contradiction. In the actuality of life such an expression would be arrogance, but in pure theory there is no contradiction. If, however, one were to think that he loves, but also that all others were unloving, we would say: no, stop; here is a contradiction in pure theory, for to be loving means precisely to assume, to presuppose, that other men are loving. Love is not an exclusive characteristic, but it is a characteristic by which or in virtue of which you exist for others. In ordinary speech we properly say, when reckoning a person's qualities, that he is wise, understanding, loving—and we do not notice what a difference there is between the last characteristic and the first ones. His wisdom, his experience, and his understanding he has for himself, even if he makes gifts of them to others. But if he truly is loving, then he does not have love in the same sense that he has wisdom, but his love consists precisely in presupposing that we others have love. When you praise him as a loving person, you mean that love is a characteristic which he possesses, which it is, too, and you feel yourself built up by him, simply because he is loving, but you do not detect the true explanation, that his love means he presupposes love in you and that you are built up precisely by this, that precisely by this is love built up in you. If it really were so that a person could be loving without its signifying the presupposing of love in others, then in the deepest sense you would not feel yourself built up, however certain it might be that he was loving; in the deepest sense you would not feel yourself built up, no more than you are in the deepest sense built up by his knowledge, no matter how certain it is that he is wise, understanding, experienced, learned. If it were possible that he could be truly loving without its signifying the presupposing of love in others, then you could not abandon yourself wholly to him, for the trustworthiness of one who loves is precisely in this, that even when you have doubts about yourself, whether there is love in you, he is loving enough to presuppose love, or better, that he is the lover, who presupposes love.—But you demanded that a person, in order truly to build up, should in truth be loving. And to be loving has shown itself to signify: to presuppose love in others. Therefore you say exactly the same as has been developed in the discourse.

Now these reflections return to the beginning. To build up means to presuppose love; to be loving means to presuppose love; only love builds up. For to build up means to draw forth something from the ground up, but, spiritually, love is the ground of everything. No man can bestow the ground of love in another man's heart; nevertheless, love is the ground, and one can build up only from the ground up; therefore one can build up only by presupposing love. Take love away —then there is no one who builds up and no one who is built up.

II

Love Believes All Things—and

Yet Is Never Deceived

" Love . . . believes all things." (*I Corinthians* 13 : 7)

" So faith, hope, and love abide, these three; but the greatest of these is love," which is, therefore, the very ground of everything, exists before everything, and remains when everything else is abolished. Love is therefore the "greatest" among "these," but that which in the sense of perfection (and what greater perfection is there for comparison than hope and faith!) is the greatest must also be able to undertake the business of the lesser ones (if I may put it this way) and make them more perfect. In a worldly sense one might at some time be outstanding without being greatest in the sense of perfection, but this is precisely the imperfection of the worldly. It certainly holds true that the greatest must be able to do what the lesser are able to do, and it holds true of love that it can take upon itself the work of faith and hope and make them even more perfect.

We shall now consider this as we ponder that

LOVE BELIEVES ALL THINGS—AND YET IS NEVER DECEIVED.

First, we shall consider how we are to understand that love believes all things and, second, how the lover, simply by believing all things, can be assured against deception, for truly not everyone who believes all things is on that account a lover, and not everyone who believes all things is on that account assured against every deception—not even faith, if it is to believe all things. And even if it might seem that to be assured against every deception is a good thing for love, a superior excellence it possesses, this subject really does not lend itself for consideration in a book on the *works* of love, because an excellence is not a work. To be assured against every deception is an act, a task, completely synonymous with believing all things, so that one can just as well say without qualification that love believes all things or that it never is deceived, since they are one and the same thing. It is not, as is customary, that acting is one thing and prudence which guards against a man's being deceived is something else. Nor is it from the standpoint of prudence that love is never deceived, for according to the language and view of prudence to love in such a way that one is never deceived is the most foolish and stupid thing a man can do. Yes, it is an offence to prudence—and therefore clearly recognisable as belonging essentially to Christianity.

Love believes all things.—Frivolity, inexperience, simplicity believe everything that is said; vanity, conceit, self-satisfaction believe everything flattering that is said; envy, spite, corruption believe everything evil that is said; mistrust believes nothing at all. Experience will teach that one acts most prudently by not believing everything—but love believes all things.

Since mistrust[10] believes nothing at all, it does just the opposite of what love does. Of course, mistrust is generally not well regarded, but from this it still does not follow either that men are agreed unconditionally to do away with all mistrust, or that they are agreed unconditionally to recommend love which believes all things. Strangely enough, men perhaps prefer to make a compromise, consequently a contentious compromise between mistrust, which loving a little nevertheless believes something, and love, which somewhat mistrustful nevertheless has this and that misgiving. Yes, if one were to draw the deep secret of mistrust out into the open, if one were to show in full magnitude the impressive form of its shrewdness, cunning, and kindness, then it might indeed tempt many. Perhaps there would be someone who would shrewdly give us to understand that this is precisely what he had discovered—and be proud of his discovery. In contrast to this, love, which believes all things, would make a very poor showing (as happens so often to the good), so that many would never again dare be known to admit that he could desire to be so simple-minded.

What, then, is the deep secret of mistrust? It is a misuse of knowledge, a misuse which straightway wishes in one breath to link its conclusion and interpretation to something which as knowledge is entirely true; this *ergo* first becomes something quite different when it is believed, upside down, in virtue of the knowledge, a procedure which is just as impossible as it is upside down, for one does not believe on the basis of knowledge. What mistrust says or presents is really only knowledge; the secret or the falsity lies in this that it straightway converts this knowledge into a belief, making belief appear to be nothing at all, making it appear as if it were something requiring no attention, since surely everyone who has the same knowledge "must *necessarily* come to the same conclusion," as if it were therefore eternally certain and absolutely decided that when knowledge is given the conclusion is also decided. The deception is that *from* knowledge (for the appearance and the falsity are that it is on the basis of knowledge) mistrust, on the *basis* of the disbelief which is in mistrust, concludes, assumes, and believes what it concludes, assumes and believes; whereas from the same knowledge, on the *basis* of belief, one can conclude, suppose, and believe the very opposite. Mistrust says: " Deception stretches unconditionally as far as the truth, falsity unconditionally as far as honesty; there is no unconditional criterion of truth or of honesty and integrity. So it is also with love; hypocrisy, artifice, wiliness, and seduction stretch unconditionally as far as love does, and they can imitate true love so strikingly that there is no absolute criterion, because in every expression of truth or of true love there exists the possibility of deception which corresponds to it exactly." And so it is; so shall it be. Precisely because existence will test *you*, test *your* love or whether there is love in you, for this very reason with the help of the understanding it presents you with truth and deception as two equal possibilities in contrast to each other, so that there must be a revelation of what is in you since *you* judge, that is, since in judging you *choose*. Alas, many think that judgment is something reserved for the far side of the grave, and so it is. But one forgets that judgment lies much closer, that it takes place every moment, because existence judges you every moment you live, inasmuch as to live is to judge oneself, to become open. For this very reason existence must be so arranged that you do not with the aid of certainty in knowledge slink out of revealing yourself in judging or in the way you judge. When deception and truth are presented as two equal possibilities in contrast to each other, the decision is whether there is love or mistrust in you. For example, one says, " Even what appears to be the purest feeling can nevertheless be a deception—certainly it is possible; it must be possible—*ergo* I choose mistrust or belief in nothing." This means that one reveals his mistrust. Let us turn the conclusion around: " Truth and falsity reach unconditionally just as far; therefore it is possible that even what appears as the vilest behaviour could be pure love "—well, now, it is possible; it must be possible—*ergo* the lover chooses to believe all things, that is, he reveals his love. A confused person certainly thinks that existence is a rather muddled setting—O, the sea is not so transparent! Therefore, if on the basis of the possibility of deception someone can demonstrate that one should believe nothing at all, I can demonstrate that one should believe all things—on the basis of the possibility of deception. If someone thinks that a man should not believe even the best person, for it is still possible that he is a deceiver, then the opposite also holds true, that you can expect the good from even the lowest fellow, for it is still possible that his baseness is an illusion.

Love is the very opposite of mistrust, and yet it is initiated in the same knowledge. In knowledge the two are, so to speak, not distinguished from each other (in the ultimate understanding knowledge is indifferent); only in conclusion and decision, *in faith* (to believe all things, to believe nothing), are they directly opposite to one another. When love believes all things, it is not at all in the same sense as frivolity, inexperience, simplicity, which believe all things on the grounds of naïveté and ignorance. No, above all, love knows better than anyone else everything that mistrust knows, yet without being mistrustful; love knows what experience knows, but it also knows that what men call experience is really a mixture of mistrust and love.

" How much of the hidden may still reside in a person or how much may still reside hidden! How inventive hidden inwardness is in concealing itself and in deceiving or in evading others; bashfully afraid of being seen and deathly afraid of becoming completely exposed, it prefers that others do not even suspect its existence! Is it not true that one man never completely understands another? But if he does not understand the other completely, then it always remains possible that what is most indisputable could still have a completely different interpretation which, mark well, would be the true interpretation, inasmuch as a hypothesis may superbly explain a great multiplicity of instances, thereby strengthening its truth, and nevertheless show itself to be untrue as soon as the instance appears which it cannot explain—and yet it was entirely possible that this instance or this somewhat more precise determination could come only at the last moment. Because of this, all patient and in the spiritual sense passionless observers who expertly seek understanding by piercing the inner man inquiringly and deeply, these very ones judge very cautiously or abstain from judgment entirely, because enriched by observation they have an enlarged conception of the enigmatic world of the hidden and because as observers they have learned to rule their passions. Only superficial, impetuous, passionate men judge straight off, men who do not know themselves and consequently do not know that they do not know others; those who know, those with insight, never act in this way. A young, inexperienced person, who has perhaps never sat on a horse before, straightway leaps up on the first horse that comes along; but the hardened, practised horse-trainer—you note with what precision he observes the strange horse the first time he is to ride, how doubtfully and carefully he goes about it, how he hardly ventures to mount but first lets it run lassoed in order to get its temper, and, further, how long he keeps on checking, long, long after the inexperienced rider has given up. The inexperienced person who knows nothing at all about horses thinks ' One horse is like all the others—*ergo* I know them all '; only the horse-trainer has a developed conception of what a great difference there can be, how one can make mistakes about a horse in the most varied and contrasting ways, and how ambiguous all the clues are, because every horse is yet somewhat different. And now the difference between man and man! How infinite! If it were not so, man would be devalued, for human superiority over the animals is not only what one most often mentions, the universally human, but it is also what one most often forgets, that within the race every individual is essentially different or unique. This superiority is the really human superiority. The first superiority is the superiority of the race over animal types. Yes, if it were not so, that the single human being, honourable, upright, respectable, God-fearing, can under the same circumstances do the opposite to what another person does, one who is also honourable, upright, respectable, God-fearing—then the God-relationship would not essentially exist, not in its deepest sense.[11] If one could with unqualified truthfulness judge every human being according to an established universal criterion, the God-relationship would essentially be done away with; then everything would turn outward, fullfilling itself paganly in political or social life; then to live would become much too easy, but also exceedingly empty; then exertion or the deepening of the self would be neither possible nor required, and yet precisely in the most difficult collision of infinite misunderstanding the God-relationship in a man develops."

Now can you tell me who said this? No, it is an impossibility. It is completely ambiguous; the most mistrustful and the most loving person, as far as knowledge is involved, could equally well have said it. No human being has said this; it is non-humanly spoken. It is a sound which first became human speech in the differentiating inspiration of the personality which gave it expression by adding voice to it. It is knowledge, and knowledge *per se* is impersonal and must be communicated impersonally. Knowledge places everything in the category of possibility, and to the extent that it is in possibility it is outside the reality of existence. The individual first of all begins his life with *ergo*, with *faith*. But most men do not even faintly notice that in one way or another at every moment of their lives they live by virtue of an *ergo*, by a faith—so carelessly do they live. In knowledge there is no decision; decision, the determinedness and determining characteristic of personalities is first in *ergo*, in faith. Knowledge is the infinite art of equivocation or the infinite equivocation; at its utmost it means precisely to place contrasting possibilities in equilibrium. To be able to do this is to have knowledge, and only he who knows how to communicate contrasting possibilities in equipoise, only he communicates knowledge. To communicate decision in knowledge or knowledge in decision is upside-down, which in these times certainly has been done—yes, it is and continues to be upside-down—but in these times it has become truly profound, the true profundity of profound thought. Knowledge is not mistrust, for knowledge is infinitely detached, the infinite indifference in equilibrium; nor is knowledge love, for knowledge is infinitely detached, is the infinite indifference in equilibrium; nor is knowledge a contamination; since it is infinitely detached. The mistrustful person and the lover have knowledge in common, and neither is the mistrustful person mistrustful because of knowledge nor is the loving person loving because of knowledge. But when a man's knowledge has placed contrasting possibilities in equilibrium and he wants or has to judge, then what he believes in becomes apparent, who he is, whether he is mistrustful or loving. Only very confused and inexperienced people think they can judge another person on the basis of knowledge. This is so because they do not even know what knowledge is; they have never devoted time and labour to developing the infinite, indifferent sense for possibilities, or with the infinite art of equivocation to grasp the possibilities and get them in equilibrium, or to reach the bottom in transparency. In a yeasty-like state they have a supine or a passionate predilection for a certain kind of possibility; a little of it is enough, they consider, and they call this judging on the basis of knowledge. And self-satisfied they think that by this—believing on the basis of knowledge (a clear contradiction)—they are assured against error—which would be faith with reservations (a new contradiction).

It is very common to hear men express great fear of making a mistake in judging. But when you listen a little more carefully to what is said, alas, there is often a sad misunderstanding in this—solemn fear. Consider the noble, wise man of ancient days. He became what he became—and it was not anything very great—neither a big business man nor high-ranking statesman in this best of all possible worlds. Impoverished, laughed at, scorned, accused, condemned, he became the noble, simple wise man, still a rarity, almost the only one who really made a distinction between what he understood and what he did not understand, and this he became precisely because he "feared most of all to be in error."[12] I wonder if it is this elevation of thought, this equilibrium of loftiness, which men have in mind when they are afraid of making a mistake in judging. Perhaps. Nevertheless, it is also quite possible that the fear is at times somewhat one-sided. All men have a natural fear of making a mistake—by believing too well of a person. However, the error of believing too ill of a person is perhaps not feared, at least not in the same degree as the other. If, then, we are not most of all afraid of being in error, we are nevertheless in error by having a one-sided fear of a certain kind of error. It puts a crimp in vanity and pride to believe or to have believed too well of a swindler, to have been foolish enough to believe him—for this is a competition between cleverness and cleverness. One is peeved with himself, or one finds rather that it is "so stupid" to have been fooled (yes, this is what we say, and indeed it does not help, or more accurately it is a deception, to use a more solemn, less popular expression in an up-building discourse). Yet should it not occur to us, to speak mildly, that it is just as stupid to have believed ill or mistrustfully to have believed nothing where there was good? I wonder if in eternity it will not become more than—"stupid." Let us use only the expression casually used in the world; it shows up just as well in relationship to the eternal! But here in the world it is not "stupid" to believe ill of a good man; indeed, it is a superciliousness whereby one gets rid of the good in a convenient way. But it is "stupid" to believe well of an evil person; therefore one guards himself —since one so greatly fears being in error. On the other hand, the lover truly fears being in error; therefore he believes all things.

The world tempts in many ways; among these is making it appear that *lovingly* to believe all things would be very restrictive, very foolish. But this is a misunderstanding! One crosses out love (alas, instead of underlining it!) and then lets the accent fall on the foolishness: to believe all things, instead of letting the primary accent fall on the *love* which believes all things. Truly, it is not knowledge which defiles a man, far from it. Knowledge is like the sheerest transparency, precisely the most perfect and purest, like the purest water, which has no taste at all. The magistrate is not defiled because he knows more about the plots than the criminal. No, knowledge does not defile a man; it is mistrust which defiles a man's knowledge just as love purifies it.

As far as judging another person is concerned, knowledge at best leads to the equilibrium of contrasting possibilities—and then the distinction becomes apparent in what is concluded. Scripture warns against judging and adds " lest you be judged."[13] It still seems as if at times one might judge without being judged in return. But this is not the case. At the very moment you judge another person or criticise another person, you judge yourself. For to judge another means ultimately only to judge oneself or to reveal oneself. Perhaps it escapes your attention; you perhaps do not notice how earnest existence is, how by showing you all these people it provides you, as it were, occasions for judging, so that you even count yourself fortunate to be among these undeservedly happily favoured ones who are nothing and therefore in unconcern have the cosy job of judging others; then it is existence which is courteous or powerful enough not to regard you as nothing; then it is existence which judges you. However greedy a man might be for judging—if he knew what it is to judge, how slow he would become! However wildly he snatches at the smallest crumb in order to have the occasion to judge—it is an opportunity to ensnare himself! Through knowledge one arrives only at equilibrium, especially when the art is perfectly practised; but the conclusion turns back into the being of the judger and makes it manifest—that he is a loving person, for he concludes: *ergo* I believe all things.

Mistrust, however, has a penchant for evil (naturally not through its knowledge, which is the infinitely indifferent, but through itself, through its unbelief). To believe nothing is right on the border where believing evil begins; the good is the object of faith, and therefore one who believes nothing begins to believe evil. To believe nothing is the beginning of *being* evil, for it shows that one has no good in him, since faith is precisely the good in a man, which does not come through great knowledge, nor need it be lacking because knowledge is meagre. Mistrust cannot maintain knowledge in equilibrium; it defiles its knowledge and therefore tends towards envy, spite, corruption, which believes all evil. But what about the one who was so eager to judge, to pour out his resentment, his powerful or puny bitterness, over another, without knowing accurately whereof he judged? What if in eternity he discovers and is constrained to confess that the one judged was not only innocent, but that he was the noblest, most disinterested, the finest spirited man! Men say that sometimes in eternity (hoping, alas, that we ourselves shall not be excluded) we shall in amazement miss one or another person whom we had definitely expected to find there; but I also wonder if we shall not see with amazement one or another whom men would have straightway excluded and note that he is far superior to us, not that he became this afterwards but was superior precisely in that which led the judgers to exclude him. But one who loves believes all things. With the blessed joy of amazement he will at some time see that he was right, and if he erred by believing too well—to believe the good is in itself a blessing. In love to believe good is indeed no error; one rather errs, therefore, by not doing it.

In mistrust *to believe* nothing at all and lovingly *to believe* everything (which are quite different from the *knowledge* of the equality of these mutually contrasting possibilities) are neither understanding nor conclusions of understanding, but a choice which makes its appearance precisely when knowledge has placed these two mutually contrasting possibilities into balance; and in this choice, which rightly is in the form of a judgment over other choices, the judger becomes revealed. That frivolity, inexperience, and simplicity believe everything is an understanding, a foolish understanding; *in love to believe* everything is a choice through the power of love. Instead of using its keenness to strengthen itself in believing nothing, as mistrust does, love uses its keenness to discover the same thing—that deception and truth both stretch just as far—and now concludes in the power of the faith which it has; *ergo* I believe everything.

Love believes everything—and yet is never to be deceived. Amazing! To believe nothing in order never to be deceived—this seems to make sense. For how would a man ever be able to deceive someone who believes nothing! But to believe everything and thereby, as it were, to throw oneself away, fair game for all deception and all deceivers, and yet precisely in this way to assure oneself infinitely against every deception: this is remarkable. And yet, even if one is not deceived by others, I wonder whether he is not deceived anyway, most terribly deceived, precisely by himself, by believing nothing at all, deceived out of the highest, out of the blessedness of devotedness, out of the blessedness of love! No, there is only one way to assure oneself against never being deceived; that is to believe all things in love.

Let us put it this way: can a man deceive God? No, in relationship to God a man can deceive only himself. For the God-relationship is the highest good in such a way that he who deceives God frightfully deceives himself. Or let us take the relationship between man and man. Can a child deceive its parents? No, the child deceives himself; there is only the illusion (consequently a deception), the fuzziness of short-sightedness, which makes it appear to the child and to one who has no better understanding than the child as if it were the child who deceived the parents—alas, whereas the poor child essentially deceives himself. One must reasonably assume that in relationship to the child the parents have such a superiority in wisdom and insight and therefore also such a superiority in true love for the child, who quite poorly understands how to love himself, that to deceive the parents would be the greatest misfortune which could befall the child, the greatest misfortune, if it were not his own fault. Indeed, then, it is—in truth—not the parents who are deceived, but rather the child, and it is an illusion (a deception) that the child deceives the parents. In a *childish and foolish* understanding the child does deceive the parents, but *consequently* it is in fact not true, since it is true only according to "childish and foolish understanding." On the other hand, would it not be a miserable, disgusting sight to see a father or mother who in relationship to the child did not have the true, serious, concerned view of superiority, grounded in an eternal responsibility to will in truth the best for the child! Would it not be miserable and disgusting to see a father or mother who could therefore sink into unseemly wrangling with the child, become irritated and embittered over their own mistakes, because the father and mother childishly had the foolish opinion that it was the child who deceived them! Such a relationship between parents and child is indeed unseemly, yes, almost as senseless as if spanking a child meant being struck by the child and in this way, by setting aside all values, uprightness, and authoritative superiority, proving only that the father and mother are stronger in the physical sense.

Therefore true superiority can never be deceived, if it remains true to itself. But in relationship to everything which is not love, therefore in relationship to every deception, true love is unconditionally superior; consequently it can never be deceived if in believing all things it remains true to itself or continues to be true love.

This certainly is very easy to comprehend. The difficulty, therefore, is elsewhere; there is a lower sphere of understanding which has no intimation of true love, of love in and for itself, and of this blessedness in itself. The difficulty is that a great multiplicity of illusions will hold a man down in this lower sphere of understanding where deception and being deceived signify exactly the opposite of what they signify *in the infinite conception of love. According to this view to be deceived signifies simply and solely to quit loving, to be carried away to the point of abandoning love in and for itself, and in this way to lose its intrinsic blessedness.* For only one deception is possible in the infinite sense—self-deception. One need not infinitely fear them who are able to kill the body; to be killed is, infinitely, no danger; nor is the kind of deception the world talks about a danger. And, again, this is not difficult to understand. The difficult thing is to fullfill the task of acquiring the true conception of love or, better yet, to become the true lover. For he defends himself against deception and fights to preserve himself in the true love precisely by believing all things. But the illusion will continually obtrude itself as does the illusion which maintains that the sun moves, although one still knows that it is the earth.

There is a lower conception of love, therefore a lower love which has no notion of love in and for itself. This view regards loving as a demand (reciprocated love is the demand) and to be loved (the reciprocated love) as a temporal, as an earthly good—alas, and yet as the highest blessedness. Yes, when this is so, deception certainly is able to play the master, just as in the commercial world. One pays out money in order to purchase this or that convenience; one pays the money but does not obtain the convenience—yes, in this way one is fooled. One makes a transaction of love; one pays out his love in exchange, but one gets no love in exchange—yes, in this way one is deceived. Consequently the deception consists in the deceiver's winning the love of the deceived, and perhaps the deceived cannot even cease loving the deceiver because he loved at least to the degree that he could love only one person, and this one person was the deceiver. It is not the intention in this sketch to deny either that the lover was deceived or that the deceiver was, yes, that he was a miserable deceiver; but it is the intention to deny that the lover was a true lover. For he who is— such an extraordinary lover—that he is able to love only one person is not the true lover but one smitten with love, and one smitten with love is a self-lover, as previously shown. But that one can deceive a self-lover the discourse has never sought to deny. Here as everywhere in existence there is something very profound. One often hears a lofty complaint about being deceived in love. The plaintiff wishes to demonstrate what a rare lover he himself is, and then again, how unusually shabby the deceiver is and was, and this he proves by affirming of himself that he can and could love only one person. He does not perceive that the more vehement his complaint becomes, the more it becomes a self-accusation which declares him to be and to have been a self-lover, who therefore quite rightly could love only one person (for the true lover loves all and without demanding reciprocated love), and therefore quite rightly could be deceived; whereas the true lover cannot. This means: everyone who essentially and decisively affirms that he has been deceived this way in love, that he has lost the best, even everything, thereby declares himself to be a self-lover; for the best is love in and for itself, and this one can always keep if one is a true lover. Therefore everyone who has only deception's lower concept of love takes good care that he does not become deceived; he learns from the financier or from those who trade in commodities what means of security are used against deceivers. Alas, and in spite of these means of security, yes, even if he succeeds in securing himself against every deception through these means—he and all like-minded persons are nevertheless essentially deceived by having their lives in the world, which is the illusion, in the world, where all are essentially victims, whether one deceived grumbles about someone else or the other person brags about not having been deceived. The difference is no greater than if in an insane asylum one patient were to consider himself better than another because he is not insane in the same way—whereas all of them are nevertheless essentially insane.

The lower conception of love and the illusion which men resort to in its service and to its honour are a temptation. The difficulty consists precisely in actively defending oneself against it, for in quiet moments it is easy enough to perceive that the true lover, who believes all things, cannot be deceived. "But still it is so stupid to be deceived." If you yourself were the true lover, who believes all things, you would nevertheless easily perceive that it is an impossibility, would perceive that you are not deceived. Is it, then, stupid to know within oneself that he is not deceived? No. "But still it is very stupid that he must seem so to others." See, here is the illusion. To know within oneself and in truth that one is not deceived and still find it stupid that one appears to have been deceived—what does one call this? One calls this vanity, or what in this case is the same, one calls it: not yet being completely the true lover. Alas, if vanity could gain power over the true lover, he would certainly be deceived, for vanity draws him down out of love into the lower world of mean-mindedness and wrangling, where one fools others and is fooled, where one is vain over being able to deceive and stupid in being fooled, and vain once again over being able to escape deception.—When we see the true lover become deceived by the sly, the intriguing, the hypocritical, we are disturbed, sometimes because we do not see visible punishment and retribution, consequently because we demand to see the theatricality of external retribution which is so satisfying to one's propensity for the imperfect and the external, consequently because we sink down into the lower conception, consequently because thoughtless and sluggish we forget that one cannot deceive the true lover. We are right in crying woe to one who leads the blind astray: it is entirely in order that here we demand to see external punishment, for one can deceive a blind person, inasmuch as being blind does not secure one against every deception; but one cannot deceive the true lover, who believes all things. In a certain sense the lover is quite aware if someone deceives him, but by not being willing to believe it or by believing all things he preserves himself in love and in this way is not deceived—therefore one sees here an example of the foolishness, the irrationality, of the bustling which thinks that knowing is superior to believing, for it is precisely believing all things which secures the lover, who in a certain sense knows that he is deceived, against being deceived.

One cannot deceive the true lover, who believes all things, for *to deceive him is to deceive oneself.* Indeed, what is the highest good and the greatest blessedness? Certainly it is to love in truth; next to this, to be loved in truth. But then it is impossible to deceive the lover, who precisely by believing all things abides in love. If it were possible to deceive someone in money matters in such a way that the so-called victim kept his money, would he then be betrayed? This is precisely the case here. By his attempt the deceiver becomes contemptible, and the lover preserves himself in love, abides in love and consequently in possession of the highest good and the greatest blessedness—therefore he certainly is not deceived! The deceiver, however, deceives himself. He does not love, and thereby he has deceived himself out of the highest good and the greatest blessedness. The next highest good is to be loved by one who loves in truth—otherwise to be loved could indeed become a great misfortune for one. Again the deceiver is on the way to deceive himself out of this, too, insofar as he prevents himself from having the true benefit of it and insofar as he should succeed, when his deception is eventually discovered, in wasting the other person's love and making the lover unhappy by his ceasing to love truly—instead of remaining in love by believing all things, secured against deception.

In order to make it quite clear, let us visualise how pitiable the deceiver looks in relationship to the true lover—for much is said of seducers and the seduced, of deception and deceivers, but men very rarely speak about or present an interpretation of the *true* lover. Therefore I imagine a sly one, an intriguer, a hypocrite; I take pleasure in endowing with all seductive talents this expert in all the secrets of deception. Now what does he want? He wishes to deceive the lover; he wishes (for in spite of his corruption he has enough understanding to perceive how great a good it is to be loved) through his craftiness to see himself beloved. But for what purpose are all these conditions, this completely superfluous arsenal of cunning and intrigue? It is the true lover he wants to deceive, but the true lover loves everyone, and therefore the deceiver is able quite simply to achieve his purpose of becoming the object of love. Yes, if the discourse were about erotic love (self-love), then there would still be some significance in the deception, for the erotic lover is able to love only the one and only, and therefore there is some point, if it is possible, in becoming the one and only through the deceptive art of cunning and craftiness. But as far as the true lover is concerned the deception is meaningless from the very beginning; from the very beginning the deceiver is put in the poorest light. But to go on—consequently the deceiver naturally succeeds in becoming loved, naturally—yes, the deceiver thinks and must naturally think that this is due to his cunning, his intrigue and art. Poor deceiver, he does not perceive that he is dealing with the true lover, who loves him because the true lover loves all men. In what meaninglessness the deceiver's contemptibleness is now trapped! It is not as if the deception failed—no, such punishment is far too mild—no, the deception succeeds and the deceiver is proud of his deception! But then where is the deception; what sort of deception does he speak of? Naturally the deception consists in this that while the lover loves him, he coldly and proudly and mockingly enjoys the self-satisfaction of not loving in return, in addition to enjoying the good of being loved. Naturally it completely escapes him (for how should the deceiver hit upon the idea that true love was present?) that he is involved with the true lover, who loves without making any demand of reciprocity, who grounds love and its blessedness precisely in not requiring reciprocity. The deceiver, therefore, has cunningly gotten the lover to love him—but this is just what the lover is infinitely willing to do; the deceiver has presumably fooled him by not loving in return—but the true lover regards the very requirement of reciprocity to be a contamination, a devaluation, and loving without the reward of reciprocated love to be the highest blessedness. Who, then, is the deceived? What sort of deception is being talked about? The deceiver mumbles in murkiness and does not himself know what he is saying, just like the man we all laugh at, the man who lay in the ditch and still thought he was riding. To deceive in this way—is it not like calling it stealing to slip money into a person's pocket? The true lover has become richer, because for every additional person he gets to love and for every additional time he gives his love with no claim of reciprocity, he becomes richer. Or is the true lover deceived if he does not get to know how unworthy an object of love the deceiver is? To love is indeed the highest good; but therefore only the love which demands reciprocity, consequently the untrue love, can be deceived by remaining ignorant of the fact that the object is unworthy. Or is the true lover deceived if he finds out how unworthy an object the deceiver is and was? To love is the highest good and the greatest blessedness. In financial transactions, for example, one who turns to a man he had depended on to lend him money and who supposedly had money is fooled if the man is insolvent and has no money. But someone who wishes to give his money away and does not demand to get it back again or desire it in the slightest way certainly is not fooled—if the recipient has no money. But the cunning deceiver, who moves with the most supple, most ingratiating flexibility of craftiness—he does not perceive how clumsily he proceeds. He imagines himself to be superior; he smiles in self-satisfaction (alas, it is like looking at the self-satisfied smile of an insane person, which is both to be laughed at and wept over!); he does not suspect that the lover is the infinitely superior one. The deceiver is blinded; he does not even notice his appalling impotence: his deception succeeds—and he performs a charitable deed; his deception succeeds—and he makes the lover still wealthier; the deception is a success for him, he succeeds—and yet it is precisely he who is deceived. Poor deceiver, even this way of salvation—that his deception fails—is cut off. If an insane person wishes to prove to one who is sane the rightness of his insane thoughts and if in a certain sense the demonstration succeeds, is not this the most appalling of all, is this not a kind of mercilessness on the part of existence, for if it did not succeed, the insane person might nevertheless in this way become aware of the fact that he is not sane, but now it is hidden from him and his insanity is quite incurable. So it is with the deceiver; but this is not merciless but rather righteous punishment upon him for the success of his deception—and in this way his very perdition.

What, then, is the conflict between the deceiver and the lover? The deceiver wants to trick him out of his love. This cannot be done; precisely by unconditionally not requiring the slightest reciprocity the true lover has assumed an unassailable position. He can no more be swindled out of his love than a man can be tricked out of the money he tenders as a gift and gives to a person. The strife, therefore, is essentially about something else—whether it could be possible for the deceiver (something which he does not in any way discern or think of) to become the occasion for the downfall of the lover, so that the lover falls away from love and sinks down into the illusory world of childish squabbling with the deceiver, because the lover has surrendered the love which loves without requiring reciprocity. But the true lover protects himself precisely by believing all things—consequently by loving the deceiver. If the deceiver could understand this, he might lose his mind. An erotic lover (the self-lover) considers himself to be deceived when the deceiver has fooled him into loving him while he does not love in return—and the true lover considers himself saved precisely when, by believing all things, he succeeds in loving the deceiver. The erotic lover regards it as a misfortune to continue loving the deceiver; the true lover regards it as a victory if he might only succeed in continuing to love the deceiver. Amazing! The deceiver may become more and more conceited because from his viewpoint the deception succeeds so extraordinarily; ultimately it ends with his regarding the lover as a poor benighted soul. And yet it is by means of just this that the true lover is eternally and infinitely secured against being deceived! Do you know, my reader, any stronger expression for superiority than this, that the superior one also has the appearance of being the weaker? *The stronger* who looks like the stronger sets a standard for his superiority; but he who, although superior, appears as the weaker negates standards and comparisons—that is, he is infinitely superior. Have you never seen in life this relationship of infinite superiority, which, of course, is not directly visible, for the infinite cannot to be seen directly? Consider someone who is infinitely superior to others in understanding, and you will see that he has the appearance of an ordinary person; only he who imagines he has greater understanding than others but is not entirely sure of himself or is limited and mediocre enough to boast of a comparison-relationship, only he strives to appear as one of superior understanding.

So it is with the lover who believes all things. Believing all things can very easily be confused with shallowness, and yet there is the depth of wisdom in this simplicity. It can very easily be confused with weakness, and yet the powers of the eternal reside in this impotence. One who believes all things can very easily give the appearance of a poor abandoned wretch whom everyone can deceive, and yet he is the only one who is eternally and infinitely secured against being deceived. But this is not directly visible. Humanly speaking the mistake is quite easily made, especially in these clever times which have become *too clever to believe in wisdom*. The mistake is quite easily made, for the lover, who believes all things, is not revealed directly. He is like those plants which are propagated in the shade: he breathes in God; he draws sustenance for his love from God; he is strengthened by God. In a certain sense he himself sees that humanly speaking he is deceived. But he knows that deception and truth stretch equally far and that consequently it still is possible that the deceiver is not a deceiver, and therefore he believes all things. For such a love has courage, courage to believe all things (truly the highest courage!), courage to endure the slights and mockery of the world (truly the greatest victory, greater than any which is won in the world, for it overcomes the world!), courage to endure the world's judgment that it is so indescribably foolish, although the world can quite clearly understand what his resolution is about but not his resolution, no more than the *mistrustful* world can understand the blessedness which the true lover has within himself.

But now suppose that in eternity it became clear that the lover *really* had been deceived! In what way—should it really be necessary to go over it once again? If to love is the highest good and the greatest blessedness, if the lover just by believing all things continued in the blessedness of love, how should he, then, be deceived in time or in eternity! No, no, there is in time and in eternity only one possible deception in relationship to true love—self-deception or giving up love. The true lover will therefore not even be able to understand the objection. Alas, but the rest of us, I regret, are able to understand it all too easily, for the lower level of conception and the pact between earthly passions and illusion are very difficult to shake loose. Just when a man has understood the truth best of all, the old ideas suddenly pop up again. The infinite, the eternal, and therefore the true are so foreign to a man by nature that it is with him as with the dog which can indeed learn to walk upright but still always prefers to walk on all-fours. One can almost constrain man's thought to the point of having to admit that, since deception stretches unconditionally as far as the truth, one man can really not judge the other, but the one judging becomes revealed himself—this is something like engaging in a test of strength with all one's might and because one does not know that it is a test of strength he thinks he is getting actual work done, although only his strength is being tested. And when one has understood all this, he can nevertheless still seek for a way out; he can relate himself inquisitively to the eternal, reckoning that it will thereby be made clear whether there *really* was a deceiver. But what does this prove? It proves that one is not the true lover with the blessedness of love within him and that he lacks the truly earnest conception of the eternal. If a man follows this impulse, it draws him straightway down into the lower domains of pettiness where the last and the highest are not the blessedness of love in itself, but rather the squabbling of special pleading.— But the true lover believes all things—and nevertheless is never deceived.

III

Love Hopes All Things and Yet

Is Never Put to Shame

Love . . . hopes all things. (*I Corinthians* 13 : 7)

Under many metaphors and with many concepts Holy Scriptures seek in various ways to give our earthly existence festivity and dignity, to win air and vision through the relationship to the eternal. And certainly this is needed. For when the earthly evaluation of life, God-forsaken, encloses itself in itself with self-satisfaction, the imprisoned air develops a poison all by itself. And when in temporality time in a certain sense skulks along loiteringly and yet so amazingly fast that in concentrated attentiveness one never becomes aware of its vanishing, or when the moment drags and becomes stagnant, and everything, everything, is mustered to turn mind and energy upon the moment: then vision is lost, and this detached, God-forsaken moment of temporality, be it longer or shorter, becomes a falling away from the eternal. Therefore in various eras there frequently is felt the need for a refreshing, enlivening breeze, a mighty gale, which would cleanse the air and drive out the poisonous vapours; a need is felt for the saving movement of a great event which saves by stirring the stagnation; a need is felt for the enlivening vision of a great expectation—so that men shall not be suffocated in worldliness or destroyed in the encumbering moment!

Yet Christianity knows only one way and one way out, although nonetheless it does always know a way and a way out; it is by the help of the eternal that Christianity at every moment procures air and vision. When busyness increases, just because the moment expands itself, when it continually hustles about in the moment, which eternally understood does not move from the spot, when busy people sow and reap and sow again and reap again (for busyness reaps repeatedly), when busy people gather stores full of what they reaped and rest upon their earnings—alas, while he who in truth wills the good in the same span of time still does not see the frailest fruit of his labour and becomes the object of mockery like one who does not know how to sow, like one who labours in vain and merely battles in the air—then Christianity procures vision through its parable of earthly life as the time of sowing and eternity the time of reaping. When the moment, simply because it stands fixed, becomes like a whirlpool (for the whirlpool does not move forward), when there is striving, winning, and losing and winning again, now at one point, now at another—but it seems that he who wills the good in truth is the only one who alone is a loser and loses everything —then Christianity procures vision through the aid of its picture of this life as a life of tribulation, of striving, and the eternal the life of victory. When the moment becomes stagnant in the wretched complexity of pettiness, which nevertheless in caricature resembles the holy, the good, and the true in miserable diminution and in caricature plays the game of distributing praise and blame, when everything is made cheap by being dragged down into the noisy, confused commotion— then Christianity procures air and vision, procures dignity and festivity for life by presenting in picturesque language the superiority of the eternal, in which it shall be eternally decided who won the wreath of honour and who was put to shame.—What solemn, earnest festivity! What in truth are honour and shame when the conditions which give infinite meaning to honour and shame are not secure! Even if a man did win honour meritoriously here in the world, what dignity does the world possess to confer significance! Suppose the pupil is deservedly put to shame or deservedly honoured—if the solemn occasion should take place on a stairway, if the teacher who dispenses praise and blame were a wretched fellow, if no one, almost no one, of those worthy persons who bring festivity by their presence was invited but only a greater crowd of misfits of dubious reputation, to say the least—what then, are praise and blame? But the eternal! Do you know any festival hall which is as loftily arched as the eternal; do you know of anything, even some house of God, where there is this holy silence as in the eternal; do you know of any group, even the most select from among the respectable, which is as secure against the presence of anyone against whom honour could have the slightest, the very slightest, objection, as secure against the presence of anyone who does not do honour to honour as the eternal is; do you know any festival hall, even though all its walls were made of mirrors, which so infinitely and exclusively reflects the requirements of honour, so infinitely excludes even the slightest, the least noticeable, crack for dishonour to hide in, the way the eternal does—if you do, it shall be put to shame!

At every moment with the help of the eternal Christianity procures vision in relationship to honour and shame, if you yourself will help by hoping. Christianity does not lead you up to some loftier place, from which you nevertheless can only survey a somewhat wider territory—this is still only an earthly hope and a worldly vision. No, Christianity's hope is the eternal, and therefore in its sketch of existence there are light and shadow, beauty and truth, and above all the depth of perspective. Christianity's hope is the eternal, and Christ is the way; his abasement is the way, but also when he ascended into heaven he was the way.

But love, which is greater than faith and hope, takes upon itself the work of hope or takes hope upon itself as the work of hoping for others. It is itself built up and nourished by this hope of the eternal and then acts lovingly in this hope towards others. This we shall now consider:

LOVE HOPES ALL THINGS—AND YET IS NEVER PUT TO SHAME;

for in truth not everyone who hopes all things is thereby the lover; nor is everyone who hopes all things thereby secured against ever being put to shame; but to hope all things in love is the opposite of despairingly hoping nothing at all, either for oneself or for others.

To hope all things or, which is the same, *to hope always*. At first glance it might seem as if to hope all things were something which could be done once for all, since *all things* indeed gathers multiplicity into one and to that extent into what one might call an eternal moment, as if hope were at rest, in repose. Yet this is not so. Hoping is composed of the eternal and the temporal; from this it arises that the expression for the task of hope in the form of the eternal is to hope all things and in the form of the temporal to hope always. The one expression is no truer than the other; rather, each of the expressions becomes untrue if it should be contrasted to the other expression, instead of unitedly expressing the same thing: in every moment always to hope all things.

To hope is related to the future, to possibility, which again, distinguished from actuality, is always a duality, the possibilities of advancing or of retrogressing, of rising up or of going under, of the good or of the evil. The eternal *is*, but when the eternal touches time or is in time, they do not meet each other in the *present*, for then the present would itself be the eternal. The present, the moment, is so quickly past, that it really is not present; it is only the boundary and is therefore transitional; whereas the past is what was present. Consequently if the eternal is in the temporal, it is in the future[14] (for the present can not get hold of it, and the past is indeed past) or in possibility. The past is actuality; the future is possibility. Eternally the eternal is the eternal; in time the eternal is possibility, the future. Therefore we call to-morrow the future, but we also call eternal life the future. Possibility as such is always a duality and the eternal relates itself in possibility equally to its duality. On the other hand, when the man to whom the possibility is relevant relates himself equally to the duality of the possibility, we say: he *expects*. To expect contains in it the same duality which possibility has, and to expect is to relate oneself to the possible simply and purely as such. Thereupon the relationship divides, inasmuch as the expecting person makes a choice. To relate oneself expectantly to the possibility of the good is to *hope*, which therefore cannot be some temporal expectancy but rather an eternal hope. To relate oneself expectantly to the possibility of the evil is to *fear*. But one who hopes is just as expectant as one who fears. But as soon as the choice is made, possibility is altered, for the possibility of the good is the eternal. It is only in the moment of contact that the duality of possibility is equivocal. Through the decision to choose hope, one thereby chooses infinitely more than is apparent, for it is an eternal decision. Only in pure possibility, consequently for the purely or indifferently expectant, is the possibility of the good or of the evil equivocal. In the differentiation (and the choice is indeed differentiation) the possibility of the good is more than possibility, for it is the eternal. This is the basis of the fact that one who hopes can never be deceived, for to hope is to expect the possibility of the good; but the possibility of the good is the eternal.

In this way one must specify more accurately what it means to hope. In ordinary speech one often calls something hope which is not hope at all, but desire, longing, longing-filled expectancy, now of one thing, now of another, in short, the relationship of an expectant person to *manifold* possibility. Understood in this way (when hope essentially signifies only expectation), hope comes quite easily to the child and the youth, because the child and the youth are themselves still a possibility; on the other hand, it is again quite in order to observe that for most men possibility and hope, or the sense of the possible, dwindle away with the years. Because of this, it may again be explained that experience speaks admonishingly about hope, as if it were only youth-fulness (which the hope of the child and of the youth certainly is), as if this were what it is to hope, like dancing, some youthful something for which adults have neither liking nor lightness. To be sure, to hope certainly means to make oneself light by the help of the eternal; hope depends on the possibility of the good. And even though the eternal is far from being youthfulness, it nevertheless has far more in common with youthfulness than with the moroseness which often enough is honoured by the name of seriousness, the slackness of age which under moderately fortunate conditions is moderately peaceful and relaxed but above all has nothing to hope for and under unfortunate conditions prefers to gnaw vexatiously rather than to hope. In youth one has expectancy and possibility enough; it develops by itself in the young like precious myrrh which exudes from the trees of Arabia. But when a man has grown older, then his life usually remains what it already has become, a dull repetition and re-writing of the same; no possibility rouses one to wakefulness and no possibility exhilarates the renewal of youth. Hope becomes something which nowhere has a home, and possibility a rarity like greenness in winter. Without the eternal one lives by the help of habit, prudence, conformity, experience, custom, and usage. In fact, take them all, put them all together, prepare the mixture over the smouldering or merely earthly ignited fire of passions, and you will discover that you can get all kinds of things out of it: variously concocted tough slime which men call a realistic view of life —but one never gets possibility out of this, possibility, the miracle which is so infinitely fragile (the most tender shoot in springtime is not so fragile), so infinitely delicate (the finest woven linen is not so delicate), and yet, brought into being, shaped, by the very help of the eternal, it is nevertheless stronger than anything else, if it is the possibility of the good!

One presumes to speak on the basis of experience in dividing a man's life into specific sections and ages, calling the first period that of hope or possibility. What foolishness! Consequently in discussing hope one completely omits the eternal—and still talks about hope. But how is this possible, inasmuch as hope is related essentially to the possibility of the good—and thereby to the eternal! And on the other hand, how is it possible to speak in such a way about hope that one assigns it to a certain period; certainly the eternal has range enough for the whole of life; therefore there is and shall be hope until the end. Therefore no particular age is the age of hope, but the whole of a man's life shall be the time of hope! One presumes, therefore, to speak about hope on the basis of experience—by sloughing off the eternal. Just as in a drama, by shortening the time and condensing the events one gets to view the content of many years in the passage of a couple of hours, likewise one speaks theatrically to arrange matters within temporality. One rejects God's plan of existence—that time is purely and simply development, prior complication, and eternity the solution. One arranges the whole of things within temporality: one uses a score of years for development, ten years for complications, then tightens the knot for a few years, and thereupon follows the untying or solution. Without a doubt, death certainly is an untying or solution and then it is past, one is buried—yet not before the dissolution of putrefaction has begun. In truth, everyone who does not understand that the whole of life shall be a time of hope is in despair, no matter, absolutely no matter whether he is conscious of it or not, whether he thinks himself fortunate in his presumed well-being or whether he wears himself out in tedium and trouble. Everyone who dismisses the possibility that his existence could be forfeited in the next moment—unless he *hopes* for the possibility of the good and therefore does not dismiss this possibility— everyone who lives without possibility is in despair; he breaks with the eternal; he arbitrarily closes off possibility and without the assent of eternity makes an end where the end is not, instead of doing as one who takes dictation and continually keeps his pencil ready for the next words so that he does not presume to put down a period meaninglessly before the meaning is complete or rebelliously to throw the pencil away.

When one wishes to help a child with a very great task, how does one go about it? Of course, one does not lay out the whole task at once, for then the child despairs and abandons hope; one lays out a portion at a time, yet always enough so that the child never reaches a stopping point as if it were all done, and yet not so much that the child cannot accomplish it. This is education's pious fraud; it really suppresses something. If the child is deceived, it is because the deceiver is a human being, who cannot vouch for the next moment. But the eternal —this is indeed the greatest task given to a human being, and on the other hand, it can certainly vouch for the next moment, but the child of time (man) relates himself to the infinite task just as a child! If the eternal were to lay out the task for man all at once and on its own terms, without regard for his poor capacities and weaker powers, man would despair. But it is a wonderful thing that the eternal, the greatest power, can make itself so small, that it is divisible in this way and yet eternally one, that clothing itself in the forms of the future, the possible, with the aid of hope it educates the child of time (man), teaches him to hope (for to hope is itself instruction, is the relationship to the eternal), if he does not arbitrarily choose austerely to be disheartened by fear or cheekily choose to despair—that is, withdraw himself from the education of the eternal. In possibility the eternal, rightly understood, continually lays out only a small piece at a time. In possibility the eternal is continually *near enough* to be at hand and yet *far enough away* to keep man advancing towards the eternal, on the way, in forward movement. In this way the eternal lures and draws a person, in the possible, from cradle to grave, if he just chooses to hope. For, as stated, possibility is twofold and is precisely therefore true education: possibility is just as rigorous or can be just as rigorous as it can be mild. Hope and possibility are not synonymous, for in possibility there can also be fear. But one who chooses hope, such a one the possible, with the aid of hope, will educate to hope. Yet the possibility of fear, rigorousness, remains hidden as a possibility, if it should be needed as an alarm for the sake of the education; but it remains hidden while the eternal lures with the aid of hope. To lure means constantly to be just as *near* as *distant*, whereby the one hoping is always kept hoping, hoping all things, kept in hope for the eternal, which in time is the possible.

This is what it means to hope all things. But *in love* to hope all things signifies the lover's relationship to other men, that in relationship to them, hoping for them, he continually keeps possibility open with infinite partiality for his possibility of the good. Consequently he hopes in love that possibility is present at every moment, that the possibility of the good is present for the other person, and that the possibility of the good means more and more glorious advancement in the good from perfection to perfection or resurrection from downfall or salvation from lostness and thus beyond.

It is readily conceded that the lover is right in holding possibility to be present at every moment. Alas, but many would perhaps more readily understand it if we permit despair to say the same thing, for in a sense despair does say the same thing. The despairing person also *knows* what lies in possibility, and yet he dismisses possibility (for to dismiss possibility is precisely what despair means), or even more accurately, he rashly presumes to *suppose* the impossibility of the good. Here again it is shown that the possibility of the good is more than possibility, for when one presumes to *suppose* the impossibility of the good, the possible dies completely for him. The fearful person *does not suppose* the impossibility of the good; he fears the possibility of evil, but he does not conclude, he does not presume to suppose, the impossibility of the good.

"It is possible," says despair, "it is possible that even the most sincere enthusiast nevertheless becomes weary, gives up the struggle, and sinks into the service of the second-rate; it is possible that even the deepest believer nevertheless at some time abandons faith and chooses disbelief; it is possible that even the most burning love at some time cools off, chilled; it is possible that even the most upright man comes to a detour and is lost; it is possible that even the best friend can become changed into an enemy, even the most faithful wife into a perjurer—it is possible: therefore despair, give up hope, henceforth do not hope all things in any man or for any man!"—Yes, indeed, this certainly is possible, but the opposite is also possible. "Therefore never in unlovingness give up a person or give up hope for him, for it is possible that even the most prodigal son can still be saved, that the most embittered enemy, alas, he who was your friend, it is still possible that he can again become your friend; it is possible that he who has sunk the deepest, alas, because he stood so high, it is still possible that he can be raised up again; it is still possible that the love which has turned cold can burn again—therefore never give up any man, not even at the last moment; do not despair. No, hope all things!"

Consequently "It is possible." To this extent the lover and one in despair are united in the same thing; but they are eternally separated, for despair hopes nothing at all for others and love hopes all things. Despair sinks down and occasionally uses possibility as a diverting stimulant, if one can really be diverted by the unstable, vain, phantasmal flashes of possibility. It is quite remarkable and shows how deeply hope is grounded in a human being that among those very men who are chilled in despair one finds a dominant tendency to play and flirt with possibility, a voluptuous misuse of the powers of imagination. Cold and defiant, the despairing one will not hope in relation to another man, even less work for the possibility of the good in him, but it amuses the despairing one to let the other man's destiny waver before him in possibility, whether of fear or of hope; it amuses him to play with the destiny of another human being, to think now of one possibility, now of another, to juggle him, as it were, in the air, while he himself, proud and unloving, scorns the whole affair.

But what justification is there for our calling desperate a person who gives up another human being? Certainly to despair is one thing and to despair over someone else another. Ah, yes, but if what the lover understands is true, and if it is true that one who is a lover understands what the lover understands, that the possibility of the good exists at every moment for the other person: then to give up the other person as hopelessly lost, as if there were no hope for him, is a proof that one himself is not a lover and consequently that he is indeed in despair, having given up hope. No one can hope unless he also loves; he cannot *hope for himself* without loving, for they are eternally inseparable; but if he loves, he also hopes for others. In the same degree to which he hopes for himself, precisely in the same degree he hopes for others, because precisely in the degree to which he hopes for himself, in precisely the same degree he is a lover. And in the same degree to which he hopes for others, precisely in the same degree he hopes for himself, for this is the infinitely exact, eternal like-for-like, which is for all eternity. Wherever love is present, there is something infinitely profound! The true lover says: " Hope all things; give up no man, for to give him up is to abandon your love for him—and if you do not give it up, then you hope. But if you abandon your love for him, then you yourself cease to be a lover." Note that generally we speak in another way, in a domineering and unloving way, about our relationship to love in ourselves, as if one were himself ruler or autocrat over his love in the same sense as one is over his money. When someone says, " I have given up my love for this man," he thinks that it is this person who loses, this person who was the object of his love. The speaker thinks that he himself possesses his love in the same sense as when one who has supported another financially says, " I have quit giving assistance to him." In this case the giver keeps for himself the money which the other previously received, he who is the loser, for the giver is certainly far from losing by this financial shift. But it is not like this with love; perhaps the one who was the object of love does lose, but he who " has given up his love for this man " is the loser. Maybe he does not detect this himself; perhaps he does not detect that the language mocks him, for he says explicitly, " I have given up my love." But if he has given up his love, he has then ceased to be loving. True enough, he adds my love " for this man," but this does not help when love is involved, although in money matters one can manage things this way without loss to oneself. The adjective *loving* does not apply to me when I have given up my love "for this man"—alas, even though I perhaps imagined that he was the one who lost. It is the same with despairing over another person; it is oneself who is in despair. Certainly it is somewhat depressing, this observation. To despair over another person is unfortunately so easy and so quick—and presumably one is so sure of himself, so full of hope for oneself. The very men who are smugly most sure of their own affairs are most ready to despair over others. But, however easily it goes, it nevertheless cannot really be done—except in thoughtlessness, which no doubt is the easiest for many men. No, here again is the eternal's like-for-like—to despair over another man is to be in despair oneself.

For the lover hopes all things, and what the lover says is true, that according to his understanding there is even at the last moment the possibility of the good, even for the most lost, therefore still hope. It is true, and it will be true for everyone in his relationship to other men, if he will keep his powers of imagination in check, undisturbed and unmuddled by unloving passions, through the eternal vision of the eternal's appearance in possibility. Therefore, when a man cannot understand what the lover understands, it must be because he is not a lover; it must be because there is something which prevents him from keeping possibility pure (for if possibility is kept pure, everything is possible) while in love he chooses the possibility of the good or hopes for the other person; it must be because there is something which weighs him down and gives him a tendency to expect the other person's discouragement, downfall, perdition. This down-drag is worldliness, the earthly passions of the unloving mind, for in itself worldliness is heavy, ponderous, sluggish, slack, dispirited, dejected and will not entertain the possible, least of all the possibility of the good, either for its own sake or for another's.—There is a *shrewdness* which, almost with pride, presumes to have special elemental knowledge of the shabby side of existence, that everything finally ends in wretchedness. How could such a person hope at the very last moment for another human being, he who early in the day already had begun to expect and be prepared for the other's downfall!—There are *anger* and *bitterness*. Even if one does not take murder upon his conscience, he nevertheless gives up the hated one as hopeless and consequently takes possibility away from him. But does this not mean to kill him spiritually? Spiritually to consign him to destruction—anger and bitterness can go this far!—There is an *evil eye;* how could an evil eye be able to catch a glimpse of the possibility of *the good*!—There is *envy*, which is quick to give up a person, and yet it does not really give him up in the sense of letting him go. No, it is ready right early to assist in his downfall. This is first apparent when envy hurries home to its dismal corner and calls out to its even more odious relatives, called malice, that they can enjoy themselves—to their own malignancy.—There is a *cowardly, fearful small-mindedness* which does not have the courage to hope anything for itself—how could it hope the possibility of the good for others? For this it is too small and too closely related to envy!—There is a *worldly, vain mentality* which would die of blushing and shame if it should go through the experience of making a mistake, of being fooled, of becoming a laughing-stock (the most terrible of all horrors) by having hoped for another person something which was not fullfilled. In this way the worldly, vain mentality protects itself by hoping nothing at the right time and considers hoping all things in love to be infinitely foolish and infinitely laughable. But right here worldly vanity makes its mistake, for what is foolish is never infinite; this was the very consolation of one who, while he lived, had to put up with so much of the world's foolishness that he could always say: it is not infinite; no, thank God, it has an end. Nor is experience right in maintaining that the greatest shrewdness is in not hoping everything for another person; yet, of course, experience is right; otherwise it would have to learn, and teach, how worthless it is to love others for the sake of one's own advantage, and only to the extent that one does this is it imprudent to hope all things.

When all of these, this shrewdness, this anger and bitterness, this envy and malice, this cowardly, fearful small-mindedness, this worldly, vain mentality, when all these or some of them are in a man and to the degree in which they are—then love is not present and to the same degree is diminished in him. But if there is less love in him, there is also less of the eternal in him; but if there is less of the eternal in him, there is also less possibility, less awareness of possibility (for possibility appears through the temporal movement of the eternal within the eternal in a human being; if there is nothing eternal in a man, the movement of the eternal is in vain and there is no possibility). But if there is less possibility, there is also less hope, just because and in the same way as there is less love, which in love could hope for the possibility of the good. The lover, on the other hand, hopes all things; for him no indolence of habit, no pettiness of mind, no picayunishness of prudence, no extensiveness of experience, no slackness of the years, no evil bitterness of passion corrupts his hope or adulterates possibility. Every morning, yes, every moment, he renews his hope and enlivens possibility, if love endures and he endures in love.

Even if the lover did not succeed in doing the slightest additional thing for another, did not succeed in bringing any other gift at all—he still brings the best gift, he brings hope. Where everything seems so hopeful and so rich in expectation for the promising youth, there love still brings the best gift: hope; but also there where men consider that they have already for a long time held out against the uttermost, there also love hopes unto the uttermost, to the "last day," for only then is hope gone. If you have seen a physician going around among the sick, you have noticed that he brings the best gift, better than all medicines, even better than all his care, when he brings hope, when it is said, "The physician has hope." Yet the physician has to do only with the temporal. Therefore it happens again and again that the moment comes when it would be false for him to deny that he has given up the patient, that the sickness is unto death. But the lover— what joy for the lover that he always dares to hope; what joy for him that the eternal vouches for him that there is always hope. For the lover, the true lover, does not hope *because* the eternal vouches for him, but he hopes *because* he is the lover, and he thanks the eternal that he dares to hope. In this way he always brings the best gift, better than congratulatory wishes for the best of luck, better than all human help in the worst of luck, because hope, the possibility of the good, is the help of the eternal. When all misfortunes descended upon the race, hope nevertheless remained.[15] In this paganism and Christianity are agreed. The difference is this, and it is an infinite difference, that Christianity has an infinitely lower conception of all these misfortunes and an infinitely more blessed conception of hope. But the hope which endures endures only in the lover. If there were no love, hope would not exist, either; it would be like a letter waiting to be picked up. If there were no love, hope would be like a letter with blessed contents, to be sure, but with no one to collect it. Love, then, although greater than hope, takes upon itself as its service and labour to bring hope.

Yet is there not some obscurity, some lack of clarity in this whole discussion so that one cannot clearly grasp what the object of love is? For "Love hopes all things" can mean that the lover hopes all things for himself and it can mean that the lover in love hopes all things for others. But these are indeed one and the same, and if anyone completely understands that they are absolutely one and the same this obscurity is precisely the clarity of the eternal. If love alone hopes all things (and Paul does not say that hope hopes all things, but that love hopes all things, for the very reason, as he says, that love is greater than hope), then it follows (from its being love and from what love is) that the lover hopes all things for others, since in fact his love qualifies his hope for himself. Only worldly comprehension (and yet its clarity is not to be recommended), only worldly comprehension, which understands neither what love nor hope is, thinks that they are two absolutely different things—to hope for oneself and to hope for others—and that love is again a third by itself. Worldly comprehension considers that a man can very well hope for himself without hoping for others, and that one does not need love to hope for oneself, although one certainly needs love in order to hope for others, those loved, and why should one hope for others besides these? Worldly comprehension does not discern that love is by no means a third by itself but is the middle term: without love no hope for one himself, with love hope for all others, and to the degree in which one hopes for himself, to that same degree one hopes for others, for to the same degree one loves.

Blessed is the lover; he hopes all things. Even at the last moment does he still hope for the possibility of the good for the most degenerate? This he has learned from the eternal; but only because he was a lover could he learn from the eternal, and only because he was a lover could he learn this from the eternal. Woe unto him who in relation to another human being gives up hope and possibility. Woe unto him, for he himself has thereby lost love!

Love hopes all things—and yet is never brought to shame. We speak of being brought to shame in connection with hope and expectation; we think that one is brought to shame when his hope or expectation is not fullfilled. In what is the shame supposed to lie? In this, that one's instrumental cleverness has not calculated accurately, that it has become evident (to one's shame) that he has injudiciously miscalculated. But, good heavens, the shame would not then be so critical; it is, after all, really critical only in the eyes of the world, to whose conception of honour and shame one should not give the honour of subscribing. What the world most highly and unanimously honours is cleverness or acting cleverly. But to act cleverly is precisely the most contemptuous of all. If a man is clever, in a certain sense he cannot help it; nor should he be ashamed of developing his cleverness—but should be all the more ashamed of acting cleverly. If men do not learn to scorn this, this acting cleverly (it is especially needful to speak of this in these clever times, when cleverness has really become something to be conquered by the help of Christianity, just as savagery and brutishness at other times), just as deeply as men despise stealing and bearing false witness —then one finally abandons the eternal entirely, and with it everything which is holy and worthy of honour—because this acting cleverly is through and through a display of false witness by one's whole life against the eternal and actually steals its existence from God. To act cleverly is basically compromise, whereby one undeniably gets farthest along in the world, wins the world's goods and favour, the world's honour, because the world and the world's favour are, eternally understood, compromise. But neither the eternal nor the Holy Scriptures have ever taught any man to strive to go far or farthest of all in the world; on the contrary, they warn against getting on too far in the world, in order, if possible, to keep oneself unspotted from the world. If this is so, then, it seems that pushing to go far or farthest of all in the world is not to be recommended.

If anything at all is to be said about being put to shame with regard to hope and expectation, the shame must lie deeper, must lie in what one hopes, so that one is consequently brought to shame whether his hope is fullfilled or not. The difference can only be that when the hope is not fullfilled it may become apparent in one's bitterness and despair how firmly one was attached to that for which it is a shame to hope. If the hope is fullfilled, the shame would perhaps not become apparent, but it would nevertheless remain essentially the same.

Yet if one hopes for something for which it is a shame to hope, regardless of whether it is fullfilled or not, one really does not hope. It is a misuse of the noble word *hope* to bring it into relationship with something like this, for to hope is essentially and eternally related to the good—therefore one can never be put to shame by hoping.

One can (to speak for a moment in an unjustifiable way) be put to shame by hoping for some kind of earthly fortune—if it does not materialise. But the shame is not essentially in that it did not materialise, that one's hope was not fullfilled. The shame is in its now becoming apparent, on the basis of the disappointed expectation, how important such an earthly success was to a person. This is not hope at all. This is desiring, craving, expecting; and therefore one can be brought to shame. One can be put to shame by giving up hope for another man, if it now becomes apparent that he is nevertheless saved or even, perhaps, that his downfall was in our imagination. Here one is really put to shame, because to give up another man is in itself a dishonour, no matter what the actual outcome is.—One can be put to shame by hoping evil for a person and it becomes apparent that everything turns out well for him. A vindictive individual says sometimes that he hopes to God that vengeance will fall upon the hated one.

But, in truth, this is not to hope but to hate, and it is impudent to call this a hope; it is blasphemy to wish to make God an accomplice in hating. The vindictive individual is not put to shame because what he expected does not happen, but he is and was put to shame, no matter what happens.

On the other hand, the lover hopes all things and is never put to shame. Scriptures speak of a hope which shall not be put to shame.[16] In this connection there first comes to mind the hope which pertains to the hoping person himself, his hope for the forgiveness of sins and of some day becoming blessed, his hope of a blessed reunion with whatever death or life has separated him from. And only in relationship to this hope, which is the hope, could there be any discussion of being put to shame, for certainly there would be no shame simply in having this hope, but rather honour, and therefore it would seem that shame comes if the hope is not fullfilled. Holy Scriptures are very consistent in this usage of terms. They do not use the name *hope* for each and every expectation, the whole crowd of expectations. They recognise only one hope, the hope, the possibility of the good, and affirm that this hope, the only one which *could* be put to shame, because to have it, say the Scriptures, is an honour, shall not be brought to shame.

Yet, when the lover's hope is for another person, would it not then be possible that the lover could be put to shame—if this hope is not fullfilled? Is it not possible that a man could be eternally lost? If the lover had hoped all things, hoped the possibility of the good for this person, then he would be put to shame by his hope.

How? If the prodigal son were dead in his sins and consequently lay in a grave of shame—and the father, who even at the last moment hoped all things, stood by: would he then stand in shame? I should think that it was the son who bore the shame, the son who shamed the father—but the father, then, must be honoured, for it is impossible to put to shame one who is shamed. Alas, the concerned father thinks least of all about honour, but nevertheless he indeed stands with honour! If there were no salvation for the prodigal son on this side of the grave, if he were eternally lost—and the father, who, as long as he lived, continued to hope all things and even in the hour of death hoped all things—would he then in eternity stand in shame? In eternity! No, the eternal certainly has the eternal's concept of honour and shame. The eternal does not even understand, it divorces from itself as vanity the cleverness which speaks only about the extent to which one's expectation has been fullfilled but does not at all consider just what the expectation was. In eternity everyone will be compelled to understand that it is not the result which determines honour and shame, but the expectation itself. Therefore, in eternity it is precisely the unloving one, who perhaps was proved right in what he picayunishly, enviously, hatefully expected for the other person, who will be put to shame—although his expectation was fullfilled. But honour belongs to the lover. And in eternity there will be heard no wearisome gossip about his nevertheless having been mistaken—maybe it was a mistake: unto salvation. No, in eternity there is only one mistake: through the fullfillment of one's picayunish, envious, hateful expectations to be excluded from blessedness! And in eternity, no mockery shall wound the lover, saying that he was foolish enough to make himself ridiculous by hoping all things, for in eternity the cry of the mocker is not heard, even less than in the grave, because in eternity are heard only the voices of the blessed! And in eternity, no envy shall touch the wreath of honour which the lover bears with honour. No, envy does not stretch that far, however far it may stretch; it does not stretch from hell to paradise!

IV

Love Seeks Not Its Own

Charity seeketh not her own.[17] (*I Corinthians* 13 : 5)

No, love does not seek its own, for to seek one's own is simply self-love, love of one's own, selfishness, or whatever other names the unloving attitude has. And yet, is not God love? But does not he who created man in his image that he might be like him, might become perfect as he is perfect[18] and consequently attain to the perfection which is God's own, become like the image which is God's own—does he not seek his own? Indeed, he seeks his own, which is love; he seeks it by giving everything, for God is good, and there is only one who is good,[19] God, who gives all. And was not Christ love? But he came into the world to become the prototype in order to draw all men unto himself that they might become like him, in truth become his own; did *he* not, then, seek his own? Yes, he sought his own, by sacrificing himself for all, that they might become like him in that which was essentially his own—in sacrificial devotion. But to seek one's own in this sense is entirely different and not at all what we have in mind when we speak of seeking one's own or of not seeking one's own. Love is essentially sacrifice; that it seeks love is again the highest love. That is, such is love in the relationship between man and God. For when a human being seeks the love of another human being, he seeks to become loved himself; this is not sacrifice; sacrifice would consist precisely in helping the other person to seek God. God alone is intrinsically capable of seeking love and being himself the object without, nevertheless, seeking his own. But no human being *is love*. Therefore, if a man seeks to become the object of another person's love, he deliberately and falsely seeks his own, for the only true object of a human being's love is love, which is God, who therefore in a deeper sense is not an object at all, since he is himself love.

Therefore, with the act of sacrificial devotion in mind (it is, then, essentially not an action, *not* a doing of this or that), let us consider

LOVE SEEKS NOT ITS OWN.

Love seeks not its own; for in love there is no mine and yours. But mine and yours are only relational qualifications of "one's-own"; consequently, if there is no "mine" or "yours," there is no "one's-own," either; but if there is no "one's-own," it is indeed impossible to seek "one's-own."

Justice is recognisable in that it gives to each his own, just as each requires its own in return. This means that justice is concerned with what is one's own: it partitions and divides; it determines what each one has the right to call his own; it judges and punishes if anyone does not make the distinction between mine and yours. With this contentious and yet legally entitled mine, the individual has the right to do as he pleases, and when he seeks his own on no other basis than that which justice grants, justice has nothing to reproach him for and no right to upbraid him for anything. In this way each one possesses his own. As soon as one is deprived of his own or as soon as one deprives another of his own, justice takes a hand, for it enforces the common security in which each has his own, whatever he rightfully possesses.—But at times change intrudes, a revolution, a war, an earthquake, or some such terrible misfortune, and all is disturbed. Justice seeks in vain to protect each one's own; it cannot maintain the distinction between mine and yours; it cannot hold the balance amid confusion; therefore it throws the scales away—it despairs!

What a terrifying spectacle! And yet, in a certain sense does not love bring about the same confusion, even though in a most life-infusing way. But love—it, too, is an event, the greatest of all and the happiest of all. Love is a change, the most remarkable of all, but the most desirable—it is precisely in the sense of something better that we say a person possessed by love is changed or becomes altered.[20] Love is a revolution, the most profound of all but the most blessed! Therefore with love, too, there comes confusion; in this life-giving confusion there is no distinction for the lovers between *mine* and *yours*. Remarkable! There are a *you* and an *I* and yet no *mine* and *yours*! For without *you* and *I* there is no love, and with *mine* and *yours* there is no love; but *mine* and *yours* (these geographical co-ordinates of possession) are in fact formed out of *you* and *I* and consequently seem necessary wherever *you* and *I* are. This holds true everywhere, except in love, which is the fundamental revolution. The deeper the revolution, the more the distinction between mine and yours disappears, and the more perfect is the love; love's perfection consists essentially in not revealing the initial and continuing distinction between mine and yours hidden at the base; therefore it consists essentially in the depth of the revolution. The deeper the revolution is, the more justice shudders; the deeper the revolution is, the more perfect is the love.

Is, then, the distinction between mine and yours dissolved in friendship and erotic love? A revolution of self-love does occur in friendship and erotic love which is motivated by self-love and by its contentious mine and yours. The beloved, therefore, has a sense of being out of himself, outside of his own, ravished, hence in a life-infusing confusion, and feels that for him and the beloved, for him and the friend, there is no distinction between mine and yours, " Because," says the lover, " everything that is mine is his and what is his . . . is mine! " How? Is then, the distinction between mine and yours dissolved? When mine has become yours and yours mine, there are indeed a mine and a yours everywhere, except that the exchange which took place betokens and signifies that it is no longer the initial, spontaneous mine of self-love which stands contentiously against a yours. Through the exchange the contentious mine and yours have become a communal mine and yours. Therefore it is a fellowship, a perfect fellowship in mine and yours. Since mine and yours exchanged become *ours*, in which category friendship and erotic love have their strength, they are strong at least in this. But ours is for the fellowship exactly the same as mine is for the individual, and ours is in fact formed—not out of the contentious mine and yours, for out of these no unity is formed, but out of the united, the exchanged mine and yours. We discern, therefore, that friendship and erotic love, as such, are only augmented and refined self-love, although erotic love is undeniably life's most happy fortune and friendship the greatest temporal good! In friendship and erotic love the revolution of self-love is just not deep enough from the ground up; therefore the original self-love's contentious distinction between mine and yours still slumbers within as a possibility. Indeed, the exchange of rings between the lovers is regarded as a very fitting symbol of erotic love; and in truth it is an absolutely fitting symbol, this exchanging, but it is a poor symbol of love. An exchange does not really mean a cessation of the distinction between mine and yours, because that for which I exchange myself becomes mine again. When friends mix their blood together, there is certainly a basic change, for when the blood is mixed a confusion arises. Is it my blood which flows in my veins?—no, it is the friend's. But, then again it is my blood which flows in the friend's veins. This means that the I is no longer itself primary but the you; yet turned around it is still the same.

How, then, is the distinction between mine and yours abrogated entirely? The distinction mine and yours is a relationship of polarity. They exist only in and with each other. Therefore if one part of the distinction is removed the other also disappears. Let us first try to take away completely the distinction yours from the distinction mine and yours. What do we have then? Then we have crime, offence. For the thief, the robber, the seducer, and the bandit recognise no yours at all in the distinction mine and yours. But precisely for this reason the distinction mine also disappears completely for him. Even if he does not understand this, even if he hardens himself against this understanding, justice understands that a criminal essentially has no mine. As a criminal he is set outside this distinction—and this is so in another way; for the richer the criminal becomes through the stolen yours, the less mine he has.—Now take away completely the distinction mine from the distinction mine and yours, and what do we have? Then we have the sacrificing one who renounces himself in all things—we have true love. But at the same time the category yours completely disappears, which is something for reflection to understand, even if for a moment it seems to be a bewildering thought. It is the curse of the criminal that his mine evaporates because he wants to do away entirely with the yours. It is the blessing of the true lover that the category yours disappears. Consequently everything becomes the true lover's; as Paul says, " All things are yours,"²¹ and as the true lover in a certain divine understanding says: all things are mine. And yet, yet this happens exclusively and only through his having no mine at all—consequently, " All things are mine—I, who have no mine at all." Nevertheless, the fact that all is his is a divine secret, for, humanly speaking, the true lover, the sacrificing one, the self-giving and in all things self-renouncing lover, he is, humanly speaking, the injured one, the most injured of all, even though he brings it upon himself by continually sacrificing himself. Thus he is exactly the opposite of the criminal, who is the injuring one. One who has fallen in love is not completely opposite to the injuring one, however else he may be different from him, for in erotic love one still seeks his own in a certain sense, often unconsciously, and thus has a mine. The category mine disappears completely only for self-renouncing love, and the distinction mine and yours ceases entirely. When in fact I know of nothing which is mine, when not a thing is mine, then everything is indeed yours, which it also is in a certain sense and sacrificing love considers it so; nevertheless, everything, unconditionally everything, cannot be yours, since yours is a relationship of polarity and there is no polarity in everything. Then something wonderful happens, heaven's blessing on self-renunciation's love: in the mysterious understanding of blessedness everything becomes his, belongs to him who had no mine, who in self-renunciation made all of his yours. God is indeed everything, and precisely by having no mine at all self-renunciation's love wins God and wins everything. For he who loses his soul[22] shall win it; but the distinction mine and yours or the mine and yours of friendship and erotic love are a preservation of the soul. Only spiritual love has the courage to will to have no mine at all, the courage to abolish completely the distinction between mine and yours, and therefore it wins God—by losing its soul. Here again is seen what the fathers understood in saying that the virtues of paganism were glittering vices.

The true lover seeks not his own. With respect to his own he knows nothing about the demands of strict law, or of justice, or even of fairness; nor does he know anything about an exchange made by the lovers, who also know how to watch out lest they be fooled (consequently know how to look out for their own); nor does he know about the fellowship formed in friendship, which also knows how to check whether like is reciprocated for like so that the friendship can be maintained (consequently knows how to look out for its own). No, the true lover understands only one thing: to be fooled, to be deceived, to give everything away without the slightest return—this is what it means not to seek one's own. O, the poor fool. How ridiculous can he get—in the eyes of the world! The true lover becomes the unmitigatedly injured one—which in a certain sense he brings on himself by his self-renunciation. Yet in this way the revolution of mine and yours achieves its highest; therefore love also achieves its highest blessedness in itself. No ingratitude, no misunderstanding, no unappreciated sacrifice, no mockery for thanks, nothing, neither present nor future can bring him to understand sooner or later that he has any mine or make it apparent that he had only for a moment forgotten the distinction between mine and yours; for he has eternally forgotten this distinction and eternally understood himself in loving sacrificially, understood himself in being sacrificed.

Love seeks not its own. For the true lover does not love his own individuality.[23]

He rather loves each human being according to the other's individuality. But for the other person "his own individuality" is precisely "his own," and consequently the lover does not seek his own; quite the opposite, in others he loves "their own."

Let us consider the external world for a moment. With what infinite love nature or God in nature encompasses the great variety which has life and being! Remember, too, what you have so frequently rejoiced in seeing, remember the beauty of the fields! There is no, not any, discrimination in love—yet what a difference among the flowers! Even the slightest, most insignificant, the most plain-looking, the poor little one overlooked even by its closest neighbours, the one you can hardly find without looking carefully, it is as if this, too, had said to love: let me be something for myself, something distinctive. And then love helped it to become something with its own distinctive, individual characteristic, but far more beautiful than what the poor little flower had ever dared hope for. What love! First of all, it makes no distinction. Second, which is like the first, it makes infinite distinctions in loving the differences. Wonderous love! For what is quite so difficult as not to make any distinctions in loving. And when one makes no distinctions at all, what is then so difficult as to make distinctions! Suppose that nature were like us human beings, strong, domineering, cold, partisan, narrow, capricious—and imagine, just imagine, what would happen to the beauty of the fields!

So it is also in the relationship of love between man and man; only true love loves every man according to his own individuality. *The strong, the domineering* person lacks flexibility, and he lacks a sense of awareness of others; he demands his own with everyone; he wills that everyone shall be recreated in his image, be trimmed according to his pattern for human beings. Or he does something which he regards as a rare degree of love; once in a while he makes an exception. He seeks, so he says, to understand completely a single human being, that is, in a definite, special—and arbitrary—way he thinks something specific concerning another person and then demands that his person shall fullfill these ideas. Whether they correspond to the other person's individuality or not makes no difference, because they are what the domineering person has thought about him. If the strong and domineering individual cannot create, he wants at least to remodel; he seeks his own so that wherever he points he can say: see, this is my image, this is my idea, this is my will. Whether the strong and domineering individual is allotted a great sphere of activity or a small one, whether he is a tyrant in an empire or a house-tyrant in a little attic room, the essence is the same: domineeringly unwilling to go out of oneself, domineeringly wanting to crush the other person's individuality or make life miserable for him. The essence is the same—the greatest tyrant[24] who has ever lived and who had the world to tyrannise became tired of it and ended tyrannising the flies, but in truth he remained the same!

As the strong and domineering individual seeks only his own, so is it also with *small-mindedness*, envious-domineering, cowardly-fearful small-mindedness. What is smallness? Is small-mindedness an intrinsic characteristic; that is, is any human being, brand-new from God's hand, small-minded? No! Small-mindedness is the creature's own miserable invention when, neither in genuine pride nor in genuine humility (for humility before God is genuine pride),[25] it behaves as if God were also small, as if he could not stand individuality, and it thereby debases God, who in love gives *everything* and nevertheless, gives everything individual characteristics. Small-mindedness must not be confused with modest gifts or with what we men small-mindedly call insignificance. Consider such an insignificant person— if he has had courage to be himself before God, he has authentic individuality. But, in truth, such an insignificant person—but what am I saying—such a nobleman is certainly not small-minded. One should carefully watch out for this confusion, and in this way one will not confuse unsophisticated, noble simplicity, which does not understand much, with petty narrowness which cowardly and restlessly wants to understand only its own. The small-minded individual has never had the courage of this God-pleasing venturesomeness of humility and pride: *before God* to be oneself—for the accent rests upon " before God," since this is the source and origin of all individuality. He who has dared to do this has authentic individuality and has come to know what God has already given to him; in the same sense he believes completely in the individuality of every single person. To have individuality is to believe in the individuality of every other person; for individuality is not mine but is God's gift by which he gives me being and gives being to all, gives being to everything. It is simply the inexhaustible swell of goodness in the goodness of God that he, the *almighty*, nevertheless gives in such a way that the receiver obtains individuality, that He who created out of nothing nevertheless creates individuality, so that creation over against him shall not be nothing, although it is taken from nothing and is nothing and yet becomes individuality. On the other hand, small-mindedness, which is *assumed being*, has no individuality, that is, it has not believed in its own and therefore cannot believe in anyone's. Small-mindedness has fastened itself tightly to a very particular shape and form which it calls its own; only this does it seek, and only this can it love. If small-mindedness finds this, then it loves. Thereby small-mindedness sticks together with small-mindedness; they grow together like an ingrown nail, and spiritually speaking it is just as bad. This association of small-mindedness is then praised as the highest love, as true friendship, as true, steadfast, sincere harmony. Men will not understand that the more they cling together in this way the more they separate themselves from true love, the greater becomes the untruth of small-mindedness—and the more corrupt, to boot, when it appropriates God for the tight little group, so that small-mindedness presumably shall be the sole object of God's love, that alone in which he is well pleased. This association of small-mindedness is just as petty in both directions: just as small in idolising an unusual individual who belongs to the company of small-mindedness as "one of its own," perhaps is its inventor, or on the other hand in idolising one who in the most detailed test is found to have, down to the least infinitesimal of small-mindedness, the countenance, the appearance, the voice, the thought-processes, the ways of speaking, and the heartiness of small-mindedness, and to be just as small-minded in wanting to supplant everything else. Just because small-mindedness is assumed being, and consequently untruth, just because it has never in openness and on the deepest level had anything to do with God but faint-heartedly has made a mess of itself and falsified God— precisely for this reason it has a bad conscience. For one who has individuality another person's individuality is no refutation but rather a confirmation or one proof more; it cannot disturb him to be shown, as he believes, that everyone has individuality. But for small-mindedness every individuality is a refutation; it feels therefore a damp, unpleasant anxiety upon observing another person's individuality and nothing is more important than to get rid of it. Small-mindedness demands of God, as it were, that every such individual characteristic be destroyed so that it can appear that small-mindedness is right and that God is a zealous God—zealous for small-mindedness. At times the excuse can be used that small-mindedness really imagines its miserable invention to be the truth; finally as a consequence forthright friendship and true fellowship mean willingness to bungle and mash everyone into a likeness with itself. When this happens, small-mindedness is fulsome in hearty ways of speaking and giving assurances. Nevertheless, although it is usually kept quiet, it is really self-defence, an instinct for self-preservation, which makes small-mindedness so active in trying to do away with everything but its own. One hears it in the narrow-chested gasping for relief, how it would perish if it did not get rid of this uncomfortableness, this anxiety; one sees it in its glance, how insecure about itself it is deep down, and therefore how cunningly and rapaciously it stalks its prey—in order that it shall become apparent that small-mindedness still is right and is victorious. Just as someone in mortal danger ventures everything, because it is a matter of life or death, small-mindedness also does likewise, except that all the means it uses are naturally to protect its own life and to deprive individuality of life—yes, they are naturally the most petty means, for although small-mindedness employs everything, one can still be certain that everything it employs is everything petty.

" But do not friendship and erotic love nevertheless love the friend and the beloved according to their individuality? " Yes, it is true, and yet it is not always completely true, for friendship and erotic love have limits: they can sacrifice everything for the other person's individuality, but not themselves, friendship and erotic love, for the other person's individuality. Suppose that the individuality of the other required precisely this sacrifice! Suppose the lover saw, to his joy, that he was loved, but also saw that this was the greatest threat to the beloved's individuality and would become the beloved's ruin—however much it might be desired, erotic love as such would not be able to make this sacrifice. Or suppose the beloved saw that the relationship would mean the lover's ruin, would completely shake his individuality—then erotic love as such would still not have the power to make this sacrifice.

But true love, sacrificing love, which loves every human being according to its own individuality, is willing to make every sacrifice—it seeks not its own.

Love seeks not its own; for it rather gives in such a way that the gift appears as if it were the receiver's possession.

When in social-economic relationships we speak of the circumstances of men, we make a distinction between those who are on their own and those who are dependent, and we desire that every man might be in a position to own his own soul, as we say. But in the world of the spirit this owning one's own soul is the very highest—and in love to help towards this, to become one's self, free, independent, his own, help him to stand on his own: this is the greatest benefaction. What, then, is the greatest benefaction? Yes, we have already mentioned it—and please note, that the lover knows how to make himself unnoticed, so that the recipient does not become dependent on him—by crediting him with the greatest benefaction. This means that the greatest benefaction is precisely *the mode* in which the only true benefaction is accomplished. It can be done essentially in only one way, even though in another sense in a multiplicity of ways; when the beneficial deed is not done in this way, it is far from being the greatest benefaction, indeed, far from being a benefit at all. Therefore one cannot straightway deduce which is the most beneficial deed, since the greatest benefaction, to help another to stand on his own, cannot be done directly.

Let us get this clear. When I say, " This man, by my help, stands on his own " and what I say is true, have I done the best by him? Let us look at this. What do I mean by this? I say, " He stands by himself, independent, by my help." But then, of course, he does not stand by himself: then he has not in fact become his own, then he is indebted to my help for all this—and he is aware of this. To help a person in this way is really to deceive him, and yet this is the way whereby the greatest benefactions are usually done in the world—that is, in the way in which it cannot be done. Yet this is the way which is especially praised in the world—which is natural, for the true way makes itself invisible and consequently is not seen, and thus the world appropriately absolves the ones concerned from all dependence. But one who is aided in the wrong and meaningless way is inexhaustible in praising and thanking me for the greatest benefaction (that he stands alone through the help of a dependent relationship to me); he and his family, each and all of them, honour and praise me as their greatest benefactor, that I lovingly have made him dependent on me or—yes, it is remarkable that one expresses his gratitude in a completely meaningless way, for instead of saying that I have made him dependent on me, he says that I have helped him stand alone.

Consequently the greatest benefaction cannot be accomplished in any way whereby the recipient gets to know that he is indebted. For if he gets to know this, it is excluded, precisely by this, from being the greatest benefaction. On the other hand, if one says, " This man stands alone—by my help," and what he says is true—then he has done for the other person the highest that one man can do for another: he has made him free, independent, unto himself, unto his own, and simply by hiding his help helped him to stand alone. Therefore: to stand alone—by another's help! There are many writers who employ dashes on every occasion of thought-failure, and there are also those who use dashes with sensitivity and taste. But a dash has truly never been used more significantly than in the little sentence above, where it is used, please note, by one who has fullfilled it, if there is such a one. For in this little sentence the infinity of thought is contained in the most profound way, the greatest contradiction overcome. He stands alone— this is the highest; he stands alone—nothing else do you see. You see no aid or assistance, no awkward bungler's hand holding on to him any more than it occurs to the person himself that someone has helped him. No, he stands alone—by another's help. But this help by another is hidden, hidden from him—from him who was helped?—no, from the eye of the independent man (for if he knows that he has been helped, he is really in the deepest sense not an independent man who helps and has helped himself); it is hidden behind a dash.

There is a noble wisdom which nevertheless, in a good sense, is infinitely cunning and inventive. It is well known. If I were to mention the foreign word[26] used for it hardly anyone in these times would fail to recognise it—by name. Perhaps there are not as many who would recognise it if one were to describe it without designating it by name. This wisdom and its name are often taken to task in the world, and still this is not strange, for the world is a very confused thinker who has neither the time nor the patience to think a single rigorous thought. That noble, simple man of ancient times was a master in this wisdom. That noble one was not exactly a plain or bad man; he was also, if I may express myself somewhat whimsically, he was, and this one cannot really deny him, he was a kind of thinker, even though not so profound as the ways of talking in modern modes of thought, even though not so admirable as they in being able to explain—for he never managed to be able to explain more than he understood.[27]

That noble rogue had profoundly understood that the highest that one human being can do for another is to make him free, to help him stand alone—and he had also understood himself in understanding this, that is, he had understood that if this is to be accomplished, the helper must be able to conceal himself in magnanimously willing his own destruction. He was, as he himself called himself, a midwife[28] in a spiritual sense, and with every sacrifice he worked disinterestedly in this service—for the disinterestedness consisted simply in keeping hidden from the one helped how and that he was helped. The disinterestedness consisted in this that the world could not understand and consequently could not esteem his disinterestedness, something it can never do, for the world simply cannot grasp why one would not be interested but it understands very well that an interested person could seek even more interestedly to be regarded as disinterested.

In such an understanding of help to another person there is agreement between the true lover and that noble rogue. He was conscious that he had done the greatest benefaction for the other person, and so it was; he was conscious of how he had worked for it, what time and industry and care it had cost him to deceive the other person into the truth, how much misunderstanding he had to endure from the one he helped by depriving him of his folly and ingeniously inducting him into the truth. For it is dangerous to practise the art of depriving one of his folly. That noble one himself said "that men became so angry at him that they sometimes wanted to bite him whenever he deprived them of a stupidity."[29] Since they regarded strengthening them in their folly as love, what wonder, then, that they were incensed when anyone wanted to take that away from them, their greatest treasure! In this way he laboured; and when the work was completed, he said very softly to himself: now this man stands alone. But at this point we come to the dash, and with the dash a smile would come upon the lips of that noble yet waggish fellow as he said, " Now this man stands alone—by my help." He kept for himself the secret of this indescribable smile. Certainly there was no trace of evil in this smile; he himself knew the good intentions of what he did; he himself knew that it is in truth a benefaction and the only mode whereby it can truly be done: but the smile, it was nevertheless the consciousness of ingenuity.

It is different with the lover. He also says: now this man stands alone. Then comes the dash. But this dash signifies for the lover something different from a smile, for however noble and magnanimous and disinterested that rogue was, he still did not in the sense of concern love the one he wanted to help. Although that rogue made himself infinitely light with the cunning of the dash, and the art is precisely in having been able to do everything for a person and to appear to have done nothing at all—for the lover the dash, even though in the sense of thought an infinite lightness, is in another sense (and it is important to observe that it is not observed) like a heavy breathing, almost like a deep sigh. For in this dash is hidden the sleeplessness of anxiety, the night-tossing of labour, almost desperate exertion; in this dash is hidden a fear and trembling which has never found an expression, and for this very reason is all the more dangerous. The lover has understood that in truth the greatest, the only benefaction one man can accomplish for another, is to help him stand alone, to become himself, to become his own; but he has also understood the danger and the suffering in the midst of the task and above all the terribleness of responsibility. Therefore with thanks to God he says: now this person stands alone—by my help. But there is no self-satisfaction in the last portion, for the lover has understood that essentially every human being stands alone—by God's help, and that the self-depreciation of love really exists only in order not to hinder the other person's God-relationship. He works without pay, for he makes himself nothing, and precisely at the moment when it could be said that he still could have the reward of proud self-consciousness, God enters in and he is again transformed into nothingness, which nevertheless for him is his blessedness. A courtier certainly has the power of making himself important to one for whom an audience with the king is very important. But now suppose that a courtier, simply by staying in the background, could aid the suppliant to obtain an audience with the king at any time. I wonder if the suppliant, in joy over audience with the king at any time, would not completely forget the poor courtier, the poor courtier who had had it in his power, by obtaining for the suppliant an occasional appointment with the king, *unlovingly* to make him very much indebted, to make himself beloved of him because of his love, the poor courtier who instead chose *out of love* to keep himself in the background and in this very way to arrange admittance for the suppliant to the king at any time, to help the suppliant to that independence which has admittance to the king at any time!

So it is with all the efforts of the lover. He truly seeks not his own, for he gives precisely in such a way that it appears as if the gift were the recipient's own possession. Insofar as the lover is able, he seeks to help a man to become himself, to become his own. But thereby in a certain sense not a thing is altered in existence, only that the lover, the concealed benefactor, is thrust outside, inasmuch as it is every human being's essential destiny to become free, independent, to become himself. If the lover in this respect has been God's co-labourer, everything has then become—as it was according to the essential destiny. If it is discerned that the lover has assisted, the relationship is disturbed, or the helper has not assisted in love and the lover has not helped properly.

What wonderful recollections the lover acquires as thanks for all his labour! In a sense he can pack his whole life together in a dash. He can say: I have laboured in spite of everyone, early and late, but what have I accomplished—a dash! (If what he had accomplished could be seen directly, he would have laboured less in love.) I have suffered as heavily as any man, inwardly as only love can suffer, but what have I gained—a dash! I have proclaimed the truth, clearly and well thought through in spite of everyone, but who has appropriated it—a dash! If he had not really been a lover, he would have directly cried out the truth less thoughtfully, and then he would immediately have had disciples who had picked up the truth—and called him master.[30]

Is, then, the life of the lover wasted, has he lived entirely in vain, since there is nothing, absolutely nothing, which witnesses to his work? Answer: is not seeking one's own the wasting of one's life? No, in truth, this life is not wasted. This the lover knows in blessed joy in himself and with God. In a certain sense his life is completely squandered on existence, on the existence of others; without wishing to waste any time or any power on elevating himself, on being somebody, in self-sacrifice he is willing to perish, that is, he is completely and wholly transformed into being simply an active power in the hands of God. This is why his labours cannot become apparent. His labour consists simply in this: to aid one or another human being to become his own, which in a certain sense they were on the way to becoming. But when one through another's help *really* has become his own, it is quite impossible to detect the help of the other, for if I see the other's help, then I really see that the one helped has not become his own.

V

Love Hides the Multiplicity of Sins

The temporal has three times and therefore essentially never *is* completely nor is completely in any one of the periods; the eternal *is*. A temporal object can have a multiplicity of varied characteristics; in a certain sense it can be said to have them simultaneously, insofar as in these definite characteristics it is that which it is. But reduplication in itself never has a temporal object; as the temporal disappears in time, so also it exists only in its characteristics. If, on the other hand, the eternal is in a man, the eternal reduplicates itself in him in such a way that every moment it is in him it is in him in a double mode: in an outward direction and in an inward direction back into itself, but in such a way that it is one and the same, for otherwise it is not reduplication. The eternal is not merely by virtue of its characteristics but in itself is in its characteristics; it does not merely have characteristics but exists in itself in having the characteristics.

So it is with love. What love does, it is; what it is, it does—at one and the same moment; simultaneously as it goes beyond itself (in an outward direction) it is in itself (in an inward direction), and simultaneously as it is in itself, it thereby goes beyond itself in such a way that this going beyond and this inward turning, this inward turning and this going beyond, are simultaneously one and the same.—When we say, "Love makes for confidence," we thereby say that the lover by his own makes others confident; wherever love is, confidence is propagated; people readily approach the lover, for he casts out fear. Whereas the mistrustful person scares everyone away; whereas the sly and cunning disseminate anxiety and painful unrest around them; whereas the presence of the domineering oppresses like the heavy pressure of sultry air—love makes for confidence. But when we say

" Love makes for confidence," we also say something else: that the lover has confidence, as in " Love gives confidence on the day of judgment."[31] That is, it makes the lover confident under judgment. —When we say, " Love saves from death," there is straightway a reduplication in thought: the lover saves another human being from death, and in entirely the same or yet in a different sense he saves himself from death. This he does at the same time; it is one and the same; he does not save the other at one moment and at another save himself, but in the moment he saves the other he saves himself from death. Only love never thinks about the latter, about saving oneself, about acquiring confidence itself; the lover in love thinks only about giving confidence and saving another from death. But the lover is not thereby forgotten. No, he who in love forgets himself, forgets his sufferings in order to think of another's, forgets all his wretchedness in order to think of another's, forgets what he himself loses in order lovingly to consider another's loss, forgets his advantage in order lovingly to look after another's advantage: truly, such a person is not forgotten. There is one who thinks of him, God in heaven; or love thinks of him. God is love, and when a human being because of love forgets himself, how then should God forget him! No, while the lover forgets himself and thinks of the other person, God thinks of the lover. The self-lover is busy; he shouts and complains and insists on his rights in order to make sure he is not forgotten—and yet he is forgotten. But the lover, who forgets himself, is remembered by love. There is One who thinks of him, and in this way it comes about that the lover gets what he gives.

Note the reduplication here: what the lover does, he is or he becomes; what he gives, he is or, more accurately, this he acquires— which is as remarkable as " Out of the eater came forth meat." Yet someone may say, " It is not so remarkable that the lover has what he gives; it is always the case that what one does not have he certainly cannot give." Well, yes, but is it always the case that one retains what he gives or that one himself acquires what he gives to another, that one acquires precisely by giving and acquires the very same which he gives, so that the given and the received are one and the same? Ordinarily this is not the case at all, but, contrariwise, what I give, another receives, and I myself do not acquire what I give to another.

In this way love is always reduplicated in itself. This also holds when it is stated that love hides the multiplicity of sins.

In Scriptures we read, and these are *love's* own words, that many sins are forgiven one who loved much[32]—because his love hides the multiplicity of sins. Yet of this we shall not speak at this time. In this little book we are continually concerned with the works of love; therefore we consider love in its outgoing movement. In this sense we shall now consider

THAT LOVE HIDES THE MULTIPLICITY OF SINS.

Love hides the multiplicity of sins. For it does not discover the sins; but not to discover what nevertheless must be there, insofar as it can be discovered, means to hide.

The concept *multiplicity* is in itself ambiguous. Thus we speak of the multiplicity of creation; yet the same expression has considerably different meanings, depending on who uses it. A man who has lived out his whole life in a remote place and, in addition, has little taste for studying nature—how little he knows, even though he speaks of the multiplicity of creation! A natural scientist, on the other hand, who has travelled around the world, who has been all over, both over and under the surface of the earth, sees the abundance of what he has seen and, in addition, with instruments discovers at a distance otherwise invisible stars or discovers at very close range otherwise invisible living things—how astonishingly much he knows—and he, too, uses the phrase, "the multiplicity of creation." And further, although the natural scientist rejoices over what he has succeeded in observing, he readily admits that there is no limit to discovery, since there is indeed no limit to discovery with respect to the instruments used for discovery; consequently the multiplicity becomes greater according to the discoveries or according to the discovery of new instruments of discovery and therefore can become even greater, that is, its even greater multiplicity becomes apparent—and yet, everything considered, it is all comprehended in the phrase "the multiplicity of creation." The same holds true of the multiplicity of sins. The phrase has quite different meanings, depending on who is speaking.

Therefore one *discovers* the multiplicity of sins to be continually greater and greater; that is, through discovery it continually reveals itself to be greater and greater, and also by means of one's appropriate discoveries it quite naturally becomes apparent how cunningly and sceptically one must conduct himself in order to make the discoveries. Consequently he who *does not discover* the multiplicity hides it, because for him the multiplicity is less.

But to discover is something praiseworthy, something admirable, even though this admiration is at times constrained in a strange way to bring heterogeneity together. One admires the natural scientist who discovers a bird, and one also admires the dog that discovered purple.[33] But we shall let this stand for what it is worth; nevertheless it is certain that discovery is praised and admired in the world. And on the other hand, he who does not discover something or who discovers nothing is rated rather low. In order to identify someone as eccentric, one who is preoccupied by his own thoughts, one readily says of him, " He doesn't really discover anything." And if one wishes to point out someone especially limited and stupid, he says, " He certainly didn't invent gunpowder"—which hardly needs doing in our time since it already has been invented; therefore it would be even more questionable if someone in our time were to think that he was the one who had invented gunpowder. But to discover something is so admired in the world that we cannot forget this enviable good fortune: to have invented gunpowder!

Thus far it is easy to see that the lover, who discovers nothing, makes a very poor showing in the eyes of the world. For to make discoveries even in the realms of evil, sin, and the multiplicity of sin, and to be a shrewd, cunning, penetrating, and perhaps half-corrupt observer who makes accurate discoveries—this is highly regarded in the world. Even the youth, in that first moment when he ventures out into life, will readily divulge that he knows and how he has discovered evil (for he does not like the world to call him a simpleton). Even a woman in her earliest youth will betray her vain desire to be a connoisseur of mankind, naturally in the direction of evil (for she does not like the world to call her a silly goose or a small-town beauty). Yes, it is incredible how the world has changed compared with ancient times— then there were but a few who knew themselves and now everybody is a connoisseur of mankind. And this is the remarkable thing—if one has discovered how basically good-natured almost everyone is, he nevertheless hardly dares make this discovery known; he fears to be laughed at, perhaps even fears that humanity might be offended thereby. However, when one discloses that he has discovered how basically shabby every human being is, how envious, how selfish, how unreliable, and what abominations can reside hidden in the purest people, that is, those regarded as the purest by simpletons, silly geese, and small-town beauties, then he conceitedly knows that he is welcome, that a premium is placed on his observation, his knowledge, and his discourse, which the world longs to hear. In this way sin and evil have greater power over men than one generally thinks: it is so silly to be good, so narrow-minded to believe in the good, so small-townish to betray ignorance or that one is uninitiated—uninitiated into the inmost secrets of sin. Here one sees quite clearly how evil and sin lie mainly on a conceited comparison-relationship to the world and to other men. For one can be quite sure that the same people who out of conceited fear of the world's judgment seek to be well-liked and entertaining in a crowd by revealing special acquaintance with evil, one can be quite sure that these same people, when they are alone in their heart of hearts where they do not need to be ashamed of the good, have an entirely different view. But in society, in daily associations, when many or even more are together, and consequently comparison, the comparison-relationship, is along in the company, something which vanity cannot possibly remain ignorant of—each one tempts the other to reveal what he has discovered.

Nevertheless, even a completely worldly-minded person at times makes an exception and passes a little milder judgment on not discovering anything. Suppose two sly fellows had something to decide together and for which they wanted no witnesses, and yet they were in such a position that they had to make their decision in a room with a third person present—and this third person was, as they knew, very much in love, head-over-heels in the first throes of falling in love—is it not true that one sly fellow would say to the other: " He can just as well stay; he will discover nothing "? They will say it with a smile and with this smile honour their own cleverness; and yet they would have a certain respect for the one in love who discovers nothing.— And now the lover! If one laughs at him, if one ridicules him, if one pities him, and whatever the world says of him, it is certain that with respect to the multiplicity of sins he *discovers* nothing, not even this laughter, this ridicule, this pity—he *discovers* nothing—and he sees only very little. He discovers nothing; of course we make a distinction between the discovering which is conscious, the planned attempt to find out, and the seeing and hearing which can happen involuntarily. He discovers nothing. And yet, whether one laughs at him or does not laugh at him, whether one ridicules him or does not ridicule him, deep down inside one has a respect for him because, resting and deepened in his love, he discovers nothing.

The lover discovers nothing; consequently he hides the multiplicity of sins which could have been found by discovery. The life of the lover expresses the apostolic injunction to be a babe in evil.[34] What the world admires as shrewdness is really an understanding of evil—wisdom is an understanding of the good. The lover has no understanding of evil and does not wish it; he is and he remains, he wishes to be and wishes to remain a child in this respect. Put a child in a den of thieves (but the child must not remain so long that he is corrupted; therefore let it be only for a short time); then let it come home and tell everything it has experienced: you will note that the child, who (like every child) nevertheless is a good observer and has excellent memory, will tell everything in the most circumstantial way, yet in such a fashion that in a certain sense the most important is left out, so that on the strength of the child's narrative anyone not previously informed will most likely not know that the child had been among thieves. What has the child left out; what has the child not discovered? It is the evil. Yet the child's narrative of what he has seen and heard is entirely factual. What, then, does the child lack? What is it which very often makes a child's narrative the most profound mockery of his elders? It is an understanding of evil and that the child lacks an understanding of evil, that the child does not even desire to understand evil. In this the lover is like the child. But at the basis of all *understanding* lies first of all an *understanding* between him who is to understand and that which is to be understood. Therefore an understanding of evil (however much one tries to make himself and *others* think that one can keep himself entirely pure, that there is a pure understanding of evil) nevertheless *involves* an *understanding with* evil. If there were no such understanding, the understander would not desire to understand it; he would flee from understanding it and would rather not understand it. If this understanding signifies nothing else, it is still a dangerous curiosity about evil, or it is cunning's way of spying out excuses for its own flaws by means of knowledge of the prevalence of evil, or it is falsity's scheme to peg up its own value by means of knowledge of others' corruption. But let one guard himself, for if out of curiosity one gives evil a finger, it will soon take the whole hand, and excuses are the most dangerous of all to have in stock; to become better or seem to be better by the help of comparisons with the badness of others is indeed a bad way of becoming better. Yet if this understanding has already discovered the multiplicity of sins, what discoveries could not be made by an even more intimate understanding which is really in league with evil! As the miser sees everything in terms of gold, likewise such a man, after he sinks himself deeper and deeper, discovers the multiplicity of sins to be greater and greater round about him

His eyes are sharpened and equipped, alas, not in the understanding of truth, rather of untruth, consequently his vision is narrowed more and more so that infected he sees evil in everything, in the impure and even in the purest—and this sight (terrible thought!) is nevertheless to him a kind of consolation, for to him it is important to discover as limitless a multiplicity as possible. Finally, there is no limit for his discovery, for now he discovers sin even where he himself knows it does not exist; he discovers it with the help of slander, backbiting, and the manufacture of lies, in which he has such long practice that finally he believes them himself. Such a one has discovered the multiplicity of sins!

But the lover discovers nothing. There is something so infinitely solemn and yet also so child-like, something reminiscent of a child's game, when the lover in this way, by discovering nothing, hides the multiplicity of sins—something reminiscent of a child's game, for this is the way we play with children; we play that we cannot see the child or the child plays that it cannot see us, and this is indescribably amusing to the child. The child-likeness, then, is that the lover, as in a game, cannot see with open eyes what takes place right in front of him; the solemnity consists in its being evil which he cannot see. It is well known that the orientals honour a deranged person; but this lover, who is worthy of honour, is, as it were, deranged. It is well known that in ancient times, for good reason, a significant distinction was made between two kinds of madness; the one was a tragic sickness and men lamented such a misfortune, and the other was called divine madness.[35] If for the moment one were to employ the pagan word *divine*, it is a divine kind of madness lovingly not to see the evil which takes place right in front of one. In truth, in these clever times which have so great a knowledge of evil, there is great need to do something to teach the honouring of this madness, because, I regret, in these times enough is done so that the love which has great understanding of the good and wants to have none of evil is taken to be a kind of derangement.

To use the highest example, consider Christ in that moment when he was brought before the Sanhedrin; consider the raging mob; consider the circle of important people—and consider then, how many a glance was directed towards him, aimed at him, only with the expectation of catching his eye so that the glance might convey its ridicule, its contempt, its pity, its scorn to the accused! But he discovered nothing; out of love he hid the multiplicity of sins. Consider, how much abuse, how much contempt, how much taunting mockery had been shouted—and to the shouter it was a matter of great importance that his voice should be heard, in order that above all it should not seem as if he had missed the opportunity, which would be indescribably stupid, as if he had not been actively participating here where the main thing was to be united all together, and thereby as an instrument of the public and consequently of the true mind, as if he had missed the opportunity of scorning, mortifying, and misusing an innocent man! But he understood nothing; out of love he hid the multiplicity of sins—by discovering nothing.

And he is the pattern. Of him the lover learns when he discovers nothing and thereby hides the multiplicity of sins, when as a worthy disciple, "despised, rejected, and carrying his cross,"[36] he walks between ridicule and pity, between scorn and lamentation, and yet out of love discovers nothing—truly something more marvellous than the episode of the three men walking unscathed in the fiery furnace.[37] Yet ridicule and contempt really do no harm when the one scorned is not injured by *discovering*, that is, by becoming embittered; for if he becomes embittered, he discovers the multiplicity of sins. If you want to illustrate clearly how the lover hides the multiplicity of sins by discovering nothing, consider love again. Suppose that this lover had a wife who loved him. See, just because she loved him she would discover the multiplicity of sins against him; offended, with bitterness in her soul she would discover every mocking glance; with knotted heart she would hear the contempt—while he, the lover, discovered nothing. And when the lover, insofar as he could not escape seeing or hearing something, nevertheless had excuse in readiness for the attackers, that he himself was at fault—then the wife would be able to discover no wrong in him, but only all the more the multiplicity of sins against him. As you consider this, do you now see what the wife, and certainly with truth, discovered? Do you see how true it is that the lover, who discovers nothing, hides the multiplicity of sins? Think of this in connection with all of life's relationships, and you will admit that the lover really hides the multiplicity!

Love hides the multiplicity of sins, for what it cannot avoid seeing or hearing, it hides in silence, in a mitigating explanation, in forgiveness.

It hides the multiplicity *in silence.*

It is sometimes the case that two lovers wish to keep their relationship secret. Suppose that in the moment they confessed their love to each other and promised each other silence a third person was quite accidentally present, but this uninvolved third was an upright and loving person to be depended upon, and he promised them to be silent: would not the love of the two nevertheless be and remain hidden? In the same way the lover conducts himself when unawares, quite accidentally, never because he has sought for it, he comes to know of a man's sin, of his fault, of some criminal act, or of how he was overcome by a weakness: the lover keeps this in silence and hides the multiplicity of sins.

Do not say " The multiplicity of sins remains just as great whether they are told or kept in silence, since silence simply cannot diminish anything and because one can be silent only about what actually is." Rather answer the question: does not the one who tells about his neighbour's sins and faults increase the multiplicity of sins? Even though the multiplicity remains just as great, whether I am silent about it or not, when I am silent about it, I nevertheless do my part by concealing. And further, do we not say that rumour tends to grow? We mean thereby that rumour tends to make the blame greater than it really is. But this is not our concern here. It is in quite another sense that one may say that rumour which reports the neighbour's faults increases the multiplicity of sins. One does not judge lightly of this witnessing to one's neighbour's faults, as if everything were all right if only the factuality of what was told had been determined. Truly, not every witness to what is true concerning his neighbour's faults is thereby innocent, and simply by becoming a witness one can himself easily become guilty. In this way rumour or one who reports his neighbour's faults augments the multiplicity of sins. That men through rumour and gossip inquisitively, frivolously, enviously, perhaps maliciously get into the habit of knowing about their neighbour's faults—this corrupts men. Certainly it is desirable that men should again learn to be silent. But if there must be gossip and consequently inquisitive and frivolous gossip, then let it be about nonsense and trifles —one's neighbour's faults are and ought to be too serious a matter; to talk about them inquisitively, frivolously, enviously is therefore a sign of corruption. But he who by reporting his neighbour's faults helps to corrupt men certainly increases the multiplicity of sins.

It is only too clear that every man, unfortunately, has a great inclination to see his neighbour's faults and perhaps an even greater inclination to want to tell about them. If it is nothing else, it is, alas, to use the mildest expression, a kind of nervousness which makes men so weak in this temptation, in this dizziness of being able to tell something evil about their neighbours, of being able for a moment to create for themselves an attentive audience with the aid of such entertaining reports. But what is already corrupting enough as a nervous urge which cannot keep quiet is sometimes a raging, demonic passion in a man, developed on the most terrifying scale. I wonder whether any robber, any thief, any man of violence, in short, any criminal is in the deepest sense as depraved as such a man who has taken upon himself as his contemptible means of livelihood the task of proclaiming on the greatest possible scale, loudly as no word of truth is heard, widely over the whole land in a way seldom achieved by something worthy, penetrating into every nook where God's word hardly penetrates, his neighbour's faults, his neighbour's weaknesses, his neighbour's sins and to press upon everyone, even upon unformed youth, this polluting knowledge—I really wonder whether any criminal is in the deepest sense so depraved as such a man, even if the evil he told were factual! Even if it were factual—but it is inconceivable that one with the earnestness of the eternal could be rigorous in taking care that the evil he told was unconditionally factual and then be able to use his life in this nauseous service of factuality: the reporting of evil. We pray in the Lord's Prayer that God will not lead into temptation. But if this should happen, if it should happen that I fell into temptation—may it please merciful God that my sin and my guilt nevertheless be such that the world regards it as detestable and revolting! But the most terrible of all must be to have guilt, heinous guilt, and to add guilt and more guilt and new guilt day in and day out—and not to become conscious of it, because one's whole environment, because existence itself had become transformed into an illusion which strengthened one in his view that it was nothing, not only that there was no guilt but that it was something almost meritorious. O, there are criminals whom the world does not call criminals, whom it rewards and almost honours— and yet, yet I would rather, God forbid, but I nevertheless would rather enter eternity with three repented murders on my conscience than as a retired scandalmonger with this horrible, incalculable load of criminality which was heaped up year after year, which was able to spread on an almost inconceivable scale, to put men in their graves, embitter the most intimate relationships, injure the most innocent sympathisers, besmirch the young, mislead and corrupt both young and old, in short, to spread itself on a scale which even the most vivid power of phantasy cannot imagine—this horrible load of criminality which I nevertheless never got time to begin repenting of, because the time had to be used for new offences, and because these innumerable offences had secured money for me, influence, prestige almost, and above all a pleasurable life! In connection with arson a distinction is made between setting fire to a house in the full knowledge of its being inhabited by many or being uninhabited. But scandalmongering is like setting fire to a whole community and it is not even regarded as a crime! We quarantine for diseases—but this disease which is worse than the bubonic plague, scandalmongering, which corrupts the mind and soul, we invite into all the houses; we pay money to become infected; we greet as a welcome guest one who brings the infection!

Now, then, is it not true that the lover hides the multiplicity of sins by keeping silent about his neighbour's faults, when you consider how one increases them in the telling.

The lover hides the multiplicity of sins *in a mitigating explanation.*

It is always the explanation which defines something that is. The fact or the facts are basic, but the explanation is decisive. Every event, every word, every act, in short, everything, can be explained in numerous ways. As we say, clothes make the man. Likewise one can truly say that the explanation makes the object of explanation what it is. With regard to another man's words, acts, and ways of thought there is no certainty, and to suppose it means to choose. Conceptions and explanations therefore exist, simply because a variation in explanation is possible—a choice. But if it is a choice, it is continually in my power, if I am a lover, to choose the most mitigating explanation. When, therefore, this milder or mitigating explanation explains what others frivolously, hastily, rigorously, hard-heartedly, enviously, maliciously, in short, unlovingly, declare straightway to be guilt, when the mitigating explanation explains this in another way, it takes now one and then another guilt away and thereby makes the multiplicity of sins less or hides it. O, if men would rightly understand what splendid use they could make of their imaginative powers, their acuteness, their inventiveness, and their ability to relate by using them to find if possible a mitigating explanation—then they would gain more and more a taste for one of the most beautiful joys of life; it would become for them a passionate desire and need which could lead them to forget everything else. Do we not observe this in other ways, how, for example, the hunter year by year becomes more and more passionately given to hunting? We do not admire his choice, but shall say nothing about this; we speak only of how year by year he devotes himself more and more passionately to this activity. And why does he do this? Because with each year he acquires experience, becomes more and more inventive, overcomes more and more difficulties, so that he, the old experienced hunter, now knows alternatives when others know none, knows how to track game where others do not, discerns signs which no one else understands, and has discovered a better way of setting traps, so that he is always rather sure of always having good hunting even when all others fail. We regard it as a burdensome task, yet in another respect satisfying and engaging, to be a detective, one who discovers guilt and crime. We are amazed at such a person's knowledge of the human heart, of all its evasions and devices, even the most subtle, how he can remember from year to year the most insignificant things just to establish, if possible, a clue, how by merely glancing at the circumstances he can, as it were, exorcise out of them an explanation detrimental to the guilty one, how nothing is too trivial for his attention insofar as it could contribute to illuminate his grasp of the crime. We admire such an official servant when by keeping after what he calls a thoroughly hardened hypocrite he succeeds in tearing the cloak away from him and making the guilt apparent. Should it not be just as satisfying and just as engaging, through perseverance with what would be called exceptionally base conduct, to discover that it was something quite different, something well-intentioned! Let the judges appointed by the state, let the detectives labour to discover guilt and crime; the rest of us are enjoined to be neither judges nor detectives—God has rather called us to love, consequently, to the hiding of the multiplicity of sins with the help of a mitigating explanation. Imagine this kind of lover, endowed by nature with such magnificent capacities that every judge must envy him, but all these capacities are employed with a zeal and rigour such as a judge would have to admire in the service of love, for the purpose of getting practice in the art and practising the art, the art of interpretation, which, with the help of mitigating explanation, hides the multiplicity of sins! Imagine his rich experience, blessed in the noblest sense: what knowledge he possesses of the human heart, how many remarkable and moving instances he knows about, in which he nevertheless succeeded, however complicated the matter may have seemed, in discovering the good or even the better, because for a long, long time he had kept his judgment suspended, until at just the right time a little circumstance came to light which helped him on the track, and then by quickly and boldly concentrating all his attention upon a completely different conception of the matter he had the fortune of discovering what he sought, by losing himself in a man's life-relationships, and by securing the most accurate information about his circumstances he was finally victorious in his explanation! Consequently " He found the clue." " He had the good fortune of finding what he sought." " He conquered with his explanation."—Alas, is it not strange that when these words are read out of context almost every man will involuntarily think they concern the discovery of a crime —most of us are far more inclined to think of discovering evil than of discovering the good. The state appoints judges and detectives to discover and punish evil. Moreover, men unite for obviously praiseworthy causes to alleviate poverty, to bring up orphan children, to rescue the fallen—but for this splendid venture, with the aid of a mitigating explanation to secure, were it ever so little, yet a little power over the multiplicity of sins—for this no association has yet been organised.

But we shall not develop further here how the lover hides the multiplicity of sins with a mitigating explanation, inasmuch as in two foregoing portions we have considered that love believes all things and love hopes all things. But to believe all things in love and in love to hope all things are the two chief means which love, this mild interpreter, uses for a mitigating explanation, which hides the multiplicity of sins.

Love hides the multiplicity of sins by *forgiveness*.

Silence really takes nothing away from the known multiplicity of sins; the mitigating interpretation removes something from the multiplicity by showing that this or that was nevertheless not sin. Forgiveness takes away what nevertheless cannot be denied to be sin. Thus love strives in every way to hide the multiplicity of sins, but forgiveness is the most significant way.

We alluded earlier to the expression "the multiplicity of creation"; let us now use this illustration once again. We say that the researcher *discovers* multiplicity; whereas the untutored person, who, to be sure, also speaks of the multiplicity of creation, knows very little comparatively. Consequently the untutored person does not know that this or that exists, but nevertheless it does exist; it is not removed from nature by his ignorance; it simply does not exist for him in his ignorance. It is quite different in the relationship of forgiveness to the multitude of sins: forgiveness takes the forgiven sin away.

This is a remarkable thought, as it is the thought of faith; for faith always relates itself to what is not seen.[38] I *believe* that the seen came into being on the basis of that which cannot be seen. I see the world, but the unseen I do not see—this I believe. Thus it is also with *forgiveness—and sin,* a relationship of faith, which, however, men are rarely aware of. What, then, is the unseen here? The unseen is in this that forgiveness takes away that which nevertheless is; the unseen is in this that what is seen nevertheless is not seen, for when it is seen, its not being seen is manifestly unseen. The lover sees the sin which he forgives, but he believes that forgiveness takes it away. This, of course, cannot be seen, although the sin can be seen; and on the other hand, if the sin did not exist to be seen, neither could it be forgiven. Just as one by faith *believes the unseen* in the seen, so the lover by forgiveness *believes* the seen away. Both are faith. Blessed is the man of faith; he believes what he cannot see. Blessed is the lover; he believes away what he nevertheless can see!

Who can believe this? The lover can. But why, I wonder, is forgiveness so rare? Is it not, I wonder, because faith in the power of forgiveness is so small and so rare? Even the better person, who is not at all inclined to carry malice and rancour and is far from being irreconcilable, is not infrequently heard to say: " I should like to forgive him, but I don't see how it could be of help." Alas, it is not seen! Yet, if you yourself have ever needed forgiveness, then you know what forgiveness accomplishes—why then do you speak so naïvely and so unlovingly about forgiveness? For there is something essentially unloving in saying: I don't see what help my forgiveness can give him. We do not say this as if a person were to become self-important by having in his power the ability to forgive another person—far from it— this is also lack of love; in truth there is a mode of forgiving which discernibly and conspicuously augments the guilt rather than diminishes it. Only love is—yes, it seems playful, but let us put it this way—only love is handy enough to take the sin away by forgiving it. When I hang weights on forgiveness (that is, when I am laggard in forgiving or make myself important by being able to forgive), no miracle occurs. But when love forgives, the miracle of faith occurs (every miracle is a miracle of faith; what wonder, then, that along with faith the miracles also are abolished!): that which is seen nevertheless by being forgiven is not seen.

It is blotted out; it is forgiven and forgotten, or, as Scriptures say of what God forgives, it is hidden behind his back.[39'] But one is not unaware of that which is forgotten, for one is unaware of that which he does not know or never knew. What one has forgotten he has known. To forget in the highest sense is therefore the opposite—not of remembering but of hoping—because to hope means to give being by

thinking and to forget is by thinking to take being away from that
which nevertheless is, to blot it out. Scriptures teach that faith is related
to the unseen, but it also says that faith is the substance of what is hoped
for.[40] This is how the object of hope, like the unseen, does not have
existence but is nevertheless given existence by *hope* thinking. When
God forgets sin, forgetting is the opposite of creating, for to create
means to bring forth out of nothing and to forget is to return it into
nothing. What is hidden from my eyes I have never seen, but what is
hidden behind my back I have seen. And this is the very way in which
the lover forgives: he forgives, he forgets, he blots out sin; in love he
turns to the one he forgives, but when he turns toward him he simply
cannot see what lies behind his back. That it is impossible to see what
is behind one's back is easy to understand, also therefore that this
expression is rightly the invention of love. But, on the other hand, it is
perhaps very difficult to become the lover, who with the help of forgiveness puts another's guilt behind his back. Generally people find
it easy, in the case of a murder, to place the guilt upon another person's
conscience; but with the help of forgiveness to put his guilt behind one's
back comes very hard. But not for the lover, for he hides the multiplicity of sins.

Do not say " The multiplicity of sins remains just as great whether
they are forgiven or not, since forgiveness neither adds nor subtracts."
Rather answer the question: does not one who unlovingly withholds
forgiveness increase the multiplicity of sins—not only because his
irreconcilability becomes one sin more, which is certainly the case, and
to that extent ought to be brought into the reckoning? Yet we shall
not emphasise this now. But is there not a secret relationship between
sin and forgiveness? When a sin is not forgiven, it requires punishment,
it cries to God or men for punishment; but when a sin cries for
punishment, it appears quite different, far greater than when this same
sin is forgiven. Is it not an optical illusion? No, it is really so. To
employ an imperfect figure, it is no optical illusion that the wound
which looked so frightful appears far less frightful when the physician
has washed and cared for it, even though it is still the same wound.
Therefore what does he do who withholds forgiveness? He increases
the sin; he acts so that it appears greater. And further, forgiveness
takes vitality away from sin; but to withhold forgiveness nourishes sin.
Therefore even though no new sin arose, and if the one and the same
sin merely continued, a new sin really comes into being, for sin grows
on sin; the continuation of a sin is a new sin. And you could have

prevented this new sin by forgiving in love and taking the old sin away, as does the lover who hides the multiplicity of sins.

Love hides the multiplicity of sins; for love prevents sin from coming into being, smothers it at birth.

Even though with respect to some undertaking or other, a task one wants to complete, one has everything prepared: one thing must still be waited for, the occasion. So it is also with sin. When it is in a man, it still waits for an occasion.

Occasions can vary greatly. Scriptures say that sin finds an opportunity in the commandment or in the prohibition.[41] The simple fact of something being commanded or forbidden becomes the occasion or opportunity. It is not as though the occasion caused sin, for an occasion never causes anything. The opportunity is like a middle-man, an intermediary, helpful only in making the exchange, merely expediting into existence that which in another sense already was, namely, as possibility. The commandment and the prohibition tempt simply because they seek to constrain evil, and now sin takes the opportunity, *takes* it, for the prohibition *is* the opportunity. Thus the opportunity is like a nothing, a fleeting nothing, which intervenes between the sin and the prohibition and in a certain sense belongs to both, although in another sense it is as if it did not exist, and yet again nothing which really has come into being has become without an occasion.

The commandment, the prohibition, is the occasion. In a sorrier sense sin in others is the occasion which evokes sin in those who come in touch with them. How often has a thoughtlessly, frivolously spoken word been enough to give occasion to sin! How often has a frivolous glance occasioned an increase in the multiplicity of sins! Just note how often one sees and hears sin and ungodliness in ordinary daily life: what rich opportunity for sin in him, what an easy shifting between giving the opportunity and taking the opportunity! When sin in a man is encompassed by sin, it is in its element. Nourished by the omnipresence of occasions it thrives and grows (if one can rightly speak of thriving in connection with evil): it becomes more and more ill-natured; it achieves more and more form (if in connection with evil one can speak of achieving form, since evil is lies and deception and thus without form); it establishes itself more and more, even though its life hovers over the abyss and therefore has no foothold.

Nevertheless, everything which is an occasion contributes insofar as the opportunity to sin is taken—to increase the multiplicity of sins.

But there is one condition which unconditionally does not give and

is not an occasion for sin: that is love. When sin in a man is encompassed by love, it is then out of its element; it is like a besieged city
with all communications cut off; it is like a man addicted to drink,
wasting away on meagre fare and vainly awaiting the opportunity to
be stimulated by intoxicants. Certainly it is possible for sin to use love
as an occasion (for what cannot a corrupt man use for corruption!); it
can become embittered about it, rage against it. Yet in the long run sin
cannot hold out against love; usually only at the beginning is there
such an advantage, just as when the drunkard in the first days, before
the medical treatment has had sufficient time to take effect, has the
strength of weakness to rage. And further, if there were such a man
whom even love had to give up—no, love never does that—but who
continually took love as an occasion to sin because he was an incorrigible, it still does not follow that there are not many who are healed.
Therefore, it remains just as completely true that love hides the
multiplicity of sins.

The authorities must often devise many shrewd ways to imprison
a criminal and the physicians often employ great inventiveness in order
to develop restraints to hold the insane: with respect to sin, however,
there are no conditions so coercive, but there are also no constraining
conditions so rehabilitating as love. How frequently anger, smouldering
within, only waiting for an occasion, how frequently it has been
smothered because love gave no occasion! How frequently evil desire,
watching and waiting for an occasion in the sensual anxiety of
curiosity, how often it has perished in birth because love gave no
occasion at all and lovingly watched lest any occasion at all be given!
How often resentment in the soul has been stilled, resentment which
was so assured and so prepared, yes, so poised to find yet a new
occasion to be wronged by the world, by men, by God, by everything,
how often it has been stilled into a quieter mood because love gave no
occasion to be wronged at all. How frequently this conceited and
defiant attitude passed away, this attitude of one who considered himself misjudged and misunderstood and thereby took occasion to become
even more conceited while merely cultivating new occasions to prove
that it was right; how frequently it passed away because love, so
alleviating, so mildly dispersive, gave no occasion at all to the sick
imagination! How often what was contemplated receded into itself,
that which sought only to find a justifying occasion; how often it
receded because love gave no occasion at all to find excuse—for evil!
O, how many crimes have been prevented, how many evil enterprises

brought to naught, how many desperate resolutions drawn into forget-fulness, how many sinful thoughts halted on the way to becoming acts, how many unconsidered words stifled in time, because love gave no occasion!

Woe unto the man by whom offence comes; blessed is the lover who by refusing to give occasion hides the multiplicity of sins!

VI

Love Abides

So . . . love abide[s]. (*I Corinthians* 13 : 13)

Yes, God be praised, love abides! Whatever the world takes away
from you, though it be the most cherished, whatever happens to you
in life, however you may have to suffer because of your striving, for
the good, if you please, if men turn indifferent from you or as enemies
against you, if no one is willing to admit acquaintance with you or
acknowledge what he nevertheless owes to you, if even your best
friend should deny you—if nevertheless in any of your strivings, in any
of your actions, in any of your words you truly have consciously had
love along: then take comfort, for love abides. What you knew with
love will be consoling to remember, more blessed than any sort of
achievement any human being could have accomplished, more blessed
than if the spirits had been submissive to you; it will be more blessed
to be remembered by love! What you knew with love will be consoling
to remember; neither the present nor the future, neither angels nor
devil, and God be praised, not even the fearful thoughts of your
unquiet mind, will be able to take it from you, not in the stormiest,
most difficult moment of your life any more than the last moment of
your life—because love abides.—And when despondency begins to
make you weak so that you lose the desire to will rightly in order to
make you strong again, as strong as despondency, alas, makes you strong
in the defiance of forsakenness; when despondency makes you all
empty, changes your whole life into a homogenised, meaningless
repetition so that you see it all together but very indifferently,
see the meadows and woods green *again*, see the manifold life in air

and water move *again*, hear the birds singing together *again*, see again and again the activity of men in all sorts of work—and you know indeed that God is, but it seems to you as if he had receded into himself, as if he were absent in heaven far away from all these insignificant things which are hardly worth living for; when despondency takes the heart out of your whole life, so that you know but only faintly that Christ has existed and nevertheless know with anxious clarity that it was eighteen hundred years ago, as if he were infinitely far removed from all these insignificant things which are hardly worth living for—O, consider, then, that love endures! For if love endures, it is equally certain that it is in the future, if this is the consolation you need, or that it is in the present, if this is the consolation you need. Against all the terrors of the future set this consolation: love abides; against all the anxiety and staleness of the present set this consolation: love abides. If it is consoling to a desert-dweller to know for sure that there is a spring and would be a spring no matter how far he travelled, what spring would nevertheless be so missed, what manner of death would be so excruciating as would be the case if love were not and would not be for all eternity!

This is a very up-building thought, that love abides. When we speak this way we speak of the love which sustains all existence, of God's love. If for a moment, a single moment, it were absent, everything would be confused. But this is not the case, and therefore, however confused everything is for you—love abides. We speak, therefore, of God's love, of its nature to abide.

Yet in this little book we are continually concerned only with the works of love, and therefore not with God's love but with human love. Naturally no human being is love. He is, if he is in love, a lover. At the same time love is present wherever there is a lover. One might believe, and usually one thinks so, that love between man and man is a relationship between two. This is true but also untrue, insofar as this relationship is also a relationship among three. First there is the lover; then the one or those who are objects; but thirdly, there is present love itself. When, therefore, in respect to human love we say that love abides, it is manifest that it is an act or that it is not a characteristic of repose which love as such possesses but a characteristic acquired at each moment and also that every moment in which it is acquired is again an active deed. The lover abides; he abides in love, preserves himself in love; in precisely this way he brings about the abiding of his love in relationship to men. He continues to be the lover by abiding in love; by abiding in love his love abides; it abides, and this is what we now wish to consider:

THAT LOVE ABIDES.

" *Love never fails* "—*it abides*

When a child has been gone all day among strangers and thinks he ought to go home again but is afraid to go alone and yet really wants to stay as long as possible, it says to an older one, who perhaps prefers to go sooner, " Wait for me"; and the older one does what the child asks. When one of two colleagues is somewhat more advanced than the other, the latter says, " Wait for me"; and the first one does as asked. When two persons have rejoiced over a decision to take a trip together, but one of them gets sick, the sick one says, " Wait for me"; and the other person does as requested. When one who owes another man money cannot pay, he says, " Wait for me"; and the other man does as asked. When a girl in love sees that there will be great and perhaps prolonged difficulties in the way of her union with the beloved, she says to him, " Wait for me"; and the lover does as asked. And this is very beautiful and praiseworthy, to wait in this way for another person, but whether or not it is actually love which does this, we have not yet seen. Perhaps the time of waiting is too brief to make completely clear the extent to which the determination of one's waiting deserves decisively to be called love. Alas, perhaps the time of waiting was so long that the older one said to the child, " No, I can't wait for you any longer"; perhaps the slower one moved so slowly that the one ahead said, " No, I can't wait for you any longer without being held back too much myself"; perhaps the sickness dragged out so long that the friend said, " No, now I can't wait for you any longer; I must travel alone"; perhaps the prospects of union with the young girl remained so remote that the lover said, " No, now I can no longer wait for you; I owe it to myself and my life not to put things off year after year for this uncertainty."—But love *abides*.

That love abides, or, more accurately, whether it really abides in this or that instance or whether it ceases: this is something which occupies men's thoughts in very many ways, frequently as the subject of their conversation, usually as the chief content in all the narratives of the poets. That love abides is presented, then, as praiseworthy, but as unworthy that it does not abide, that it ceases, that it becomes altered. Only the first is love; the other by its alteration shows itself not to be love—and consequently that it never was love at all. The case is this, one cannot cease to be loving; if one in truth is loving he continues to be so. If one ceases *to be* loving, then one never *was* loving anyway. Therefore ceasing, in respect to love, has a retroactive power. Yes, I can never become weary of saying and pointing this out: wherever love is, there is something infinitely profound. For example, a man may have had money, and when it is gone, when he no longer has money, it nevertheless remains absolutely true and certain that he *has had* money. But if one ceases to love, he *has never been* loving at all. What is so mild as love and yet so rigorous, so strict with itself, so disciplining as love!

And further. When love ceases—when in erotic love, in friendship, that is, when in the love-relationship between two persons something intervenes and love ceases—then, as people say, these two have a falling out. Love was the connecting factor, in the good sense was between them. Then when something comes between them love is displaced; it ceases. The bond between them is broken, and the break becomes divisive. Therefore the relationship reaches a breaking point. But this expression Christianity does not recognise, does not understand, is not willing to understand. When one speaks of reaching a breaking-point, this is because one is of the opinion that in love there is only a relationship between two rather than a relationship among three, as has been shown. This talk about a break between two is very frivolous; thereby it is made to appear as if the love-relationship were a matter between the two persons, as if no third were concerned at all. If, then, the two are agreed to break with one another, no objection at all could be made. Furthermore, because these two break the relationship with each other, it does not follow that these same two might not be loving in relationship to others; therefore they retain the characteristic of loving, but their love is now brought into play only in relationship to others. Furthermore, the one who was guilty of provoking the break would have the advantage, and the innocent one would be defenceless. But this certainly would be wretched, if an innocent one should be the weaker. So it is in the world, to be sure, but eternally understood it can never hold together this way. What does Christianity do about it? The earnestness of Christianity immediately concentrates the attentiveness of the eternal upon the single individual, upon each single individual of the pair. Now when two persons relate themselves in love to each other, each one of them all by himself is related to *love.* Now the break does not come easily at all. Before they reach the breaking-point, before one comes to break his love in relationship to the other, he must first fall away *from* LOVE. This is the important thing. Therefore Christianity does not speak of a couple's breaking with each other but about that which essentially only the individual can do—falling away from *love*. A break between two smacks all too much of the bustle of temporality, as if the matter were not very dangerous; but to fall away from *love*—this has the seriousness of the eternal. Now everything is in its place; now the eternal maintains discipline and order; now in and through the break the innocent sufferer shall certainly be the stronger, if he also does not fall away from *love*. If love were simply and only a relationship between two, then one person would continually be in the other's power, insofar as the other was a base person who would break the relationship. When a relationship is only between two, one always has the upper hand in the relationship by being able to break it, for as soon as one has broken, *the relationship* is broken. But when there are three, one person cannot do this. The third, as mentioned, is love itself, which the innocent sufferer can hold to in the break, and then the break has no power over him. And the guilty one shall certainly not congratulate himself for making a good bargain out of the affair, for to fall away from *love*, yes, this is the highest price; a quite different kind of seriousness is involved than in this hasty breaking with a single person—and then, after all, to be a good and loving person in every respect.

But the true lover never falls away from *love*; therefore he can never reach the breaking-point, for love abides. Yet, in a relationship between two persons can one prevent the break when the other breaks? One would certainly think that one of the two is enough to break the relationship, and if the relationship is broken, the break simply exists. In a certain sense it is so, but just the same, if the lover does not fall away from *love*, he can prevent the break, he can perform this miracle; for if he perseveres, the break can never really come to be. By abiding (and in this abiding the lover is in compact with the eternal), he maintains superiority over the past; thereby he transforms what is a break in the past and through which a break exists, into a possible relationship in the future. Seen from the angle of the past the break becomes clearer and clearer day by day and year by year; but the lover, who abides, by abiding belongs to the future, the eternal, and from the angle of the future the break is not a break, but rather a possibility. But the powers of the eternal are needed for this, and therefore the lover, who abides, must abide in *love*; otherwise the past still gets power little by little and thereby the break gradually becomes apparent. O, the powers of the eternal are needed at the decisive moment straightway to transform the past into the future! But it is capable of being this power.

How shall I now describe this work of love? O, that I might be inexhaustible in describing what is so indescribably joyous and so up-building to reflect upon!

And so the breaking-point between the two is reached. It was a misunderstanding; yet one of them broke the relationship. But the lover says, " I abide "—therefore there still is no break. Imagine a compound word which lacks the last word; there is only the first word and the hyphen (for the one who breaks the relationship still cannot take the hyphen with him; the lover naturally keeps the hyphen on his side); imagine, then, the first word and the hyphen of a compound word, and now imagine that you know absolutely nothing more about how it hangs together—what will you say? You will say that the word is not complete, that it lacks something. It is the same with the lover. That the relationship has reached the breaking-point cannot be seen directly; it can be known only from the angle of the past. But the lover wills not to know the past, for he abides; and to abide is in the direction of the future. Consequently the lover expresses that the relationship which another considers broken is a relationship which has not yet been completed. Although it lacks something, it neverthe-less is not for that reason a break. Therefore the whole thing depends upon how the relationship is regarded, and the lover—he abides.— And so it came to the breaking-point; there was an argument which separated the two. But one broke off; he said: " It is all over between us." But the lover abides; he says, " All is not over between us; we are still midway in the sentence; it is only the sentence which is not complete." Is it not so? What a difference there is between a fragment and an unfinished sentence! In order to call something a fragment, one must know that nothing more is to come. If one does not know this, he says that the sentence is not yet completed. From the angle of the past, we say when it is determined that nothing more is to follow, " It is a broken fragment." From the angle of the future, waiting for the next part, we say, " The sentence is not complete; it still lacks something."—And so it came to the breaking-point. It was dis-harmony, cooling-off, indifference which separated them. But one made the break; he says, " I am not speaking to that person any more; I never see him." But the lover says: " I abide; therefore we shall still speak with one another, because silence also belongs to conversation at times." Is this not so? But suppose now that it is three years since that they last spoke together. See, here it comes again. That it was three years ago one can know only in the sense of the past; but the lover, who daily renews himself by the eternal and abides, over him the past has no power at all. If you saw two persons sitting silent together and you knew nothing more, would you thereby conclude that it was three years since they spoke together? Can any one determine how long a silence must have been in order to say now, there is no more conversation; and if one can determine this, in a particular instance one can nevertheless know only from the angle of the past whether this is so, for the time must indeed be past. But the lover, who abides, continually emancipates himself from his knowledge of the past; he knows no past; he waits only for the future. Does the dance cease because one dancer has gone away? In a certain sense. But if the other still remains standing in the posture which expresses a turning towards the one who is not seen, and if you know nothing about the past, then you will say, " Now the dance will begin just as soon as the other comes, the one who is expected." Put the past out of the way; drown it in the forgetfulness of the eternal by abiding in love: then the end is the beginning and there is no break! When the faithless man forsakes a girl, but she sits by the window in "the red glow of twilight" and waits, she thereby expresses every evening: now he comes, he comes very soon; every evening it seems as if there had been no break, because she abides. That she has sat this way every evening for three years is certainly not expressed each evening; the passer-by discovers this no more than she herself knows it, if she really abides in love. But perhaps the girl really was in love with herself. She desired union with the beloved for her own sake; it was her only desire; her soul was as one with this desire. In gratitude for its fulfilment she would do everything to make the beloved's life as beautiful as possible—yes, it is true—but yet, yet it was for her own sake that she desired the union. If this is so, she becomes weary; she becomes attentive to the past, to the duration of time—now she no longer sits at the window; she expresses that the break exists. But love abides.—And so it came to a breaking-point, whatever the occasion might have been—one broke the relationship. It was terrible; in all probability hate, eternal and irreconcilable hate will fill his soul in the future. " I will never see that person any more; our paths are forever separated; the abysmal depth of hate lies between us." He indeed concedes that insofar as life is still a path, they are on the path together, but not in any other sense; he goes about very circumspectly so that his path does not cross that of the hated one; to him the world is almost too small to house them both; to him it is agony to breathe in the same world where the hated one breathes; he shudders at the thought that eternity will house them both. But the lover abides. " I abide," he says: " therefore we are still on the path together." And is this not so? When two balls collide (something everyone can try) in such a way that the one simply by repulsion carries the other along in its path, are they not in the path together? That it happens through repulsion cannot be seen; it is something past which must be known. But the lover wills not to know the past; he abides, he abides on the path with the one who hates him; consequently there is still no break.

What marvellous strength love has! The most powerful word which has been said, yes, God's creative word, is: " Be." But the most powerful word any human being has ever said is, if said by a lover: I abide. Reconciled to himself and to his conscience, God's friend, in league with all good angels, the lover goes without defence into the most dangerous battle; he only says: " I abide." And as he is truly the lover, he will still conquer, conquer by his abiding, conquer even more gloriously than that Roman did with his delay,[42] for the abiding of love is in itself far more noble. As he truly is the lover, there is no misunderstanding which sooner or later will not be conquered by his abiding, there is no hate that ultimately will not have to give up and yield to his abiding—in eternity if not sooner. Note—he who has acquired another person's love and therefore is in possession of it must at every moment be afraid of losing it. But he who is hated because of his love is eternally certain of winning love. If time cannot, at least the eternal shall wrench away the other's hate, open his eyes for *love* and thereby also for the love which endured all through life and now abides in eternity.—In this way love never fails—it abides.

Love abides—it never wastes away

That a certain spontaneous good nature, a certain benevolent co-operativeness and helpfulness still has time to give in affectionately waiting we certainly appreciate with rejoicing; that it becomes weary as time stretches out or moves slowly and therefore drags—this is only too clear. Duration, duration of time is indeed the demand which brings the majority into bankruptcy. In the commercial world it is more customary for an establishment to go under because suddenly in a single stroke too great a demand is made upon it, but in the world of the spirit it is the duration which does this with so many. People have strength enough for a moment; on the long haul, however, they become insolvent. But love endures. O, what ability the poets and orators have to characterise the changeableness of everything, to show the power of time over everything which comes into time, over the greatest, the most powerful, the most magnificent underakings, over the wonders of the world, which in time have become talmost unre cognisable ruins, over the most imperishable name, which in time ends in the vagueness of legends!

But, while love abides, cannot something happen, even though it abides, so that nevertheless it becomes changed in time, except that this is not its fault but is a suffering? Then the relationship would be: love abides; no circumstance changes it or gets it to forsake itself, and yet it is altered through a change which we call *wasting away*, although we may say of this same love that it never falls out of love.

Let us consider for a moment what occupies men very much, erotic love, or this girl who, according to the poet's words, sits every evening at the window "in the red glow of twilight" and waits for the beloved, "alas," while "time comes and goes." Now this was long ago, for it was, so says the poet, "in the time long since gone." The girl did not mark how time came and went while she waited—although time marked her. We usually say, " Time goes "—O, it goes so quickly for the fortunate, so indescribably tediously for the sorrowing. Or we say, " The time will come "—O, it comes so slowly for those who hope, only too quickly for the fearful. But here the poet says, and felicitously, that time comes and time goes, because he wants to describe one who is waiting, and for such a person it does not only go or only come— it comes and goes. Out of sympathy with the waiting girl time under- took to do, as it were, what the faithless man should have done. When the time came that " He " should come, time came, but " He " did not come; then time went again until the time came when it was time that " He " should come who did not come. In this way time lulled the waiting girl by coming and going until cradled in this movement she rested in expectation. Amazing! One should think that expecta- tion would be most likely to keep a person awake; yet expectation, when one gives himself to it completely, is very soporific, and this is not so amazing. If you have lain down to sleep and while you slept someone suddenly turned on a powerful, high-gushing fountain, you would wake up terrified. But if you were to lie down beside a fountain to rest: never had you slept more sweetly, never more refreshingly, never more deliciously than when lulled by the playing of the fountain!

Therefore time came and time went; to be sure, the girl did not fail in her love, but nevertheless she wasted away—for it was not time which wasted away; no, it came and it went, but the girl wasted away. Honour be to this faithful soul! Indeed, she has the honour, the greatest honour among men: that a poet has celebrated her, not as an occasional poet does for money or perhaps because the poet had known her. No, her name is not known, only her beautiful act which inspired the true poet. Let us never forget that to remain faithful in one's love is a noble womanly deed, a great and glorious act. It shall be held in high honour as long as a poet exists in the world, in spite of all the talk about the wretchedness of domestic life; and if the world becomes so wretched that no poet exists any more, the race must learn to despair over the extinction of poets, and thereby a poet will again come who holds her in honour.

She wasted away—a sacrifice to love. And yet precisely this is the highest which can be said of any human being. The question, however, is this, whether that for which one is sacrificed is the highest. But, eternally understood, to be sacrificed is and continues to be, as long as the world remains the world, a far greater achievement than to conquer; for the world is not so perfect that to be victorious *in the world* by adaptation to the world does not involve a dubious mixture of the world's paltriness. To be victorious in the world is like becoming something great in the world; ordinarily to become something great in the world is a dubious matter, [43] because the world is not so excellent that its judgment of greatness unequivocally has great significance— except as unconscious sarcasm.

Hence the girl wasted away, a sacrifice to erotic love. But erotic love is not in the highest sense love and is not the highest love—for this she wasted away, loving in death as she had in life, but dis- tinguished by the fact that erotic love had been for her the highest. Erotic love is desire for this life; therefore time had power over her; therefore she wasted away in love, until it, too, wasted away, although she nevertheless knew that she had power over time, for she did not fall away from her love.

But love abides—it never wastes away. For spiritual love contains in itself the spring which flows unto eternal life. That this lover also ages through the years and then dies in time proves nothing; for his love nevertheless remains eternally young. In his love he is not bound to temporality, is not dependent upon temporality, as in erotic love; the eternal is the right season for his love. When he dies, he is right at the goal; when he dies, it just proves that he did not expect in vain. Alas, when the young girl died, we simply said: unfortunately it seems that she waited in vain. How, then, should the love which abides waste away? Can, then, immortality become weak? But what is it which gives a human being immortality, what else but the love which abides? For erotic love, the most beautiful but nevertheless frail invention of temporality, belongs to time. Hence there is a deeper contradiction here. On the girl's part there was no wrong; she was and remained true to her love. Yet her love became somewhat changed through the years. This inheres in erotic love itself. The contradiction, then, is this: that with the most incorruptible will, willing to be sacrificed, one nevertheless cannot, more deeply understood, be unconditionally faithful or abide in that which does not itself eternally abide —and this erotic love does not do. The girl herself perhaps had not understood this, these inter-relationships, but this structure of self-contradiction was the sadness of her death. That she is sacrificed does not have the solemnity of the eternal and therefore is not inspiring and up-building; rather it has the sadness of temporality and thus is inspiring to the poet.

The young girl wasted away. Even if " He " had come, consequently had come before death, it nevertheless still would have been too late. She abided, but time had weakened in her the desire by which she lived, and yet this same desire consumed her. On the other hand, the lover in the deepest sense, he who abides, does not waste away; his love does not consume. If someone who misunderstood him, if someone who had cooled off towards him, if someone who hated him returned to him again, he would find him unchanged, unchanged in the same longing for the eternal and in the same quiet calmness amid the temporal. His love is eternal, relates itself to the eternal, rests in the eternal. Therefore he expects *at every moment* the same as he expects *eternally*, and therefore without disquiet, for in the eternal there is time enough.

If love's expectation is able to make a man, essentially understood, weak, it must be because his expectation stands in a dependent relationship to time; so that time has the power to decide whether or not the expectation becomes fullfilled or not. That is to say, the expectation is principally a temporal expectation, but such an expectation the love which abides does not have. That an expectation is exclusively temporal makes for unrest in expectation. Time essentially does not exist without unrest; it does not exist for animals, which are completely without unrest; and the clock, which tells time, cannot do this when the unrest ceases. But when, as in the case of the purely temporal expectation, unrest swings between fullfillment and non-fullfillment in such a way that the movement becomes accelerated in time because the elapsing of time, the fact that it passes, elicits disquietude, then the fullfillment, if it does not occur in time, cannot occur at all—when this is the case, expectation consumes. Finally, the unrest apparently vanishes; alas, this is precisely when the sickness develops into consumption. But the lover, who abides, has an eternal expectation, and this eternal gives proportion in the unrest which in time swings between fullfillment and non-fullfillment, but independently of time, for the fullfillment is not at all made impossible because time has passed: this lover is not consumed.

What faithfulness in the love which abides! It is far from our intention to depreciate the loving girl, as if there were a kind of faithlessness in her (alas, a faithlessness—toward a faithless one!) because she weakened through the years and wasted away and her love became changed with the change which is the change in erotic love itself over the years. And yet, yet—yes, it is a strange criss-crossing of self-contradicting thoughts, but it cannot be otherwise with even the highest faithfulness in erotic love than that it almost seems to be faithlessness, because erotic love itself is not the eternal. The contradiction does not lie in the girl; she remained faithful. The contradiction, which the girl suffered, lies in this that erotic love is not the eternal and consequently in this that it is impossible to relate oneself with *eternal* faithfulness to that which in itself is *not* the *eternal*. On the other hand, what faithfulness in love, to remain completely unchanged, without the least weakening, the same at every moment—no matter at what time or hour the misunderstanding, the unfriendly, the hateful may turn again to this lover! That he who abides never wastes away is for him an eternal gain; but it is also, and so we regard it here as he does himself, a work of love in faithfulness toward the ones he loves.

What would be more distressing, yes, almost to the point of desperation, than if, when the moment came that the misunderstanding one turned again and sought understanding, when the unfriendly one turned again and sought friendship, when the one who had hated turned again and sought reconciliation—what would be more distressing than if the lover has wasted away so that neither understanding, nor resurrection of friendship, nor reconciliation's renewal in love could genuinely come about with the blessed joy of the eternal! And on the other hand, what can make the moment of pardon, the transition of reconciliation so natural, so easy, as this that the lover (as sketched previously), by abiding, has continually discarded the past; for then from his side the reconciliation already exists, as if there had been no separation at all. When both have a conception of the past or of the long duration of the separation, forgiving is often a difficult collision and the relationship perhaps never becomes fully re-established. But the lover knows nothing of the past; therefore he performs even this last act in love; he takes the shock away so that no collision can occur: the transition of forgiving cannot take place more easily. How frequently reconciliation has almost been reached between two persons, but one remained offended, as we say. When this is the case, it is because something from the past unlovingly comes forth, for it is impossible to be hurt by that which is softer than the softest, by love. Truly, no boat which glides easily through smooth water over the softest sand till the rushes halt and enclose it can be so protected from the slightest shock as one who turns again and seeks reconciliation with the love which abides!

Such is the lover. That the most beautiful of all, the moment of reconciliation, should become a fruitless attempt, a vain journey, because by that time he had become changed: this he *prevents*, because he abides and never wastes away. That the transition of forgiving may be as easy as meeting with a person one had seen just recently, that the dialogue of love might flow as naturally as with a person one engages in conversation, that the journeying together might be as rhythmically swift as it is between two people who for the *first* time begin a new life —in short, that there might be no hitch, none at all, which could shock in the least, not for a second and not for a split second: this the lover *accomplishes*, for he abides and never wastes away.

VII

Mercifulness, a Work of Love, Even
if It Can Give Nothing and Is
Capable of Doing Nothing

" Do not neglect to do good and to share "[44]—but also do not forget
that this perpetual worldly talk about doing good and well-doing and
charity and charities and gifts and gifts is almost mercilessness.[45] Let
journalists and tax-collectors and parish clerks talk about charity and
calculate and calculate; but let us never fail to hear that Christianity
speaks *essentially* of mercifulness, that Christianity would last of all
reward this mercilessness, as if poverty and wretchedness were not only
lacking in money, *etc.*, but also were excluded from the highest of all,
from being able to practise mercifulness, because they are excluded
from the capacity of being charitable, well-doing, beneficent. But men
preach and preach ecclesiastically-worldly and worldly-ecclesiastically
about charity, well-doing—men forget, even in the sermon, mercifulness. This is, Christianly understood, indecent. The poor man who
sits in church must groan, and why must he groan? Could it be that
aided by the pastor's preaching his groaning might be able to open up
the purses of the rich? Oh, no, he must groan, in the Biblical sense[46]
he must "groan against" the pastor because precisely when one is so
eager to help him the greatest injustice is done to him. Woe unto him
who devours the inheritance of widows and orphans,[47] but woe also to
the preachers who are silent about mercifulness in order to talk about
charity! Preaching should be solely and only about mercifulness. If
you know how to speak effectually *about this*, charity will follow of
itself and come by itself to the degree to which the individual is capable.
But consider this: if by speaking of charity a person gathered money,
money, money, consider that by being silent about mercifulness he

acted unmercifully towards the poor and the wretched for whom he nevertheless procured relief with the help of rich charity's money. Consider this: if the poor and the wretched disturb us with their requests, we certainly can see about getting help for them through charity; but consider that it would be far more terrible if we constrained the poor and the wretched to "hinder our prayers," as Scriptures say (I Peter 3 : 7), by their groaning against us to God, because we insultingly rebuffed the poor and the wretched by not speaking about how *they* can practise mercy.

We shall hold to this point in our discussion of mercifulness and take care lest mercifulness be confused with external conditions, which love as such does not really have within its power; whereas true love has mercifulness within its power, just as love has a heart in its bosom. Because a person has a heart in his bosom, it does not follow that he has money in his pocket, but the first is nevertheless by far the more important and certainly is decisive with respect to mercifulness. And truly, if one did not have money but understood how to speak of mercifulness in a way encouraging and inspiring to the poor, the wretched: I wonder if he would not have done just as much as he who tossed the poor some money or preached benevolences out of the pockets of the rich!

We shall, then, consider:

MERCIFULNESS, A WORK OF LOVE, EVEN IF IT HAS NOTHING TO GIVE AND IS CAPABLE OF DOING NOTHING.

We shall, with the powers we have, seek to make this as enlightening as possible, as alluring as possible, to bring as close as possible to the poor the consolation he has in being able to be merciful. We shall speak of this by discarding some worldly illusions. Insofar as it is needed, we wish also—this is our desire, if possible—to contribute something by what we say to make him who can be charitable and well-doing ashamed in such a way as is God-pleasing, to make him blush in that holy shyness which becomes a Christian, to make him willing to give and yet unwilling to admit that it is alms, to make him as one who turns his gaze away in order not to have the shame of seeing that *others see* that he has honour in it or as one whose left hand really does not know what the right hand is doing.

Mercifulness has nothing to give. It follows of itself that if the merciful person has something to give, he gives it very willingly. But this is not what we want to concentrate our attention upon but on this, that one can be merciful without having the least to give. And this is of great importance, since really *to be able* to be merciful is a far greater perfection than to have money and consequently *to be able* to give.

If that man famous through eighteen hundred years, the merciful Samaritan,[48] if he had come walking, not riding, on the way from Jericho to Jerusalem where he saw the unfortunate man lying, if he had brought nothing with him whereby he could bind up his wounds, if he had then lifted up the unfortunate man and placed him on his shoulders, carried him to the nearest inn where the keeper would take in neither him nor the unfortunate one because the Samaritan did not have a penny, if he could only beg and beseech the hard-hearted inn-keeper nevertheless to be merciful because it involved a man's life—if therefore he had not . . . but no, the tale is not yet done—consequently, if the Samaritan, far from losing patience over this, had gone away carrying the unfortunate man, had sought a softer resting-place for the wounded man, had sat by his side, had done everything in his power to halt the loss of blood—but the unfortunate man died in his arms: would he not have been just as merciful, equally as merciful as that merciful Samaritan, or is there some objection to be lodged against calling this the story of the good Samaritan?—Take the story about the woman[49] who placed the two pennies in the temple-treasury, but let us poetise a little variation. The two pennies were for her a great sum, which she had not quickly accumulated. She had saved for a long time in order to get them saved up, and then she had hidden them wrapped in a little cloth in order to bring them when she herself went up to the temple. But a swindler had detected that she possessed this money, had tricked her out of it, and had exchanged the cloth for an identical piece which was utterly empty—something which the widow did not know. Thereupon she went up to the temple, placed, as she intended, the two pennies, that is, nothing, in the temple-treasury: I wonder if Christ would not still have said what he said of her, that "she gave more than all the rich?"

Yet, mercifulness without money, what does this signify? Yes, ultimately the worldly presumption of charity and well-doing even goes so far as to ridicule mercifulness which possesses nothing! Truly it is unjust and revolting enough, the mercilessness of this worldly existence, that when the poor person gives his last dime the rich man comes along and gives hundreds of dollars so that everybody sees the hundreds of dollars, that is, that the rich man with his gift completely overshadows the poor man's gift—his mercifulness! But what madness, if what

Christ says is nevertheless true, that the poor gave the MOST; what lunacy, that he who gives less (the rich man—and the large amount) overshadows him who gives more (the poor person—and the little mite), yes, overshadows even him who gives most! Yet, obviously, the world does not say this. It says that the rich man gives the most, and why does the world say this? Because the world has understanding only for money—and Christ only for mercifulness. And just because Christ alone had understanding for mercifulness, he is therefore so accurate about its being only two pennies which the widow gave, and precisely for this reason he would say that not even this much was needed or that one could give even less and nevertheless give more in giving even less. Wonderful computation, or rather, what a wonderful mode of calculating—not to be found in any mathematics book! A remarkable expression is used about this widow, that " She gave of her poverty." But the greatness of the gift increases in proportion to the greatness of the poverty, consequently in reverse of what the world thinks (that the greatness of the gift is in proportion to one's wealth); therefore one who is even poorer than this widow by giving one penny out of his poverty gives even more than this widow, who in comparison to the rich still gave the most. Yes, to the world this certainly must appear to be the most tedious kind of reckoning, in which one penny can become so important, become the most significant gift. The world and the world's charity would rather deal with large, impressive amounts, and one penny certainly does not impress—any more than mercifulness is impressed by glittering virtues. Eternally understood, however, this kind of reckoning is the only true kind and can be learned only from the eternal and by forsaking the illusion of worldliness and temporality. For the eternal has the sharpest eye and the most developed understanding for mercy, but no understanding for money, no more than the eternal has financial problems or, as the saying goes, has anything to use money for. Yes, one could both laugh and weep over it. It would undeniably be a splendid invention for laughter to imagine the eternal in financial difficulties—Ah, but let us weep a little over the fact that temporality has completely forgotten the eternal and forgotten that money is eternally less than nothing! Alas, many think that the eternal is a construction of the imagination, money the reality—in the understanding of the eternal and of truth it is precisely money which is a construction of the imagination! Think of the eternal whatever way you will; only admit that in temporal existence there are many temporal things which you have desired to find again in eternity, that you have desired to see trees and flowers and stars again, to hear the singing of birds and the murmuring of brooks again—but could it occur to you that there should be money in eternity? No, then heaven would indeed become a land of wretchedness again, and therefore this cannot possibly occur to you; it is no more possible than for one who considers money to be reality to imagine that there is an eternity. Of all that you have seen there is nothing you can be so sure will never enter heaven as—money. On the other hand, there is nothing heaven is so certain about as mercifulness. Therefore you see that mercifulness infinitely stands in no relationship to money.

Nevertheless money, money, money! That foreign prince[50] is supposed to have said as he turned his back on mighty Rome, " Here lies a city for sale and only awaits a buyer." How often might one not have been tempted despondently to turn his back on all of existence with these words, " Here lies a world which is for sale and only awaits a buyer"—insofar as one will not say that the devil has already bought it!—What is the earnestness of life? If you in truth have considered this serious question, then remember how you answered it to yourself, or let me remind you how you yourself answered it. Earnestness is a person's God-relationship; wherever the thought of God accompanies what a man does, thinks, and says, earnestness is present; therein lies earnestness. But money is the world's god; therefore it thinks that everything which has to do with money or has a relationship to money is earnestness. That noble, simple wise man of old would not accept money for his teaching,[51] and the apostle Paul preferred to work with his own hands rather than to besmirch the Gospel and devalue his apostolic service and falsify the proclamation of the Word by taking money for it.[52] How does the world judge such people? Yes, let us not foolishly ask how the world judges that noble, simple one and the sainted apostle, because the world has learned to speak by rote a kind of eulogy over them. But if a contemporary at this moment wanted to do as these two, how would our age judge it? It would judge it to be eccentricity, to be fanaticism; it would judge such a person to be " lacking in earnestness." Because earnestness is to make money; to make lots of money, even if it is by selling men—this is earnestness; to make great amounts of money by contemptible slander—this is earnestness. To proclaim something true—and at the same time make considerable money—this is earnestness (that it is true is not basic but rather that one makes money). Money, money—this is earnestness. So we are brought up, from earliest childhood, trained in ungodly money-worship. Permit me to cite an example, the first, the best among thousands and thousands—there are not more herring ahead of a boat working its way through a shoal of herring than there are examples of up-bringing in money-worship. Think of a household in which the head of the family recommends that on the next day (which is Sunday) all of them go to church together. But what happens? Sunday morning finds the girls not dressed in time. What does the father say then— earnest father, who earnestly brings up his children to worship money? Yes, he naturally says nothing, or as good as nothing, because there is no occasion here for a warning or a reprimand; he just says, " If the girls are not ready, we have to stay home; there is nothing else to do." But imagine, imagine how terrible it would be if the girls were to have gone to the theatre and they were not ready at the appointed time. How do you imagine this earnest father would carry on then, and why? Because in this case they had wasted considerable money; whereas by staying at home on Sunday they had saved at least the offering-money. Now the daughters will get a stern—earnest— paternal reprimand. Now it is a fault, a great sin not to have been ready—and therefore this earnest father, who with earnestness brings up his children, for sake of the next time must not let this go by unpunished. That there is slovenliness on the girls' part is the least of the matter—otherwise the guilt was just as great on Sunday; no, the seriousness lies in this, that money has been lost. And this is called being a father; this is called having paternal worthiness and making responsible use of paternal dignity; this is called up-bringing! To be sure, this is indeed up-bringing; only one does not bring up human beings this way, but rather fools and inhuman beings!

But if one has this conception of money, what conception can one then have of mercifulness which lacks money? Such mercy must be regarded as a kind of madness, a fancy. Indeed, the eternal and Christianity must also be regarded as a kind of madness, a fancy. A pagan emperor supposedly said that one should not smell of money.[53] Christianity, on the other hand, rightly teaches to smell of money. It teaches that money in itself has a bad odour. Therefore some strong perfume is always needed to drive out the stench. Have mercy: then giving money takes care of itself; without it money has a bad odour. See, a beggar can also say this, and he ought to become just as immortal through his expression as that emperor—and financier. Mercifulness is a strong perfume. If prayer is an offering of the lips and is God-pleasing, mercifulness is essentially an offering of the heart and is, as Scriptures say, a sweet scent in the nostrils of God. O, never forget it, when you think of God, that he has not even the poorest understanding for money!

My reader, if you were a speaker, which task would you choose: the one of speaking to the wealthy about practising charity or the one of speaking to the poor about practising mercifulness? I know well enough which one I choose or, better, which one I have chosen—if only I were a speaker. O, there is something so indescribably reconciling in speaking to the poor about *practising* mercifulness! And how necessary it is—if not for sake of the poor, then for your own sake—you can readily ascertain yourself. Only try it, and you shall immediately see the concept shift in your hands, as if it were of no help to speak to the poor about mercifulness, since they simply have nothing to give, and that one therefore ought to speak to the rich about mercifulness towards the poor. In this way the poor man is trapped in his poverty and, in addition, is excluded in the world's view from the capacity to practise mercifulness, and consequently is designated and abandoned as the pitiable object of mercy, who can at best bow and thank—when the rich are so good as to practise mercy. Merciful God, what mercilessness!

So the discourse turns to you, you poor and wretched! O, be merciful! Preserve your heart in your bosom, this heart which in spite of poverty and wretchedness yet has sympathy for another's wretchedness, this heart, which before God has the fearlessness to know that one can be merciful, yes, that one can be precisely this on the supreme level, merciful in a remarkable and pre-eminent sense, when one has nothing to give. "O, be merciful!" See, here it is again: who does not immediately and involuntarily think of the cry of the poor man, of the beggar, to the rich, "Be merciful"—however erroneous this speech-usage is, since the cry is for charity. Therefore we use the language more correctly, we who say to the poor, to the poorest of all: O, be merciful! Do not let the envious pettiness of this worldly existence finally corrupt you in such a way that you are able to forget that you can be merciful, corrupt you in such a way that a false shame squelches the best in you. A false shame—yes, for true shame comes first—O, that it would always come, but in every case it ought to come—with money. If you get money and because of this are able to give, then, then first will you have something to be ashamed of. Be merciful, be merciful toward the rich. Remember that you have this within your power, although he has the money! Therefore do not misuse this power; do not be unmerciful enough to call down the punishment of heaven upon his mercilessness! Yes, we know well what the world cares about a poor man's sigh to God when it complains of the rich; that sigh wafted away, that inaudible word, is indeed the most insignificant thing of all; but still, still, although not unfamiliar with loud cries, I am carried away by them, lest any poor person should with reason be able to complain of me to God in return. O, be merciful! If the rich man is stingy and tight, or even if he is tight not only with money but also reserved and stingy with words: then you be rich in mercifulness! For mercifulness works wonders; it makes two pennies into a great sum when the poor widow gives them; it makes the little gift into a great sum when the poor person mercifully does not call the rich to account; it makes the morose giver less guilty when the poor mercifully cover his peevishness. O, how many has money made merciless—if money shall also have the power of making merciless those who have no money: then the power of money has certainly conquered completely! But if the power of money has conquered completely, then mercifulness is altogether abolished.

Mercifulness is able to do nothing.

The sacred narratives have this remarkable characteristic, among others, that in all their simplicity they nevertheless always get everything said which should be said. This is also the case in the Gospel concerning the rich man and the poor man. Neither Lazarus's wretchedness nor the rich man's luxuriousness is minutely elaborated and described; yet there is one detail added which is worth noticing. It is told that Lazarus was laid full of sores at the rich man's door, but the dogs came and licked his sores. What is it that is to be portrayed about the rich man? Lack of mercy or, more accurately, inhuman unmercifulness. In order to illuminate mercilessness one can use a merciful person placed at his side. This is done in the story of the merciful Samaritan, who by contrast illuminates the Levite and the priest. But the rich man was inhuman; therefore the evangelist makes use of the dogs. What contrast! We shall not now exaggerate and say that a dog can be merciful; but in contrast to the rich man it was as if the dogs were merciful. And this is the shocking thing, that when men have abandoned mercy, then the dogs must be merciful.—But there is something else in this comparison between the rich man and the dogs. The rich man had it richly enough in his power to be able to do something for Lazarus; the dogs were able to do nothing—and yet it was as if the dogs were merciful.

Note that this is precisely what we are speaking about in these reflections. It follows naturally of itself that if the merciful person can do something, he does it most gladly. But we do not wish to concentrate attention upon this, but rather upon the fact that one can be merciful without being able to do the slightest. And this is of great importance, inasmuch as being able to be merciful is a much greater perfection than to be able to do something.

Suppose that there was not one man who journeyed from Jericho to Jerusalem but that there were two, that both were overpowered by thieves, disabled, and that no one came travelling by—suppose then that one of them knew of nothing else to do but groan, while the second one forgot and overcame his own suffering in order to speak comforting, friendly words or, something which involved great pain, dragged himself to a little creek in order to get a refreshing drink for the other; or suppose that both were bereft of speech, but one of them in silent prayer sighed to God for the other one also: was he not then merciful? —If someone has cut off my hands, I cannot play the zither, and if one has cut off my feet, I cannot dance, and if I lie disabled at the brink, I cannot throw myself into the sea to save another person's life, and if I lie with broken arm or leg, I cannot dash into the flames to save another's life: but for all that I can be merciful.

Frequently I have thought of how a painter might portray mercy, but I have been convinced that it cannot be done.[54] As soon as a painter does it, it becomes doubtful whether it is mercy or something else. Mercy is evident most definitely when the poor one gives the two pennies which are his whole possession, when the helpless one is able to do nothing and yet is merciful. But instead art will portray the gift, consequently charity, and instead it will portray that which looks best in painting, the great exploit. Try to paint it: a poor widow who gives another the only bread she possesses—and you will easily discern that you cannot express what is most important; you can express that it is one piece of bread but not that it is the only piece she possesses. Danes are well acquainted with the dangers at sea. There is a work which portrays a courageous sailor[55] who is responsible for rescuing many human lives by pilot-boat. His figure is depicted and lower to one side a wreck, on the other side a pilot-boat. Note that this can be painted. And it is indeed splendid, to steer like a rescuing angel through the billows and to do it bravely, courageously, and, if you will, also mercifully. O, but if you have never seen it, you have nevertheless imagined such wretchedness or the wretchedness of those who perhaps from childhood or later in life are so unfortunately deformed, so badly defaced, that they are unable to do anything at all, nothing at all, are hardly able even to express sympathy in intelligible words: shall we then unmercifully add this new cruelty to their misery by denying their capacity for mercifulness—because this certainly cannot be portrayed, since such a person cannot be properly portrayed except as an object of mercy! And yet it is true that the mercifulness of precisely such a person is the most beautiful and most true and has yet one value more in that he is not stupefied by his own suffering and has thereby lost sympathy for others.

Think of a widow in poverty. She has only one daughter, but nature has stepmotherly denied this daughter almost every gift which could mitigate the mother's condition. Think of this unfortunate girl, who sighs under the heavy burden and yet with the small endowment granted her is inexhaustibly inventive in doing the little, the nothing, she is capable of in order to alleviate her mother's life. See, this is mercifulness! No rich man will squander thousands of dollars to have a painter paint this, for it cannot be painted. But every time the society patron who helps the mother visits them, the poor girl is put to shame, because "he," he can do so much—his mercifulness overshadows that of the girl! O, yes, in the eyes of the world, perhaps even to the eye of the painter and of the art connoisseur.

So the discourse turns to you, you wretched one, who can do nothing at all: do not forget to be merciful! Be merciful. This consolation, that you can be merciful, let alone the consolation that you are that, is far greater than if I could assure you that the most powerful person will show mercy to you. Be merciful to us more fortunate ones! Your care-filled life is like a dangerous criticism of loving providence; you have it therefore in your power to make us anxious; therefore be merciful! In truth, how much mercifulness is shown toward the powerful and the fortunate by such an unfortunate! Which, indeed, is more merciful—powerfully to alleviate another's need or by suffering quietly and patiently to take care mercifully lest one disturb the joy and happiness of others? Which of these two loves more: the fortunate one who has sympathy for another's suffering, or the unfortunate one who has true sympathy for another's joy and happiness?

" *But the main thing is still this, that need be met in every way, and that everything possible be done to remedy every need.*" This is the way temporality speaks, well-intentioned, and it cannot very well speak otherwise. On the other hand, the eternal says: there is only one danger, this, that mercifulness is not practised; even if aid were given in every need, there is still no certainty that it was done in mercifulness, and if this was not the case, this wretchedness, that mercifulness was not practised at all, would be greater than all temporal need.

The fact is that the world does not understand the eternal. Temporal existence has a temporal and to that degree an activist conception of need and also has a materialistic conception of the greatness of a gift and of the ability to do something to meet need. " The poor, the wretched may die—therefore it is very important that help be given." No, answers the eternal; the most important is that mercifulness be practised or that the help be the help of mercifulness. " Get us money, get us hospitals, these are the most important! " No, says the eternal; the most important is mercifulness. That a man dies is, eternally understood, no misfortune, but that mercifulness has not been practised is. It is worth noting the caption beneath the painting which portrays a wreck on one side and a pilot-boat on the other: Poverty— and Violent Death; Prosperity—and Natural Death: consequently death on both sides. The eternal maintains with immovable firmness that mercifulness is the most important. No thinker can be so stiff-necked as the eternal is about its thought; no thinker can be so calm, so undisturbed by the urgency of the moment and the danger of the moment which seem to enforce the view that it is most important of all that help be given in every way; no thinker is so calm, so undisturbed, as the eternal. And no thinker is so certain as the eternal is that men must finally, nevertheless, come around and think his thoughts, for it says: just wait; we shall talk about this in eternity, and we shall talk simply and only about mercifulness and simply and only about the distinction—merciful/not-merciful. O, that I could portray the countenance the eternal will assume when the rich man answers the question whether or not he has been merciful: I have given hundreds of thousands to the poor! For the eternal will look at him amazed, as one who cannot get into his head what he is talking about; and then it will again put the question to him: have you been merciful? Imagine that a man went out to confer with a mountain about his affairs or that someone had dealings with the wind about his enterprises—the eternal will not understand any better what the rich man says of hundreds of thousands and what the powerful man says of having done everything.

Does mercifulness consist in giving hundreds of thousands to the poor? No. Is it mercifulness to give a halfpenny to the poor? No. Mercifulness is *how* it is given. Therefore the hundreds of thousands and the halfpenny are a matter of indifference; that is, I can see mercifulness just as well in one as in the other, that is, there can be mercifulness and it can be fully as apparent in the halfpenny which is given as in the hundreds of thousands. But if I can see mercifulness in the halfpenny just as well as in the hundreds of thousands, I can really see it better in the halfpenny, for the hundreds of thousands have an accidental significance which easily draws physical attention to itself and thereby distracts me from seeing the mercifulness. Is it mercifulness when one who can do everything does everything for the wretched? No. Is it mercifulness when one who can do just about nothing does this nothing for the wretched? No. Mercifulness is *how* this everything and this nothing are done. But I can just as readily see mercifulness in this everything and in this nothing; and when it is so, I can really see it better in this nothing, for to be able to do everything is a spectacular externality which has an accidental kind of significance which nevertheless strongly affects the sensuous in me, easily draws attention to itself, and distracts me from seeing the mercifulness.

Let me illustrate this again. If you wanted to observe the movements, the rings, which a stone causes and forms when it is thrown into the water: would you then travel to some distant land where the mighty waterfall turbulently plunges down and throw out the stone, or would you throw it out into the tumultuous sea? No, this you would not do. For although the stone would cause movements and form rings here as everywhere, you would be distracted from seeing them aright. Therefore you would rather seek out a small quiet pond, almost the smaller the better, throw out the stone, and then undisturbed by all irrelevancies really concentrate your attention upon observing the movements.—What do you understand by a significant person? Certainly a person who has significant intrinsic worth? If, then, it is your concern really to will to become engrossed in the observation of such a person, could you wish to see him surrounded by enormous riches or fitted out in stars and ribbons; or would you not think that precisely this would distract you from concentrating your mind wholly upon discerning his significant inwardness? So it is with mercifulness. Mercifulness is the *truly significant*; the hundreds of thousands or in a worldly way to do everything is the *significant gift*, the *significant aid*. But the truly significant is indeed that which must be looked *at*; the secondarily significant is indeed that which must be looked away *from*. And out of mistrust of yourself you therefore desire the removal of *that* from which you must look away—alas, but the world thinks it is much easier to achieve awareness of mercifulness when it gives hundreds of thousands than when it gives a halfpenny and consequently thinks to become aware of mercy most easily by looking at *that* from which one must look away if he is to see mercifulness aright.

Yet let us not forget that mercifulness can be seen in both cases, in the halfpenny and in the hundreds of thousands, in the everything which the powerful do and in the nothing which the wretched do. But even if it is conceded that mercifulness is present, you will nevertheless easily ascertain that the greater, the more spectacular the gift is, the more wondrous the aid, the greater is the hindrance to one's dwelling wholly upon the mercifulness. It is told of the apostle Peter[56] that one day when he went up to the temple he met a cripple who begged for alms. But Peter said to him, " I have no silver and gold, but I give you what I have; in the name of Jesus Christ of Nazareth, walk." And he took him by the right hand and raised him up; and immediately his feet and ankles were made strong. And leaping up he stood and walked. Who would dare doubt that this is a work of mercifulness, and yet it is in fact a miracle. But a miracle immediately draws attention to itself and thereby to a degree away from the mercifulness, which never becomes clearer than when it can do nothing at all; for then there is nothing at all to hinder seeing definitely and accurately what mercifulness is.

The eternal has understanding only for mercifulness; therefore if you want to learn to understand about mercifulness, you must learn from the eternal. But if you are to have understanding for the eternal there must be stillness around you while you wholly concentrate your attention upon inwardness. Alas, the hundreds of thousands—they make a racket; at least they can very easily make a racket; you almost go out of your wits at the thought of being able to give away hundreds of thousands just as easily as giving away five pennies; you become expansive; you come to think of the magnificence of being able to do good on such a scale. But in this way there is a side-tracking of the eternal: that the glorious, blessed, holiest state is to practise mercifulness. And now consider power and might! They again very easily disturb the mind; one comes to be amazed over the externalities. But when you are amazed, you can be sure that it is not mercifulness which you see, for it does not arouse amazement. What is there to be amazed about when even the most wretched, and precisely such a one best of all, can practise mercifulness? But mercifulness, if in truth you see it, does not arouse amazement; it moves you and just because it is inwardness it makes the most inward impression upon you. But when is inwardness clearer than when no externality at all is present or when the externals because of their poorness and insignificance are more like a refutation and sensuously understood are really a hindrance to seeing inwardness? And when this is the case with respect to mercifulness, then we indeed have the mercifulness which has been discussed here, which is a work of love, even if it has nothing to give and is able to do nothing.

VIII

The Victory of Reconciliation in Love

Which Wins the Vanquished

" And having overcome all, to stand " (Ephesians 6 : 13)![57] But is this not rather easy, does it not follow automatically that one stands or continues to stand[58] when he has overcome everything? When one has really overcome everything, what then should be able to pull one down; if one has really overcome everything, is there anything more for him to stand against? O, the experienced apostle knew what he was talking about! It follows automatically that he who cowardly and fearful never ventures into danger also never conquers and never overcomes anything; however, because he gave up it is presupposed that he is the one vanquished. But on the other hand, when a person has overcome all, precisely then is he perhaps closest to losing everything —if he loses anything at that moment, he just as well loses everything, which is possible only for one who has won all. Precisely the moment of victory is perhaps the most difficult, more difficult than any moment of striving; the very victory-cry, " Everything is decided," is perhaps the most equivocal of all expressions if the second it is uttered it signifies " Now it is decided that all is lost." Consequently there is still something to be said about standing after having overcome everything; yes, it is really from this moment on that it can properly be spoken of. This is implicit in the concept. When you say that someone vanquishes something, you think of him bent forward to thrust against the opposition. Consequently there cannot even in the deepest sense be talk about standing; for although the opposition stands opposed, it nevertheless in another sense holds on to him, as it were, him who thrusts forward. But now, now all is overcome. Now it is a question of his standing and continuing to stand, of his not losing the victory

as soon as he wins it. Is it not so? The weak and fearful bow down
to the opposition; but when the courageous person falls, one who
boldly ventures into danger, he prefers to fall, as the saying goes, over
his own feet: as a courageous person he vanquishes the opposition, and
yet he falls. He does not fall amid the perils but in his progress,
consequently because he did not stand.

Somewhere else Paul says that in faith we more than conquer.[59]
But can a man more than conquer? Yes, one can, if after having
conquered one stands, keeps the victory, continues in the victory. How
frequently it happens that one who has conquered has so exerted
himself that he did not even need, like that general,[60] one more such
victory—because this one was enough for his downfall! How frequently
it happens that one who lifted a weight could not carry the weight
because of having lifted it, or that one who without exhaustion pressed
forward victoriously against the storm could not in his exhaustion hold
out during that moment of calm ushered in by the victory, or that one
who in his hardiness could bear all the changes of weather, heat and
cold, could not endure the victory-moment's breeze! And how often
a victory has been taken in vain, so that the victor became proud,
conceited, arrogant, self-satisfied and thereby has lost simply by having
conquered!

If, then, we were to express in a reflective phrase what lies in this
apostolic word (to stand after having overcome all) we might say: there
are, spiritually understood, always two victories, a first victory and a
second in which the first victory is preserved. One cannot express the
distinction between the divine and the worldly more accurately than
this: the worldly continually reckons with only one victory; the divine
continually with two. That no man shall count himself happy before
he is dead (thereby leaving it to posterity)—this the worldly mentality
can also get into its head; but on the other hand, the worldly mentality
will become impatient if it hears talk about the second victory. If
anything is to be said to some purpose about a second victory or about
standing after having conquered, one misses what the worldly mind
naturally places highest value on, misses *that* for the sake of which one
has endured all the hardships of battle—because if a second victory is
considered, a person never gets to be proud of his victory; for this
purpose not even a moment's time is granted to him. On the contrary,
in the moment when he has conquered and is about to make prepara-
tions for the triumphal festival, precisely in this very moment godly
reflection leads him into a new struggle, the most difficult of all,

because it is the most inward, because he struggles with himself and with God. If he falls in this struggle, he falls by his own hand; physically and externally understood I can fall by the hand of another, but spiritually there is only one who can slay me, and that is myself; spiritually a murder is not conceivable—certainly no violent assaulter can murder an immortal spirit; spiritually suicide is the only possible death. And if a person is victorious in this second struggle, it clearly signifies that he did not receive the honour for the first victory, because to be victorious means in this context to give God the honour. In the first struggle the battle is for victory against the world and it is won; in the second struggle the battle is with God over this victory. After having vanquished all a man stands only when in the very moment of victory he yields the victory to God. As long as he strove, it was the opposition which in a certain sense helped him stand; but when he has given God the honour of victory, God is the support by whose help he stands. That he conquered with God's support is certainly possible (although the victory in an external sense can indeed also be won without God's support); but God's support first becomes clearly evident when a person has triumphed. O, what foolishness in the eyes of the world, to need God's support most when one has triumphed!

This sort of double struggle or double victory we shall now make the more detailed object of consideration in speaking about:

THE VICTORY OF RECONCILIATION IN LOVE WHICH WINS THE VANQUISHED.

Inasmuch as this discussion is about the *vanquished*, a first victory which has been won is presupposed. What is this? It is to triumph over evil with the good. The struggle may have been quite protracted and strenuous, for if the lover is to overcome evil with good, this is not decided all at once or in one blow; rather, the battle often becomes more and more rigorous and, if you will, more dangerous—if one is willing to understand what the danger is. The more good the lover has done toward the unloving, indeed, the longer he has persevered in repaying evil with good, the closer, in a certain sense, lies the danger that evil nevertheless finally overcomes the lover, if in no other way than by making him cold and indifferent toward such an unloving person. O, a great kingdom's depth of goodness, which only the lover has, the steady warmth of an unquenchable, purified fire, is needed to hold out for a long time of repaying good with evil!—But this victory is won; the unloving one is the vanquished.

Now what is the situation in this struggle? On one side stood the lover (or we could also call him the good, the noble, for in the first struggle it is not yet entirely clear that he is the lover), and he had the good on his side. On the other side stood the unloving one, fighting with the help of evil. Thus they strove. The lover had the task of maintaining himself in the good so that the evil should not gain power over him. Therefore he had to do not so much with the unloving person as with himself; it was not for the sake of the unloving person but for the sake of the good, also in the noble sense for his own sake, that he strove to win in this struggle. Therefore the two are related combatively yet externally to one another, in a certain sense irreconcilably striving, since the strife is between good and evil; the one strives with the help of the good and the other in league with the evil, and the latter becomes the vanquished.

Now the relationship is altered; it now becomes clearly apparent that it is the lover who is in the struggle, for he battles not only so that the good may come to be in him, but he battles *reconcilingly* in order that the good might be victorious in the unloving one, or he battles *in order to win the vanquished*. Consequently the relationship between the two is no longer an out-and-out relationship of combat, because the lover works on the side of the opponent for his advantage; he wills to battle the cause of the unloving one through to victory.

This is *reconciliation in love*. When the enemy or someone who has done you wrong comes to you and seeks restoration—and you are then willing to forgive: this is truly beautiful and laudable, and also loving. But, O, how slow! Do not say, " I did it *immediately, as soon as* he asked for it "—consider rather in what haste for reconciliation the true lover is compared with this, compared with this haste which by being dependent upon another's haste or slowness in asking for forgiveness is thereby *essentially* slowness, even though on occasion it comes very quickly. Long, long before the enemy thinks of seeking reconciliation, the lover is already reconciled with him; not only this, no, he has gone over to the enemy's side, battles for his cause, even though the enemy does not or does not want to understand it, and works to bring about reconciliation. Indeed, one can call this a battle of love or a battle in love! To battle with the help of the good *against* the enemy—this is laudable and noble; but to battle *for* the enemy—and against whom? —against oneself, if you will: this is, yes, this is loving or this is reconciliation in love! This is the way reconciliation is presented in Holy Scriptures. The words read,[61] " So if you are offering your gift at the altar, and there remember"—yes, now what should one expect would and must follow, most likely that you have something against someone? But it does not continue this way. It reads, and if you "there remember that your brother has something against you, leave your gift there before the altar and go: first to be reconciled to your brother, and then come and offer your gift." But is this not too much to demand? Who is it, then, who needs forgiveness, the one who did wrong or the one who suffered wrong? Certainly he who did wrong is the one who needs forgiveness. But, O, the lover who suffered wrong needs to forgive or needs restoration, reconciliation, words which do not like *forgiveness* make a distinction by remembering right or wrong but in love note that both stand in need. In the perfect sense forgiveness is not reconciliation when forgiveness is asked for; but it is reconciliation to need to forgive beforehand long before the other person is perhaps thinking of seeking forgiveness. Therefore the Scriptures say,[62] " Make friends quickly with your accuser," but one cannot ever be more agreeable than when one himself is the one in need; and one cannot be *quicker* to forgive than when one does it before it is asked for, yes, battles for the opportunity even when it meets resistance—not against the giving but against the receiving of forgiveness. Note well what the relationship is, for the truly Christian is always just the opposite of what the natural man most easily and naturally understands. " To battle for forgiveness"—who does not immediately understand this as battling to get forgiveness?—alas, for humanly speaking this is often difficult enough. And yet this is not at all what we are talking about; we speak here about battling in love so that the other will accept forgiveness, will permit himself to be reconciled. Is not this Christianity? It is indeed God in heaven who through the apostle says,[63] " Be reconciled"; it is not man who says to God: " Forgive us." No, God loved us first; and again it was God who came first a second time, since it had to do with reconciliation—although from the standpoint of justice he certainly was the one who could well have waited. It is the same in relationship between man and man: there is true reconciliation when a person who does not, this is important to note, does not need the forgiveness is the one who offers reconciliation.

And so the lover battles in reconciliation in order to win the vanquished. *To win one vanquished!* What a beautiful linguistic use of the word *win*. Listen, now. When we say *win* a victory, one immediately hears the intensity of the strife. But when we speak of winning someone, to win one for oneself, what infinite mildness there is in it! What is quite so ingratiating as the thought and the expression "to win someone"; how could there now be any thought of strife! Two are required in every strife, and now there is only one: the unloving one, for the lover is in reconciliation his best friend, who wishes to win the vanquished. To win the vanquished. What a wonderful reversal there is in the whole thing! One would think that to win is less than to *overcome*, because *over* suggests something which surpasses winning, and yet the discourse here is really on the ascent, is about the higher, although it is about winning one who is overcome. Perhaps in the understanding of pride it is greater to overcome, but in the understanding of love the lesser is the greater, "to win the one overcome." Beautiful strife, more beautiful than a lover's struggle, when the lover must be alone, and therefore all the more loving when he must be alone in battling through to reconciliation! Beautiful victory, most beautiful of all victories, when the lover succeeds in winning the vanquished.

To win one vanquished. Now you see the double victory the discussion is about! For when the lover wills to wage only one battle to overcome evil with good and has finally conquered, then he looks sharp to it that he stands after having conquered all. O, his downfall is only too close at hand if he does not permit love and godly consideration to lead him straightway into the next strife, to win the vanquished. If this is done, he is rightly guided past the dangerous reefs where one becomes proud of having held out in repaying evil with good, where one becomes self-important by having repaid evil with good. For when you go immediately into the next strife, who then becomes the more important one? The very one you strive to win? But then you are not the more important. Precisely this is the humbling which only love can endure, that everything goes backwards, as it were, while one goes forward, that things are reversed: when one himself has overcome all, the vanquished becomes the more important one. Let us suppose that the prodigal son's brother had been willing to do everything for his brother—one thing he still could never have gotten into his head: that the prodigal brother should be the more important one. It is really difficult to get it into one's head; it does not occur to a human being that way.

But to win one vanquished is always difficult and in the relationship we are discussing it involves a special difficulty. It is humiliating to be vanquished; therefore the vanquished person avoids particularly the one who vanquished him, because his downfall becomes greater by contrast and no one makes his downfall more clear than the one who vanquished him. And yet here it is the victor who is to win the vanquished, and consequently they must be brought together. Furthermore, the relationship involves a special difficulty. In less important matters it could be done something like this: in the presence of the vanquished the victor could hide the fact that he was the vanquished, piously deceive him as if it were he who was right, reconcilingly yield even by affirming him to be right where he nevertheless was wrong. We shall not decide to what extent this is ever permissible, but in the relationship under discussion the lover least of all dares to do this. It would be weakness, not love, to delude the unloving person into thinking that he was right in the evil which he did; it would not be reconciliation but treachery which would strengthen him in the evil. No, it is of special importance, and implicit in the work of love, that through the help of love the unloving person becomes clearly aware of how irresponsibly he has acted so that he deeply feels his wrong doing. This the lover has to do, and then he will also win the vanquished— but, no, it is not *also*, for it is one and the same since he truly desires only to win him to himself or to win him to truth and to himself, not to win him to himself by deceiving him. But the more deeply the vanquished comes to feel his wrong and to that extent his downfall, the more he feels himself thrust away from him who—in love deals him this *coup de grâce*. What a difficult task: simultaneously to thrust away from oneself and to win to oneself, simultaneously to be rigorous as the truth requires and yet be mild in such a way as love desires in order to win the one against whom rigour is employed! Truly it is a miracle if it succeeds, because it is, like everything Christian, directly opposite to the proverb: One cannot do two things at the same time. That the vanquished looks for the place where he falsely gets the easiest examination is easy to understand; but to win him to oneself with the help of truth's rigorous examination—this is difficult.

The deliberation now pauses in the task. Consider what would happen if the unloving person were pitted against another unloving one who had nourished and excited all his evil passions. Consider this *while you pause in order to see rightly how the lover conducts himself.*

The unloving one is vanquished. But what is the significance here of his being overcome? It means that he is vanquished by the good, the true. And what is it the lover wants? He wants to win him for the good and the true. But to be overcome, if this means to be won for the good and the true—is this so humiliating? Pay attention now to love and reconciliation. The lover gives no indication at all, nor does it even occur to him, that he is the one who has conquered, that he is the victorious master—no, it is the good which has conquered. In order to remove the humiliation and mortification, the lover interpolates something higher between the unloving one and himself and thereby gets himself out of the way. When there is no third in the relationship between man and man, every such relationship becomes unsound, either too ardent or embittered. The third, which thinkers would call the idea, is the true, the good, or more accurately, the God-relationship; this third is a cooling factor in certain phases of a relationship and in others a soothing agent. In truth, the lover is too loving to take a posture over against the vanquished and himself be the victor who revels in the victory—while the other is the vanquished; it is simply unloving to want to be master of another person in this way. With the help of the third, which the lover gets placed between them, both are humbled: for the lover humbles himself before the good, whose needy servant he is, and, as he himself admits, in frailty; and the vanquished one humbles himself not before the lover but before the good. But when both are humbled in a relationship, there is no humiliation for either one of them alone. How resourceful love can be, what a handyman it is! Would you rather, as you say, that I should speak more seriously? O, you can be sure that the lover thinks it best for me to speak in this way, for there is a joy, even over the success of a concern rooted in the earnestness of the eternal, which makes one prefer to speak in this way. Furthermore, there is in this way of speaking a kind of shyness and to that extent again a concern for the one who is in the wrong. Often, perhaps, a reconciliation in love does not succeed, alas, because one goes at it too earnestly; this is because one has not learned from God (and this one learns from God) to be earnest enough himself to be able to go about it as lightly as the truth actually permits. Do not ever believe that earnestness is surliness; do not ever believe that earnestness is the grim countenance which spreads evil on sight: no one was ever earnest who has not learned from earnestness that one can also seem too earnest. If it has really become second nature to you to will to win your enemy, you will become so familiar with this kind of tasks that they will concern you as technical problems. When a fresh influx of love is continuously in you, when this supply is in order, then there is also time enough for being resourceful. But when there is resistance within the person himself, when in observing the rigorous commandment of love one has to force himself to go out to reconcile himself with his enemy, the matter easily becomes too serious and fails precisely because of—great earnestness. But this "great earnestness," however estimable it may be, particularly in contrast to irreconcilability, is not something we should strive for. No, the true lover is indeed resourceful.

In this way the lover also hides something from the vanquished. But not the way the weak and indulgent person does it, one who hides the truth: the lover hides himself. In order not to disturb, he is, as it were, present but concealed; whereas that which is really present is the exalted majesty of the good and the true. If one only pays attention to this, there is also present something so majestic that the slight difference between man and man easily disappears. This is the way love always conducts itself. The true lover, who could not for any price find it in his heart to let the beloved girl feel his superiority, brings her the truth in such a way that she does not notice that he is the teacher; he lures it out of her, puts it upon her lips and hears her say it, not himself, or he draws truth forward and hides himself. Is it humiliating then, to learn the truth in this way? And so it is with the vanquished, of whom we speak here. Expression of grief over the past, remorse over this wrong, petition for forgiveness—in a certain sense the lover receives all this, but he immediately lays it aside in holy abhorrence, as one lays aside that which is not his: that is, he intimates that it is not due him; he places it all in a higher category, gives it to God as the one to whom it is due. This is the way love always conducts itself. If the girl, indescribably happy over the joy she finds in association with the beloved, were to thank him for it, I wonder if the beloved, if he were genuinely a lover, would not halt this horrifying thought, saying, " No, my dear, this is a slight misunderstanding, and there must be no misunderstanding between us; you should not thank me, but you should thank God if it is as important as you think. If you do this, you are secured against every mistake; for suppose that your happiness were not so great, then it would still be a great happiness that you thanked God for it."—This, which is inseparable from all true love, is: holy shyness. A woman's shyness has to do with earthy concerns, and in this very shyness she feels herself superior, although the contrast hurts; but this holy shyness exists through God's being present, and in shyness a person feels his insignificance. As soon as there is the remotest hint of anything that modesty is unacquainted with, shyness appears in a woman; but as soon as a person considers that God is present, then holy shyness is present. One is not shy before the other person but before the third who is present, or one is shy before the second insofar as one thinks of how the presence of the third would affect the other person. This is the way it is even in human relationships. For when two people are talking together and the king is present as a third, but known only to one, then this one is quite different, because he is somewhat shy—before the king. The thought of God's presence makes a person shy in relationship to the other person, for God's presence makes the two essentially equal. Whatever difference there may be between two persons, even if humanly speaking it were most extreme, God has it in his power to say: "When I am present, certainly no one will presume to be conscious of this difference, because that would be standing and talking with each other in my presence as if I were not present."

But when the lover himself is the shy one, when he hardly dares lift his eyes to look at the vanquished, how can it be so humiliating to be the vanquished! One is indeed shy when another stares at him; but if this other person, who by looking at him makes him shy, himself becomes shy, there really is no one staring at him. But if there is nobody looking at one, there certainly cannot be anything humiliating in humbling oneself before the good or before God.

Consequently the lover does not look at the vanquished. This is the first thing, which is to prevent humiliation. But in another sense the lover nevertheless does look at him. This is the second thing.

O, that I could describe how the lover looks at the vanquished one, how joy beams from his eyes, how this loving look rests gently upon him, how it alluringly and beckoningly seeks to win him! For it is indescribably important to the lover that no disturbing element enters in, that no ill-omened word inadvertently falls between them, that no fateful glance should accidentally be exchanged, which would perhaps spoil everything again for a long time. This is the way the lover looks at him, and, furthermore, he is as calm as only the eternal can make a person. Certainly the lover desires to win this vanquished one, but his desire is too sacred to have the sort of passion which desire otherwise has. The passion of desire usually makes a man somewhat confused; whereas the purity and sacredness of this desire gives the lover an elevated calm which then aids him so that he can win the victory of reconciliation, the finest and the most difficult, for here strength is not enough—the strength must be in weakness.

But is there, then, something humiliating in feeling that one is so important to another person? Is there something humiliating for the girl in the lover's trying to gain her love; is there something humiliating for her in the obviousness of his great concern to win her; is there something humiliating for her to foresee his joy if it succeeds? No, certainly there is not. But the lover, who wants to win the vanquished in reconciliation, is in the very situation of trying to gain the other person's love in a far higher sense. And the lover knows only too well how difficult it is to set one free, to set one free from the evil, to set him free from being humiliated in being the vanquished one, to set him free from thinking dejectedly about the forgiveness which he needs: and ultimately, in spite of all these difficulties, to win his love.

Yet the lover succeeds in winning the vanquished. Every disturbance, every conceivable hindrance is eliminated as if by a charm; while the vanquished seeks forgiveness, the lover seeks the love of the vanquished. O, but it is not true that one always gets an answer if one asks; Christianity has rendered this adage, like all the proverbs of human cleverness, untrue! For when the vanquished asks, " Have you now forgiven me? " the lover asks, " Do you really love me now?" But he does not give an answer to what is asked. No, this he does not do; he is too loving for this; he will not even answer the question about forgiveness, because these words, especially if emphasis is laid upon them, could easily make the matter too serious in a damaging sense. What a wonderful kind of conversation! There is, it would seem, no meaning in it; one asks a question in the eastern hemisphere and the other answers in the western hemisphere: yet the conversation is about one and the same thing.

But the lover has the last word. For after some time has passed between them, when the one says, " Have you now really forgiven me?" the other answers, " Do you now really love me? " But note, no one, no one, can hold out against a lover, not even one who begs for forgiveness. Finally he becomes disaccustomed to asking for forgiveness. Then the lover has conquered, for he has won the vanquished one.

IX

The Work of Love in Remembering One Dead

When one fears that somehow he will not be able to maintain an understanding grasp of something complex and extensive, he tries to find or to make for himself a brief summary of the whole—for the sake of a comprehensive view. Thus death is the briefest summary of life or life reduced to its briefest form. Therefore to those who in truth meditate on human life it has always been very important again and again to test with this brief summary what they have understood about life. For no thinker has power over life as does death, this mighty thinker who is able not only to think through every illusion but can think it analytically and as a whole, think it down to the bottom. If you are perplexed when you consider the multiplicity of life's ways, then go out to the dead, "where all ways meet"—then the over view is easy. If you get dizzy continually seeing life's diversities and hearing about them, then go out to the dead, *there* you have power over the diversities: among "the kin of the mould" there is no distinction, only a close family-relationship. That all men are blood-relatives, consequently of one blood, this kinship of life is very often denied in life; but that they are of one mould, this kinship of death, this cannot be denied.

Yes, once again go out to the dead in order *there* to get a look at life: this is the way the sharp shooter operates—he seeks out a place where the enemy cannot attack him but from which he can attack the enemy and where he can have perfect quiet for observation. Do not choose an evening hour for the visit, for the evening quiet of an evening spent among the dead is often not distinguishable from a kind of overstraining which tenses and "surfeits with unrest" and gives rise to new riddles instead of explaining those already given. No, go out there earlier in the morning, when the morning sun peeps in among the gravestones with shifting lights and shadows, when the beauty and friendliness of the woods and the different forms of life and the twittering of the birds almost let you forget that you are among the dead. Then it will seem as if you had entered into a foreign land which has remained unacquainted with the confusion and fragmentation of life, into the world of childhood, consisting only of small families. Out here, in fact, there is an attainment of what in life is vainly sought: equal distribution. Every family has a little piece of ground for itself, all about the same size. The view is about the same for all of them; the sun shines equally over all of them; no building rises so high that it takes away the sun's rays or the refreshing rain or the fresh air of the wind or the music of bird-song from a neighbour or the one across the way. No, here there is equal distribution. In life it sometimes happens that a family which has lived in luxury and prosperity must cut back, but in death all of them have had to cut back. There can be a slight difference—perhaps a foot in the size of the plot, or one family may have a tree, which other inhabitants do not have on their plots. Why do you suppose this difference exists? It is a profound jest to remind you by means of its littleness how great the difference was. How loving death is! For in this inspiring joke it is precisely death's love which with the help of this little difference reminds one of the great difference. Death does not say, "There is no difference at all"; it says, "There you can see what the difference was: half a foot." If there were not this little difference, death's summary would not be completely reliable. In this way life turns through death back to childhood. In the period of childhood there was also the great difference, that one had a tree, a flower, a stone. And this difference was a suggestion of what later in life would appear according to a completely different standard. Now life is passed, and among the dead this little suggestion is retained as a remembrance, softened in a jest, of how things were.

See, out here is the place to think about life, to get an overview with the help of this brief summary which abbreviates all the complicated extensiveness of relationships. How, then, in a piece on love could I leave unused this occasion for making a test of what love essentially is? In truth, if you really want to make sure about love in yourself or in another person, then note how he relates himself to one who is dead. When one wishes to make observations of a person, it is very important, for the sake of the observations, that one looks at him alone even though looking at him in the relationship. When one actual person is related to a second actual person and there consequently are two, the relationship is compounded and observation of the one alone is made difficult. The second man may hide something from the first, and in addition the second may have such great influence upon the first that he may appear quite otherwise than he is. Consequently a double accounting is needed here; the observation must run a special reckoning of the influence of the second person, of the effect of his personality, his characteristics, his actions, and his mistakes, upon the first person, who is the object of observation. If you could perchance watch someone shadow-boxing in earnest, or if you could get a dancer to dance alone in a dance he customarily dances with a partner, you would best be able to observe his movements, better than if he boxed with another actual person or if he danced with another actual person. And if you understand the art of making yourself *nobody* in conversation, you get to know best what resides in the other person. But when one relates himself to one who is dead, in this relationship there is only one, for one dead is nothing actual. No one, absolutely no one, can make himself *nobody* as one dead can, for he is *nobody*; consequently there can be no talk here about irregularities in observation; here the living becomes revealed; here he must show himself exactly as he is, because one who is dead—yes, he is a clever fellow—has withdrawn himself completely; he has not the slightest influence, either disturbing or helping, on the living person who relates himself to him. One who is dead is not an actual object; he is only the occasion which continually reveals what resides in the one living who relates himself to him or which helps to make clear how it is with one living who does not relate himself to him.

But we *do* have duties towards the dead. If we are to love the men we see, then we are also to love those whom we have seen but see no more because death took them away. One must not disturb the dead with his complaints and cries; a person should move about one who is dead as he moves about one who is sleeping, one whom he has not the heart to wake up because he hopes the sleeper will wake up by himself. "Weep softly over one dead, for he has found rest," says Sirach[64] (21, 12); and I know of no better way to describe true memory than by this weeping softly, which does not begin sobbing one moment —and then quickly subsides. No, one must remember the dead; weep softly, but grieve long. How long cannot be decided in advance, because no one remembering can with certainty know how long he shall be separated from the dead. But he who in love remembers one dead can make his own some words from the psalm of David[65] in which there is also discussion of remembering: " If I forget thee, let my right hand forget its cunning; let my tongue cleave to the roof of my mouth if I do not remember thee, if I do not prefer thee above my chief joy"—only he is to remember that the task is not to say it straightway on the first day but in this frame of mind to be true to himself and the one dead even if he is silent about it, which is frequently preferable for the sake of certainty and also a certain seemliness. It is a task, and one need not have seen much of life to have seen enough to assure himself that there is need for emphasising that it is a task, a duty, to remember the dead: left alone by itself the bankruptcy of human feeling never appears more complete than in precisely this relationship. Yet the feeling and its mighty outpouring are not therefore untrue; that is, one means what he says and one means it at the time he says it, but one satisfies himself and the passion of his uneducated feelings by giving expression in speech which binds in such a way that rare is the man who by later expression does not render the first untrue, although at first it was true. O, one often speaks of what a completely different view of human life one would get if everything which life hides were made apparent—alas, if one dead were to come out with what he knows about the living: what a terrifying contribution to the knowledge of man which at least does not directly promote love of mankind!

Therefore, among the works of love, let us not forget this, let us not forget to consider

THE WORK OF LOVE IN REMEMBERING ONE WHO IS DEAD.

The work of love in remembering one who is dead is a work of the MOST UNSELFISH *love.*

If one wants to make sure that love is completely unselfish, he eliminates every possibility of repayment. But precisely this is eliminated in the relationship to one who is dead. If love nevertheless remains, it is in truth unselfish.

Repayment in connection with love can be quite varied. For that matter one can have outright profit and reward, and this is indeed the persistently common way, the "pagan" way, "to love those who can make repayment." According to this view the repayment is heterogeneous, something different from the love itself. But there is also a repayment for love which is homogeneous with love: requited love. And there is still so much good in the majority of men that as a rule they will regard this repayment, repayment in the form of gratitude, of thankfulness, of devotion, in short, of requited love, as the most significant, although in another sense they will perhaps not admit that it is repayment and therefore consider that one cannot call love selfish insofar as it seeks this repayment.—But in no sense do the dead make repayment.

In this respect there is a similarity between lovingly remembering one who is dead and parents' love for children. The parents love their children almost before they exist and long before they become conscious, therefore as non-beings. But one dead is also a non-being. And the two greatest benefactions are these: to give life to a human being and to remember one dead; yet the first act of love has repayment. If there were no hope at all for parents, no prospect at all ever of having joy in their children and reward for their love—yes, there are still many fathers and mothers who would nevertheless lovingly do everything for children: but there are also many fathers and mothers whose love would grow cold. It is not our intention hereby directly to declare such a father or mother to be unloving; no, but their love is nevertheless so weak or self-love so strong that they need this joyous hope, this encouraging prospect. And with this hope, this prospect, everything would be right again. The parents could say to each other: " Our little child certainly has a long time ahead of him; there are many years; but in all this time we still have joy in him, and above all, we have the hope that at some time he will reward our love, will in repayment make our old age happy, if he does nothing else."

The dead, however, make no repayment. One who remembers lovingly can perhaps also say: " A long life lies before me, dedicated to remembering, but the prospect first and last is the same; in a certain sense there is no threat at all in the prospect, for there simply is no prospect." O, in a certain sense it is so hopeless; it is such a thankless job, as the farmer says, such a disheartening occupation to remember one who is dead! For one who is dead does not grow and thrive toward the future as does the child: one who is dead merely crumbles away more and more into certain ruin. One who is dead does not give joy to the rememberer as the child gives joy to its mother, does not give him joy as the child gives her joy when to her question about whom he loves most he answers, " Mother "; one who is dead loves no one most, for he seems to love no one at all. O, it is so dejecting that he remains quiet this way down there in the grave while the longing after him grows, so dejecting that there is no change conceivable except the change of dissolution, more and more! True, he is not difficult as the child can be at times; he does not cause sleepless nights, at least not by being difficult—for, remarkably enough, the good child does not cause sleepless nights, and yet one who is dead causes the more sleepless nights the better he was. O, but as far as the most difficult child is concerned there are still the hope and prospect of repayment of love: but one dead makes no repayment at all. Whether you are sleepless and expectant on his account or you completely forget him seems to be completely a matter of indifference to him.

If, therefore, you wish to test for yourself whether or not you love disinterestedly, note sometimes how you relate yourself to one who is dead. Much love, doubtless most, would upon closer examination certainly show itself to be self-love. But the situation is this, in the love-relationship among the living there is still the hope, the prospect, of love as repayment, at least the repayment of reciprocated love, and generally repayment is made. But this hope, this prospect, together with the fact that repayment is made, makes a man unable to see with clarity what is love and what is self-love, because one cannot see with clarity whether repayment is expected and in what sense. In relationship to one who is dead, however, the observation is easy. O, if one were accustomed truly to love unselfishly, one would certainly remember the dead differently from the way one usually does after the first period, frequently rather brief, in which one loves the dead inordinately enough with cries and clamour.

The work of love in remembering one who is dead is a work of the freest love.

In order properly to test whether love is entirely free, one eliminates everything which in some way could constrain a person to an act of love. But precisely this is absent in the relationship to one who is dead. If love nevertheless remains, this is the freest love.

That which can constrain an act of love from a person is extremely varied and can hardly be catalogued. The child cries, the poor man begs, the widow importunes, considerations squeeze, wretchedness forces, and so on. But all love in action which is extracted in this way is not entirely free.

The stronger the compulsion, the less free is the love. Usually we consider this with reference to parents' love for their children. If one wants to make an adequate description of helplessness and to sketch it in its most compelling form, one usually recalls an infant lying there in all its helplessness, forcing, so to speak, love from its parents—it forces, *so to speak*, because it really forces love only from the parents who are not what they ought to be. Therefore the infant in all its helplessness! And yet, when a person first lies in his grave with six feet of earth over him, he is more helpless than the child!

But the child cries! If the child could not cry—yes, there have been many a father and mother who nevertheless cared for the child in the fullness of love; but, O, there have also been many a father and mother who at least many times would forget the child. Our thought is not therefore to call such a father or a mother outright unloving; but nevertheless love in them was so weak, so self-seeking, that they needed this reminder, this constraint.

On the other hand, one dead does not cry like a child; he does not call himself into memory as the importunate do; he does not beg as does the pan-handler; he does not squeeze with consideration; he does not force you by visible wretchedness; he does not besiege you as the widow did the judge:[66] one dead is silent and says not a word; he remains completely still and does not move from the spot—and perhaps he does not suffer evil either! There is no one who inconveniences the living less than one who is dead and no one who is easier for the living to avoid than one dead. You can leave your child with a baby-sitter in order not to hear its cry; you can say you are not at home in order to avoid the solicitation of beggars; you can go about disguised so that no one will know you: in short, in relationship with the living you can use many precautions which perhaps still do not give you complete security, but in relationship to one who is dead you do not need the least precaution, and yet you are entirely secure. If anyone is of such a mind, if it best suits his scheme of life to be rid of the dead the sooner the better, without being challenged at all or becoming the object of any sort of prosecution, he can turn cold in approximately the same moment the dead one becomes cold. If only out of shame (certainly not for the sake of the dead) he remembers to weep a little in the newspapers on the burial day, if he merely takes care to show the dead this last honour, out of shame: then he can for all that, spit right in the dead man's—no, not right in his eyes, for they are now closed. Naturally one who is dead has no rights in life; there is no public authority whose job concerns whether you remember the dead or not, no authority who mixes into such a relationship as sometimes in the relationship between parents and children—and one dead certainly takes no step to inconvenience or compel in any way.—If, therefore, you want to test whether you love freely, observe some time how over a period of time you relate yourself to one who is dead.

If it did not seem frivolous (which it certainly is not—except to one who does not know what earnestness is), I would say that as an inscription over the graveyard gate one could place " No compulsion here " or " With us there is no compulsion." Yet I may as well say it, and I may well have said it, and I may as well stand by having said it; for I have thought too much about death not to know that he cannot speak earnestly about death who does not know how to employ (for awakening, please note) the subtlety and all the profound waggery which lies in death. Death is not earnest in the same way the eternal is. To the earnestness of death belongs precisely that remarkable capacity for awakening, that resonance of a profound mockery which, detached from the thought of the eternal, is an empty and often brash jest, but together with the thought of the eternal is just what it should be, utterly different from the insipid solemness which least of all captures and holds a thought with tension like that of death.

O, there is a lot of talk in the world about how love must be free, that one cannot love if there is the slightest constraint, that in matters of love absolutely nothing must be obligated. Well, let us see how things stand with this free love when one gets right down to this— how the dead are remembered in love, for one who is dead does not compel one at all. Yes, in the moment of separation, when one cannot get along without him who is dead, there is a shriek. Is this the free love so much talked about, is this love for one who is dead? And thereupon, little by little, as the dead crumbles away, the memory crumbles away between the fingers and one does not know what becomes of it; little by little one becomes free of this—burdensome memory. But to become free in this way—is this free love, is this love for one who is dead? The saying puts it well: out of sight, out of mind. And one can always be sure that a proverb speaks accurately of how things go in the world; it is quite another matter that every proverb, Christianly understood, is untrue.

If everything said about loving freely were true, that is, if it happened, if it were carried out, if men were accustomed to love in this way, men would also love the dead quite differently than they do. But the actual situation is that as far as other human love is concerned there is usually something coercive, daily sight and habit if nothing else, and therefore one cannot definitely see to what extent it is love which freely holds its object fast or it is the object which in one way or another coercively lends a hand. But with respect to one dead everything is made clear. Here there is nothing, nothing coercive at all. On the other hand, the loving memory of one dead has to protect itself against the actuality around about lest by ever new impressions it gets full power to expel the memory, and it has to protect itself against time: in short, it has to protect its freedom in remembering against that which would compel it to forget. The power of time is great. One perhaps does not notice it in time, because time slyly steals a little bit away at a time. Perhaps one will get to know this clearly for the first time in eternity when one is required to look back again and around to see what he has managed to get together with the help of time and forty years. Yes, time has a dangerous power; in time it is so easy to make a beginning again and thereby to forget where one left off. Even when one begins to read a very big book and does not completely trust his memory, he puts in a bookmark. But, O, with respect to his whole life, how often one forgets to put in a marker in order to be able to find his place! And now through the years to have to remember one dead, while he, alas, does nothing to help one, or whether he does anything or simply does nothing, everything goes to show one how completely indifferent he is! In the meantime the multiplicity of life's demands beckons to one, the living beckon to one and say: come to us, we will take care of you. One who is dead, however, cannot beckon. Even if he wanted to, he could not beckon. He cannot do a single thing to make us captive to him; he cannot move a finger; he lies and crumbles away—how easy for the powers of life and of the moment to overcome such a weakling! O, there is no one as helpless as one who is dead, and in his helplessness he exercises absolutely not the slightest compulsion! Therefore no love is as free as the work of love which *remembers* one who is dead—for to remember him is something quite different from not being able to forget him at first.

The work of love in remembering one dead is a work of the most faithful love.

In order properly to test whether or not love is faithful, one eliminates everything whereby the object could in some way aid him in being faithful. But all this is absent in the relationship to one who is dead, one who is not an *actual* object. If love still abides, it is most faithful.

Not infrequently there is talk about the lack of faithfulness in love among human beings. Then one blames the other and says, " It was not I who changed; it was he who changed." Good. And what then? Do you then remain unchanged? " No, as a consequence I naturally changed too." We shall not here point out how meaningless this presumably necessary consequence is, whereby it follows of itself that I change *because* another changes. No, we are speaking of the relationship to one dead, and here it cannot be said that it was the one dead who changed. If an alteration enters into this relationship, I must be the one who changes. Therefore, if you will test whether or not you love faithfully, note some time how you relate yourself to one who is dead.

But the situation is this: it is certainly a difficult task to maintain oneself unchanged throughout time; the situation is also this: that human beings love to deceive themselves by all sorts of imaginings more than they love both the living and the dead. O, how many do not live in the conviction so firm that they would die for it—that if the other person had not changed, he, too, would have remained unchanged. But if this is so, is every living person in fact completely unchanged in relationship to one who is dead? O, perhaps in no relationship is the change so remarkable, so great, as that between one living and one dead—although the one dead is nevertheless not the one who changes.

When two living persons are joined in love, each holds on to the other and the relationship holds on to both of them. But no holding together is possible with one who is dead. Immediately after death it perhaps can be said that he holds on to one, a consequence of the relationship together, and therefore it is also the most frequent occurrence, the customary thing, that he is remembered during this time. However, in the course of time he does not hold on to the one living, and the relationship is broken if the one living does not hold on to him. But what is faithfulness? Is it faithfulness that the other holds on to me?

When death interposes separation between the two, the survivor—faithful during the first period—says, " I shall never forget him who is dead." O, how uncircumspect, because the one who is dead is a canny one to talk with, only that his cunning is not like that of the person of whom it is said, " You never find him where you left him," for the canniness of one dead consists precisely in this, that one does not get him back again from where one left him. We are often tempted to think that men believe they can say to the dead just about what they wish, in view of the fact that he is dead, hears nothing, and answers nothing. But—but—take the greatest care of all for what you say to one who is dead. Perhaps you can say quite calmly to one living, "You I will never forget." And after a few years have passed, both of you probably will have good and well forgotten the whole thing—at least it would be unusual if you were unfortunate enough to meet up with a less forgetful person. But watch out for the dead! For one who is dead is a resolute and determined man; he is not like the rest of us who are able in fairytale fashion to go through many droll experiences and seventeen times forget what we have said. When you say to one dead, "You I will never forget," it is as if he answered you, "Good, rest assured that I shall never forget that you have said this." And even though all your contemporaries would assure you that he had forgotten it: from the lips of the dead you shall never hear this. No, he goes his own way—but he is *unchanged*. You will not be able to say to one dead that he was the one who grew older and that this explains your altered relationship to him—for one who is dead does not get older. You shall not be able to say to one who is dead that he was the one who in the course of time grew cold—for he has not become colder than he was when you were so warm, or that he was the one who became less attractive, for which reason you could love him no more —for he has become essentially no less attractive than when he was a beautiful corpse, something which does not, however, lend itself as the object of love, or that he was the one who has made new associations with others—for one dead does not make associations with others. No, whether or not you will begin again where you two left off, one who is dead begins again with the most scrupulous accuracy where the two of you left off. For one who is dead is a strong man, although one does not see this in him: he has the strength of unchangeableness. And one who is dead is a proud man.. Have you noticed that a proud person, particularly in relationship to someone he scorns most deeply, tries very hard to give no hint, to appear completely unchanged, to let the matter be as nothing, thereby to permit the despised one to sink deeper and deeper—only the one cherished by the proud person is benevolently made aware of injustices, of errors, in order thereby to be assisted towards improvement. But one who is dead—who is proudly able as he to give no hint at all, even if he despises the one living who forgets him and his good-bye promise—one who is dead still does everything to make himself forgotten! One dead does not come to you and remind you; he does not look at you in passing; you never meet him; and if you were to meet him and see him, there would be nothing involuntary in his countenance which against his will could betray what he thought and judged of you, for one dead has his countenance under control. We should be truly careful about poetically drawing forth the dead for the sake of remembrance: the most frightful of all is that one dead gives no hint at all. Beware, therefore, of the dead! Beware of his kindness; beware of his definiteness, beware of his strength; beware of his pride! But if you love him, then remember him lovingly, and learn from him, precisely as one who is dead, learn the kindness in thought, the definiteness in expression, the strength in unchangeableness, the pride in life which you would not be able to learn as well from any human being, even the most highly gifted.

One who is dead does not change; there is not the slightest possibility of excuse by putting the blame on him; he is faithful. Yes, it is true. But he is nothing actual, and therefore he does nothing, nothing at all, to hold on to you, except that he is unchanged. If, then, a change takes place between one living and one dead, it is very clear that it must be the one living who has changed. On the other hand, if no change takes place, it is, then, the one living who in truth has been faithful, faithful in lovingly remembering him—alas, although he could do nothing at all to hold on to you, alas, although he did everything to show that he had forgotten you and what you had said to him. For no person who has really forgotten what one had said to him can express more definitely than one who is dead that it is forgotten, that the whole relationship to him, the whole affair with him, is forgotten.

The work of love in remembering one who is dead is thus a work of the most disinterested, the freest, the most faithful love. Therefore go out and practise it; remember one dead and learn in just this way to love the living disinterestedly, freely, faithfully. In the relationship to one dead you have the criterion whereby you can test yourself. One who uses this criterion will with ease abbreviate the prolixity of the most complicated relationship, and he will learn to loathe the mass of excuses which actual life usually has right at hand to explain that it is the other person who is selfish, the other person who is guilty of being forgotten because he does not bring himself into remembrance, the other person who is faithless. Remember one who is dead, and in addition to the blessing which is inseparable from this work of love, you will also have the best guidance to rightly understanding life: that it is one's duty to love the men we do not see, but also those we do see. Our duty to love the men we see cannot be set aside because death separates them from us, for the duty is eternal; but consequently our duty toward the dead cannot separate our contemporaries from us so that they do not remain objects of our love.

X

The Work of Love in Praising Love

" It is one thing to say it, another to do it." This is a proverbial remark which is quite true if one wisely excludes the situations and relationships in which the main thing is "to say it." For it would indeed be strange if anyone were to deny that the poet's art is precisely "to say it," since, after all, not everyone can say *it* as the poet says it, *in such a way* that he thereby shows that he is a poet. To a degree this is also true of the art of one who discourses.

But with respect to love it is neither partially nor totally true that the art is in the saying or that being able to say it in some way depends essentially upon the accident of talent. For just that reason it is very up-building to speak of love, because one must continually reflect and say to himself: " This is something everyone can do or everyone should be able to do "—whereas it would be strange talk to say that everyone is or could be a poet. Love, which overcomes all distinctions, which dissolves all bonds in order to bind all in the bonds of love, naturally watches out lovingly lest suddenly a special sort of differentiation schismatically asserts itself.

Because speaking of love is structured in this way, because it is no *art* to praise love, for that very reason to do it is work, an act, for *art* is related to the accident of talent, and work is related to the universally human.[67] Therefore the proverb can be used in a special way. If in this sense one were to say in a quickly tossed off remark, in a snappy suggestion (which in these times seems to be especially favoured), " It would be good if someone undertook to praise love," one might answer, " It is one thing to say it, another to do it "—although *to do it* in this case would mean to say it, which nevertheless, as pointed out, with respect to love is not art. Consequently it is the art and yet not an art but a work. The work, then, is to undertake the labour of carrying out such a praise of love, for which both time and industry are required. If it were an art to praise love, the relationship would be different, for certainly not everyone has the endowments for practising an art, even if he wishes to use time and industry and wishes to undertake the labour. Love, on the other hand, O, it is not like an art, envious for itself, and therefore granted only to a few. Everyone who wishes to have love, to him it is given, and if he wishes to undertake the work of praising it, he will be able to do this also.

Therefore let us now consider

THE WORK OF LOVE IN PRAISING LOVE.

It is a work and naturally a work of love, for it can be done only in love, more accurately defined, in love of truth. We shall try to make clear how this work may be carried out.

The work of praising love must be done inwardly in self-renunciation.

If praising love is to be done effectively, one must persevere for a long time in thinking one thought, in maintaining it, spiritually understood, with the greatest abstemiousness concerning everything heterogeneous, alien, irrelevant, disturbing, in maintaining it with the most punctilious and dutiful renunciation of every other thought. But this is very strenuous. By this route it is quite easy to leave meaning, coherence, and understanding behind; and this will be the case if the single thought which occupies one is a single finite conception, not an infinite thought. But if it is one thought, one which saves and preserves the understanding, it is still very strenuous. Consequently, to think one thought in the direction of inwardness away from all distraction, step-by-step, month-after-month, to make stronger and stronger the hand which tightens the cord of thought, and then from the other side step-by-step to learn ever more dutifully, ever more humbly, to make the hand lighter and more supple at the joints, the hand which, at any second if necessary, can be momentarily relaxed or eased in tension, in order with rising passion to grasp more and more tightly, more securely, and, if the moment requires it, with deepening humility more and more readily to let go: this is very strenuous. And yet it cannot remain concealed from one that this is the requirement, nor can it remain concealed if one does it; because if one thinks only one thought, the direction is inward.

It is one thing to think in such a way that one's attentiveness is solely and constantly directed towards an external object; it is something else to be so turned in thought that constantly at every moment one himself becomes conscious, in reflection, conscious of one's own condition or how it is with oneself under reflection. But only the latter is essentially what thinking is; it is, in fact, transparency.[68] The first is unclear thinking which suffers from a contradiction: that which in thinking clarifies something else is itself basically unclear.[69] Such a thinker explains something else by his thought, and lo, he does not understand himself; externally in the direction of the object he perhaps utilises his natural talents very penetratingly but in the direction of inwardness he is very superficial, and therefore all his thought, however fundamental it seems to be, is still basically superficial. But when the object of one's thought is complicated in the external sense, or when one transforms what he is thinking about into a scientific object, or when one moves from one object to another, one does not discover this last discrepancy: that an unclearness constitutes the basis for all its clarity —instead of discovering that true clarity is only in transparency. When, on the other hand, a man thinks only one thought, he does not have an external object, he has an inward direction towards self-deepening, and he makes a discovery concerning his own inner situation; and this discovery is at first very humbling. Human-spiritual powers are not like physical powers. If one works beyond his physical capacity, well, he is injured and nothing is gained thereby. But if one does not strain his spiritual powers in their spirituality simply by choosing the inward direction, he discovers nothing at all, or he does not discover in the deeper sense that God is; and if this is the case, he has certainly lost the most important, or the most important has essentially evaded him. In physical powers as such there is indeed nothing selfish, but in the human spirit as such there lies a selfishness which must be snapped if the God-relationship is to be won in truth. One who thinks only one thought must experience this; he must experience the occurrence of a halting wherein everything is, as it were, taken from him; he must risk his life, a hazard which involves losing life in order to win it. He must go ahead on this path if he is to bring something deeper to light; if he shies away from this difficulty, his thought becomes superficial— although in these clever times it has certainly been assumed among men, yet without raising the question before God and the eternal, that such exertion is not needed, in fact is an extravagance. Granted that this is not needed in order to have a comfortable life in thoughtlessness or in order to satisfy one's contemporaries with an admired perfection which in every jot and tittle is like everyone else's. Nevertheless, it is certain that without venturing into this difficulty and without this exertion one's thought remains superficial. For spiritually understood it holds true that precisely when a person has strained his spiritual powers as such, then and only then can he become an instrument. From this moment on, if he honestly and believingly perseveres, he will gain the best powers, but they are not his own; he possesses them in *self-renunciation*.—O, I do not know to whom I am speaking concerning this, to what extent he is someone who is concerned about such things. But this I know, that such persons have lived, and this I know, that precisely those who have effectively praised love have been experienced and competent in these dangerous waters which are almost unknown to the majority in our time. And for such persons I can write, consoling myself with the splendid words:[70] " Write! " " For whom? " " For the dead, for those whom you have loved in time past! " —and in loving them I shall also meet with the dearest among the living.

When one thinks only one thought, one must in relationship to this thinking discover self-renunciation, and it is self-renunciation which discovers that God is. Precisely this becomes the blessing, disturbing contradiction: to have one all-powerful as co-worker. For one all-powerful cannot be a co-worker with you, a human being, without its signifying that you are able to do nothing at all; and on the other side, if he is your support, you are able to do everything. The strenuousness lies in the simultaneity of the contradiction so that you do not experience the one to-day and the other to-morrow; the strenuousness lies in this that the contradiction is not something you are conscious of once in a while but something you must be conscious of every moment. In the same moment that you feel capable of everything—and the selfish thought that it is you who are capable sneaks in—at that moment you can lose everything; and at the same moment when the selfish thought surrenders itself you can have everything again. But God is not seen and consequently since God uses this instrument which one has made himself in self-renunciation, it appears as if it were the instrument which is capable of everything, and the instrument itself is tempted to understand things in this way— until it again is capable of nothing. Granted the difficulty of working together with another human being—O, but to work together with the almighty! Yes, in a certain sense it is easy enough, for what is he not capable of—well, I can simply leave it for him to do. The difficulty lies therefore in this that I am to work together, if not with someone else, then with the constant understanding that I am capable of nothing at all, which is not to be understood once and for all. And this is difficult to understand, to understand it not in the moment when one is actually capable of nothing, when one is sick, disabled, but to understand it in the moment when one seemingly is capable of everything. Of course there is nothing as swift as a thought and nothing which lands on one as heavily as a thought when it falls upon him. And now out in the sea of thought, out in "70,000 fathoms deep"—before one learns to be able, when night comes, to sleep undisturbed *away from* the thoughts in the confidence that God, who is love, has them in superabundance, and to be able to wake up, confident, *to* the thoughts, assured that God has not slumbered! A powerful oriental emperor had a servant who daily reminded him of a certain matter—but that a poor human being may turn the relationship around and say to God, the all-powerful one, "Be sure to remind me of this and that"—and that God does it! Is this not enough to make one lose his mind, that a human being should have permission to sleep securely and sweetly if he only speaks to God, much like the emperor to his servant—be sure to remind me of this or that! Yet this all-powerful one is so jealous that merely one selfish word in this rash freedom which he permits, and all is lost; then God remembers not only this or that, but it is as if he would never forget the this or that which is deserved. No, then it is far safer to be capable of a little less and then to imagine in ordinary human fashion that one is sure of being able to do it; it is far safer than this strenuousness: absolutely literally and actually to be capable of nothing and yet in a certain figurative sense, as it were, to be capable of everything.

Yet only in self-renunciation can one effectually praise love, for God is love, and only in self-renunciation can a human being hold God fast. What a human being of himself knows about love is very superficial; he must get to know the deeper love from God, that is, in self-denial he must become what every human being can become (for self-renunciation is related to the universally human and thus is distinguished from special vocation and selection), an instrument for God. Therefore every human being can get to know everything about love, just as every human being can get to know that he is, as every human being is, loved by God. The difference is only that some consider (which does not seem so remarkable to me) this thought to be more than adequate even for the longest life, so that even in the seventieth year they do not think they have marvelled over it enough; and others, however, consider (which seems to me very queer and reprehensible) this thought to be very insignificant, since to be loved by God is no more than what every man shares—as if it therefore were less significant.

Only in self-renunciation can a man effectually praise love. No poet can do it. The poet can sing of erotic love and friendship, and ability to do this is a rare gift, but *the poet* cannot praise love. Because the poet's relationship to his inspiring muse is nevertheless to him like a jest, the invocation of its presence like a jest (this could well correspond to self-renunciation and prayer), his natural talent the decisive factor, and the yield of the relationship to the inspiring muse the main concern to him, it is poetry, a poet-production, which is the yield. But for him who is to praise love (which everyone can do, it is not a talent) self-renunciation's relationship to God or in self-renunciation to be related to God ought to be everything, ought to be the earnestness; whether or not there is a production ought to be a jest, that is, the God-relationship itself ought to be more important to him than the yield. And in self-renunciation it is his utterly earnest conviction that it is God who helps him.

O, if in self-renunciation a person could properly get rid of all illusion, as if he were capable of something, if he could rightly understand that he himself is capable of nothing—that is, if a person could properly win the victory of self-renunciation and then to the victory add the triumph of self-renunciation, truly and honestly to find all his blessedness in not being capable of anything himself—how wonderfully such a person should be able to speak about love! For in the extreme strenuousness of self-renunciation, in this swooning and fainting of all one's own powers to be blessed, to feel himself blessed, what is this other than to love God in truth? But God is love. Who, therefore, should better be able to praise love than he who in truth loves God, because he is related to his object in the only proper way; for he is related to God and is truly loving.

This is inwardly the condition or the mode by which praising love must be done. To carry it out has naturally its own intrinsic reward, although in addition it also has the purpose, through praising love insofar as one is able, of winning men to it, to make them properly aware of what in reconciliation is round about every man, namely, the highest. He who praises art and science emphasises the cleavage between the talented and untalented among men. But he who praises love equalises all, not in a common poverty nor in a common mediocrity, but in the community of the highest.

The work of praising love must OUTWARDLY *be done in sacrificial disinterestedness.*

In self-renunciation one achieves the ability to be the instrument by inwardly making himself nothing before God; in sacrificial dis-interestedness he externally makes himself nothing, an unprofitable servant: inwardly he does not become important to himself, for he is nothing, and externally he does not become important to himself either, for he is nothing; he is nothing before God—and he never forgets that he is before God, right where he is. Alas, it can happen that a man makes a mistake at the last moment, that, truly humble before God, nevertheless by orienting himself towards men he becomes proud of what he can do. This is a temptation of comparison, which becomes his downfall. He understood that he could not compare himself with God; before him he remained conscious of himself as a nothing; but in comparison with men he seemed to himself nevertheless to be some-thing. That is, he forgot self-renunciation; he is ensnared in an illusion, as if he were before God only during certain hours, just as when one has audience with the king at a certain hour. What tragic confusion! For with respect to a human being one may quite properly speak differently with him in his presence than about him in his absence, but may this be done in speaking about God—in his absence? [71] If this is rightly understood, sacrificial disinterestedness is one and the same as self-renunciation. It would also be the most terrible con-tradiction if anyone wanted to dominate others—by praising love.— Thus sacrificial disinterestedness is in a certain sense, inwardly under-stood, a consequence of self-renunciation or one with self-renunciation.

But sacrificial disinterestedness is required outwardly if love is in truth to be praised; and in love of truth to will to praise love is precisely a work of love. One can easily enough gain worldly advantage and, what is saddest of all, win the approval of men by proclaiming all sorts of deception. But truly this is not done in love. For loving is the very opposite: in love to the truth and to men to will to bring every sacrifice in order to proclaim the truth and nevertheless not to be willing to sacrifice the least bit of the truth.

Essentially the truth must be regarded as polemic in this world. The world has never been so good, and so good it will never be, that the majority will the truth or have the true conception of it so that upon its proclamation it promptly and necessarily wins the approval of all. No, he who wills in truth to proclaim something true must prepare himself in some other way than with the aid of such a beguiling expectation; he must be willing essentially to relinquish the moment. Even an apostle says that he strives "to win men,"[72] yet with the addition, " But before God we are revealed." Therefore there is absolutely no thought in these words of this selfish or cowardly, fearful craving to win men's approval—as if it were the approval of men which decides whether something is true or not. No, the apostle is revealed before God when he seeks to win men; therefore he does not want to win them for himself but for the truth. As soon as he sees that he can win them in such a way that they become devoted to him but misunderstand him, distort his teaching, he will straightway keep them at a distance in order to win them. He does not wish to win them in order that he himself should have some advantage, but using every sacrifice, and consequently also the sacrifice of their approval, he wants to win them for the truth—if it is possible for him: it is this which he wants. Therefore the same apostle says elsewhere (I Thessalonians 2 : 4-6): " So we speak, not to please men, but to please God who tests our hearts. For we never used either words of flattery, as you know, or a cloak for greed, as God is witness; nor did we seek glory from men, whether from you or from others, though we might have made demands as apostles of Christ." What sacrifice this involves! He has not sought any advantage, has not received recompense, not even insofar as he could rightfully have claimed it as an apostle of Christ. He has renounced their honour, their applause, their devotion. Forearmed he has exposed himself to their misunderstanding, their mockery: and all this he has done—in order to win them. Yes, according to this method it is permissible to do everything, even if this means giving one's life by being executed, in order to win men, for precisely this is self-sacrificial and disinterested abandonment of all those momentary means by which one wins the moment—and loses the truth. Rooted in the eternal the apostle stands. He it is who will win men through the powers of the eternal in self-sacrifice. It is not the apostle who has need of them to maintain himself and therefore grasps opportunistically for the cleverest means to win them—rather than to win them to the truth, because for this such means cannot be used.

And now in these times. How necessary disinterestedness is in these times when everything is done to make everything momentary and the momentary is regarded as everything!—Is not everything done to make the present moment as supreme as possible, supreme over the eternal, over the truth, is not everything done to make the present moment self-sufficient in almost proud ignorance of God and the eternal, so con-

ceited in presumed possession of all truth, so presumptuous in the idea
of itself being the discoverer of the truth! How many of the better ones
have not bowed down before the power of the present moment and
thereby made the moment even worse; for the very one who is superior,
when weakly or selfishly he gives in, must in the very noise of the present
moment seek to forget his downfall and now must work with all his
might to make the present moment even more puffed up. Alas, the
time of thinkers seems to be past![73] The quiet patience, the humble
and obedient monotony, the magnanimous abandonment of momentary
influence, the infinite distance from the momentary, the love devoted
to his thought and his God, which is necessary in order to think one
thought: this seems to disappear; it is almost on the way to be a
laughing-stock to men. " Man " has again become "the measure of
everything "[74] and completely in the understanding of the moment.
All communication must be contrived opportunely into a light
pamphlet and be supported by untruth upon untruth. Yes, it is as if all
communication must finally be so contrived that it can be presented
in at most an hour before a gathering which spends half an hour for
noises of approval or disapproval and for the other half-hour is too
confused to gather the ideas. And yet this is considered to be the
highest. Children are brought up to regard this as the highest: to
be heard and to be admired for an hour. In this way the coinage
standard of being a human being is debased. Nothing is said any more
of the highest, of being acceptable to God, as the apostle says, or of
pleasing the noble men who lived in the past, or of pleasing a few of
excellence who are contemporary: no, to satisfy for an hour a hap-
hazard gathering of men, "the first the best," who themselves have had
neither time nor occasion to reflect on the truth and who consequently
crave superficiality and half-truths if they are to bestow the reward of
their approval: this is the aspiration.—That is, in order to make
aspiration worth anything at all, one helps along with a little untruth,
men flatter each other that those assembled are very wise, that every
gathering consists of the very wise. It is just as it was in the time of
Socrates, according to the information of the accusers: " Everyone
understood how to instruct the young men; there was only a single
one who did not understand this—that was Socrates."[75] Thus in our
time *all* are the wise; only here and there is a solitary one who is a fool.
The world is so close to having achieved perfection that now *all* are the
wise; if there were not the individual eccentrics and fools, the world
would be completely perfect. Amid all this God sits, as it were, in

heaven and waits. No one longs to be away from this noise and tumult of the moment in order to find the quiet wherein God dwells; although men admire men and admire God—because he is like all the rest—no one longs for the solitude in which one prays to God; no one in longing after the standard of the eternal disdains this cheap secession from the highest.—Such is the importance the immediate moment has come to have in itself. Therefore sacrificial disinterestedness is required. O, that I could portray such a truly disinterested figure! But this is not the place for it, a discourse essentially about the work of praising love —hence there is another desire here: would that the immediate moment, if such a one were portrayed, had time to consider him!

What holds true for all love of truth in relationship to the present moment also holds true of truly praising love. Before one seeks to win the approval of the moment with his praise of love, one must first of all ascertain to what extent the present moment has the true conception of love. Does the present moment which now is or can the present moment ever have the true conception of what love is? No, impossible. Love according to the understanding of the present moment or the immediate is neither more nor less than self-love. Consequently it is selfish to talk in this way about love and selfish to win this approval. True love is self-renunciation's love. But what is self-renunciation? It is precisely to give up the present moment and the immediate. But then it is completely impossible to win the approval of the present moment by a true discourse on the love which is love precisely by giving up the present moment. It is impossible, so impossible that the speaker, if the truth is more important to him than the approval of the present moment, should himself point out the misunderstanding insofar as he might inadvertently win the approval of the moment. From what has been developed here it is easily seen that the conclusion is by no means correct which without qualification concludes: he who praises love must himself be or become loved—in a world which crucified him who was love, in a world which persecuted and liquidated so many witnesses to love.

If conditions in this respect have changed, even if conditions are no longer so extreme and inexorable that witnesses to the truth must give up blood and life: the world has nevertheless not become essentially better; it has merely become less impassioned and more petty. Therefore what the world generally considers to be worthy of love the eternal will naturally regard as somewhat censurable and punishable. What the world calls a lovable man is one who above all is careful not to take to heart the demands of the eternal or of God for an essential or an essentially strenuous existence. The lovable man knows about all the possible excuses and escapes and clever maxims for higgling and haggling and chiselling; and he is loving enough to let a little of his cleverness rub off on others, by whose help he organises his own life advantageously, easily, and comfortably. In the company of the lovable man one finds himself secure, very comfortable; one is never prompted by him to imagine the possibility of thinking that there is something eternal, or what demand this makes upon the life of every human being, or that the eternal lies so close to one that the demand could concern the day today. This is the lovable man. But he is regarded as unlovable who, without requiring anything of anyone, by rigorously and earnestly requiring much of himself yet is a reminder that there is such a requirement. In his company the excuses and escapes do not look very good; all that one lives for takes on an unheroic cast. In his company one cannot simply take his ease; even less does he help one adjust the pillow of ease by temporal or even by good-natured-pious indulgence. But what is this love-worthiness of the lovable person? It is traitorousness towards the eternal. This is why temporality thinks so well of it. And this is why the world is always offended by the words, " Love to God means hatred of the world." When the demand of the eternal is made properly relevant, it seems as if such a person hated everything which most men live for. How disturbing, therefore, how peculiar, how unlovable! On the other hand, how lovable and how loving to strengthen and help human beings in their beloved error. But is it really love to deceive people; is it certain that this is love because the deceived regard it as love, because they thank the deceiver as if he were their greatest benefactor; is it love to love in deception and to have love requited in deception? I should believe that love is: in personally communicating the truth to will to bring every sacrifice, but not to be willing to sacrifice the least bit of the truth.

Yet, even if we want to forget actuality, forget how the world is, and poetically cast the entire relationship within the world of imagination: it lies in the very nature of the matter that *in the relationship between man and man* disinterestedness is required for truly praising love. Let us risk such a poetic venture wherein we have nothing at all to do with the actual world but with the distance of thought poetically go through the thought of praising love. If, poetically understood, a human being is to speak about true love in complete truth, there is a double requirement: *the speaker must make himself the self-lover* [76] *and the content of the discourse must be about loving the un-lovable object.* But when such is the case, there is no possible advantage in praising love, for there is advantage in this only when the speaker is regarded as the true lover or the content of the discourse is ingratiating and about loving the lovable object. And when it is impossible to get any advantage out of praising love, there is no interest in doing it.—Consider that simple wise man of ancient times who knew best of all how to speak about the love which loves the beautiful and the good. He was, yes, he was the homeliest man in the whole town, the homeliest man among the most beautiful people. One might think that this would have frightened him out of speaking about the love which loves the beautiful—one certainly prefers to avoid speaking about rope in the house of a hanged person, and even the beautiful prefer to avoid speaking about beauty in the presence of the extraordinarily ugly. But, no, he was eccentric and strange enough to find just this to be engaging and inspiring, consequently eccentric and strange enough to put himself in the most disadvantageous position possible. For when he spoke of the beautiful, when by the reflective utterance of longing for the beautiful he transported his listeners away—they inadvertently looked at him, he became even homelier than as he was before, he who already was the homeliest man in the populace. Indeed, the more he spoke, the more beautifully he spoke of beauty, the homelier he himself became by contrast. He certainly must have been an eccentric, this wise man; he must have been not only the homeliest man in the populace but also the most eccentric person in the whole populace; otherwise what could have made him do this? I believe that if he had only had a beautiful nose (which he did not have—strikingly noticeable among the Greeks, all of whom had beautiful noses), he would not have been willing to speak a single word about loving the beautiful. He would have been opposed to it out of fear that someone might believe that he spoke of himself or at least of his beautiful nose. This would have grieved his spirit, as if he defrauded the object of the discourse, the beauty about which he spoke, by drawing attention to his beauty. But in the assurance of his being the homeliest, he believed that with good conscience he could say everything, everything, everything in praise of beauty without gaining the slightest advantage from it, he who thereby only became homelier and homelier. Nevertheless the love which loves the beautiful is not true love, self-renunciation's love. To speak of true love, the speaker must transform himself into the self-lover, if everything is to be in order and poetically perfect. To praise self-renunciation's love and then to want to be the lover is certainly a lack of self-renunciation. If the speaker is not a self-lover, he easily becomes unsure and unauthentic; either he will be tempted to gain advantage for himself out of the praise, which would be a defrauding of the object, or he will fall into a kind of embarrassment so that he does not even dare to say everything about the gloriousness of love, for fear that someone might think he is talking about himself. But if the speaker is a self-lover or, to conceive of this in ultimates, the most selfish in the whole populace whom the loving speaker calls the people of love,[77] then, yes, then he can speak freely of self-renunciation's love, happier in having made himself the most selfish than that simple wise one in being the homeliest. In an actual situation lengthy preparation would certainly be required in order to be able to speak of self-renunciation's love. But the preparation would not consist in reading many books or in being honoured and respected for one's universally recognised self-renunciation (if it is generally possible that one can show self-renunciation by doing that which *all* understand as self-renunciation on his part), but just the opposite, in transforming oneself into the self-lover, in managing to become regarded as the most selfish of all. And this would still not be easy to accomplish. To become distinguished through competition and to get the poorest reputation, the very poorest, are just about equally difficult, and therefore there is about an equally large number of each.—So much concerning the speaker. The content of the discourse should be: about loving the unlovable object. Consider that simple wise man of ancient times who knew how to talk so beautifully about the love which loves the beautiful; at times he spoke otherwise and spoke of *loving the ugly*. He did not deny that to love is to love the beautiful, but he nevertheless spoke, yes, it was a kind of jest, about loving the ugly. What, then, is to be understood by *the beautiful*? *The beautiful* is the immediate and direct object of immediate love, the choice of inclination and of passion. One certainly need not recommend that men should love the beautiful. But the ugly! This is not something to offer to inclination and passion, which turn away, saying, " What is that to love! " What, then, is *the beautiful* according to our conceptions of love? It is the beloved and the friend. For the beloved and the friend are the spontaneous and direct objects of spontaneous love, the choice of passion and of inclination. And what is *the ugly*?[78] It is *the neighbour*, whom one SHALL love. One SHALL love him—that simple wise man knew nothing of this; he did not know that one's neighbour exists and that one should love him; what he said about loving the ugly was only teasing. One's neighbour is the unlovable object, not something to offer to inclination and passion, which turn away from him and say, "What is that to love!" But for that very reason there is no advantage connected with speaking about having to love the unlovable object. And yet the true love is precisely love to one's neighbour, or it is not finding not the lovable object but finding the unlovable object to be lovable.—When, in order that there can be completely true speaking about the true love, the speaker has had to transform himself into the most selfish of all and the content of the discourse must be about loving the unlovable object: then every advantage or reward is impossible. The speaker in recompense does not become loved, for the degree of his selfishness becomes more apparent in contrast, and the content of the discourse is not designed to ingratiate oneself with men, who prefer to hear what inclination and passion very easily and so gladly understand but do not like to hear what is not at all desired by inclination and passion.— Yet this poetic attempt is entirely correct and can, among other things, perhaps serve to illuminate a fraud or misunderstanding which has appeared again and again in all Christendom. Men take Christian humility and self-renunciation in vain in that they certainly deny themselves in one respect but do not have the courage to do it decisively; for this reason men take care to be understood in their humility and self-denial, and consequently they become respected and honoured for their humility and self-denial—which, nevertheless, is certainly not self-renunciation.

Consequently, in order to be able to praise love, there is need for *inward* self-denial and *outward* sacrificial disinterestedness. If, then, one undertakes to praise love and is asked if it really is out of love on his part that he does it: the answer must be, " No other person can decide this accurately; possibly it is vanity, pride—in short, of evil—but it is also possible that it is love."

Conclusion

In the foregoing writing we have tried "many times and in many ways"[79] to praise love. As we thank God that we have been able to complete the writing in the way intended, we shall now conclude by introducing John the apostle, saying: "Beloved, let us love one another."[80] These words, which consequently have apostolic authority, also have, if you will consider them, a middle tone or a middle mood with respect to the contrasts in love itself, which has its basis in that they are said by one who was perfected in love. You do not hear in these words the rigorousness of duty; the apostle does not say, "You *shall* love one another"; but neither do you hear the intensity of inclination, of poet-passion. There is something transfigured and blessed in these words, but also a sadness which broods over life and is tempered by the eternal. It is as if the apostle said, "Dear me, what is all this which would hinder you from loving; what is all this which you can win by self-love: the commandment is that you *shall* love, but when you understand life and yourself, then it is as if you should not need to be commanded, because to love human beings is still the only thing worth living for; without this love you really do not live; to love human beings is also the only salutary consolation for both time and eternity, and to love human beings is the only true sign that you are a Christian"—truly, a profession of faith is not enough. Christianly understood, love is commanded; but the commandment of love is the old commandment which always remains new. It is not with the love-commandment as with a human command, which becomes old and dulled with the years or is changed by the mutual agreement of those who should obey it. No, the love-commandment remains new until the last day, just as new even on the last day when it has become most ancient. Consequently the commandment is not altered in the slightest way, least of all by an apostle. The only change can be, then, that the lover becomes more and more intimate with the commandment, becomes more and more of one with the commandment, which he loves: therefore he is able to speak so mildly, almost as if it had been

344

forgotten that love is the commandment. If, however, you forget that it is the apostle of love who speaks, then you misunderstand him, for such words are not the beginning of the discourse on love but are the consummation of love. Therefore we do not dare talk this way. That which is truth in the mouth of the veteran, perfected apostle could in the mouth of a beginner easily be flirtation whereby he would seek to leave the commandment's school much too soon and escape the *school-yoke*. We introduce the apostle speaking; we do not make his words into our own but make ourselves into hearers of: " Beloved, let us love one another."

Now only one thing more. Remember *the Christian like-for-like, the like-for-like of the eternal*.[81] This Christian like-for-like is such an important and decisively Christian category that I could wish to end with this thought, if not every writing in which I develop the Christian categories as I am able, at least one work.

In these times Christianity is relatively less spoken of (in relationship, I mean, to what otherwise is talked about so much). But in the talk which is heard (for the attacks are in no way a discussion of Christianity), it is not infrequent that Christianity is presented in a certain almost enervated form of coddling love. It is always love, love; spare yourself and your flesh and blood; have pleasant days or delightful days without self-made cares, for God is love, love—of strenuousness nothing must be heard; everything must be the easy talk and easy nature of love. But understood in this way, God's love easily becomes a fanciful and childish conception, the form of Christ too mild and mawkish for it to be true that he was and is a stumbling-block to the Jews, to the Greeks foolishness: it is as if Christianity were in a second childhood.

The matter is very simple. Christianity has abandoned the Jewish like-for-like: " An eye for an eye, a tooth for a tooth";[82] but it has established the Christian, the eternal's like-for-like in its place. Christianity turns attention completely away from the external, turns it inward, makes your every relationship to other human beings into a God-relationship. Therefore you shall receive sufficient like-for-like according to both the one and the other understanding. Christianly understood one has ultimately and essentially to do with God in everything, although one nevertheless must remain in the world and in the relationships of earthly life allotted to him. But having in everything to do with God (consequently one is never delayed on the way, half-way, by information, by human judgment, as if this were decisive) is simultaneously the highest consolation and the utmost strenuousness, the greatest mildness and rigour. This is man's education, for the relationship to God is an education; God is the educator. But the true education must be as rigorous as it is mild and as mild as it is rigorous. Now, when a human teacher has many children to educate at one time, how does he go about it? There naturally is not time for much talk, reproof, and verbosity. And if there were time, the education naturally becomes worse through much talking. No, the competent educator educates rather with the help of the eyes. He takes the individual child's eyes away from him; that is, he constrains the child, amid everything, to look at him. God does it in the very same way. With his glance he guides the whole world and educates these countless human beings. For what is conscience? In the conscience it is God who looks upon a human being so that the human being now must look to him in all things. In this way God educates. But the child who is being educated easily imagines that his relationship to his comrades and to the little world which they create is reality; the educator, however, teaches him with his glance that all this is used for educating the child. Similarly the adult easily imagines that his transactions with the world are reality; but God educates him to understand that all this is used simply for his education. In this way God is the educator; his love is the greatest mildness and the greatest rigour. It is just as in nature, where heaviness is also lightness. The heavenly body swings easily in the infinite—by gravity; but if it gets out of its course, it becomes too light, and then the lightness becomes heaviness and it falls heavily—because of its lightness. In this same way God's rigour is mildness for the loving and humble, but for the hard-hearted his mildness is rigorous. This mildness, that God has willed to save the world, becomes the greatest rigour in those who will not accept salvation, an even greater rigour than if God had never willed it but only willed to judge the world. See, here is the unity of mildness and rigour; that in all things you relate yourself to God is the greatest mildness and the greatest rigour.

If you listen carefully, therefore, you will hear rigour also, even in what very definitely must be called gospel. Thus when it was said to the centurion from Capernaum, " Be it done for you, as you believed," [83] no happier tidings could be imagined, no milder, more compassionate word! And yet, what is said there? It says, " Be it done for you as you believed." If we use these words for ourselves, we must say, " Be it done for you as you believe; if you have faith unto salvation, then you are saved." How mild, how compassionate! But is it so certain that I have faith, for the fact that the centurion believed I cannot without ado transfer to myself as if I had faith because the centurion had it. Let us suppose that one asked Christianity, " It is certain, then, that I have faith? "—Christianity would answer, " Be it done for you as you believe." I wonder what Christ would have thought if the centurion, instead of coming to him believing, had come to him privately to find out whether he had faith or not! " Be it done for you as you believe," that is, it is eternally certain that it will be to you as you believe; Christianity vouches to you for this; but this, whether or not you, precisely *you*, have faith, does not belong to Christianity's doctrine and proclamation so that it should tell you that you have faith. When you are disturbed by fearful concerns that you perhaps do not have faith, then Christianity repeats, unchanged, " Be it done for you as you believe." How rigorous! From the story of the centurion you learn that he had faith; this does not really concern you at all. And then you learn the essentially Christian, that it was done for him as he believed—but you are, indeed, not the centurion. Let us suppose that someone said to Christianity, " It is absolutely certain that I have been baptized; is it therefore also absolutely certain that I have faith? " Then Christianity would answer, " Be it done for you as you believe." The centurion, although not baptized, believed. Therefore it was done for him as he believed; in his faith *the* Gospel is first *a* gospel. If the centurion, although he came and asked Christ for help, had nevertheless been somewhat dubious in soul about how much Christ might be able to help him, and Christ had then said the same thing, " Be it done for you as you believed": what then? Would this have been a gospel? No, not for the centurion, for it would have been a judgment upon him. This " Be it done for you" appears so quickly, but it is coupled tightly to the next part, "*as* you believe." With this text one can preach rigour just as well as mildness, for there is also rigour in this word, Christian rigour, which certainly does not mean the exclusion of the timorous from the kingdom of God or, perhaps more accurately, does not mean to teach that the timorous exclude themselves; consequently one can just as little make his way into the kingdom of God defiantly as one can timidly and weakly make his way in by whining. But in these times when in social-political relationships there is so much talk about security and security, men finally extend this into Christianity and let baptism be the security—which it certainly is, if you really believe that it is the security of " Be it done for you as you believe."

If it were right without further ado to make baptism into security, then rigour would certainly be done away with. But God does not allow himself to be mocked, nor does he let himself be made a fool. He is far too transcendent in heaven for it to occur to him that a human being's striving should be something meritorious to him. Yet he requires it, and then one thing more, that the man himself does not presume to think that it is something meritorious. But God is also too transcendent in heaven childishly to play the good God with a cowardly and negligent human being. It is eternally certain that it will be done for you as you believe, but the certainty of faith, or the certainty that you, you in particular, believe, you must win at every moment with God's help, consequently not in some external way. You must have the help of God to believe that you are saved by baptism; you must have the help of God to believe that in communion you receive the gracious forgiveness of your sins. Certainly if forgiveness of sins is declared, it is declared also to you, but the pastor has no right to say to you that you have faith, and yet it is declared to you only if you believe. Be it done for you as you believe. But everything in you which is of flesh and blood, of timorousness and attachments to the earthly, must despair so that you cannot get an external certainty, a certainty once for all, and, in the most convenient way. You see, it is the striving of faith in which you get occasion to be tried every day. The gospel is not the law; the gospel will not save you with rigour but with mildness. But this mildness will save you; it will not deceive you; consequently there is rigour in it.

And if this like-for-like holds true even with respect to what most definitely must be called the gospel, how much more, then, when Christianity itself proclaims the law. It says, " *Forgive, and you will also be forgiven.*"[84] Meanwhile, one might nevertheless manage to understand these words in such a way that he imagined it possible to receive forgiveness without his forgiving. Truly this is a misunderstanding. Christianity's view is: forgiveness *is* forgiveness; your forgiveness is your forgiveness; your forgiveness of another is your own forgiveness; the forgiveness which you give you receive, not contrariwise that you give the forgiveness which you receive. It is as if Christianity would say: pray to God humbly and believing in your forgiveness, for he really is compassionate in such a way as no human being is; but if you will test how it is with respect to the forgiveness, then observe yourself. If honestly before God you wholeheartedly forgive your enemy (but remember that if you do, God sees it), then you dare hope also for your forgiveness, for it is one and the same. God forgives you neither more nor less nor otherwise than *as* you forgive your trespassers. It is only an illusion to imagine that one himself has forgiveness, although one is slack in forgiving others. No, there is not a more exact agreement between the sky above and its reflection in the sea, which is just as deep as the distance is high, than there is between forgiveness and forgiving. It is also conceit to believe in one's own forgiveness when one will not forgive, for how in truth should one believe in forgiveness if his own life is a refutation of the existence of forgiveness! But one imagines that he himself is related to God and nevertheless with respect to another human being is simply related to the other person, instead of being related in all things to God.—*Therefore to accuse another person before God is to accuse oneself, like-for-like.* And if a person, humanly speaking, actually suffers an injustice, he nevertheless is wary of getting over-heated with accusations against the guilty before God. O, men so gladly deceive themselves; men so gladly imagine that a person should for his part have, as it were, a private relationship to God. But relationships to God are like relationships to authorities: you cannot speak privately with one in authority about things which are his business—but God's business is to be God. If a valet, if you happily can afford one, has committed a crime, a theft, for example, and you do not know what you should do with the case: above all, you would not go privately to the highest magistrate in office, because he has no under-standing of anything private in matters of theft—he straightway has the guilty one arrested and opens the case. Now, then, if you wish to pretend to be completely outside the matter in hand and wish privately before God to complain of your enemies, God makes short work of it and opens a case against you, because before God you yourself are a guilty person —to complain against another is to complain against oneself. You think that God should, as it were, take your side, that God and you should to-gether turn against your enemy, against him who did you wrong. But this is a misunderstanding. God looks without discrimination upon all and is wholly that which you want to regard him as being only partially. If you petition him in his role as judge—yes, it is a kind of mildness on his part that he warns you to omit this, because he knows well enough what the consequences would be for you. But if, nevertheless, you will not desist from speaking and turn to him in his character as judge: it does not then help any that you intend that he shall judge someone else, for you yourself have made him your judge, and he is, *like-for-like*, simultaneously your judge, that is, he judges you also.

If, on the other hand, you do not engage in accusing someone before God or in making God into a judge, God is then a merciful God. Let me illuminate this with an example. There was once a criminal who had stolen some money, including a hundred-dollar bill. [85] He wanted to get this changed and therefore turned to another criminal in the house. The second criminal took the money, went into the next room as if to change it, came out again, acted as if nothing had happened, greeted the visitor as if seeing him for the first time: in short, he swindled him out of the hundred-dollar bill. The first man became so embittered over this that in his resentment he brought the case to the authorities and reported how shamefully he had been deceived. Naturally the second man was imprisoned on the charge of fraud— alas, in the trial the first question which the authorities raised was: how did the accuser get the money? In this way there were two trials. The first man understood quite correctly that he was in the right in the case of fraud. Now he wanted to be the upright man, the good citizen, who applies to the authorities to get his rights. Yes, but the authorities do not function privately or with regard to an isolated matter one is pleased to lay before them, nor do they always approach the case from the angle of the accuser and plaintiff: the authorities see more deeply into the relationships. So it is with respect to God. When before God you accuse another man, there straightway are two cases; simply because you come and report another man, God happens to think of how it involves you.

Like-for-like; yes, Christianity is so rigorous that it even affirms a rigorous inequality. It is written: " Why do you see the speck that is in your brother's eye, but do not notice the log that is in your own eye? " [86] A pious man has piously interpreted these words in this way: the log in your own eye is nothing more or less than seeing for the purpose of judging the speck in your brother's eye. But the most rigorous like-for likeness would be that seeing the speck in another's eye becomes a speck in one's own eye. Yet Christianity is even more rigorous: this speck, or in judgment to see it, is a log. And if you do not even see the log and if no man sees it—God sees it. Consequently the speck is a log. Is this not rigorousness, this which makes a gnat into an elephant? O, but if you consider that Christianly and truly understood God is continually present in everything, that everything revolves about him and him alone, then you will indeed be able to understand this rigorousness, you will understand that seeing the speck in your brother's eye—in God's presence (and God is in fact always present) is high treason. If, in order to see the speck, you could only use a moment and a place where God were not present! But Christianly understood this is what you must learn by heart, that God is always present, and if he is present, he also sees you.[87] In a moment when you rightly think God to be present, it certainly will not occur to you to see some speck in your brother's eye nor will it occur to you to employ this terribly rigorous standard—you, who yourself are guilty. But the situation is this, that even if every better person applies himself to having the thought of God's omnipresence present as far as his own life is concerned (and nothing more preposterous can be thought of than thinking of God's omnipresence at a distance), he nevertheless often forgets God's omnipresence in his relationships to other men, forgets that God is present in the relationship, and is satisfied with a merely human comparison. Thus one has security and ease for discovering the speck. What, then, is the fault? This, that you yourself forget that God is present (and in fact he is always present), or that you forget yourself in his presence. How uncircumspect to judge so rigorously in God's presence, so that a speck is judged—like-for-like, if you will be so rigorous and God can be even more rigorous—to be a log in your own eye. The authorities have already regarded it as a kind of audacity on the part of that criminal whom we have already discussed to want to play the righteous man pursuing his rights by law and court, alas, a criminal who shall himself be pursued by the law and court—but God sees it as presumption that one would play the role of purity and judge the speck in his brother's eye.

How rigorous is this Christian like-for-like! The Jewish, the worldly, the activist like-for-like is: see to it that in the long run you do unto others what others do unto you. But the Christian like-for-like is: as you do unto others, God does unto you in the very same mode. Christianly understood you have absolutely nothing to do with what others do to you; it does not concern you; it is curiosity, an impertinence, a lack of consciousness to mix into things which are no more your business than if you were absent. You have to do only with what you do unto others or with the way you receive what others do unto you; the direction is inwards; essentially you have only to do with yourself before God. This world of inwardness, the new version of what other men call reality, this is reality. In this world of inwardness the Christian like-for-like is at home. It wants to turn you away from the external (but without taking you out of the world), upwards or inwards. For, Christianly understood, to love human beings is to love God and to love God is to love human beings; what you do unto men you do unto God, and therefore what you do unto men God does unto you. If you are embittered towards men who do you wrong, you are really embittered towards God, for ultimately it is still God who permits wrong to be done to you. If, however, you gratefully take the wrongs from God's hand "as a good and perfect gift," you do not become embittered towards men either. If you will not forgive, you essentially want something else, you want to make God hard-hearted, that he should not forgive, either: how, then, should this hard-hearted God forgive you? If you cannot bear the offences of men against you, how should God be able to bear your sins against him? No, like-for-like. For God is himself really the pure like-for-like, the pure rendition of how you yourself are. If there is wrath in you, then God is wrath in you; if there is mildness and mercifulness in you, then God is mercifulness in you. Infinite love is this, that above all he wills to have to do with you and that no one, no one, so lovingly discovers the slightest love in you as God does. God's relationship to a human being is the infinitising at every moment of that which at every moment is in a man. You know well enough that echo dwells in solitude. It corresponds exactly, O, so exactly, to every sound, to the slightest sound, and duplicates it, O, so exactly. If there is a word which you prefer not said to you, then watch your saying of it, watch lest it slip out of you in solitude, for echo duplicates it immediately and says it to *you*. If you have never been solitary, you have also never discovered that God exists. But if you have been truly solitary, then you also learned that everything you say to and do to other human beings God simply repeats; he repeats it with the intensification of infinity. The word of blessing or judgment which you express concerning someone else, God repeats; he says the same word about you, and this same word is blessing or judgment over you. But who believes in echo if night and day he lives in urban confusion! And who believes that such an observer is present, that like-for-like is done so exactly; who believes this if from his earliest childhood he is accustomed to live in confusion! If one so confused hears of Christianity he is nevertheless not in position to hear it rightly; as Christianity does not resound rightly in the inwardness of his being, he never discovers the resonance which is the Christian like-for-like. Here in the noise of life he perhaps does not discern God's or the eternal's repetition of the uttered word; he perhaps imagines that the repayment should be in the external or in an external mode; but externality is too dense a body for resonance, and the sensual ear is too hard-of-hearing to catch the eternal's repetition. But whether or not a man discovers it, the word he himself said is nevertheless said of him. Such a person lives out his life as one who does not know what is said about him. Now, if a man remains oblivious to what the town says about him, it is perhaps good; besides, what the town says of him may be untrue: but, O, what good is it for a moment or for a long time to remain oblivious to what the eternal says about him—which, however, is the truth!

No, like-for-like! Certainly we do not say, nor is it our thought, that a person ultimately earns grace. [88] O, what you learn first of all in relating yourself to God is precisely that you have no merit at all. Test this merely by saying to the eternal, " I have merited "; then the eternal answers " You have merited . . ." If you wish to have merit and think you have merited something, punishment is all it is; if in faith you are not willing to appropriate the merit of another, then you will receive according to merit.—We do not say this as if it were our thought that it would be better for one to sit in the anxiety of death, day in and day out, listening for the repetition of the eternal; we do not even say that it would be better than the smallness of spirit which in these times uses God's love for the purpose of selling excuses from all more dangerous and more rigorous striving. No, but just as the well-brought-up child has an unforgettable conception of rigour, so also must the human being who relates himself to God's love, if he is not "foolishly" (I Timothy 4 : 7) or light-mindedly to take it in vain, have an unforgettable fear and trembling, even though he rests in God's love. Such a person will certainly avoid speaking to God about the wrongs of others towards him, about the speck in his brother's eye, for such a person will rather speak to God only about grace, lest this fateful word justice lose everything for him through what he himself has called forth, the rigorous like-for-like.

Notes to Introduction

Page references in the notes without a given title refer to this volume, *The Works of Love*. References to Kierkegaard's *Journals or Papirer* I-XI (København: Gyldendalske Boghandel, 1909-1948) are to the Danish edition. The translations of quoted portions are by the present translators unless the excerpt is found in Alexander Dru's selections from the *Papirer* (*The Journals of Kierkegaard*. London: Oxford University Press, 1938), in which case the entry number from Dru's volume follows in parentheses: *Papirer* I A3 (D1).

[1] *Papirer* VIII¹ A6 (D629).

[2] *Papirer* VIII¹ A294.

[3] *Papirer* VIII¹ A308.

[4] *The Gospel of Suffering* (translated by David F. Swenson and Lillian Marvin Swenson. Minneapolis: Augsburg Publishing House, 1948), p. 119.

[5] *Papirer* VIII¹ A165 (D676).

[6] *Papirer* VIII² B73, p. 131: "Just because we are conscious that our efforts are truly disinterested in this sense, I dare call this volume a work of love. It is honestly done in order to make love as beautiful as it is, and it is our desire that he who reads it might be won for love. This is our task. Whether or not the volume has readers is not our affair; our task does not therefore become less disinterested because there are no readers. . . ."

[7] *Papirer* X¹ A161 (D890): "I have not, as yet, said a direct word about myself; the epilogue to the *Final Postscript* contains nothing of the kind, I simply assumed responsibility for the pseudonyms and spoke *hypothetice* ('as I understood it') about their ideas. The explanations concerning the structure of the works of the pseudonyms which are to be found in the *Final Postscript*, are by a third person. The conclusion of *Works of Love* (the work of love which is

to praise love) contains nothing direct about me, on the contrary, that 'the greatest egoist should be the one who undertakes to praise love.' There is just one little hint about me in the review of *The Two Ages*, but that again is not direct communication but concealed as though I had learnt it from the novel."

[8] *Papirer* VIII[1] A250 (D694).

[9] *Ibid.*

[10] See *Papirer* VIII[1] A33 (D643)—A38 for a discussion of punctuation and mode of writing.

[11] *Papirer* X[1] A489 (D932): "Here Luther is again completely right. No one can see faith; it is unseen: therefore no one can decide whether or not a man has faith. But faith shall be known by love. Now men have indeed wanted to make love into an unseen something, but against this Luther, together with Scriptures, would protest, for love is Christianly the works of love. It is really an un-Christian conception of love to say that it is a feeling and the like. This is the esthetic definition of love and therefore fits the erotic and everything of that nature. But Christianly love is: the works of love. The love of Christ was not inner feeling, a full heart, *etc.*; It was rather the work of love, which is his life."

[12] *Papirer* VIII[1] A196.

[13] Søren Kierkegaard, *Værker I Udvalg*, edited by F. J. Billeskov Jansen (København: Gyldendalske Boghandel, 1950), IV, p. 199.

[14] Pp. 424-425.

[15] *Papirer* III A240. See also *Papirer* III A240, VIII[1] A89, A196, A327 and A650 (D754).

[16] *Papirer* VIII[1] A4.

Notes to Part One

[1] See Introduction for Kierkegaard's distinction between Christian reflections and Christian discourses.

[2] Compare pp. 53, 80-1, 160. " The single individual " is of great importance in the whole authorship and has been greatly misunderstood. For Kierkegaard's own consideration see " *The Single Individual, Two Notes Concerning my Activity as an Author* " (Appendix to *The Viewpoint For My Activity as an Author*) and his brief *Concerning My Activity as an Author*. See also *Papirer* VII[1] A176, VIII[1] A23, A123-6, A538, VIII[2] B190-195.

Papirer VIII[1] A482 (D723): " ' The individual ' is the category through which, from a religious point or view, our age, our race and its history must pass. And the man who stood and fell at Thermopylae was not as convinced as I am, who stand at the narrow pass 'the individual.' It was his duty to prevent the hordes from forcing their way through that narrow pass; if they got through he was lost. My duty is, at any rate at first sight, much easier and seems to place me in far less danger of being trodden down; as though I were an unimportant servant who, if possible, was to help the masses trying to go through the narrow pass, 'the individual,' through which, be it noted, no one can ever go without first becoming 'the individual.' "

Papirer VIII[1] A19 (D637): " ' The masses': that is really the aim of my polemic; and I learnt that from Socrates. I wish to make people aware, so that they do not squander and dissipate their lives. The aristocrats assume that there is always a mass of men lost. But they hide the fact, they live withdrawn and behave as though these many, many men did not exist. That is what is godless in the superiority of the aristocrats; in order to have things their own way they do not even make people aware. But I do not want that."

Papirer VIII¹ A108 (D657): "There is another respect in which conditions are certain to change, and in the future every effort at reformation, if the man concerned is a true reformer, will be directed against the 'masses,' not against the government. Government (royal power) is really representation, and to that extent Christian (Monarchy), the dialectic of monarchy is historically both tried and settled. Now we are going to begin at another point, namely, upon the intensive development of the state itself. In that way there arises the category: 'the individual,' the category which is so wedded to my name that I wish that on my grave might be put 'the individual.' "

Papirer X⁵ B208: ". . . 'the individual' must be gone through with ethical decisiveness as a middle term in order to make sure that 'congregation' is not taken in vain as being synonymous with 'public,' 'the many,' *etc.*, although it must be remembered, what is well-known, that it is not the individual's relationship to the congregation which determines his relationship to God, but his relationship to God which determines his relationship to the congregation. Ultimately, in addition, there is a supreme relationship in which 'the individual' is absolutely higher than the 'congregation,' the individual κατ' ἐξοχην, the God-man, the judge in the Old Testament, the apostle in the New Testament, however God-fearingly they acknowledge having their divine authority in order to serve the 'congregation.' But *religiously* there is (in contrast to 'public,' 'many,' *etc.*, which can have validity *politically*) only the individual. And Christianly-religiously there is less than ever of 'public,' 'many,' *etc.* (which had, has, and can have validity in paganism and worldliness), because 'the possibility of offence,' which Christianly is *the middle-term* in connection with becoming a Christian, unconditionally makes a person first of all and qualitatively an 'individual,' whereby the concept ' Christian congregation' is secured as qualitatively different from 'public,' 'many,' *etc.*, although of course absolutely every human being can be the individual."

Papirer VIII¹ A8 (D631): " I am accused of leading young men to rest satisfied in their own subjectivity. Perhaps, for a moment. But how is it possible to get rid of all the illusions of objectivity such as the public, etc., without drawing forth the category of the individual? Under the guise of objectivity people have wished to sacrifice individualities completely. That is the whole question."

Papirer VIII[1] A9 (D632): "The whole development of the world tends to the importance of the individual; that, and nothing else is the principle of Christianity. Yet we have not got very far in practice, although that is recognised in theory. That explains why people still consider it proud and haughty and presumptuous to talk about the individual when it is of course the really human attitude, namely, that everyone is an individual.

" Sometimes misunderstandings are expressed piously. When the late Bishop Møller says (in the introduction to his *Instructions*) that it would be sad if truth (*in specie* Christianity) were only accessible to a few individuals and not to everyone, he certainly said something true, but at the same time false. For Christianity is certainly accessible to all but—be it carefully noted—only provided everyone becomes an individual, becomes 'the individual.' But people have neither the moral nor the religious courage. The majority is quite terrified of becoming each one of them, an individual. This is how the question oscillates: at one moment it is pride to preach that opinion of the individual and then, when the individual tries it out, he finds the thought is too great for him, in fact overwhelming."

" *Concluding Unscientific Postscript* (Princeton: Princeton University Press: 1941), pp. 317-18: The more the collective idea comes to dominate even the ordinary consciousness, the more forbidding seems the transition to becoming a particular existing human being instead of losing oneself in the race, and saying 'we,' 'our age,' 'the nineteenth century.' That it is a little thing merely to a particular existing human being is not to be denied; but for this very reason it requires considerable resignation not to make light of it. For what does a mere individual count for? Our age knows only too well how little it is, but here also lies the specific immorality of the age. Each age has its own characteristic depravity. Ours is perhaps not pleasure or indulgence or sensuality, but rather a dissolute pantheistic contempt for the individual man. In the midst of all our exultation over the achievements of the age and the nineteenth century, there sounds a note of poorly conceived contempt for the individual man; in the midst of the self-importance of the contemporary generation there is revealed a sense of despair over being human. Everything must attach itself so as to be a part of some movement; men are determined to lose themselves in the totality of things in world history, fascinated and deceived by a magic witchery; no one wants to be an individual human being. Hence perhaps the many attempts to continue clinging to Hegel, even by men who have reached an insight into the questionable character of his philosophy. It is a fear that if they were to become particular existing human beings, they would vanish tracelessly, so that not even the daily press would be able to discover them, still less the critical journals, to say nothing at all of speculative philosophers immersed in world-history. As particular human beings they fear that they will be doomed to a more isolated and forgotten existence than that of a man in the country; for if a man lets go of Hegel he will not even be in a position to have a letter addressed to him."

[3] Compare VIII¹ A173.

[4] Compare Proverbs 4 : 23.

[5] Compare I Timothy 6 : 16.

[6] Compare Ephesians 4 : 30.

[7] Compare Matthew 12 : 34.

[8] Compare Kierkegaard's use of *suum cuique* or distributive justice and Plato's in *The Republic*, Book I.

[9] Sirach or Ecclesiasticus, writer of one of the apochryphal books. The Book of Sirach was in the Danish authorised Bible until 1871.

[10] Compare *Papirer* VII¹ A205. The Danish expressions are *fra Hjertet* and *sætte Hjertet*. Kierkegaard sometimes uses effective combinations of similar-sounding words with distinctions in meaning which cannot be translated adequately. We think he would approve of the above translation although it is not required by the particular sentence.

[11] Compare Matthew 6 : 1-18.

[12] II Samuel 12 : 1-7.

[13] Compare Matthew 7 : 24 ff.

[14] Compare Matthew 10 : 28.

[15] Apparently a reference to Hegel and his Danish followers.

[16] Genesis 32: 31.

[17] See pp. 59-60.

Papirer VIII¹ A269 (D696): " One must really have suffered very much in the world, and have been very unfortunate before there can even be any talk of beginning to love one's neighbour. It is only in dying to the joys and happiness of the world in self-denial that the 'neighbour' comes into existence. One cannot therefore accuse the immediate person of not loving his neighbour, because he is too happy for the 'neighbour' to exist for him. No one who clings to earthly life loves his neighbour, that is to say his neighbour does not exist for him."

[18] James 2 : 8.

[19] Compare Matthew 5 : 46-47.

[20] II Corinthians 5 : 17.

[21] Compare I Corinthians 7 : 29-31.

[22] Compare I Corinthians 2 : 9.

[23] Matthew 10 : 16.

[24] Matthew 9 : 20 ff.

[25] A reference to Solon's observation on the insecurity of happiness: " Call no man happy until he is dead." Herodotus I, 32.

[26] Compare Romans 8 : 37.

[27] Compare James 3 :10.

[28] Compare Matthew 25 : 1 ff.

[29] Darius, whom Herodotus (5, 105) reports to have had a slave who repeated daily: " Remember the Athenians."

[30] For an extended consideration of *to exist* or *to become a self* as contrasted qualitatively to simply being or subsisting, see Kierkegaard's *Either-Or*, *The Sickness Unto Death* (especially the crucial first two pages), and *Concluding Unscientific Postscript*. The entire authorship, in its complexity of substance and form, can properly be regarded as concerned with these same interlocked questions: What is it to become a human being? What does it mean to exist? What does it mean to become a self? What does it mean to become a Christian? See also page 65.

[31] For further consideration of despair, see Kierkegaard's *The Sickness Unto Death*, *The Concept of Dread* [Angst], and *Either/Or*.

[32] *Possibility* and *impossibility*, *faith* and the *absurd* are pursued further in Kierkegaard's *Fear and Trembling*, *Repetition*, *For Self-Examination*, and *The Sickness Unto Death*. The categories of *possibility*, *reality* and *actuality* are treated extensively in *Concluding Unscientific Postscript*.

[33] Compare Kierkegaard, *Either/Or*, especially Volume II, and *Papirer* VIII[1] A196 for additional discussion of love and erotic love.

[34] II Corinthians 10 : 5. See also pp. 56 and 67 and *Papirer* VIII[1] A739 on the comparative defence of Christianity as better and deeper and the accompanying loss of " You shall."

[35] For more on the creative artist and the ethical-religious life, see Kierkegaard's *Fear and Trembling*, *Repetition*, *The Sickness Unto Death*,

Concluding Unscientific Postscript, For Self-Examination, and *Training in Christianity,* as well as his *Viewpoint.* Also see note II, 54.

³⁶ The following few pages from this non-pseudonymous work constitute considerable difficulty for those who would interpret Kierkegaard's thought as a cultural-social isolationism. At the same time they are a brief sample of Kierkegaard's ethical-religious critique of cultural-religious confusions and fragmentation. See also pp. 59, 157, and 179-180.

³⁷ The phrase *without authority* frequently appears in both the pseudonymous and signed portions of the authorship of Søren Kierkegaard. This phrase means a number of things: on the one hand Kierkegaard's awareness of his nonordained place in his church and on the other the limits of a second person's role in the essential learning and decisive becoming of another. (Compare pp. 64-65 on spiritual love.)

³⁸ Compare Kierkegaard's consideration of Socrates on this point in *Philosophical Fragments.*

³⁹ Compare *Concluding Unscientific Postscript* on the tragedy of neither retaining the poetic nor gaining the religious.

⁴⁰ Compare *Fear and Trembling* and *Postscript* for further discussion of passion. Usually in Kierkegaard's writings *passion* does not refer to feeling and emotion. (Compare " Diapsalmata," *Either/Or,* I.) It means rather the concentration of the person. Esthetic passion is therefore a great thing, marred by its exclusiveness and by its spontaneous and episodic character. Qualitatively different is the passion generated in ethical resolution and in the venture of faith. Passion, reflection, resolution, and the leap of faith are distinguishable but not distinct. The emphasis is upon the integrity of the person, upon the wholeness of selfhood in itself and in transparent (see note II, 53) relationship ultimately to the "power that posited it" (*The Sickness Unto Death*). The becoming of the person, or "stages *on life's way,*" thereby involves "cutting the tap roots" of the esthetic, the ethical, and the immanental religious, but not abrogating them, and in the life of faith catching them up in "spontaneity after reflection."

⁴¹ On *fleshly fanaticism* see *Papirer* X² A241 (D1005).

⁴² I Corinthians 7 : 9.

⁴³ Augustine, *The City of God,* ch. 19, 25. See p. 227.

⁴⁴ *Papirer* VII¹ A190: " Erotic love and marriage are really only a deeper corroboration of self-love by becoming two in self-love. For this very reason marriage becomes so satisfying, so vegetatively

thriving—because pure love does not fit this way into earthly existence as self-love does. Therefore the solitary lacks the self-love which married people express thus: he is selfish—since married people proceed from the concept that marriage is love."

Papirer VII¹ A231: "There is an especially good remark which now, strangely enough, I find in my old journal for 1839 (E.E.) in which there is otherwise not much of real felicity or finish: that marriage is not genuine love and that therefore the expression is used that the two become *one flesh*—not one spirit, inasmuch as two spirits cannot possibly become one spirit. This remark could have been used quite fittingly in *The Works of Love*."

⁴⁵ See footnote 30.

⁴⁶ Martin Buber's important *I and Thou* is a fruitful development of the basic concept found here on pp. 60 and 66.

⁴⁷ This and the next two paragraphs are a compressed characterisation of Kierkegaard's essential Christian humanism which, like a stick, has two ends, which are neither to be identified or confused nor regarded as unrelated. Here is epitomised his dialectic of immanence and transcendence of individual and universal, and of *the single individual* and community.

⁴⁸ See note 34.

⁴⁹ The possibility of offence is frequently considered in the authorship (see Appendix to *The Sickness Unto Death*) and *Journals*.

Papirer VIII¹ A381: "The various occasions on which Christ himself says: blessed is he who is not offended by me. These places could be gathered together in order to show how Christ himself at various points sets the possibility of offence alongside. For example, as soon as he speaks of his glory, he straightway adds as an antidote that he must suffer, and then he adds again: blessed is he who is not offended. Likewise in the answer to John the disciple."

Papirer VIII¹ A510 (see also A381, A579, A585, and A673): "Christ says: blessed is he who is not offended by me. How very concerned Christianity is about offence—but consequently how close offence lies to Christianity. If that which is now called Christianity were Christianity, this doctrine, which especially satisfies the cultured as the highest of culture—where in all the world would there be room for such concern: blessed is he who is not offended by me? Where in all the world should any man be able to be offended by modern Christianity! Yes, I know only one form (which, however, one does not think of enough) which a simple man would be offended by: that the truth and Christianity might be unapproachable for him. But in this sense one could also be offended by the arts and sciences and by tight-rope dancing, *etc.*

" Has Mynster [Bishop in Copenhagen at the time] ever dared to say that this is Christianity: do the good and then be punished for it. And why has he not done it? Because he himself wants to be honoured and respected because he does the good, wants to be conscious of deserving the respect he enjoys, since he indeed does the good. But this is paganism. In part it also has another basis, because Mynster has an activist conception of practical life and reality: that it does not help at all to demand so much. Certainly it does not help—except that it can help one to experience what Christianity speaks of. But then Christ was indeed the most impractical of all.

" There is primarily a great confusion about the practical. In contrast to an empty formalism and vaunted scholarship, *etc.*, one speaks of the practical and praises Christianity as practical. And when it comes to a show-down one is served little enough by Christianity's practice and he may find it decidedly impractical. Is there anything more impractical than to sacrifice one's life for the truth, anything more impractical than not to look out for one's own advantage, anything more impractical than to make one's life burdensome and strenuous and to be rewarded with insults, is there anything more impractical than to be singled out not by titles and honours but by abuse and mockery. And yet I should indeed think that this is Christianity; and yet I should indeed think that old father Socrates was infinitely farther along than all of this contemporary geographical Christendom. But, of course, Socrates, who in contrast to the speculative philosophers is called practical, is equally impractical, almost just as impractical as Christianity. How impractical not to take money for teaching, how impractical not to defend himself in a way which he himself knew would effect his acquittal, how impractical not to escape from jail, how impractical to die for the truth. That a sailor dies out at sea—where he ventured in the hope of gain, that a soldier falls in battle, where he ventured in the hope of becoming a general: that is worth talking about, something practical—but to die for the truth! "

[50] John, with his camel-hair cloak. Matthew 3 : 4.
[51] I John 4 : 8. *Papirer* X² A49: " Loving Father, everything goes wrong for me—and nevertheless you are love. O, I also fail to hold

fast to this, that you are love—and yet you are love. No matter how I shift about, this alone I cannot do without or be without—that you are love. And therefore I believe that when I fail to hold fast to this, that you are love, that you permit even this to happen out of love. O, infinite love! "

[52] Compare I Corinthians 3 : 9. The Danish translation is *Guds Medarbeider*.

[53] Allusion to Genesis 2 : 22.

[54] Presumably an allusion to the caste system in which outcasts are regarded as "not born."

[55] Compare John 17 : 15.

[56] For other discussions of political-social and ethical-religious equality see *The Book on Adler* (English title: *On Authority and Revelation*) and " Two Notes Concerning My Activity as an Author."

[57] Compare Psalm 1 : 1.

[58] See p. 433. Compare *Papirer* VIII A63 (D649): " The love of God is the only happy love: but on the other hand it is also something terrible. Face to face with God man is without standards and without comparisons; he cannot compare himself with God, there he is nothing, and in the presence of God he may not compare himself with others, for that is a distraction. And so in everyone we find a clever fear of really having anything to do with God, because by having to do with God they become nothing. And even though, humanly speaking, a man honestly tries to do the will of God: before God it is all one, his atom of progress vanishes to nothing before God's holiness. And so we find in everyone a clever fear of really having to do with God: they desire the relationship at a distance and so spend their life in the distractions of time:— all that making a business of life is really only a distraction."

For another use of distance (infinite qualitative difference) see *Papirer* X² A72 (D973).

[59] Luther at the Diet of Worms. See pp. 222 ff. Compare *Papirer* VIII¹ A97, 155.

[60] See pp. 223-226 and note I, 116. Compare *Papirer* VIII¹ A155.

[61] Compare Exodus 20 : 17.

[62] For further consideration of our common humanity see Kierkegaard's *The Lilies of the Field* (in English edition together with *The Gospel of Suffering*).

[63] Compare the first discourse of *The Gospel of Suffering*.

Papirer VIII A3¹1-32: " There is something very up-building in the thought that what is written of Christ also holds true of suffering: what he suffered, he suffered once. One must suffer only once: the victory is eternal. (In a worldly way one hears this talk often enough: enjoy life—you live only once.)

"[marginal note] One suffers only once—but is victorious eternally. Insofar as one is victorious, this is also only once. The difference, however, is that suffering's *once* is momentary (even though the moment were seventy years) but victory's *once* is the eternal. Suffering's *once* (even though it lasted seventy years) can therefore not be pictured or portrayed in art. On the altar of Our Saviour's Church there is a work which presents an angel who holds out to Christ the cup of suffering. The error is that it lasts too long; a picture always endures for an eternity. It appears interminable; one does not see that the suffering is momentary, for in the concept or in the idea of conquering all suffering is momentary. The victory, however, is eternal; this (insofar as it is not spiritual) can be portrayed, because it endures. . . ."

⁶⁴ Martin Buber's *I and Thou* is a very valuable development of this theme.

⁶⁵ The Danish is "*At love* er *ærligt*, men at *holde* er *besværligt*." This is a good example of some of the problems of translation. Shall one use the most approximate English maxim ("To promise is easy: to keep it is hard") and lose all play on words (*ærligt* and *besværligt*) and part of the meaning (*ærligt*) as well as the repetition of a term (*honourable*) in the discussion following? The translators have chosen to translate it, "To promise is honourable, but to keep a promise is onerous," although this can hardly be called an "old proverb" in English.

⁶⁶ Compare *Papirer* VIII¹ A29.

⁶⁷ Romans 13 : 10.

⁶⁸ Socrates.

⁶⁹ Compare Luke 10 : 29.

⁷⁰ Compare I Corinthians 3 : 19.

⁷¹ See also "Diapsalmata" in *Either/Or*, I, and *The Sickness Unto Death* for brief, trenchant characterisations of busyness.

⁷² *Purity of Heart* (New York: Harper Torchbook, 1956), companion ethical volume to *The Works of Love*, is centred on the meaning of wholeness, willing one thing, and the multitudinous ways men contrive for sake of evasion.

⁷³ Compare John 8 : 46.

⁷⁴ I Peter 2 : 22.

[75] Luke 10 : 42. Compare *Papirer* VIII¹ A111.

[76] Compare Luke 22 : 61.

[77] Compare Luke 10 : 17.

[78] Matthew 26 : 40.

[79] Compare Matthew 12 : 49.

[80] Compare John 9 : 4.

[81] *Explanation* (Danish: *Forklaring*) and *transfiguration* (*Forklarelse*). These tightly knitted terms with their deep distinction are difficult to render in English. The meaning here is that truth is being, the embodied explanation, the ultimate of "subjectivity is truth."

[82] Compare *Papirer* VIII¹ A77.

[83] Compare Colossians 2 : 17.

[84] The RSV translation of this verse, as well as that in the 1931 authorised Danish version are alike in themselves and in being somewhat different from earlier translations which a hundred years ago used *sum, Summen* (Danish), and *Hauptsumme* (German). Here a rendition of the older Danish is given because of the continuity of thought in the paragraph. Compare p. 157 (I Timothy 1 : 5), where the RSV has been followed (as elsewhere except where unsuitable) in translating " Men Summen of Budet er Kjerlighed. . . ."

[85] Here Kierkegaard uses *understanding* in the quite common narrow sense of technical or discursive reason, not as he usually uses it in the sense of the totality of one's human powers. Kierkegaard is not an anti-intellectualist, an irrationalist (see pp. 416-417). His distinction in regard to faith rarely takes the form employed here, for he sees the basic distinctions as being despair/faith, man/God, impossibility/possibility, rather than reason/faith in the narrower sense. In *Philosophical Fragments* some difficulty is occasioned by his using both conceptions of understanding. See excellent quotation from David Swenson in the introduction to the Anchor edition of *Fear and Trembling* and *The Sickness Unto Death* (New York: Doubleday, 1955), pp. 15-17.

[86] Matthew 16 : 23.

[87] This paragraph may well be read in conjunction with the " Grand Inquisitor " chapter of Dostoievsky's *Brothers Karamazov*. Although chronologically (Kierkegaard 1813-1855, Dostoievsky 1821-1881) there conceivably could have been some knowledge one of the other, apparently the closeness of relationship in common substance is independent of direct influence.

[88] Ephesians 2 : 12. The essential definition of secularism.

[89] This sentence and this long paragraph express Kierkegaard's

basic criticism of romanticism and the Enlightenment: the self-deification of man. Yet in this work and in the entire authorship there is a dialectical view of man which can best be termed a Christian humanism: man's essential humanity is possible only in the God-relationship. Without this man becomes less than human in the midst of his assertive cosmic impiety. See p. 417.

⁹⁰ Compare *Papirer* VIII¹ A283.

⁹¹ Compare *Papirer* VIII¹ A80.

⁹² Compare first discourse in Kierkegaard's *The Gospel of Suffering* and

Papirer VIII¹ A303: " Current Christendom really lives in such a way as if Christ were the great hero and do-gooder who once for all has secured salvation for us—and now we are only to be happy and pleased with the innocent goods of earthly life and let him take care of the rest. But Christ is essentially the pattern; consequently we are to be like him and not merely have advantage through him."

⁹³ Socrates in Plato's *Apology*.

⁹⁴ Compare *Papirer* VII¹ A237, VIII¹ A40 and A75, for references to killing time, time and solitude, time as mitigation.

⁹⁵ Compare *Papirer* VIII¹ A312 and A511 for discussions of inwardness and expression.

⁹⁶ Kierkegaard read pp. 157-158 to King Christian VIII during an audience at which time he presented the king with a copy of *Kærlighedens Gjerninger*. *Papirer* X¹ A42.

⁹⁷ I Corinthians. Compare Homer's *Iliad* 5, 340.

⁹⁸ Compare I Peter 2 : 5, 2 : 9.

⁹⁹ Compare *Papirer* VIII¹ A60.

¹⁰⁰ Kierkegaard's discussion here seems to separate his view from that of some contemporary existentialists who, like Sartre, affirm that existence is prior to essence, that an essentialist philosophy of man is in principle impossible. See also pp. 170-171, 179-180 and *The Sickness Unto Death*.

¹⁰¹ Matthew 26 : 53.

¹⁰² Compare I Corinthians 8 : 4.

¹⁰³ A version of Aristippus's criticism of Plato's doctrine of the reality of universals: " Horses I see, but 'horseness' I do not see." Here it is positively used as an analogy of the hiddenness, yet reality, of universals to the hiddenness and reality of Christian love. See G. Malantschuk, " Søren Kierkegaards Teori om Springet og hans Virkelighedsbegreb," *Kierkegaardiana* 1955 (København: Ejnar

Munksgaard, 1955), pp. 7-8, for a compact presentation of concept and phenomenon.

[104] Compare *Papirer* VIII¹ A89.

[105] The philosopher Kierkegaard valued most was Socrates, "that simple wise man of old," as he calls him in this work (p. 203) and in others. The statement about self-ignorance is no doubt a reference to that significant fragment of a sentence in Socrates's trial-address as presented in Plato's *Apology*: ". . . the unexamined life is not worth living."

[106] Genesis 2 : 18.

[107] *Papirer* VIII¹ A370 (D706): " If Christ had been merely a man then Peter would clearly not have denied him; Peter was too deep and honest for that. But whereas in general the parsons talk nonsense in the opposite sense and say that it was doubly irresponsible of Peter because Christ was God; one ought to say: no, that is precisely what explains Peter. Had he simply looked upon Christ as a man then he could well have endured the thought that he should be treated thus, and Peter would not have forgotten himself but would have been true to him. But the seeming madness that Christ was God, that he had it in his power to call legions of angels at any moment he wished: that is what utterly overwhelmed Peter. Just as one can lose the power of speech from fright, in the same way all Peter's ideas left him and in that, as it were, apopleptic condition he denied him."
See also *Papirer* VIII¹ A130.

[108] Compare James 5 : 9-10.

[109] I John 4 : 20.

[110] Compare II Corinthians 4 : 16-18.

[111] Mark 7 : 11.

[112] Compare *Papirer* VIII¹ A17.

[113] Compare *Papirer* VIII¹ A296.

[114] Compare John 3 : 13.

[115] Socrates. The quotation is from Plato's *Symposium*. Socrates in his speech attributes the words to Diotima.

[116] Compare *Papirer* IX A414 (D843): " The danger of being a Christian is a double one. First of all the sufferings of inwardness involved in becoming a Christian: parting with one's understanding and being crucified upon the paradox—here belongs the *Final Postscript*, which presents this as ideally as possible. Then the danger that the Christian must live in the world of worldliness and in it

express the fact that he is a Christian. Here belong all the later productions which will culminate in what I have ready."

[117] A version of a line from St. Augustine, *The City of God*: 19, 25.

[118] Compare *Papirer* VIII¹ A113: " When a man has a toothache the world says: poor man; when a man has trouble making a living, the world says: poor man; when a man's wife dies, the world says: poor man; when a man is arrested, the world says, poor man; when God lets himself be born and suffers for the world, the world says: poor man; when an apostle of God is favoured with a call to suffer persecution and death in God's service, the world says of the apostle: poor man.—Poor world!

[119] Compare I Corinthians 1 : 23.

[120] As in John 16 : 2.

[121] See footnote 85.

[122] Matthew 18 : 7, according to Danish version (*Forargelsen:* the offence).

[123] Compare *Papirer* VII¹ A192.

Notes to Part Two

[1] This paragraph, although concerned with the double use of language, is developed against a summary background of Kierkegaard's philosophy of man. It epitomises his central affirmations that man is an intended being (related to spirit), a becoming being who in freedom ought to become what as a human being he is intended to be (spirit), and a being who in becoming lives in qualitative categories (esthetic, ethical, religious) which are displaced (esthetic and ethical) but which are subsumed in new relationships and under new orientation ("the first portion of life shall not, however, be cast aside when the spirit awakens"). *Spirit* is used in a wide sense to designate the ethical-religious qualitative spheres of existence. To become spirit is to become a self, and a whole self healed signifies the life of faith. Compare *The Sickness Unto Death* (beginning and end): " Man is spirit. But what is spirit? Spirit is the self. But what is the self? The self is a relationship which relates itself to itself [not "to its own self" as in the present American translation] . . ." When despair is eradicated, the self " ' by relating itself to itself and by willing to be itself is grounded transparently in the Power which established it.' And this characterisation, as has often been noted, is the definition of faith."

[2] Matthew 14 : 13-21.

[3] Schrempf, in the early German translation, handled the difficulties of translating Kierkegaard's exploitation of ordinary terms and phrases (and other difficulties) by leaving out entire sentences and portions of paragraphs. The temptation is strong, because wholly corresponding terms are not always available. In this paragraph, however, one can be quite faithful to the Danish and utilise ordinary language with some profit of the kind the author intended.

[4] I Corinthians 13 : 1.

[5] I Corinthians 8 : 1.

[6] II Corinthians 12 : 19.

⁷ Compare Proverbs 16 : 32.

⁸ Compare Luke 7 : 47.

⁹ Abraham of St. Clara, *Werke*, X, 392.

¹⁰ In the following pages the distinction is being drawn between *Mistroiskhed* and *Tro*, which seem best translated *mistrust* and *faith* although the common root is obscured in this pair of English words. Faith here (pp. 264-269) is not Christian faith but the need for the decision and venture of personal involvement in freedom on the part of the existing knower as contrasted to the abstract, detached categories of knowledge; and yet even in the latter case Kierkegaard emphasises the inescapable involvement of the person on the presuppositional and judgmental levels.

Papirer VII¹ A215: "A conviction [*Overbeviisning*] is called a conviction because it is beyond [*over*] proof [*Beviisning*]. For a mathematical proposition there is a proof, but in such a way that no contradictory proof is logically conceivable. For this reason one cannot have a conviction with respect to mathematics. But with respect to every existential proposition for every proof there is a contradictory proof; there are a *pro* and a *contra*. One who is convinced [*den Overbeviste*] is not unaware of this, he knows very well what doubt is able to say: *contra*. Nevertheless or, more accurately, precisely for this reason he is convinced [*Overbeviist*] because he has made a decision and willingly swings up above the dialectic of proofs and is convinced."

Papirer VIII¹ A186: "Knowledge is infinitely indifferent (in the sense of elevation). Knowledge is like an auctioneer who puts existence on the block. The auctioneer then says: ten dollars (the value of the property), but it means nothing. Only when someone says ' I bid ', only then is the bid ten dollars."

¹¹ Compare *Fear and Trembling*, " Is there a Teleogical Suspension of the Ethical? "

¹² Socrates. Plato's *Apology*.

¹³ Matthew 7 : 1.

¹⁴ Compare *Papirer* VIII¹ A305: "This is the turning point in world-history. Christianity the religion of the *future*. Paganism was the religion of the present or of the past (pre-existence). Even Judaism was too present-minded in spite of its prophetic character; it was a futurity in the present; Christianity is a present *in futuro*."

[15] An allusion to the Greek legend about Pandora's box. Hesiod, *Theogony*, 521.

[16] Compare Philippians 1 : 20.

[17] Here the King James translation is used rather than the RSV because it is closer to the Danish translation used by Kierkegaard and to the development in the chapter.

[18] Compare Matthew 5 : 48.

[19] Matthew 19 : 17.

[20] The Danish *bliver forandret* (to be changed) also means colloquially *to get married*. In *Repetition*, Constantine finds that very little in Berlin is as it was on an earlier visit. Even his former bachelor landlord is changed.

[21] I Corinthians 3 : 21.

[22] Compare Luke 17 : 33.

[23] In the following few paragraphs *Eiendommelighed* (characteristic, peculiarity, distinction) is translated as *individuality* or as *authentic individuality*. By analogy (compare *Papirer* VIII[1] A462) to the flowers Kierkegaard points out that there are natural particularising characteristics within a species. For human beings, however, there is the possibility in freedom of becoming a self, an authentic individual, by willing before God to be oneself. The ethical-religious implication of this authentic individuality is to esteem the individuality of others as they are and their being intended for the authentic individuality of the ethical-religious life.

[24] The Roman emperor Domitian. Compare Suetonius, *Domitian*, III.

[25] Compare *Papirer* VII[1] B92, p. 306: ". . . for pride, as I understand it, is something so glorious that he who knows what it is, that he is. Pride is humility before God and humility before God is pride. What men call pride is a confused mixture of modesty and vanity."

[26] Irony.

[27] Compare quotation from Hamann used opposite the title page of the *Concept of Dread*.

[28] Socrates said he was a midwife of ideas, one who helps another give birth to his ideas, similar to his own mother who was a practising midwife.

[29] Socrates in Plato's *Theaetetus*. See *Philosophical Fragments*, I, B, C.

[30] This kind of paragraph is not unrelated to the Kierkegaardian authorship itself, to the indirect method which Kierkegaard employed

in it. (See *Concluding Unscientific Postscript* and *The Viewpoint for my Activity as an Author*.) It is also a warning against " Kierkegaardians" and " Kierkegaardianism" as expressions of an essential misunderstanding of Kierkegaard's thought and intentions.

[31] Compare I John 4 : 17. For a succinct yet comprehensive study of Kierkegaard's expression *reduplication* see G. Malantschuk, " Begrebet Fordobelse hos Søren Kierkegaard " in *Kierkegaardiana II* (København: Ejnar Munksgaard, 1957).

[32] Luke 7 : 47.

[33] Pollux, *Onomast*. I, 45-46.

[34] I Corinthians 14 : 20.

[35] Plato's *Phaedrus*. See also the last page in *Fear and Trembling*.

[36] From Kingo's hymn " Go Stand under Jesus' Cross."

[37] Daniel 3 : 21-30.

[38] Compare II Corinthians 4 : 16-18.

[39] Compare Isaiah 38 : 17.

[40] Compare Hebrews 11 : 1.

[41] Romans 7 : 8.

[42] Quintus Fabian Maximus and the Fabian delaying tactic.

[43] *Papirer* VIII[1], A298: "concerning a portion in Christian reflections, Part II, Chapter VI—to become something great in the world is a dubious matter—it must be noted here that the reference is not to the state. In this way Mynster may well be said to have become something great, but he has a strong tendency towards being in the minority."

[44] Hebrew, 13 : 16.

[45] Compare *Papirer* VIII[1] A299: " Section VII, Part II, about mercifulness is also rightly turned against communism. It is no art to speak of such things in ordinary expressions which mean nothing, but here the matter is given a completely different turn which is certainly Christian."

[46] Compare James 5 : 9.

[47] Compare Matthew 23 : 14.

[48] Luke 10 : 30 ff. In *Papirer* (VIII[1] A311) is another unused variation on the Samaritan: ". . . But suppose that the one who had been attacked, the one whom the merciful [*barmhjertige*] Samaritan was concerned with—was dead in his hands, and then suppose that the Samaritan consequently had to report this to the police, and suppose that the police had said: we must keep you under arrest until further developments—what then? Then his

contemporaries would have laughed at him, saying that he had been stupid enough to expose himself to such nonsense and that either he must have been completely ignorant of the ways of the law and been a " block-head," or, if he did have prior knowledge of what could happen, that he must have been "nuts."—See, this is the reward of mercifulness."

[49] Luke 21 : 1 ff.

[50] Jugurtha. Compare Sallust, *Jugurtha* 35.

[51] Socrates (Plato, *Apology*), in contrast to the Sophists, accepted no money for his teaching, although he said ironically that if he had had anything to teach it would have been fitting to receive compensation for his teaching.

[52] I Thessalonians 2 : 5-9, II Thessalonians 3 : 8.

[53] Compare Suetonius, *Vespasian*, 23. Vespasian is supposed to have held up some money to his son Titus, who complained because a tax had been levelled against urine, and asked whether the smell was offensive. When Titus said no, he replied, " But it is from urine." A somewhat inaccurate reference here.

[54] Compare *Papirer* VII[1] A88: " All art really involves a dialectical self-contradiction. The truly eternal can neither be painted nor sketched nor sculptured in stone, for it is spirit. But the temporal cannot really be painted or sketched or sculptured in stone either, because when it is portrayed in these ways it is portrayed eternally in that every picture expresses a fixation of the moment. When I paint a man putting a spoon to his mouth or blowing his nose, he is immediately eternised: the man continues to blow his nose this one time as long as the piece endures."
See note I, 35.

[55] P. N. Sølling, who about 1800 introduced a new type of pilot-boat for use along the Norwegian coast. The lithograph referred to was very popular and appeared in at least three editions. It is reproduced in O. C. Nielsen's *Peter Norden Sølling og Bombebøssen* (København, 1936). Compare *Papirer* VIII[1] A207.

[56] Acts 3 : 1 ff.

[57] Compare RSV Ephesians 6 : 13. The phrase is here translated as used in the text, inasmuch as the RSV translation ("... and having done all, to stand") broadens the meaning so it is not as directly related to the development of section VIII.

[58] Compare *Papirer* VIII[1] A279: " The category *to continue to stand*

can be used in connection with Asia. The Jews continued to stand; China has continued to stand; India has continued to stand.— On the other hand, the category in Europe is: to go under. Rome went under. Greece went under."

[59] Compare Romans 8 : 37.

[60] Pyrrhus.

[61] Matthew 5 : 23-24.

[62] Matthew 5 : 25.

[63] II Corinthians 5 : 20.

[64] See note I, 9.

[65] Psalm 137: 5-6.

[66] Luke 18 : 2 ff.

[67] On the esthetic differential of artistic-intellectual talents and the universally human of the ethical, see *Papirer* VIII[1] A160, also note II, 69.

[68] *Transparency* is a particularly significant term in this work, also in *The Sickness Unto Death* (see note II, 1) and in the entire authorship. Transparency in thought means not only clarity and adequacy of conceptualisation but the thinker's own relationship to his thought, particularly in terms of the ethical-religious life, which can be thought but essentially is to be realised existentially. Thinking in which human existence is ignored may be descriptively and instrumentally important but it is irrelevant. Objective ethical-religious reflection, close to the personal centre but without the relationship of inwardness, is existentially irrelevant and thereby unclear, or the thinker lacks the transparency of being in this thought. Ultimately transparency is spontaneity after reflection, the individual before God, healed in faith. See note I, 40.

See *Papirer* VIII A649, A650 (D753, D754), for Kierkegaard's use of spontaneity or immediacy after reflection, a characterisation of faith.

[69] Compare with illustrative and explanatory portion in *Papirer* VII[1] A200 (D619): " The main objection, the whole objection to natural science may simply and formally be expressed thus, absolutely: it is incredible that a man who has thought infinitely about himself as a spirit could think of choosing natural science (with empirical material) as his life's work and aim. An observant scientist must *either* be a man of talent and instinct, for the characteristic of talent and instinct is not to be fundamentally dialectical, but only to dig up things and be brilliant—not to understand himself (and to be able to live on happily in that way, without

feeling that anything is wrong because the deceptive variety of observations and discoveries continuously conceals the confusion of everything); *or* he must be a man who, from his earliest youth, half unconsciously, has become a scientist and continues out of habit to live in that way—the most frightful way of living: to fascinate and astonish the world by one's discoveries and brilliance, and not to understand oneself. It is self-evident that such a scientist is conscious, he is conscious within the limits of his talents, perhaps an astonishingly penetrating mind, the gift of combining things and an almost magical power of associating ideas, etc. But at the very most the relationship will be this: an eminent mind, unique in its gifts, explains the whole of nature—but does not understand itself. Spiritually he does not become transparent to himself in the moral appropriation of his gifts. But that relationship is scepticism, as may easily be seen (for scepticism means that an unknown, an X, explains everything. When everything is explained by an X which is not explained, then in the end nothing is explained at all). If that is not scepticism then it is superstition."

[70] Herder, *Zur schönen Literatur und Kunst.*

[71] See pp. 389 and 432-433.

Compare *Papirer* VIII[1] A55: " Father in heaven! In our relationships with men it often happens that we say one thing in their presence and, sad to say, something else when they are gone. We speak differently about them in their presence than in their absence. But of you, our God, how should we be able to speak in your absence, you who are everywhere present, how could we possibly speak in a different way of you, you who are always the same! Grant unto us, O God, diligence in combating the absentmindedness in which we imagine that you are absent, in order that, for our concentration of mind and its up-building, for our discipline of mind and its purification, we may keep in mind that you are always present."

[72] Compare II Corinthians 5 : 11. Kierkegaard's use of *win* follows the Danish translation. See the opening of *For Self-Examination* for further use of this line.

[73] Compare *Papirer* VIII[1] A627 (D746): " In *The Works of Love* I said: the age of thinkers is passed. Soon one will have to say: the age of thought is passed."

[74] The position of the Greek Sophists, notably Protagoras, and a particular object of attack by Plato. See also *Philosophical Fragments*, III.

Papirer VII¹ A235: "Protagoras's proposition that man is the measure of everything is, in the Greek understanding, properly a parallel to the jest of a noncommissioned officer to his companion. When the barmaid did not have the half-pint measure handy and there was no time to waste since taps were being blown, he said: just give me the bottle; I have the measure in my mouth."

⁷⁵ Plato, *Apology*.

⁷⁶ Compare *Papirer* VIII¹ A295: "He who will speak of self-renunciation's love need not take the great pains to appear to be a self-lover, for if he is the true lover, the world must regard him as the self-lover."

⁷⁷ Compare *Papirer* VIII¹ A309: "In the reference to the people of love there is also a fling at Grundtvig: for it is really presumptuous that a group will call itself 'the people of love': it is vain and selfish."

⁷⁸ Compare *Papirer* VIII¹ A189: "What Socrates says about loving the ugly is really the Christian doctrine of loving the neighbour. The ugly is the reflected, consequently the ethical object; whereas the beautiful is the immediate, which therefore all of us more than willingly love.—In this sense *the neighbour* is the *ugly*."

⁷⁹ Compare Hebrews 1 : 1.

⁸⁰ I John 4 : 7.

⁸¹ Compare pp. 254 and 295, *Papirer* VIII¹ A114, and *Papirer* VII¹ A228: "The word to the captain from Capernaum: be it done unto you as you believe is a consoling, joyous word, but it also contains the judgment: if you really have faith. Therefore one could speak on these words in this way: the judgment and the joy in always being done unto as a man believes."

⁸² Exodus 21 : 24.

⁸³ Matthew 8 : 5-13.

⁸⁴ Compare Matthew 6 : 12, 14-15.

⁸⁵ Compare *Papirer* VII¹ A87.

⁸⁶ Matthew 7 : 3.

⁸⁷ See p. 389 and note II, 71.

⁸⁸ Compare *For Self-Examination* and *Papirer* VIII¹ A19: "Good works in the sense of meritoriousness are naturally an abomination to God. Yet works are required of a human being. But they shall be and yet shall not be; they shall be and yet one ought humbly to be ignorant of their being or that they shall be of any significance. It is like a dish which is that particular dish because of the way

in which it is served: good works therefore should be done in humility in faith. Or it is as when a child gives his parents a present procured, however, with what the child has received from his parents; all the pretentiousness which otherwise resides in giving a gift disappears when the child has received from his parents the gift which he gives to the parents."

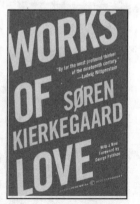

ISBN 978-0-06-171869-4

ISBN 978-0-06-156161-0

ISBN 978-0-06-176631-2

ISBN 978-0-06-155024-9

ISBN 978-0-06-176521-6

ISBN 978-0-06-163265-5

ISBN 978-0-06-176824-8

ISBN 978-0-06-187599-1

ISBN 978-0-06-120919-2

Available wherever books are sold, or call 1-800-311-3761 to order.